The Building of

ADARE MANOR

First published by Eastwood Books, 2023
Dublin, Ireland
www.eastwoodbooks.com
@eastwoodbooks

First Edition

Eastwood Books is an imprint of the Wordwell Group

Eastwood Books
The Wordwell Group
Unit 9, 78 Furze Road
Sandyford
Dublin, Ireland

ISBN: 978-1-913934-30-9 (hardback)

Endpapers: Adare Manor, Adare. Design for dining room fireplace and panelling by A. W. N. Pugin, 1846. Courtesy of the Dunraven family.

British Library Cataloguing in Publication Data.
A catalogue record for this book is available from the British Library.

Printed in Spain by Gráficas Castuera, Navarra.

The Building of

ADARE MANOR

A Family Chronicle

Anna-Maria Hajba

Eastwood

To Geraldine, Countess of Dunraven,
with gratitude

Contents

QUIN FAMILY PEDIGREE
(ABRIDGED)

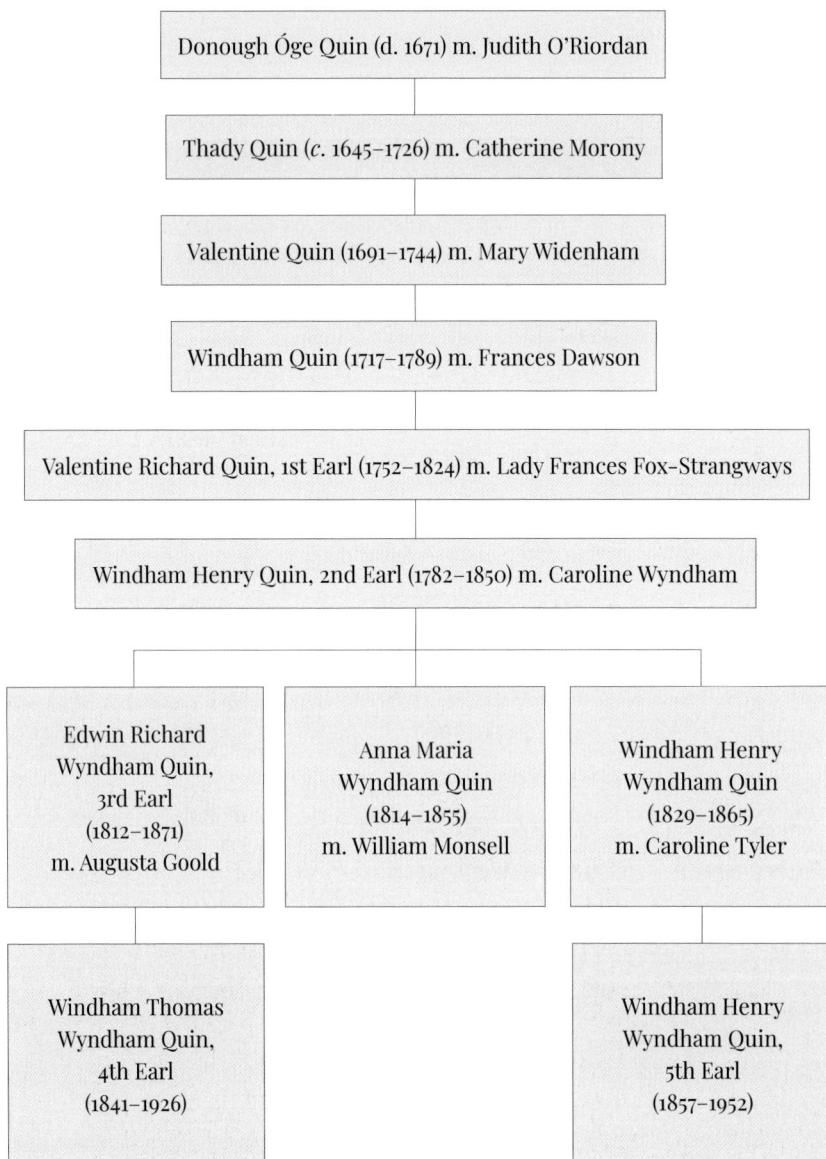

Donough Óge Quin (d. 1671) m. Judith O'Riordan

Thady Quin (*c.* 1645–1726) m. Catherine Morony

Valentine Quin (1691–1744) m. Mary Widenham

Windham Quin (1717–1789) m. Frances Dawson

Valentine Richard Quin, 1st Earl (1752–1824) m. Lady Frances Fox-Strangways

Windham Henry Quin, 2nd Earl (1782–1850) m. Caroline Wyndham

Edwin Richard Wyndham Quin, 3rd Earl (1812–1871) m. Augusta Goold

Anna Maria Wyndham Quin (1814–1855) m. William Monsell

Windham Henry Wyndham Quin (1829–1865) m. Caroline Tyler

Windham Thomas Wyndham Quin, 4th Earl (1841–1926)

Windham Henry Wyndham Quin, 5th Earl (1857–1952)

WYNDHAM FAMILY PEDIGREE
(ABRIDGED)

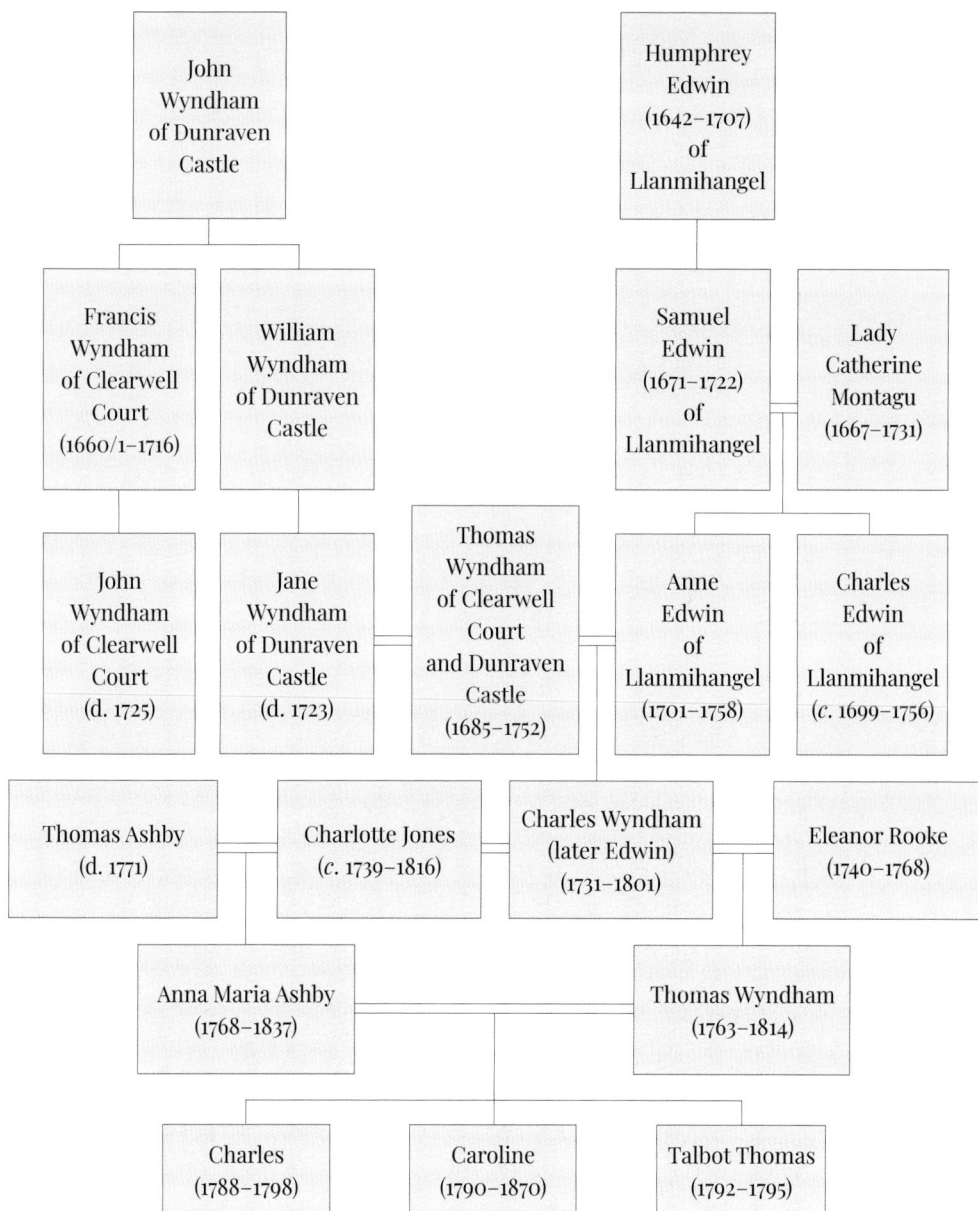

```
John                                    Humphrey
Wyndham                                   Edwin
of Dunraven                             (1642–1707)
Castle                                      of
                                        Llanmihangel


Francis              William            Samuel              Lady
Wyndham             Wyndham             Edwin             Catherine
of Clearwell        of Dunraven        (1671–1722)         Montagu
Court                 Castle               of            (1667–1731)
(1660/1–1716)                          Llanmihangel


                     Thomas
John                Wyndham             Anne               Charles
Wyndham            of Clearwell         Edwin               Edwin
of Clearwell          Court               of                 of
Court             and Dunraven        Llanmihangel        Llanmihangel
(d. 1725)            Castle           (1701–1758)        (c. 1699–1756)
         Jane       (1685–1752)
       Wyndham
       of Dunraven
        Castle
        (d. 1723)


Thomas Ashby      Charlotte Jones     Charles Wyndham     Eleanor Rooke
 (d. 1771)        (c. 1739–1816)      (later Edwin)       (1740–1768)
                                      (1731–1801)


       Anna Maria Ashby              Thomas Wyndham
         (1768–1837)                  (1763–1814)


        Charles            Caroline          Talbot Thomas
      (1788–1798)        (1790–1870)          (1792–1795)
```

Preface

It is not too much of an exaggeration to claim that this book took almost as long to write as Adare Manor took to build. My investigations began with a visit to the Glucksman Library at the University of Limerick in 2002 for a quick perusal of the Dunraven Papers. Curiously, this brought in its wake a career change, which now finds me in the role of an archivist in the Glucksman Library's Special Collections and Archives Department. As a result, my decades-long interest in the Wyndham Quin family and their building activities, coupled with my current role has given me the unique opportunity to delve deeper and deeper into this most engaging of subjects.

The gradual transformation of Adare Manor from a modest early Georgian country seat to an exuberant sampler of Gothic Revivalism is, of course, in its broad brushstrokes already familiar to students of Irish architectural history. The first to explore the topic in detail was John Cornforth, whose articles on the subject, based in part on research carried out by the late Knight of Glin, were published in three consecutive issues of *Country Life* in May 1969. More recent contributions include Judith Hill's scholarly essay, 'Gothic in Post-Union Ireland', published in *The Irish Country House: Past, Present and Future* (2011), and the more wide-ranging *Adare Manor: The Renaissance of an Irish Country House* (2019) by Turtle Bunbury. David Lee's biography of James Pain (2005) also contains a section on Adare Manor, and passing references to the building can be found in publications such as *Twilight of the Ascendancy* (1987) and *Life in an Irish Country House* (1996) by Mark Bence-Jones; *Great Irish Houses and Castles* by Jacqueline O'Brien and Desmond Guinness (1992); *The Irish Country House* by Peter Somerville-Large (1995); *The Big House in Ireland* by Valerie Pakenham (2000); *The Pursuit of the Heiress* by Anthony Malcomson (2006); and *Painting Ireland*, edited by William Laffan (2006).

While these accounts provide valuable insights into the construction process and architectural features of Adare Manor, they are perhaps less successful in capturing the human story behind the stones. An absence of reflection on the family may have arisen for a number of reasons. Cornforth's detailed and comprehensive articles may have disinclined subsequent scholars towards making further forays into the family records. Researchers may equally have been put off by the fact that the Dunraven Papers and related collections are at present divided between three repositories in two countries, with a fourth portion remaining in private hands.[1] The sheer volume of the Irish material alone makes it complex to navigate, and the considerable time-span of building works exacerbates the challenge. The journals of the second earl's wife, for instance, extend over six decades and require a particular patience to decipher. The spread of material is also uneven. Little of the second earl's correspondence survives, while that of the third earl is voluminous to excess. One may even question the need for such an undertaking, since it is unlikely to change the broad picture of what is already known. As this book demonstrates, however, an in-depth study of the primary sources available in this instance allows for a much more nuanced narrative to emerge. The story of the building of Adare Manor is inseparable from the story of the family who built it. Construction works ebbed and flowed in line with the rise and fall of family fortunes, as three generations of Wyndham Quins went about their daily lives within the expanding walls of their home. Beyond the demesne boundary, there was scarcely a family in the village of Adare who did not benefit from employment provided by the building works. Many young stonemasons and wood-carvers learnt their trade working alongside their fathers on the construction site, while women honed their skills of weaving and needlework to produce textiles for the new interiors. Equally, and viewed in the widest context, the ideas and thinking that created Adare Manor reveal the importance of British and Continental influences on the architectural development of the Irish country house and the manner and speed with which Gothic Revivalism gained popularity in the first half of the nineteenth century.

In addition to enriching the building history of Adare Manor, this book will dispel a number of commonly held misconceptions. The first of these, that Windham, the second Earl of Dunraven, single-handedly designed the greater part of the building and supervised its construction without the assistance of an architect, was actively promoted by his widow and eldest son in their jointly authored work, *Memorials of Adare Manor* (1865). There is no doubt that the appearance of Adare Manor strongly reflects the second earl's personal tastes, cultivated and refined by years of close study of medieval architecture. Yet, for all his carefully nurtured proficiency in the finer points of Gothic Revivalism, the second earl was no draughtsman, as his feeble attempts at sketching reveal. He needed an architect, if only to give a shape to his ideas. His account books and his wife's journals attest to James and George Richard Pain's regular visits to Adare in the mid-1830s to oversee the building works and to amend the working plans as and when required. While the second earl took a more prominent role as designer when the construction of the south front got under way in the early 1840s, even then he was to rely not on his own skills but on those of architects attuned to his personal vision. The role played by Lewis Nockalls Cottingham in this respect has sometimes been questioned, since only one working drawing signed by him has come to light. As we shall see, however, family correspondence puts the second earl's association with Cottingham and the architect's importance to the design process beyond doubt.

Another misconception, first promulgated by John Cornforth, is that the second earl began rebuilding Adare Manor as a way of occupying his time, as by the early 1830s he was so crippled by gout that he could no longer enjoy other pursuits such as shooting or fishing. His wife's journals, however, which record the ailments and illnesses of family members in meticulous detail, reveal that gout did not become a recurrent problem until the autumn of 1835, and that it was not until the early 1840s that the attacks became so persistent and debilitating as to render the second earl incapable of pursuing daily activities. Consequently, it is more appropriate to say that the building works continued in spite of his increasingly severe bouts of illness.

This book is by no means a comprehensive study of every aspect of the construction of Adare Manor. It is first and foremost a family chronicle, in which building works play a prominent role. A number of key elements require further elucidation. For instance, only brief reference is made to the wealth of heraldic and other carvings and their historical allusions within and without the building, which merit a book in their own right. The correspondence and account books concerning the completion of the south front by the third earl and his architect Philip Charles Hardwick are equally too extensive to include in this book in their entirety but would make a wonderful subject for a doctoral dissertation. Lastly, and taking a local perspective, it is true to say that, while the names and activities of some of the masons and carvers who built Adare Manor have reached the pages of this book, those of scores of other workmen continue to lie unexplored in the family archive. In this and many other respects I hope that this book will encourage new generations of researchers to make their own discoveries and add to this evolving story to the benefit of all.

This book has benefited from the assistance of a great number of people and it is now my pleasant duty to thank them. I must first of all express my indebtedness to the Dunraven family, without whose lifelong commitment to the preservation of their family history I would not have had a story to tell. Lady Dunraven and Lady Ana Johnson opened not only their home but their hearts to me and allowed me to explore their remarkable store of family memorabilia, many items of which now enrich the pages of this book. I am very thankful for the trust they placed in me and can only hope that I have done it justice.

I am grateful to Dr Andrew Tierney of Trinity College, Dublin and the late and much-lamented Dr Geoffrey Brandwood for peer-reviewing the text and providing valuable feedback; Teresa Connolly for sharing with me her passion for the Connolly family and bringing to my attention seminal printed sources which otherwise would have eluded me; Glucksman Library's Special Collections Librarian Ken Bergin for his flexibility and support during the most intense stages of book production; my colleagues Olivia O'Keeffe, Diarmuid O'Callaghan and Seán Cafferkey for their unwavering readiness to retrieve and reproduce documents, often at a moment's notice; Christabel Scaife for introducing me to Eastwood Books and my editor Ronan Colgan and his superb design team for producing a book that exceeded all my expectations.

Images form an integral part of this publication. In addition to the Dunraven family, whose private collection forms the backbone of the book, I must thank the many archivists and curators who went out of their way to help me with my queries and to provide me with exceptional images from their collections. You are too numerous to list individually but your kindness has not been forgotten. I therefore wish to offer my collective appreciation to the staff of the following institutions and organisations: akg-images, Art

UK, Bibliothèque nationale de France, British Museum, Bonhams, Buxton Museum & Art Gallery, Derbyshire Record Office, Eton College, Historic England, Indianapolis Museum of Modern Art, Irish Architectural Archive, National Galleries of Scotland, National Gallery of Ireland, National Library of Wales, National Museum Wales, Royal Collection Trust, Royal Institute of British Architects, Stair Galleries of Hudson, New York, Tate Gallery, University of Limerick, University of Reading and Yale Center for British Art. In addition, my special thanks are due to Senan Furlong OCB of Glenstal Abbey, Lavinia Graham-Vivian, William Laffan, David Lee, Lowell Libson, Thomas Lloyd, Thomas Methuen-Campbell, Anne Robinson, Richard Suggett, Emma Thompson and Ruth Waycott for providing me with images from private collections or helping me to track them down.

Last but by no means least I wish to express my gratitude to my fellow architectural historian Michael O'Sullivan for the photographic miracle he performed on inhospitably gloomy winter mornings in Adare. The images his camera produced of the Dunraven memorabilia show no evidence of the grief caused by the effort to capture a decent shot in the middle of a blizzard! Not only is Michael an exceptional photographer, but his knowledge of every corner of Adare Manor is unsurpassed. His willingness to share that knowledge made this a much better book than what I would have been able to produce on my own. Indeed, by rights this work should have been written by him, but since he wouldn't, I had to!

My heartfelt thanks to each and every one of you.

Anna-Maria Hajba
Doneraile
April 2023

Introduction

In 1749, the writer, historian and Whig politician Horace Walpole began rebuilding a small cottage in his possession at Twickenham, London. Irregular in shape and embellished with pinnacles, pointed windows and other Gothic decorative features, Strawberry Hill stood in notable contrast to the Classical symmetry of the buildings of the day. While not the only or even the first dwelling of its kind, its construction in several stages between 1749 and 1776 signalled the emergence of the Gothic Revival, a style which was to feature so prominently in nineteenth-century Britain.

Gothic architecture originated in twelfth-century northern France and England and flourished throughout Europe until the early sixteenth century. Its defining elements were the pointed arch, the rib vault, the flying buttress, elaborate window tracery, pinnacles, spires, stained glass and a strong vertical emphasis. As the sixteenth century progressed, the style gave way to Renaissance and Baroque architecture, but it never died out completely. It continued to be used in church-building and in a number of urban contexts, such as the universities of Oxford and Cambridge.

Gothic elements reappeared in domestic architecture in the early eighteenth century, heralding the rise of Romanticism. This movement developed in the latter half of the eighteenth century as a reaction to the Industrial Revolution and the Age of Enlightenment, with its emphasis on reason, rationality and progress. Romanticism, in contrast, sought intense emotion, venerated nature and harboured a nostalgic longing for the past, particularly the Middle Ages. At this time Edmund Burke, Richard Payne Knight and Uvedale Price, among others, developed their theories of the Picturesque, while William Gilpin published guidebooks aimed at middle-class domestic tourists in search of the most romantic beauty spots in Wales, Scotland and the Lake District. The historical novels of Sir Walter Scott, the passionate verse of Lord Byron and the Lake Poets, and the emerging Gothic fiction which, like Strawberry Hill, originated with Horace Walpole and his 1764 novel *The Castle of Otranto* increased interest in medieval times and rekindled an appreciation of Gothic architecture. In Wales, John Nash joined forces with landscape designer Humphry Repton and devised an asymmetrical and picturesque architectural style which ultimately caught the eye of the prince regent.

In the early decades of Gothic Revivalism, Gothic elements were used mainly for their picturesque and romantic qualities. They lacked any historical authenticity and little interest was expressed in the original structural function of the style, sometimes with disastrous consequences. By the early 1820s, however, a more serious interest in the Gothic style had emerged. One of its pioneers was the restorer and architect Lewis Nockalls Cottingham, who in 1814 began to collect medieval carvings and other artefacts from demolished buildings and later assembled them into a museum which he opened to the public to better demonstrate the art of medieval architecture. The French émigré Auguste Charles Pugin, who worked as a draughtsman for John Nash, spent years minutely examining medieval structures in Britain and on the Continent and published his findings in a series of illustrations, *Specimens of Gothic Architecture*, between 1821 and 1823. His son, Augustus Welby Northmore Pugin, co-designer with Charles Barry of the Houses of Parliament, became one of the outstanding exponents of the style and contributed significantly to the theory of Gothic Revivalism through the publication of *Contrasts* in 1836. Pugin's belief that Gothic was true Christian architecture resonated strongly in an age when the growth of religious nonconformism and increased secularisation were giving rise to a demand for the reawakening of Christian traditions. Such demands, promoted by the Oxford Movement, also known as Tractarianism, fuelled a further revival of interest in church architecture and led to the formation of the Cambridge Camden Society in 1839. Through its journal, *The Ecclesiologist*, the society championed a return to a medieval style in church architecture and advised builders on the finer points of design.

Gothic Revivalism also appealed to the secular market. All across the British Isles, compact, symmetrical and regularly proportioned Classical homes gave way to the new style of buildings, some of them conscientious studies of medieval authenticity, others wildly embellished riots of random pinnacles and pointed windows. An entire army of manufacturers sprang up in major cities to produce stained glass, encaustic tiles, woodwork, mosaics, wallpaper, textiles, grates, firedogs, locks, hinges and door handles in appropriate Gothic designs to ornament domestic interiors. Antique dealers peddled armoury, weaponry and works of art to fill the newly constructed cavernous halls, while heraldry and heraldic imagery became the very emblems of fashionable taste. The finest domestic examples of Gothic Revivalism created by the fabulously rich became popular tourist destinations among the genteel classes.

It was this exciting and vibrant cultural milieu that created Adare Manor, a Tudor-Gothic country house located beside the village of Adare on the western bank of the Maigue River some 18km south-west of Limerick city. Built by two generations of the Quin, later Wyndham Quin family, Earls of Dunraven, it represents Gothic Revivalism at its finest while at the same time possessing a quality that marks it out as unique. Composed, as noted by the author Mark Bence-Jones, of a variety of elements rather loosely tied together,[2] its picturesque façade abounds in playful carvings and other features of interest. Although the building lacked architectural purity, it retains a pleasing cohesiveness, suggestive of a house built over centuries rather than decades.

The builders of Adare Manor, Windham Henry Quin and his Welsh wife Caroline Wyndham, embarked on their architectural journey almost by accident, when a downturn in family finances in the early 1820s forced them to retrench to Wales. They built a cottage in the scenic Vale of Neath and, while waiting for its completion, began a light-hearted exploration of John Nash's picturesque designs in Wales. The timely discovery of coal on their Welsh estates enabled them to return to Ireland, where the old family home, having stood idle for this time, needed repairs. The initial decision to add a kitchen wing to the property led over time to a meticulous study of Gothic architecture and extensive tours of England, Wales and the Continent in search of ideas, and culminated in the creation of a Tudor-Gothic work of art in stone. Three generations of the family lived, laboured and died before the house was finally completed in 1871.

While the second earl enjoyed country pursuits, he had abandoned them since his youth, along with the gaming table and the 'polished, & frivolous circle of gay, & fashionable intrigue', as the main objects of his life, having found that none of them answered his expectations.[3] Architecture, on the other hand, captivated him and served as a source of deep personal satisfaction. Many of the features of Adare Manor—an emphasis on the horizontal line but with a vertical thrust created by turrets and corner towers rising above the main roofline, skylines decorated by ornamental parapets, a forest of tall chimneys and an abundance of carved detail—reflect his architectural tastes. They were borrowed from or inspired by medieval domestic buildings in England and Wales such as Longleat, Knole, St Donat's and Haddon Hall, all of which he visited and deeply admired. Architecture, however, was not merely a diverting occupation to the second earl but also a vehicle for doing good. The poet Aubrey de Vere recalled him as a man who 'was much given to reflection on practical, not abstract, subjects, and held strong opinions on the ethics of life'.[4] This focus on ethics became all the stronger as the second earl's own position in society grew. It is no mere happenstance that the start of the reconstruction of the family home coincided with his succession to the family title. For him, great power always came with equally great responsibility towards those in lower and more vulnerable positions in life.

The second earl's wife shared both her husband's ethos and his interest in building works. In many respects, Countess Caroline remains the unsung champion in the story of Adare Manor. It was not only her money that made the transformation of the family home possible but also her personal tastes that shaped the appearance of both Adare Manor and the adjoining village. The thatched cottages for which Adare is today famous have their parallel in the hamlet of Merthyr Mawr in South Wales near Caroline's home, and it was her interest in the Picturesque that contributed to the landscaping of the demesne. Her father's extensive renovations at Dunraven Castle in the early 1800s kindled her interest in building works from an early age, as did the art of draughtsmanship that she learnt from her mother. While her husband sat in the House of Commons, Caroline travelled in England and Wales copying patterns from churches, abbeys and country houses and brought them to Adare, where she instructed the masons in the skill of preparing working drawings. Her interest in architecture continued to the end of her life and gave her solace after the death of her husband in 1850 and her subsequent return to Wales.

The work on Adare Manor was completed by the couple's eldest son, Edwin, the third Earl of Dunraven. His sense of duty towards those in less advantageous positions in society, which he inherited from his parents, was heightened by, or perhaps contributed to, his conversion to Catholicism in 1855. It was Edwin's Catholic leanings and his close friendship with the prominent Roman Catholic convert Ambrose Lisle Phillipps that brought Pugin to Adare in 1846. Religion was also a contributing factor in his choice of Philip Charles Hardwick, a fellow Tractarian, as the architect to complete the south front of Adare Manor following the second earl's death in 1850. An ardent follower of Pugin's doctrines, the third earl lacked his father's enthusiasm for architectural exploration and instead sought purity, even austerity, of design. His efforts were not fully appreciated by his surviving parent; yet it was the third earl's collaboration with Hardwick that gave Adare Manor its perhaps most recognisable feature, the Wyndham Tower, and its most beautiful detail, the oriel window on the west wall. Edwin's religious views also found little favour, particularly with his wife, and caused an almost insurmountable rift within the family which cast a deep shadow over the final years of his life.

Few houses in Ireland enjoy such a long and well-recorded building history as Adare Manor. As the family dynamics reveal, however, the story of Adare Manor is much more than the sum of its building materials. It is intrinsically linked to domestic upheavals, to the rise and fall of family fortunes and, on a broader scale, to the events that shaped and moulded the nineteenth century in Ireland and beyond: the Industrial Revolution, the Napoleonic Wars, Catholic Emancipation, the Great Famine and mass emigration. Natural forces also played their part. Storms, shipwrecks, volcanic eruptions and epidemics all contributed, directly or indirectly, to the building of Adare Manor. Although no longer the home of the Dunraven family, the house stands as testament to their remarkable endeavour to create a building without parallel in Ireland.

This is their story.

CHAPTER ONE

A Welsh Heiress

In December 1806 Windham Henry Quin of Adare, Co. Limerick, a young Irish gentleman and freshly minted MP, travelled to London for the first meeting of the new Parliament. Having crossed the Irish Sea to Wales, he broke the journey at Penrice near the Bristol Channel on the Gower Peninsula, home of his father's old friend Thomas Mansel Talbot. Thomas and Valentine Richard Quin had first met in Rome in May 1773, when Richard was visiting the city as part of a Grand Tour to get his portrait painted by the celebrated and highly fashionable artist Pompeo Batoni.[1] At the same time, Thomas was touring Italy to purchase statues and works of art on a grand scale for his park and house at Margam in Glamorgan, South Wales, which he had inherited in 1758 at the age of ten. The classical villas of Italy and the country's uncultivated, romantic scenery had also inspired Thomas during an earlier journey to commission the Gloucestershire architect Anthony Keck to design a new house for him at Penrice in 1772.[2]

The easy friendship that developed between the two young men gained added importance in 1777, when Richard Quin married Frances Muriel Fox-Strangways, fourth daughter of the first Earl of Ilchester of Melbury House, Dorset, and Penrice became a welcome pit stop for members of both families on their way to and from Ireland. Windham, born to the couple in September 1782, and his younger brother Richard, born in April 1789, were

Portrait of Valentine
Richard Quin (1752–1824).
Painted by Pompeo Batoni,
1773. Courtesy of the
Dunraven family.

among these commuters on their regular journeys to Eton in the 1790s. By this time it was not only friendship but also kinship that linked Thomas and the Quins. In 1792, Lady Frances Quin's brother Henry was travelling to Ireland with some of his children when a sudden attack of gout detained him at Penrice for a month instead of the usual few days. By the time Henry was well enough to set out again, the 44-year-old Thomas had fallen in love with his friend's sixteen-year-old daughter, Mary. Although the only emotion the young lady had initially expressed towards Thomas's romantic overtures was utter bewilderment, she returned to Penrice just two years later as his bride.[3]

It was also very possibly under the roof of Penrice that Windham Henry Quin first met his future wife, Caroline Wyndham, whose home, Dunraven Castle, lay just 40 miles south-east of Penrice and whose parents counted Thomas and Mary Talbot among their friends. Marriage was certainly at the forefront of Windham's mind at the start of his political career, albeit for the most prosaic of reasons—money. The Quin family's fortunes were by the early 1800s on a decidedly downward spiral, mostly owing to Windham's grandfather and namesake, a high society rake and member of the Limerick branch of the notorious Hellfire Club, who was far more interested in raucous merrymaking than in minding the fortune amassed by the previous two generations of the family. His grandfather, Thady Quin, a clever businessman of native Irish stock, had in 1671 inherited from his father a valuable freehold estate and a beneficial farm worth more than 100 pounds a year in Adare, a small trading post on the banks of the Maigue River in north County Limerick.[4] In spite of the Penal Laws, Thady managed not only to hold on to his Catholic faith but also to considerably expand his inheritance by obtaining thousand-year leases of two substantial portions of land in County Limerick, confiscated by the Crown from the Fitzgerald family, Earls of Kildare, after the so-called Desmond Wars of the late sixteenth century.

Thady's son Valentine further strengthened the family's foothold by purchasing the remainder of the property of the Earls of Kildare in and around Adare and the fee-simple (a purchase outright) of the lease acquired by his father.[5] The estate now incorporated not only the lands and ruins of Desmond Castle, a stronghold built in 1200 by Geoffrey de Marisco, but those of three religious houses established by the Fitzgerald family, for the

Trinitarian Order in 1230, the Augustinian Order in 1315 and the Franciscan Order in 1464. With such wealth to protect, Valentine was not prepared to continue the cat-and-mouse game that his devoutly Catholic father had played with the Protestant authorities. Taking a more pragmatic view of the matter, Valentine converted to the Protestant faith in 1739.

Valentine's son paid little heed to the efforts made by his forefathers. By the time of his marriage in 1748, Windham was in such a financial bind that his future father-in-law Richard Dawson took it upon himself to clear some 6,000 pounds' worth of his debts, and in years to come was obliged to repeat the exercise more than once.[6] When Richard Quin succeeded to the estate in 1789, it was so heavily encumbered and the family coffers so depleted that after a fruitless struggle of some years he had no choice but to abandon his Irish home for a scaled-down life in England. For his eldest son, who one day would inherit this financial burden, Richard had nothing but cold comfort to offer. 'I think it probable that you will wish to settle yourself in England', Richard advised Windham in 1799. 'You will have no fortune upon my death to enable you to live out of Ireland, and during my life, and I am still young, it never will be in my power to afford you an allowance to make you independent.'[7] When Windham began his studies at Oxford, his father cautioned him against 'the various debaucheries of that University' and warned him 'to refrain from excess in Wine' and 'never to hazard at play any money which can in the least inconvenience you to lose'. Aware that he could not offer his son a carefree future, Richard instead urged Windham to cultivate advantageous friendships at college to improve his chances in the world, and to focus on the study of belles-lettres rather than the Classics because 'the acquirement of such knowledge as will make your company sought for, & acceptable in polite & fashionable society, will be in your situation of life, of more advantage to you'.[8]

What Richard had not allowed for, however, was his eldest son's practicality and strong sense of duty, or his financial genius and acuity for good management. Windham detested the reckless actions of 'Windham the Drone', as he called his grandfather, and refused to hang his portrait on the same side of the room as that of his great-grandfather Valentine Quin, to whom he felt the family owed a debt of gratitude. 'What have not my predecessors done for me', Windham noted humbly, '& should I not be a

Portrait of
Valentine Quin
(1691–1744).
Courtesy of
the Dunraven
family.

selfish, poor spirited creature to fill myself with the fruit of their labour &
not to act in my generation as they acted for me.'[9] Yet, as determined as
Windham was to save the family's Irish estates from ruination, he was not
blind to the fact that such plans required money. Hard work and a prudent
lifestyle alone would not produce the quantities he needed, but marriage to
a wealthy woman would. It was with this in mind that Windham was now
casting his net in matrimonial waters.

Adare, Co. Limerick. View of the medieval ruins from Ardshanbally Hill at the close of the eighteenth century. From *Memorials of Adare Manor* (1865). Courtesy of Special Collections and Archives, Glucksman Library, University of Limerick.

While Penrice was the likeliest place for Windham to have met Caroline, there were other ways in which he might have come into contact with the Wyndham family. His regular journeys through Wales on his way to and from Eton, Oxford and London and his kinship with the Earls of Ilchester had provided him with many social connections in the principality. More importantly, Caroline's father, Thomas Wyndham, was an MP for Glamorgan, South Wales, and sat in the House of Commons at the same time as Windham. Although Thomas's appearances in London were by 1806 increasingly rare owing to ill health, the poised and ambitious young Irishman is bound to have come to his notice, not least because of his unusual first name, so redolent of Thomas's surname. It derived from Windham's paternal great-grandmother, Mary Widenham, a wealthy heiress from County Limerick, whose money had enabled her husband Valentine Quin to solidify the family's land assets and to establish himself firmly in the upper echelons of the social hierarchy of the day. It was the very same path that Windham was now determined to tread.

❖ ❖ ❖

Windham's potential father-in-law offered, in principle at least, excellent prospects for a young gentleman in need of money. Thomas Wyndham was a landowner whose rather complex family history had brought into his possession no fewer than three estates—Dunraven Castle, a medieval hall-house in a dramatic position on a rocky outcrop on the coast of South Wales, some eight miles west of the busy market town of Cowbridge in Glamorgan; Clearwell Court in Gloucester, constructed by Thomas's grandfather in 1728 as one of the country's first Gothic Revival mock castles; and Llanmihangel, an Elizabethan manor house two miles south of Cowbridge. Dunraven Castle, the largest and most striking of the buildings, was Thomas Wyndham's main residence. It had been in his family since 1642, when it was bought by his ancestor, Humphrey Wyndham of Somerset, as a gift for his Welsh wife, Joan Carne, who hailed from Ewenny Abbey near Cowbridge. It later passed to their great-granddaughter, Jane Wyndham, who married a cousin, Thomas Wyndham of Norfolk. When Jane died without surviving issue in 1723, aged just 35, the property passed to her husband.

Clearwell Court came into the family through Jane's uncle, Francis Wyndham, who purchased it in 1698. A generous benefactor, Francis established a library in Cowbridge for the use of local clergy and schoolteachers, and founded six charity schools and an almshouse for widows in the village of Newland in Gloucestershire.[10] His personal life, however, was wrought with tragedy. His wife became mentally ill, many of his children died in infancy and his own life ended prematurely in 1716, when he was just 46 years of age.[11] His only surviving son, John Wyndham, inherited the property. As John was a minor at the time of his father's death, his cousin Jane of Dunraven Castle took charge of his affairs and held the Clearwell estate in trust for him until he reached maturity. John fared no better in the longevity stakes than did his cousin and died in 1725. Having no other family to call his own, he bequeathed Clearwell Court to Jane's husband, Thomas Wyndham.[12]

In 1728 Thomas commissioned Roger Morris to replace the old and rather rambling manor house which had existed at Clearwell since at least the fifteenth century. London-born Morris had begun his career as an

Dunraven House, Glamorgan. A view from the north, 1776. Private collection.

Portrait of Windham 'the Drone' Quin (1717–89) with his dog. Painted by Stephen Slaughter, *c.* 1745. Courtesy of the Dunraven family.

assistant to the pioneering Scottish architect Colen Campbell. Through him, Morris also came into contact and collaborated with Henry Herbert, ninth Earl of Pembroke, whose interest in architecture earned him the sobriquet 'architect earl' and whose influence opened the door for Morris to enjoy the patronage of a number of distinguished clients.[13] Although he was particularly popular for his classical Palladian villas, Morris was not averse to experimenting with unusual design styles. At Clearwell Court he combined Georgian symmetry with elements of medieval domestic architecture: arched windows on the principal floor, diagonal buttresses at the outer corners of the building and an embattled roof parapet adorned by the Wyndham crest. With this combination of features Morris created one of the earliest of the country's Georgian Gothic castles, pre-dating such landmark buildings as Inveraray Castle (designed jointly by Morris and William Adam in 1746) and Horace Walpole's Strawberry Hill (begun in 1749).[14] Inside, the most notable features included the entrance hall and the long, axially placed library at the rear.[15] The English antiquary Francis Grose noted in his *Antiquarian Repertory* (1775) that, 'though the stile of Architecture gives it a sort of gloomy solemnity, it is on the whole a very desirable Mansion'.[16]

Some years after the death of his first wife, Thomas Wyndham remarried. His second wife, Anne Edwin, brought Llanmihangel, by far the largest and most profitable of the three estates, to the Wyndham family landholdings. Her grandfather, Sir Humphrey Edwin, a wealthy merchant and one-time lord mayor of London, had purchased the property in 1685 as a mark of his wealth and success in the world. A colourful and controversial character, Humphrey was parodied by the satirist Jonathan Swift in his *A Tale of a Tub* as 'Jack who gets on a great horse and eats custard'.[17] His business acumen and keen desire for self-advancement raised Humphrey from humble origins to financial and social prominence, a standing which his eldest son and successor, Samuel Edwin, actively cultivated. An usher in the court of receipt of the Exchequer in London, Samuel married Lady Catherine Montagu, daughter of the third Earl of Manchester and lady-in-waiting to Queen Caroline. He added over 3,300 acres to the Llanmihangel property by purchasing the castle and manor of Coity in 1718. His son, Charles Edwin, further strengthened the family's aristocratic connections by marrying Lady Charlotte, daughter of the fourth Duke of Hamilton. Charles also enjoyed success as an MP, first for the city of Westminster and, from 1747, for Glamorgan. He had an elegant London residence on Upper Grosvenor Street and considerably increased the size of his holdings in Wales by purchasing several manors in the Vale of Glamorgan formerly belonging to the Stradling family of St Donat's Castle.

Charles Edwin had no offspring of his own. When he died in 1756, the vast Llanmihangel estate passed to his sister Anne's eldest child, Charles Wyndham, who had also inherited Dunraven Castle and Clearwell Court following the death of his father in 1752. The legacy contained a sting, however: Lady Charlotte enjoyed a life interest in the property and was to survive her husband by 21 years, an imposition which Charles Wyndham, described as a man 'destitute of anything like gentlemanly breeding', bore with ill grace. When Lady Charlotte eventually died in 1777, Charles became Glamorgan's largest landowner, second only to Thomas Mansel Talbot, with over 24,000 acres of land providing an annual rental income of £3,600.[18]

Having changed his surname to Edwin in accordance with the terms of his uncle's will, Charles wasted no time in turning his assets into ready cash, most notably by felling the timber on the demesne lands of Llanmihangel. Estate owners often disposed of timber as part of a woodland management programme, but Charles wielded the axe with a vigour his neighbours considered excessive. Charles also regarded the three houses he now owned as too antiquated for a man of his status and for a time busied himself with plans for a more grandiose building to be constructed just north of the manor house of Llanmihangel. These plans were soon abandoned, however, and Charles evidently lost all interest in the property, choosing instead to lease it to a succession of tenant farmers.[19]

Before changing his surname to Edwin, Charles Wyndham had married Eleanor Rooke, daughter of Major James Rooke of Bigsweir House in the Forest of Dean. Their only child, Thomas Wyndham, Windham's future father-in-law, was born in March 1763. Thomas's early years were shadowed by the death of his mother when he was but five years old. His solitary childhood was compounded by the fact that Charles showed no interest in remarrying.

Clearwell Court, Forest of Dean, Gloucestershire. From Grose's *Antiquarian Repertory* (1807 edition). By permission of Llyfrgell Genedlaethol Cymru/The National Library of Wales.

In 1780 Charles decided to enter politics and was returned as MP for Glamorgan without contest. As a political representative, he acted in keeping with his dour character. Soon after his election, the *English Chronicle* made the sardonic observation that Charles Edwin 'possesses a large fortune in the county of Glamorgan, and it was probably due to the influence of that consideration alone that he owed the honour of his parliamentary delegation, as he is not distinguished for any other circumstances, than the omnipotent one of enjoying ten thousand pounds a year, and being the modern Nimrod of the neighbourhood where he resides'. Charles, the paper concluded, 'is above corruption, and as far as a *silent* vote can go, will, in all probability, prove the sincere friend of the minister'.[20] His graceless character was brutally attacked not only by newspapers but also by his very neighbours, who snubbed Charles for being as 'illiterate as he is rude' and accused him of having 'not one character of a gentleman, but hunting'. Even in this sphere he failed, when he was expelled from the local hunt for ill-treating his hounds.[21]

Portrait of Charles Wyndham (1731–1801) and his son Thomas Wyndham (1763–1814). Painted by Johann Zoffany, c. 1773. Private collection. Courtesy of Stair Galleries & Restoration, Inc., New York. Charles later changed his surname to Edwin in accordance with his uncle's will.

Charles Edwin's evident lack of social charm was an unfortunate trait in a politician, particularly at election time. It may have been a contributing factor in his decision to resign his parliamentary seat in 1789. The official reason was increasing ill health, but it is more likely that the step was taken to open the way for his son to contest the seat and enter politics. To canvass support for Thomas, Charles turned to the Duke of Beaufort, who held political control in Glamorgan through his command of an alliance of wealthy aristocrats. Beaufort, however, announced the alliance's intention to back Captain Thomas Windsor, second son of the Earl of Plymouth, regardless of the fact that Windsor was absent on naval duties at the time of the election. An aristocratic stranglehold on local politics and Beaufort's haughty and high-handed manner had for some time been a bone of contention among the county's electorate and calls for independence from such control were growing. When Thomas Wyndham, popular as a young and energetic magistrate, was put forward as a candidate, the independent freeholders and wealthy industrialists of the county seized the moment and announced support for him. Thomas Mansel Talbot of Penrice sealed their success by defecting from Beaufort's alliance to back Thomas. His victory in the stiffly fought election of 1790 was a hard pill to swallow for Beaufort. Among Thomas Wyndham's supporters, however, it was hailed as a triumph for independence, inspiring the great Welsh bard Iolo Morganwg to celebrate the occasion with a song, *Wyndham and Liberty*. In truth, with an income of £10,000 a year and connected by marriage to the county's most influential families, Thomas's politics were little different from those of his aristocratic peers, yet his popularity secured him an uncontested seat in Glamorgan for years to come.[22]

❖   ❖   ❖

In 1783, six years before Thomas Wyndham entered the political scene of Glamorgan, his father finally decided to remarry. Charles Edwin's second wife, Charlotte Jones, was the daughter of Robert Jones of Fonmon Castle in the Vale of Glamorgan. The Joneses were among the most prominent families of South Wales, devoted Wesleyan Methodists and champions of political reform who stood firmly on Thomas Wyndham's side during the 1790 election campaign. At the time of Charlotte's marriage to Charles Edwin, her brother Robert was living at Fonmon Castle as the head of the family, their father having died in 1742 when still in his thirties. In 1762, Robert began the process of remodelling the fortified medieval castle which had served as the family home since the mid-seventeenth century. He remained faithful to the building's original medieval form, seeking inspiration from places like St Donat's, a medieval castle in the Vale of Glamorgan. He employed the Bristol architectural and building firm of Thomas Paty to create a spacious staircase hall in the east wing and to combine the two first-floor rooms of the old keep into a long salon-library which ran the full width of the building. The noted Bristol-based stuccadore Thomas Stocking was commissioned to decorate interior rooms with high-quality rococo plasterwork.[23]

By the time she met Charles, Charlotte Jones, then in her mid-40s, had already been twice widowed. Her first husband, Thomas Ashby, an illegitimate but recognised son of an MP of the same name, had died in 1771, less than four years after the couple's wedding. In June 1779 Charlotte married Lieutenant-Colonel Charles Mawhood, an accomplished military officer who had served as the British commander during the 1777 Battle of Princeton. This marriage was even more short-lived than the first, for Charles died a mere fourteen months later during the Siege of Gibraltar—not from a bullet wound heroically received on a battlefield, but from an attack of gallstones. From her first marriage Charlotte had one daughter, Anna Maria Charlotte Ashby. Born in November 1768, she was still under age at the time of her mother's marriage to Charles Edwin, and her new stepfather assumed guardianship of the young girl. Their relationship was not always easy. Whenever Charles fell out with his charge, Mrs Edwin could but advise her daughter to 'regain his love, by yielding to his desires as much as you can'.[24] Much more agreeable was Anna Maria's rapport with Charles's son Thomas. Over a few short years, a romance blossomed between them. On 15 March 1787 the young couple exchanged marriage vows at St Mary's church in Marylebone, London. They were now in the exceptional position that their parents were also their in-laws.

Portrait of Charlotte Edwin née Jones (c. 1739–1816) and her daughter Anna Maria Ashby (1768–1837), painted c. 1778. Courtesy of the Dunraven family.

Anna Maria's antipathy towards her stepfather may have arisen from the latter's prickly nature, but financial matters are likely to have played a significant part. By 1792, debts on the family's Welsh and English estates amounted to £25,680, leaving the Wyndhams in a financially untenable position. To solve the problem, Anna Maria's mother and stepfather pressured her to dissolve a trust fund that she had inherited from her father to clear the family's debts. When Anna Maria objected, her mother warned her that not releasing the funds would leave her destitute should Thomas suddenly die with such debts hanging over him. She softened the blow by reassuring her daughter that upon her own death money would be made available to Anna Maria from Mrs Edwin's private fortune—not a substantial amount, but enough to allow her to live in relative comfort. Although determined to get her way, Mrs Edwin was not unsympathetic to her daughter's plight and acknowledged with some bitterness that 'Women having power is in general of little avail they are either kissed or kicked out of it'.[25] Anna Maria eventually relented, but the release of her funds provided only temporary relief. Despite Charlotte Edwin's hope that Thomas would not incur more debt, within ten years the Wyndhams were once more facing financial crisis.

❖ ❖ ❖

Thomas and Anna Maria Wyndham lived at Dunraven Castle, which befitted Thomas's status as representative of Glamorgan. Their parents, meanwhile, lived at Clearwell Court, which Charles Edwin had always preferred. Although separated by a distance of some 65 miles, the relationship between the two families remained close. Contact was maintained by copious correspondence, and at regular intervals the Wyndhams made their way to Clearwell Court to visit their parents. Indeed, of their three children, the two eldest were born there: Charles in April 1788 and Caroline in May 1790. Only the youngest, Talbot Thomas, came into the world at Dunraven Castle, in November 1792.

The Wyndhams could not have been more attached to their offspring: 'they are in every respect the finest, & pleasantest children I ever saw', was their father's opinion.[26] Even the prickly Charles Edwin softened into a doting grandfather whenever the little brood visited Clearwell Court. Its vast sloping grounds formed an ideal playground and were held in great favour by the three children. Their days here were spent in glorious idleness, fishing in the nearby Noxon Lake, running up and down the grassy slopes surrounding the home of their uncle, General Rooke, in the nearby Bigsweir, and making excursions to local beauty spots such as Tintern Abbey on the banks of the Wye River. Caroline in particular, whose earliest memories were of Clearwell Court's comfortable rooms, developed a deep and lifelong affection for the place. It was also here, in the beautiful valley of the Wye, that William Gilpin first popularised his aesthetic ideal of the Picturesque, a concept that was to play an important role in Caroline's later life.

When Charles Edwin died in 1801, Thomas Wyndham, as the new head of the family, embarked on extensive and much-

Portrait of Caroline Wyndham (1790–1870). Painted in 1796. Courtesy of the Dunraven family.

needed renovation works at Dunraven Castle. The building was of considerable antiquity and, with its walled-up arches and grotesque carvings, resembled a religious house more than a castle.[27] It had been primarily used as a hunting lodge until Thomas took up permanent residence in 1790, but some previous attempts at modernising the building had been made, as Francis Grose noted in 1775 that it had been 'patched on in all directions in the Gothic style'.[28] Not that there was anything unusual about such buildings in South Wales. Up until the last quarter of the eighteenth century, the region was characterised by ancient country seats, unmodernised and unfashionable to such a degree that one tourist complained of never having seen 'so few seats worthy of the residence of gentlemen even in middling fortune.'[29] As the century drew to a close, the rising agricultural prices fuelled by the Napoleonic Wars provided many a country squire with the means to improve his building stock. This opportunity Thomas Wyndham now eagerly grasped.

Thomas did not employ a professional architect to provide designs for the scheme. Instead, the task of draughtsmanship fell to his wife, Anna Maria, who possessed considerable artistic talent and whose portraits and landscapes in oils and pastels adorned the walls of Dunraven Castle. Her chosen style for the additions and alterations was Gothic. Apart from its emerging popularity as an architectural idiom, the style suited the castle's medieval origins and its dramatic location on a clifftop on the edge of the sea. Anna Maria reconstructed the entire north-west-facing sea front and enlarged it by adding dining and drawing rooms and a passage with a suite of bedrooms above them. The south-east front she altered by adding to it a central octagonal entrance tower, flanked by two massive castellated projections, much in the style of Clearwell Court. Inside, a grand staircase became the focal point of the entrance hall. Roughcast rendering was applied to the exterior walls to give the somewhat rambling form of the house a more unified appearance and to protect it against the worst effects of the weather. A large stable block was added to the north-west end of the large, three-compartmented walled garden, which adjoined the house. The tops of the garden walls were raised with rendered battlements and the walls of an old deer park to the north and east of the house, stocked with deer from Clearwell Court, were similarly altered. The pleasure-grounds surrounding the castle were redesigned and new walks and drives introduced.[30] The task of executing these alterations was given to a Mr Willis and work was begun in the summer of 1802 with the construction of the stables and the lower part of the house. The bulk of the building materials, both timber and stone, were taken from different parts of the estate and hauled to the building site.[31]

Thomas and Anna Maria's activities were observed with considerable interest by their daughter Caroline, who provided detailed accounts of progress in letters to her grandmother. In June 1803, the thirteen-year-old reported that the workmen 'have nearly finished roughcasting the inside part of the stables it looks twice as pretty since it has been done. The roof is raised to the other wing and that is nearly covered in. Tomorrow they will go on with the battlements … The house has been swimming all the time of this wet weather, for the rain penetrates through the roof, the staircase and the passage are both very wet now.'[32]

Dunraven House, Glamorgan. Drawing by Samuel Hieronymus Grimm, *c.* 1776. By permission of Llyfrgell Genedlaethol Cymru/The National Library of Wales.

By the autumn of 1803 the main body of the house had been roofed and rain was no longer a problem. Internally, however, the family had to make several adjustments to their living arrangements, as the new rooms had not yet been completed and ongoing building works and interior alterations hindered the use of existing ones. As a consequence, Caroline and her parents wandered from space to space within the building as in a game of Musical Chairs: '… the stripe room will soon be ready for Mama to go into, and then we shall sit in the Orange Room, where Mama sleeps now', Caroline reported in October. 'For the present we are in the Red Room which has been painted pink and made comfortable. The old bow window room is so cold that no one uses it, as it has no chimney to it. The Saloon is then the only sitting room Mama has but in a short time the library and Morning room will be ready, they are stuccoed grey. Papa sleeps in his study which is the most comfortable and least noisy room in the house. They have made a passage from underneath the new drawing room to the other passage which leads to his room which will be very convenient as the servants need no longer go round the court.'[33]

Dunraven Castle, Glamorgan, following the 1802–05 renovation works by Thomas Wyndham. From Neale's *Views of the Seats of Noblemen and Gentlemen in England, Wales, Scotland and Ireland*, vol. 4 (1821). Courtesy of Special Collections and Archives, Glucksman Library, University of Limerick.

Works continued throughout 1804. By August of that year, many of the rooms were ready, the new staircase was beginning to take shape and, Caroline was pleased to tell her grandmother, her father's set of rooms were prepared and furnished. In her opinion, the rooms looked well even though they were not particularly handsome. She also liked the effect produced by a stained-glass window placed in the tower.[34] Even so, another year was to pass before Caroline's father could finally record in his diary the completion of the house on the last day of 1805.[35]

The newly furbished house provided Thomas Wyndham with an excellent stage from which to continue his seemingly endless rounds of entertainment. Local magistrates and members of parliament were expected to give careful attention to the needs of their constituents in the form of social functions and charitable works, and in all these activities Thomas excelled.[36] Unlike his father, Thomas was a genial and sociable man who liked nothing better than entertaining guests under his roof. Dunraven Castle was an open house to local inhabitants and offered boundless hospitality in the form of dances, dinner parties, theatricals and the ruling passion in Thomas's life, field sports. He was also generous in his benevolence, contributing to charitable funds and distributing gifts of food, clothes and fuel to the needy. In the early 1800s, to provide work opportunities in the neighbourhood, he established a large woollen manufactory in the nearby town of Bridgend, which employed about 100 people in the production of yarn.[37]

Inevitably, Thomas Wyndham's lavish lifestyle had consequences. By the early 1800s his estates were heavily encumbered with mortgages, the financial obligations of which Thomas struggled to meet.[38] Moreover, from the mid-1790s onwards, his attendance to parliamentary affairs became irregular and accusations of neglect and indifference were levelled at him. It was not disinterest, however, that caused the prolonged absences of duty but something far more prosaic. Thomas suffered from what Lord Chesterfield termed 'the distemper of a gentleman'—gout. Widely viewed as a disease exclusive to the upper classes, it achieved something of a social cachet, becoming a mark of good breeding, wealth, social status and cultural superiority. This did not, of course, in any way diminish the acute misery it caused. One nineteenth-century sufferer described the pain quite aptly: 'Apply a thumb-screw to the thumb, and turn it until the pain is as severe as can possibly be endured, and that is *rheumatism*. Now give it one more turn, and you have *gout*.'[39] Thomas's diaries reveal increasing episodes of confinement, often for months on end, particularly during the winter and around Christmas, when the consumption of rich food and large quantities of alcohol played a significant part in triggering attacks. There was no known cure, but Thomas treated his problem with blood-letting and generous swigs of Dr Beddow's gout medicine, which was effectively nothing more than bottled lemon juice. Wine in particular was Thomas's great weakness. His diaries contained copious entries on how 'to prevent one from getting intoxicated with Drinking', 'to recover a person from intoxication' and 'to cure those who are too much addicted to drink wine'. The 'cure' was particularly drastic and no doubt effective: 'put in a sufficient quantity of wine, 3 or 4 large eels, which leave there till quite dead. Give that wine to the person you want to reform.'[40]

Thomas's illness came at an unfortunate time. As the eighteenth century drew to a close, international unrest was mounting and those in power could ill afford to lose their grip. Against the backdrop of the Napoleonic Wars, commodity prices soared, food was scarce and bankruptcies and banking crises frequent. Poverty and hunger found expression in popular unrest. In April 1801, a group of starving women and children marched in protest on a corn warehouse in Swansea. One of the onlookers, Herbert Evans, was moved to complain that, while the labouring people struggled to stay alive, their parliamentary representatives behaved in a shameful manner: 'Mr Talbot in an insular part of the County doing nothing, and our member Mr W[yndham] sitting at home and getting drunk'.[41] Thomas also came under pressure from merchants and industrialists who, having previously supported him, were now disgruntled with those who held their parliamentary seats by virtue of social charm and did little to address real issues such as local improvement, fair taxation and industrial development.[42] It was an unfair charge to level at Thomas, who throughout his political career had demonstrated a strong interest in such matters, but this did not prevent ill feeling. Thomas's political career reached a crisis point in 1806, when he was publicly criticised for his non-presence. He narrowly avoided losing his seat by giving assurances of future attendance, but persistent bouts of illness made such promises difficult to keep.[43]

If Thomas Wyndham's political life was wrought with crises, these were nothing compared to the tragedies that overshadowed his personal life. In April 1795 his youngest child Talbot, then aged two and a half years, was struck down with croup and died within days of contracting the infection. Three years later, in June 1798, his ten-year-old son and heir Charles fell from a horse and died from his injuries. In this tragic and unprecedented manner, Thomas's daughter and last surviving child, Caroline, became the sole heiress to the Dunraven, Clearwell and Llanmihangel estates.

Portrait of Charles Wyndham (1788–98). Painted in 1796. Courtesy of the Dunraven family.

Charcoal landscape by Caroline Wyndham, 8 January 1808. Caroline inherited her skill at drawing from her mother. Courtesy of the Dunraven family.

Caroline's parents did not let her sex deter them from giving her the best possible grounding in life. While most girls were educated at home by a governess, Caroline began her schooling in 1800 in London, where she received a formal education in an establishment on Great Cumberland Street run by a Mrs Cleiland. Two years later, she returned home to study under the tutelage of Anna Weymer, a German governess who not only was her teacher but became a close and trusted friend. By the time Caroline completed her education, she was fluent in French and Italian and had a broad knowledge of history, geography and science. Aside from more serious studies, she devoured romantic poetry (Sir Walter Scott's *Lady of the Lake* being among her favourites), played the harp with exceptional skill and produced scores of drawings and sketches, a talent inherited from her mother. Anna Maria also passed to her daughter an interest in architecture and landscape, while Thomas instilled in her the virtues of charity and hospitality. Caroline's friendships were carefully cultivated. Her circle of friends included the daughters of well-to-do families in England and South Wales. Among them were Arabella, Caroline, Harriet and Maria Bucknall, whose father, Thomas Skip Dyot Bucknall, had won a seat in parliament in 1796 and, having voted faithfully with the government, was granted one of the rent-free grace and favour apartments at Hampton Court Palace. The palace and its famous gardens became a familiar place for Caroline during her many visits to London to enjoy the city's amusements.

Also friendly with Caroline were Mary and Jane Talbot, the eldest of Thomas and Mary Talbot's seven daughters. The two families frequented each other's homes and spent jovial evenings over dinner and exchanging news and gossip over a game of cards.[44] Caroline's father and Thomas Talbot were not only close political allies but also distantly connected through marriage, and the strong sense of mutual kinship was reflected in Thomas and Anna Maria's choice of the name Talbot for their younger son. The two families' interest in building, charitable works and social reform was also shared by Windham Henry Quin. When introduced to the Wyndhams, his interest in Caroline was immediately aroused. Landed and monied, well connected but not aristocratic, she was of the right social standing and held the promise of bringing considerable wealth his way. Ever the pragmatist, these reasons alone were sufficient for Windham to commence his courtship.

CHAPTER
TWO

Adare House

In 1808 Caroline Wyndham attained her eighteenth birthday. To mark this important milestone and to provide her with the best possible entrée into society, her parents arranged for Caroline to be introduced at court. Beyond the aristocratic classes, only girls with the most impeccable backgrounds or those fortunate enough to enjoy the attachment of a wealthy patroness were considered for such a privilege. Caroline had both wealth and good connections on her side, thanks to her grandmother, Charlotte Edwin, who throughout her life had cultivated distinguished acquaintances. Among her closest friends was Lady Jane Harewood, wife of Edwin Lascelles, first Baron Harewood, whom she married as her second husband in 1770. Through her mother, Lady Harewood was a direct descendant of Edward, first Duke of Somerset, whose sister, Jane Seymour, was Henry VIII's third wife. Both Lady Harewood and her two daughters were in favour with members of the royal family, whom Lady Harewood entertained to tea in her apartment on Portman Square during her regular visits to London. It was owing to influential friendships of this kind that Caroline gained the privilege of curtseying to Queen Charlotte in June 1808.[1]

Among the first visitors to congratulate Caroline after her visit to the palace was Windham Henry Quin. By this time Caroline's parents were well acquainted with the young Irish gentleman and had no hesitation in welcoming him to their London home on Queen Anne Street. Windham's exceptional maturity and poise, his prudence and strong sense of obligation towards his family inspired those who knew him to heap praise on him. 'He is a credit and an honor to the family, I think him a singular young Man', is how a friend of the day congratulated Windham's father. 'I have never failed to discover in him a facility of improvement that in the end will carry him (trust me) to very great heights. He has an admirable understanding, a quiet sense of what is right—the nicest sentiments of honor, considerable industry for his Rank & Years and above all a legitimate and laudable Ambition which are rarely to be found in so young a Man … I look to Windham Quin laying the foundations of a *great* family. He is every way fitted for it.'[2]

Such affable qualities, coupled with the family's considerable estates in Ireland, even though heavily encumbered, made Windham an attractive object in the marriage market, while Caroline's prospective wealth and good connections made her equally desirable in the eyes of young men from prominent families anxious to salvage or add to their financial prospects. Among Windham's rivals was Charles James Lewis, the younger son of Charles Lewis of St Pierre in Monmouthshire. A highly respected family, the Lewises possessed an estate worth some £2,000 per annum and held an important position in the social and political life of South Wales. Charles was a regular dancing partner of Caroline's in the parties of the 1808 London season, but, in spite of an evident attraction between the two, Charles's worldly prospects were probably not sufficient to satisfy Caroline's parents. Although the pair continued to socialise in Wales later in the year, there was no indication of a romantic attachment between them.

A far more eligible contender for Caroline's affections was James Lindsay, eldest son and heir of the sixth Earl of Balcarres, a Scottish peer and industrial entrepreneur who, in addition to coal mines and iron foundries, owned a third share

Miniature portrait of Caroline Wyndham (1790–1870) as a young woman. Courtesy of the Dunraven family.

A drawing-room at St James's Palace, London. From *The Microcosm of London* by Rudolph Ackermann [London, 1808–1810]. University of Reading, Special Collections.

in a company supplying slaves to the British Army. Upon his father's death, James stood to inherit an earldom with an annual income of £10,000 and an estate which, as his father was quick to point out, was affected by neither 'one shilling of debt nor Incumbrance of any kind'.[3] Throughout the 1808 season James accompanied Caroline to numerous entertainments in London. By late June, matters had advanced so far that his father saw fit to pay a visit to Caroline's grandmother to establish whether a marriage between the pair might be feasible. Nevertheless, when James felt sufficiently encouraged to propose to Caroline, she turned him down, much to everyone's surprise. Charlotte Edwin was not at all pleased with her granddaughter, for such prospects as James offered were not to be discarded lightly. Determined to change Caroline's mind, she maintained surreptitious negotiations with the Earl of Balcarres for a full year before finally admitting defeat.[4]

Caroline's reluctance to accept James Lindsay's offer of marriage arose from the fact that she had by that time developed strong feelings for Windham. The young Irishman was by now a frequent visitor to Queen Anne Street and almost daily in Caroline's company on her jaunts to the opera and the theatre. To Caroline's bitter disappointment, however, a proposal of marriage was not forthcoming. As the parliament concluded its business and the London season drew to a close in July 1808, Windham paid a brief visit to Queen Anne Street to take leave of the Wyndhams, departing from London without a backward glance and without any evident desire to continue their association. Caroline made a valiant attempt to fool herself into believing that her depression of spirits was merely a consequence of the oppressive summer heat, but eventually she grew so wretched and agitated that her mother felt it best to take her to the spa at Tunbridge Wells to help her shake off 'all the cares which for various reasons had inflamed my romantic imagination'.[5]

Caroline had no idea what had caused this sudden coolness in her suitor. Windham, however, made no secret to his father of the reasons behind his reticence. Although he admitted to liking Caroline, he discontinued the relationship 'because ambition mastered the liking, as I thought I might form a great match perhaps, where the fortune would be *present*'.[6] Caroline's wealth, albeit considerable, was tied up in the family's three estates, and marriage with her would not bring Windham the ready cash he so badly needed to clear the debt that crippled his property in Adare. Worse still, as Thomas Wyndham's estates also remained heavily encumbered, instead of solving Windham's financial dilemma, marriage with Caroline would complicate it.

For nine months Windham pursued his goal of finding a woman equal to his ambition, yet all the while his thoughts kept returning to Caroline. After lengthy reflection, he gradually came to realise that 'I know no person who is a fit match for me whom I think more amiable, & hold so high'. Moreover, paying court to women was not something in which Windham had much interest. He noted rather pragmatically to his father that 'these habits which led me where acquaintances with Girls are formed, occupy a time which I now with more pleasure devote to parliamentary pursuits, & that therefore if I did not take this opportunity I might long wait for another'.[7] Whether driven by love or cold logic, Windham decided to look no further and returned his attentions to Caroline. They were engaged in London in May 1810, an occasion which even moved Thomas Wyndham to make one of his by now increasingly rare appearances in the city to congratulate the happy couple. His only regret was the great distance between Wales and Ireland, which would separate Caroline from her parents, but he acknowledged philosophically that 'we must sacrifice our own inclinations where the personal happiness of one so dear is concerned'.[8]

❖ ❖ ❖

In late August 1810, Windham made his way to Wales to pay his first visit to Dunraven Castle, a place he would one day own. Overjoyed at seeing him, Caroline organised a number of outings to share sites and places close to her heart with her future husband. There were walks on the sandy beach of Southerndown in Dunraven Bay, carriage drives to the nearby thatched hamlet of Merthyr Mawr and a daylong picnic at St Donat's, a medieval castle in the Vale of Glamorgan, with which Windham fell in love at once and insisted on visiting again and again. Built by the Stradling family in the early years of the fourteenth century and expanded in subsequent centuries, the castle stood on the edge of a steep ravine against the backdrop of the wide sweep of the Bristol Channel. In its multiperiod form, the building incorporated all the elements that appealed to Windham: castellated parapets, heavily mullioned windows, projecting bay and oriel windows, and a magnificent fifteenth-century great hall with a mural fireplace and vaulted timber ceiling. Of equal interest to him was Coity Castle, which he and Caroline visited in early October. Having spent an entire morning exploring the ruins, the couple concluded their visit with a sunlit picnic on top of one of the towers, where the ringing of the nearby church bells added to their enjoyment.[9]

As the year drew to a close, the couple's wedding day arrived. Shortly after three o'clock in the afternoon of 27 December 1810, a small family group gathered at St James's church in the village of Wick to witness the ceremony. Groups of cheering locals lined the road to catch a glimpse of the young bride on her way to church.[10] After the ceremony, the assembled guests were ushered to Dunraven Castle for a wedding feast, while the bride and groom stepped into a carriage and set off for Llanmihangel, where they spent the first two days of their married

St Donat's Castle, Glamorgan. Watercolour painted by John Glover (1767–1849). Yale Center of British Art, Paul Mellon collection.

Coity Castle, Glamorgan. Watercolour, attributed to Paul Sandby, late eighteenth century. © The Trustees of the British Museum.

life. The building was made available to the couple by its then occupant, John Franklen, who had been hired by Caroline's grandmother in the early 1770s to manage the family's estates and who, although now well into his 70s, continued in that role. The semi-castellated Elizabethan manor house with its irregular shape, buttressed walls, charming corner windows and grotesque stone carvings was one of Caroline's favourite buildings. Inside, the house incorporated a fine oak-panelled hall, which also served as a dining room and was dominated by a sixteenth-century fireplace, on the mantelpiece of which several coats of arms were carved in stone.[11] The sloping gardens that surrounded the house were dominated by avenues of magnificent yew trees, in the shade of which the newly married couple walked in pleasant winter sunshine.

In January 1811 the couple settled in London at Spring Gardens, a fashionable quarter near St James's Park. Favoured by politicians and civil servants owing to its proximity to the House of Commons, the district was dominated by handsome three-storey brick buildings with stone cornices, ornamental iron railings and wrought-iron balconies. While Windham attended to parliamentary business and sat for a new portrait, Caroline busied herself with domestic arrangements by hiring servants, choosing curtains and buying things for the house, including a piano and a harp to allow her to further cultivate her musical talent. Caroline also availed of the opportunity to acquaint herself with Windham's sister, Harriot Payne, who was staying in London for the season, and to spend time with her childhood friends the Bucknall sisters at Hampton Court Palace. Windham's new portrait was completed in February and deemed by his wife an excellent likeness. Only a few days after the portrait had been hung up in the house, Caroline suffered an early miscarriage, which left her weak and anxious. Windham, who was about to set off for Ireland, postponed his departure by a week to make sure that his wife was out of danger.

✧ ✧ ✧

Notwithstanding the attractions of London, Windham and Caroline decided early on to make Adare their permanent home. At the time of their marriage, the debts on the Quin estate amounted to some £44,000 Irish currency

Llanmihangel House, Glamorgan. Ink drawing by W. H. Taynton, copied from an earlier drawing by Philip Henry De la Motte; early nineteenth century. By permission of Llyfrgell Genedlaethol Cymru/The National Library of Wales.

and Windham's disposable income was £2,200 a year.[12] Although Caroline's marriage portion, which added an estimated £1,500 a year to the couple's disposable income, had alleviated the most immediate of Windham's financial problems, they were far from being fully resolved.[13] His determination not to sell as much as an acre of his property, while sensible in the long term, had left the couple cash-strapped and made maintaining a house in an expensive part of London unsustainable. Life in Ireland offered the best prospects for their future. Concentrating their efforts on one property would save money, besides which permanent residence in Adare would enable Windham to supervise his many building and planting projects with greater consistency than his brief and irregular dashes across the Irish Sea had heretofore allowed. For her part, Caroline, who shared her husband's instinct for financial prudence, was content to lead a quiet country life and to stay in Adare while her husband attended to his parliamentary duties in London. Windham was deeply grateful for his wife's common sense. 'Where should we have been now', he was to recall many years later, 'if my wife's heart … had been set upon being a fine lady in London, and I had encouraged her, and it had brought me every year deeper in debt?'[14]

To that end, Windham travelled to Ireland in 1811 to prepare the family estate for Caroline's arrival and to discuss its long-term management with his father. While Richard was in favour of selling parts of the property to raise much-needed capital, Windham argued that doing so would only put the estate in greater peril. Instead, he pushed for the establishment of a sinking fund in the hands of trustees, whereby any profits generated by the estate would be set aside for the gradual repayment of the debt which encumbered it. He defended this option by reasoning that 'the invariable effect of diminishing the debt on an estate, is the removal of the necessity of selling it'. Regardless, and respectful of his father's authority in such matters, Windham vowed to submit to whatever decision Richard should choose to make, but warned him that if something were not done they would all come to rue it bitterly.[15] Aware of his son's superior business skills, Richard decided to trust his judgement and gave him a free hand to forge ahead with his plan. In April 1811 he put his seal and signature to an assignment in which he relinquished his entire estate to his eldest son, retaining ownership in name only.[16]

Windham wasted no time in taking much-needed steps to improve the age-old family home, which had remained only partly occupied for a number of years and was showing signs of neglect. Adare House was of considerable antiquity and incorporated a square or oblong tower, most likely a remnant of Thady Quin's home and place of birth. In the early years of the eighteenth century a south-facing front was added to the tower to form a T-shape. The new portion, built in the Anglo-Dutch style still popular in Ireland in the early 1700s, was of two storeys and seven bays and sported a three-bay pedimented breakfront and a steeply pitched roof with dormer windows, tall chimney-stacks and an ornamental bracket cornice. Although small, the house was elegant and enjoyed a superb position on the banks of the Maigue River in view of the ruins of the Franciscan friary.[17]

Adjacent to the house an ornamental garden was laid out, dominated by topiary in exacting geometric forms. A broad avenue lined on either side by a double row of tall elm trees approached the building from the south. Similar avenues ran between the house and the stables and from the demesne proper to a walled deer park, which adjoined it to the south-west. Extensive woods of elm and oak were planted on the estate from the 1650s onwards, first by Thady's father, Donough Oge Quin, and later by Thady. His son Valentine, who continued this work, took such pride in it that he added a clause to his will to prevent his three sons from wasting or destroying a single tree, avenue or hedgerow within the demesne.[18] The agriculturalist Arthur Young, who visited Adare in October 1776, was much taken by the verdure of the place and provided a rare early glimpse of it in his *Tour of Ireland*: 'Few places have so much wood about them as Adair', he noted. 'Mr Quin has above 1,000 acres in his hands, in which a large proportion is under wood. The deer park of 400 acres is almost full of old oak and very fine thorns, of a great size; and about the house, the plantations are very extensive, of elm and other wood, but that thrives better than any other sort. I have no where seen finer than vast numbers here.' Young also admired the fine river that ran beside the house and the three medieval monastic ruins within view, 'two of them remarkably beautiful, and one has most of the parts perfect, except the roof'.[19]

Adare House in the early eighteenth century. First permutation of the building later renamed Adare Manor. Courtesy of the Dunraven family.

In the latter half of the eighteenth century, Adare House was occupied by Windham 'the Drone', while Richard lived with his wife and children in Kilgobbin House, then known as The Farm, located on the estate some two and a half miles north-west of Adare House in the northern extremity of the parish. When Windham died in 1789, Richard and Frances at once began a programme of improvements to upgrade the family seat and bring the grounds into line with modern tastes. The house was raised by a further floor, a bow window was added to the drawing room and the entrance on the south front was moved to the north-west side.[20] The wide avenues and strict geometric forms which previously defined the grounds were removed and replaced by sweeping parkland and islands of deciduous woodland to conform to the dictates of the then-fashionable English landscape movement. Luxuriant elm trees continued to dominate the demesne, particularly along the banks of the Maigue River, but many of the old lime and ash trees from Thady Quin's time were so decayed and mutilated by storms that they were cut down and replaced by new planting. A fine yew hedge running along the edge of a roadway close to the house was cut into arches, and a row of beech trees was planted to the west of the house.[21]

Richard Quin also took an interest in developing the village of Adare and the preservation of its medieval buildings, which even in the eighteenth century were increasingly popular with tourists. Realising the need to safeguard the picturesque assets of the village, Richard carried out repairs to the Desmond Castle and constructed walls on the northern and eastern boundaries of the demesne to protect the Augustinian and Franciscan friaries 'from the dilapidations of the ignorant multitude'. His efforts were praised by George Holmes, a visitor to Adare in 1797, who declared that Richard's refined taste and liberality made Adare one of the most interesting objects with which the tourist could hope to meet.[22]

Windham, who at the time of the family's move to Adare House was seven years old, followed his father's activities with mounting interest as the latter roamed the estate surveying the grounds, supervising workmen or examining the medieval ruins for signs of damage and deterioration. Such experiences became deeply ingrained in Windham's mind and nurtured in him a lifelong appetite for building works and landscape design. His father's example also distilled in Windham a strong altruistic leaning, the desire to benefit not only

Adare House in 1812. Second permutation of the house later renamed Adare Manor. From *Memorials of Adare Manor* (1865). Courtesy of Special Collections and Archives, Glucksman Library, University of Limerick.

Desmond Castle, Adare, with the Franciscan friary in the background. Watercolour by Louisa Payne-Gallwey, *c.* 1837. Courtesy of Lavinia Graham-Vivian.

himself but also those dependent on him. The pride that Richard felt in the family estate and his preoccupation with the medieval ruins may also have awakened in his eldest son an interest in history, tradition and the concept of continuity, elements which defined Windham's disposition as an adult.

All these proficiencies Windham was now able to put to good use. He began with the grounds and revitalised the badly overgrown demesne by felling some 10,000 ash trees and planting exotic specimen trees to improve the stock. In anticipation of his wife's arrival in Adare, he kept her up to date with developments. 'I have planted five mahogany trees which came over in seeming good health', he wrote to Caroline on St Patrick's Day. He continued, somewhat tongue-in-cheek, 'I gave the sixth to Mr Smyth, a great friend of mine, who desires to preserve it in his garden, & not plant it out he says, till I have a son born. I think it right to afford you this intelligence, as you are a party concerned. I have planted several cedars which probably will grow well, as three or four, which were put out thirty, or forty years ago, are fine looking trees. There is a yew tree in one of the abbeys on which a desponding lover, some time ago, carved his mistress's name. The example was too good to be resisted; & since then, all his companions have done the same. Unless you come over quickly & take compassion on it, the poor tree will die of Love.'[23]

Knowing Caroline's interest in gardening, Windham improved the grounds which adjoined Adare House to the south. Many of the plants for the gardens and greenhouses were supplied from Wales by Caroline's mother and grandmother, both of whom were experienced and enthusiastic plantswomen and had created luxurious gardens at Clearwell Court and Dunraven Castle. Windham also progressed with the construction of brick-walled melon beds with flues to heat them. The melon yard lay adjacent to tool and compost sheds and a commodious garden house, where, Windham was fully confident, he should be able to produce cucumbers 'as large as beer barrels', blackcurrants 'the size of grapes' and lettuce 'I can't tell how tall'![24]

Adare House itself was also the focus of Windham's critical attention. The family home had been without female care since the sudden and unexpected departure of Windham's mother, Lady Frances, in the autumn of 1793, when she returned to England and was never again seen in Adare. Quite what precipitated this abrupt flight is not known, but infidelity may have played a part. Frances's sister, Susan O'Brien, visited her in Bristol and observed in her diary that 'Penitence and misery seemed personifyed in her figure, her manner, her words, her actions. Such a lesson to her sex was hardly ever given, of every virtue and amiable quality lost to herself and her family by imprudence, unjustifiable imprudence, and *fear*, for that occasioned all her errors.' Richard's difficult personality may also have been a contributing factor. Frances's niece, Elizabeth Talbot, considered Richard 'as mad as a March hare', while Susan was of the opinion that 'his temper would always have made him unhappy in any situation'. He did, however, allow his children to visit their mother in England—a generous measure by eighteenth-century standards, which denied women any rights to their children—and made provisions for her maintenance, albeit, according to Susan, so mean that Frances was 'obliged to deny herself every enjoyment, nay almost necessarys, from the smallness of the income'.[25]

Consequently, having for several years served as Windham's sole retreat, Adare House was unsuitable as a residence for a lady. 'I find a Bachelor in his house', Windham noted, 'is very much like the dry rot, which quietly decays everything.'[26] To remove such rot, Windham gave orders to have the rooms aired and cleaned and took dimensions of the floors for his wife to order new carpets.[27] He also consulted Nicholas Hannan, a builder who shared an office with his brother William on Taylor Street in Limerick, about some minor structural alterations to the house. Hannan arrived in Adare in March 1811, and the two men spent a day measuring, planning and plotting. 'We must shorten the staircase window very much for our painted glass', Windham decided, 'which Hannan thinks will have the effect of leaving the stairs steady enough, but making us trip in the dark—but never mind that people must walk the more carefully.'[28] When the old cellar beneath the house was put to rights by a team of workmen, Windham was grieved to discover several dozen bottles of valuable wine gone to waste as a result of decay. He consoled himself, however, that 'it is better to be cheerful with the possession [of] vinegar than repine at the loss of Wine'.[29]

The couple's plans to relocate to Ireland came to a temporary halt in the early autumn of 1811, when Caroline discovered to her delight that she was once again expecting. Fearful of another miscarriage, she and her husband spent the winter months quietly with Caroline's parents at Dunraven Castle. In February 1812 Windham escorted his wife back to London, where they settled to await

Adare House, Adare. View of the old hall. Sepia drawing by Louisa Payne-Gallwey, June 1833. Courtesy of the Dunraven family.

Adare House, Adare. The old drawing room by Louisa Payne-Gallwey, December 1833. Courtesy of the Dunraven family.

Above left: Miniature portrait of Lady Frances Fox-Strangways (1755–1814), wife of Valentine Richard Quin and mother to the second Earl of Dunraven. Courtesy of the Dunraven family.

Above right: Miniature portrait of Edwin, the future third Earl of Dunraven (1812–71). Painted by Joseph Pastorini, 14 April 1815. Courtesy of the Dunraven family.

the birth of their child. Having cast about for more affordable accommodation for several days, they settled on an apartment in Park Place, Baker Street North.[30] It was here, in the early hours of 19 May 1812, that their first child was born. He was christened Edwin Richard five days later on Caroline's 22nd birthday. A month later, the family packed their possessions, took leave of their London friends and set their course for the ferry crossing at Holyhead.

For Caroline's immediate family, the news of her departure for Ireland filled them with sentimental gloom. Lord Balcarres did his best to console Caroline's grandmother. 'It will be a sad parting when her husband runs away with her', he wrote to Charlotte Edwin, 'but so far I think you have been fortunate that as a Married Woman you have had her so long with you and I presume you will only part to meet soon again.'[31]

CHAPTER
THREE

All My Beautiful Territories

S hortly after four o'clock on 22 July 1812, Windham's carriage made its
way from Limerick city towards Adare. News of its approach spread
like wildfire. People from every corner of the parish rushed to line
the road to greet the young landlord and to catch the first glimpse of his
wife and infant son. Four miles from the village, the Quins were stopped
by a large crowd of cheering country people carrying garlands of flowers.
Forty beautifully dressed men uncoupled the horses from the carriage and
proceeded to draw it towards Adare. A band of musicians led the procession,
while soldiers lining the road saluted as it passed. The squeeze of the gathered
crowd was so immense that the military had to interfere to prevent people
from getting crushed under the carriage wheels.

Having entered the demesne, the coach stopped in front of the house, where
the Adare infantry was lined up before the drawing room windows. As the
young couple emerged from the vehicle, the soldiers fired their rifles three times
as a mark of respect. Windham then turned to the great crowd of gathered
neighbours and proudly introduced his startled wife and newborn son to his
friends. More than a little dazed by the day's events, Caroline could but marvel
at the affection in which her husband was held by all those around him.[1]

The warm welcome did much to soften any anxiety she may have felt about relocating to Ireland, a move which had separated her not only from her friends and relatives but also from every scene familiar to her since early childhood.

Having sufficiently recovered from her long journey and the excitement caused by the family's arrival, Caroline began to explore her new surroundings. She was pleased to find the house much better than she had expected and the grounds exceptionally beautiful. She was enchanted by the ruins of Desmond Castle and the Franciscan friary, glimpsed views of which were afforded from the adjacent grounds, and by the beautiful wood near the river to the south of the family seat.[2] In this wooded pleasure-ground, Caroline made her first mark as the new chatelaine of Adare House by planting a group of Lebanon cedars to commemorate her arrival.[3]

Limerick city. A view from Bank Place. Painted by William Turner de Londe, early nineteenth century. Private collection, USA. Courtesy of Lowell Libson & Jonny Yarker Ltd.

For the next seven years, the couple engaged in developing and improving their home. Like any newly married wife, Caroline wanted to make changes to her new surroundings to reflect her personal tastes. Her early years in Adare were spent repainting the rooms, buying and rearranging furniture, hanging pictures and curtains and laying down new carpets. Windham meanwhile continued his activities to improve the demesne and the adjoining deer park. By now the old oaks and thorns so admired by Arthur Young in 1776 had been reduced to such a pitiable state that the greater part of them had to be cut down.[4] A nursery of young oak trees was established on the grounds and large consignments of trees and shrubs ordered from London and planted by teams of workmen to rejuvenate the old stock of timber on the estate. The pleasure-

Adare House, Adare. View of the drawing room. Watercolour by Louisa Payne-Gallwey, c. 1830s. Private collection.

grounds to the south of the house, which covered twenty acres, also received attention. Bounded by oaks and elms of enormous size, the finest feature of this expanse was a row of 30 English elm trees, each more than 150ft in height, which lined the bank of the Maigue River. To these were now added several exotic specimen trees and ornamental plants. In addition to the cedars of Lebanon planted by Caroline, there were Portugal laurels, evergreen oaks, acacias, a hickory tree, silver firs and walnut, almond and Spanish chestnut trees, while fragrant magnolias, myrtles, camellias, pomegranates and a great profusion of other ornamental plants dominated the southernmost end of the picturesque glen.[5]

One of Windham's more ambitious undertakings was to open a series of new walks and drives within the demesne. This activity was followed closely by his father, who in his more prosperous days had begun a similar project before financial constraints put an end to his endeavours. Richard's hope had been to utilise the picturesque effect of the Maigue River and the medieval ruins on its banks to create a lengthy and circuitous drive to take the visitor from the main entrance diagonally across the demesne, crossing the river in two places by means of rustic bridges for a view of the ruins of the Franciscan friary and Desmond Castle at the northernmost end of the estate. 'This well executed, I will venture to say, there would not be in the United Kingdom so charming a home drive', he wrote to his son in an attempt to entice Windham to adopt the idea. 'I see the whole of this beautiful drive at this moment, I trace minutely every yard of it, and every object is brought into view.'[6]

In spite of Richard's eager representations, Windham did not execute his father's proposal in every detail, although he did include elements of it in his plan. The long drive that he created followed the southern and western banks of the Maigue as it wound its way through the demesne, affording views of the medieval ruins on the opposite bank before taking the visitor through the riverside pleasure-grounds and down to the south-western tip of the estate at Boulabally. Rustic seats made of ash trees were placed along the walk. Between October and November 1816, a team of workmen constructed a pavilion on the river's edge at the southern tip of the pleasure-grounds for a similar purpose.[7] Known as the Heath House, this was a small ornamental building with a thatched roof in the style of a *cottage orné*, copied from a similar structure at Dunraven Castle. When completed, it was very popular, particularly on summer evenings when friends were invited for tea and picnics, often accompanied by a bugler or other musicians. Although within walking distance of Adare House, the pavilion was far enough to merit visiting it in a horse-drawn carriage or, for romantic effect, by boat on moonlit evenings.

Windham's efforts at rejuvenation extended to the village which adjoined the estate and which had for some time struggled to survive. In general, given the bad condition of Irish roads, settlements in a riverside location enjoyed a crucial trading advantage. In Adare, however, the tidal and sinuous nature of the Maigue did not immediately lend itself to commercial activity. As a result, Adare by the early 1800s was reduced to a small group of thatched cottages near the castle on the east side of the river and around the ruins of the Trinitarian abbey on the west. At the time, the only commercial building in the village was a thatched inn, which doubled as a fox-hunting clubhouse. In 1809, to revive

Dunraven Castle, Glamorgan. Rustic 'temple' in the grounds. Watercolour by Miss Trehome, early nineteenth century. Courtesy of the Dunraven family. The building served as a template for Caroline's Heath House at Adare.

the settlement and to improve its physical appearance, Windham commenced a systematic programme of demolishing existing properties when their leases expired and granting new leases for the construction of terraced stone houses on either side of the main street at its western end. To encourage uniformity and speed up the building works, Windham boldly imposed a penalty of £200 sterling on tenants who failed to meet the construction deadline of one to two years, depending on the size of the building, or to follow the building specifications detailed in each lease. As the development depended on the expiration of old leases, the village grew only gradually; by 1811, however, Windham's programme was beginning to bear fruit.

Windham also continued his father's efforts to preserve the medieval ruins in the family's ownership. Of particular concern to him were the remains of the Trinitarian abbey which dominated the heart of the village. This thirteenth-century monastery complex had suffered badly during the Desmond and Cromwellian Wars. By the early 1800s only fragments of the tower, the nave and part of the choir survived. The ruins were used as a ball court and rows of market stalls lined its southern wall, which ran parallel to the main street. When a proposal was put forward to have the entire church fitted up as a market house, Windham was appalled and declared that he 'would never allow it to be a den of thieves'.[8] An ideal opportunity to restore the building and return it to its original use presented itself in 1810, when the Catholic church in the parish was destroyed in an accidental fire. Windham at once announced his intention to provide the local residents with a new place of worship. Construction work commenced shortly after to repair and reroof the Trinitarian church. When the interiors were fitted up, Windham pointedly had a panel inserted in a window in the south wall depicting Christ driving the sellers out of the temple, with the words 'My house is a house of prayer, but you have made it a den of thieves' inscribed underneath. The act of providing the local Catholic community with a place of worship in the heart of the village reflected Windham's ecumenism. Although the Quins had converted to the Protestant faith, they remained favourably attuned to Roman Catholics. Windham in particular was a staunch supporter of Catholic Emancipation, not only in his private life but also in his role as an MP.

The remains of the Augustinian friary on the north side of Adare were also put to good use by Windham. Up to the early 1800s, the former Catholic parish church of St Nicholas had been used for Sunday service by the Protestant community of the village. Moreover, its gabled division in the western end of the nave had been allocated to the local Methodist congregation as a preaching house. Owing to its great age, however, the building was in poor repair and gradually grew too small for the purpose. The construction of a new Methodist hall in 1803 provided partial relief. To solve the problem once and for all, Windham offered the church of the Augustinian friary to the local vestry as a viable alternative in 1808. The agreement was formalised three years later, and the church was restored by the Ecclesiastical Commissioners between 1811 and 1814. One of the major alterations carried out to the interior involved work to the four pointed arches separating the aisle from the nave, three of which were combined into two. The idea behind the change was to afford the congregation a better

Adare village, Adare. View of the village at the turn of the eighteenth century, showing the remains of the Trinitarian monastery on the right. From *Memorials of Adare Manor* (1865). Courtesy of Special Collections and Archives, Glucksman Library, University of Limerick.

view of the service, which otherwise would have been partly obscured by the rectangular piers carrying the arches. Not everyone was pleased with the result, however. Many years later, Windham's eldest son Edwin criticised it as being out of character with the medieval building but shrugged it off as 'not the only instance of barbarism in architecture perpetrated under the sanction of the Ecclesiastical Commissioners'.[9]

Windham kept a close eye on the progress of the work. In April 1811 he had reason to congratulate himself for this, as 'I discovered a mistake in the work carrying on at the new Church, which unless rectified would have been a great blemish, & have caused a great expense'.[10] Caroline, too, became involved in the refurbishment of the building. Since her arrival in Adare she had developed an interest in the education of children. Between 1813 and 1815 she visited several schools patronised by her peers. These included John Anderson's establishment in Fermoy, Co. Cork, and Lady Kingston's institutions in Mitchelstown, also in Cork, which consisted of spinning and weaving schools, a circulating library and an orphanage in which twelve children at a time were fed, clothed and educated. Inspired by such examples, Caroline went on to establish a school in Adare. In 1814 she arranged for the old refectory in the Augustinian monastery complex which adjoined the now-completed church to be reroofed and converted into a schoolhouse.[11] Accommodating some 200 pupils on average, the establishment was one of the largest of its kind in the area. It accepted children irrespective of their religion, although objections made by Roman Catholic bishops to such an irregular arrangement meant that the number of Catholic children rarely exceeded two dozen.[12] Caroline not only funded the school out of her private money but also regularly taught the children and was always present at the twice-yearly school inspections and examinations. She also provided a treat for the pupils at the end of each school year on the grounds of Adare House, with generous quantities of food and an equally generous supply of games,

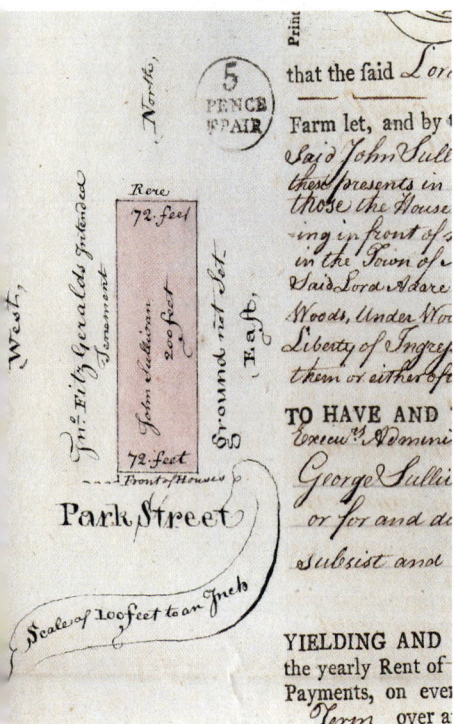

Detail of a building lease issued in 1809 to John Sullivan for the construction of a property on Park Street, Adare. Courtesy of the Dunraven family and Special Collections and Archives, Glucksman Library, University of Limerick.

fireworks, magic-lantern displays and other forms of entertainment.

In addition to the education of children, Caroline took an interest in the welfare of local women and provided them with employment opportunities by distributing spinning-wheels and quantities of flax and wool to be worked into yarn and cloth, which could then be sold on for profit. Such generous acts of charity not only benefited the local inhabitants but also strengthened Caroline's own role in the community and reinforced a sense of belonging in her new Irish home. Her ultimate rationale, however, remained religious. 'As I advance in years', she noted in 1816, 'the wish of becoming useful to my fellow creatures increases in ardour, & I feel the necessity of making out my faithful stewardship to my heavenly Master, as the business of the highest importance to me.'[13]

❖ ❖ ❖

In June 1813, Caroline's grandmother, Charlotte Edwin, arrived for a much-awaited visit to Adare, a visit which was to last not for a few precious weeks but for a full fourteen months. It was not her first journey to Ireland nor her first glimpse of Adare House, as she had been received there on her way to visit Killarney with some friends in the mid-1770s. Mrs Edwin recalled how deeply struck she had been by the magnificence of the elm avenues leading up to Adare House on that first visit.[14] Much to her delight, some of these avenues were still in place in 1813, but they were not to last much longer. In November 1814 an enormous storm blew down the entire double row of elm trees which had lined the walk between the house and the original stable yard. In addition, some 700 other trees on the wider estate, three quarters of which were full-grown mature specimens, were also destroyed.[15]

The Augustinian church, Adare, showing Caroline's schoolroom on the right. From *Memorials of Adare Manor* (1865). Courtesy of Special Collections and Archives, Glucksman Library, University of Limerick.

During Mrs Edwin's lengthy stay in Adare, her granddaughter treated her to several visits to local beauty spots. In August 1813 she was taken to Askeaton, a town some nine miles north-west of Adare, to view the great banqueting hall of its castle and the handsomely carved cloisters of its abbey. A month later, Mrs Edwin and the Quins made a journey to County Tipperary to admire the fine carved woodwork at Kilcooly Abbey and to explore the stonework at Holy Cross Abbey, which all three unanimously deemed superior to anything they had seen.[16] There were numerous visits to the elegant seats of the county's élite, boating on the Maigue when the tide was favourable, and firelit winter evenings accompanied by readings from Ann Radcliffe's Gothic novel *Mysteries of Udolpho*, which the entire family devoured with rampant interest. The highlight of the year, however, was a week-long journey to Killarney, where Mrs Edwin invited the Quins to join her. Although the excursion was partly marred by wet weather, it did little to diminish the couple's enchantment with the place. On their first day they visited Ross Castle in jaunting cars and there got into a boat to sail across the lake, while in another boat a full military band provided musical entertainment. The musicians attended the Quins everywhere as they explored the many beauty spots the lakes had to offer—the medieval abbey, O'Sullivan's Cascade, Dinis Island and the Herbert family's beautiful demesne at Muckross. Occasionally, musicians were replaced by the firing of cannons or a lone bugler sounding a melancholy note to demonstrate to dramatic effect the echo which reverberated from the surrounding mountains and for which the lakes of Killarney were famous. Such was the influence of this excursion on the Quins that for several years afterwards a week-long trip to Killarney as summer turned to autumn became a fixture in their social calendar.

Visits to places of picturesque interest formed an important part of the lives of the young couple, not so much as a distinct or clearly defined activity with a specific objective but as part of a more general effort to plant their roots into Irish soil. They formed an essential part of a comfortable routine, which patterned and gave shape to the year: excursions to local beauty spots in the summer, shooting parties and hunts in the autumn and winter, Limerick Races and visits to Tralee spa in the spring. All too soon, however, this pleasant routine was jolted by two sudden deaths in the family, both of which occurred in 1814.

Killarney, Co. Kerry. View of the lakes.
Watercolour by Augusta Goold, *c.* 1830s.
Courtesy of the Dunraven family.

❖ ❖ ❖

The first tragedy to strike the family was the death of Windham's mother, Lady Frances Quin, in March as a result of heart failure. While Windham reacted badly and plummeted into deep depression for several weeks, his father must have received the news with something approaching relief. Estranged from his wife for 21 years, Richard had effectively lived the life of a lonely widower but without the ability to remarry. As soon as the obligatory two-year mourning period was over, Richard tied the knot with Margaret Mary née Coghlan, a twice-married Roman Catholic widow,[17] who gave her husband a present of £2,600 before they were married. Unfortunately, their union was unhappy and ended in separation within a year. Mary's brother, Colonel Edmund Coghlan, regarded the annuity of £150 that Richard had settled on his wife at their parting as derisory. He accused Richard of treating

Miniature portrait of Caroline's father Thomas Wyndham (1763–1814). Painted in the late eighteenth century. Courtesy of the Dunraven family.

his sister in a cruel and unmanly manner, especially considering her generosity to him, and badgered him for years with 'puerile and unjustifiable menaces' in an attempt to double the annuity. All Richard could do was to retort bitterly, 'She got more when I left her than I got from her when I married her'.[18]

In November it was Caroline's turn to suffer bereavement when her father died. Crippled by gout, Thomas Wyndham had travelled to Bath in December 1813 in an attempt to improve his health, but a persistent cold had hindered his attempts at taking the waters. Charlotte Edwin's friend Emma Evans, who was also visiting the spa, was 'sorry to see him so afflicted, but he has the use of his hands & I saw him walk from one room to another by his crutch's, but it was performed with much difficulty'.[19] Nevertheless, his spirit and thirst for life remained strong. In spite of being confined to his wheelchair, Thomas travelled to London with his wife in May 1814 to attend the House of Commons. He showed equal ebullience in August, when Windham and the now heavily pregnant Caroline escorted Mrs Edwin on her return journey to Wales and settled at Dunraven Castle to await the birth of their second child. Elated by the joy of seeing his daughter for the first time in two years, Thomas celebrated her arrival by throwing a grand fête for his tenants in the grounds of his house, with tables laid in a circle for lunch in the garden and dancing organised on the green.

In late October, however, Thomas complained of ill health and took to his bed. His symptoms were sufficiently mild not to cause any alarm among family members, well used by now to his bouts of sickness. Great was their shock, therefore, when on the morning of 8 November Thomas suddenly fell into a coma and died.[20] The funeral of this generous, hospitable and kind-hearted man took place at St Bride's church near Bridgend a week later and is said to have been the largest ever known in the locality.[21] Caroline, who was deeply attached to her father, was devastated by his death. There was, however, a silver lining to this dark cloud. On 21 November Caroline went into labour and gave birth to a daughter who 'came like a little angel to revive our agonised spirits'.[22] The baby was quietly baptised Anna Maria Charlotte eight days after the birth, but her official christening was postponed until the family's minds were 'more attuned to joy' in 1818.[23]

With Thomas Wyndham's death, his Welsh and English estates passed to Caroline as his only surviving child—or rather, as married women were not entitled to own property in their own right, to her husband. To meet the conditions outlined in his father-in-law's will, Windham assumed the additional surname of Wyndham before that of Quin by royal sign manual in 1815. For him, succession to the Welsh and English estates was a double-edged sword. While it increased the couple's annual income by £1,150, it also left Windham's already badly stretched purse further burdened with two neglected and heavily encumbered estates in addition to the Irish property, which continued to swallow money at a rapacious rate.[24] Windham's first thought was to sell one of the properties, but this quickly proved impossible. He would not part with Adare, while his wife's mother and grandmother did everything in their power to prevent the sale of Dunraven Castle. Caroline in turn refused to consider letting go of Clearwell Court, a property to which she had a deep sentimental attachment as the place of her birth. Her more pragmatic mother questioned the sense of her determination to hold on to it: 'why you should reckon Clearwell your sheet-anchor, I cannot conceive', she wrote, 'for you must always receive more from the Welsh estate, and being chiefly on old leases and underlet, that will pay when the Gloucester estate will not'.[25] Caroline, however, remained unyielding, which left her husband at an impasse.

Miniature watercolour of Edwin (1812–71) and Anna Maria Quin (1814–55). Painted c. 1816. Courtesy of the Dunraven family.

Left: Miniature portrait of Caroline's mother, Anna Maria Wyndham *née* Ashby (1768–1837). Painted in the late eighteenth century. Courtesy of the Dunraven family.

Right: Miniature portrait of Windham Henry Wyndham Quin (1782–1850). Watercolour by George Orleans Delamotte, November 1820. Courtesy of the Dunraven family.

Windham's second suggestion was for the families to economise by living together in Adare. The idea had first been put forward when Windham and Caroline decided to make Ireland their permanent home and invited Caroline's parents to join them.[26] While touched by the generosity of the offer, the couple demurred. Now, some three years later, Mrs Wyndham showed no sign of having changed her mind. She pointed to her delicate state of health, which, she argued, required her to remain close to a physician accustomed to her constitution. She also contended that there would be no financial benefit to her from such an arrangement, as her household expenses were small and 'all my standing expences would be the same, excepting one footman, for I would not on any account part with Davies, Henry Smith or Kitty'.[27] Instead, she suggested that they could all live together at Dunraven Castle. This Windham in turn was loath to do, even though Mrs Wyndham pointed out how easy it would be for him to cross over from Wales to Waterford whenever his Irish concerns required his presence in that country.

The issue of economy came to the fore yet again when Caroline's grandmother died in June 1816. On this occasion it transpired that Mrs Edwin and Mrs Wyndham had for some time been sharing household expenses on the strength of a bond of £900 in Mrs Edwin's possession, from which her daughter continued to benefit.[28] The revelation led to a dispute between Mrs Wyndham and her son-in-law, who questioned her entitlement to the bond and insisted on having it for his own use. This Mrs Wyndham refused to do, firstly because she could not afford it and secondly because she felt that handing it over to Windham would have been contrary to her mother's wishes. Caroline was now placed in the unenviable position of having to put pressure on her mother to release the bond to please her husband while trying to avoid a falling out with a loyal and affectionate parent. In response to a particularly cool letter from Caroline, Mrs Wyndham, appalled by her daughter's antics and angered by Windham's fixation with Adare to the detriment of the Welsh and English estates, curtly reminded Caroline that at the time of her marriage 'I was the person, who caused your having so large an allowance supposing that if Mr Quin did not like residing at Dunraven, you would keep it up on your pin money, do your duty towards the poor there & at Clearwell—*certainly*, it was not given you to spend on clothes or in Ireland'.[29]

In spite of the awkward standoff, or perhaps in an attempt to defuse it, Mrs Wyndham accepted an invitation from her daughter and son-in-law to visit them in Ireland in the autumn of 1816. The visit extended from early August to early November, and Caroline went out of her way to make her mother feel welcome by introducing her to her friends and neighbours and showing her the beauties of her Irish home. An avid gardener, Mrs Wyndham took a particular interest in the pleasure-grounds and the three eighteenth-century walled gardens which adjoined to the west. The brick-lined enclosures were linked to each other by means of great double stone arches and together covered more than three acres of ground. In addition to borders of flowers, the topmost enclosure contained apricot and peach trees, while the middle garden had as its centrepiece a large fig tree, which produced two crops of fruit every summer. The walls of the southernmost part, which contained a selection of cherry and quince trees, were at some stage altered according to Caroline's wishes and given a castellated top identical to the walled gardens at Dunraven Castle.[30] Something about the arrangement of these gardens was not quite to Mrs Wyndham's liking, however, and the two women spent much of October altering them. In general, when not entertaining friends to dinner, the evenings were passed pleasantly at cards or in reading out chapters from Jane Austen's *Mansfield Park*.

Such pleasant domestic scenes were, alas, almost immediately forgotten. No sooner had Mrs Wyndham parted from the Irish shores than the argument over the bond of £900 resumed. In February 1817, when Mrs Wyndham invited her daughter and two grandchildren to stay at Dunraven Castle, Caroline responded by saying that her mother's selfishness in not relinquishing the bond meant that she couldn't possibly afford such an expensive journey. Tired of fighting with her only surviving child, and perhaps reminded of the futility of her struggle to maintain financial independence against her stepfather in 1792, Mrs Wyndham capitulated. She placed the bond in the hands of two trustees, who agreed to pay Caroline the arising interest after an interval of three years. Perhaps reflecting her mistrust of Windham with his promise to hold on to Dunraven Castle, Mrs Wyndham vouched not to claim the principal of the bond as long as the property remained in the couple's ownership.[31] Windham was jubilant on hearing the successful outcome. 'I always told you you would get this Bond by one means or other', he wrote approvingly to Caroline from London, 'a steady perseverance in refusing to be humbled by her, has its effect.'[32] Going against her mother had unsettled Caroline, however. When she discovered that some £4,000 of her father's debts remained unpaid, she determined to follow her mother's advice and assign most of her private income to clear the balance.[33] This, she hoped, would also reduce her mother's fears of Dunraven Castle being sold.

Adare House, Adare. Drawing by Miss Hanmer, *c.* 1831. Courtesy of the Dunraven family.

In July 1818 Mrs Wyndham caused a shock of a different kind, when she suddenly announced her decision to marry John Wick Bennett, owner of a small estate in the parish of Laleston near Dunraven. Caroline was mortified by the news. The Bennetts, although prominent and respectable members of the local gentry, were far from wealthy; to add to the embarrassment, John, while an amiable man in every respect and evidently sincerely attached to his wife-to-be, was 26 years Mrs Wyndham's junior and five years younger than Caroline.[34] This inevitably aroused the family's suspicion of him as a fortune-seeker. Mrs Wyndham took measures to alleviate such fears by reassuring her daughter that 'I have given directions for a new will, with the same annuities as before, and a small legacy to you, but will leave *very little* to Mr Bennett, and so have ever told him'.[35] Far from happy with her mother's decision, Caroline did her best to assist her with the wedding arrangements but, although in London at the time, could not bear to attend the ceremony at St James's church. Instead, she retreated to Tunbridge Wells in a state of high nervous agitation. Her husband, however, took a more rational approach and expressed no hesitation in welcoming John Wick Bennett into the family.

◈   ◈   ◈

While improvements on the family estate progressed, Windham continued his annual absences from Adare to attend to his parliamentary duties in the House of Commons. At the start of his political career he had been endorsed by the Lord Chancellor, George Ponsonby, as a young man of excellent character, and great hopes were expressed that he would vote with Pitt's coalition of Tory politicians and pro-government Whigs. To Pitt's disappointment, Windham remained firmly in the Whig opposition, where, among other things, he voted systematically in support of the Catholic cause.[36] As the years passed, however, his attitude towards government softened. There were a number of reasons for this, the most important of which included his determination to hold his seat as a representative of County Limerick against increasingly difficult political odds, and the desire expressed by his father for promotion in the peerage.

Adare House, Adare. Plan of the late eighteenth-century building. From *Memorials of Adare Manor* (1865). Courtesy of Special Collections and Archives, Glucksman Library, University of Limerick.

PLAN OF THE OLD MANOR HOUSE.

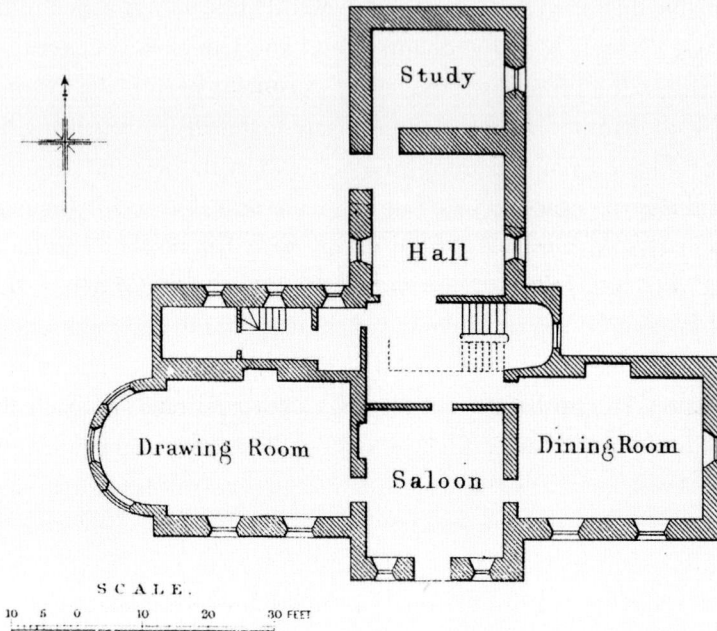

Study

Hall

Drawing Room

Saloon

Dining Room

SCALE.

10   5   0   10   20   30 FEET

The Quin family's progression along this path had begun in 1768, when Windham 'the Drone' successfully canvassed for a seat as MP for Kilmallock, Co. Limerick. His sudden move, it seems, did not stem from a burning interest in politics or social reform, for a review carried out in 1774 revealed that he seldom attended the House of Commons.[37] Instead, his ambitions most likely lay in a far more prosaic direction: a desire for social advancement in the form of a peerage. The usual route towards this goal began with the acquisition of a large country estate to demonstrate the person's dignity, followed by a seat in parliament, a baronetcy and an Irish peerage.[38] The ultimate prize, an English peerage, brought its possessor into a club as exclusive as it was rare: in the entire course of the eighteenth century, just 1,003 persons held such a title. Along with a peerage—whether English or Irish—came influence, social leadership and enormous deference from all classes. Such prestige was hard to come by and took many years of effort and frequent applications to the king. In the Quin family's case it took an entire generation, for it was Richard Quin and not his father who in June 1781 was created a baronet of Great Britain. Richard's next opportunity for advancement came in 1799, when he was elected MP for Kilmallock just in time to vote in favour of the union of the kingdoms of Great Britain and Ireland, which resulted in the abolition of the Irish parliament in 1800. As a consequence, Lord Cornwallis, who had been instrumental in preparing the ground for the Act of Union, recommended Richard for a peerage, to which he was raised on 31 July 1800 as Baron Adare.

Richard showed as little interest in politics as had his father and did not seek a seat in the House of Commons after the Union. His son's election in 1806 rekindled his interest in social advancement, however, and in the pursuit of it Windham proved a willing assistant. By April 1815 the government could look upon him as its new ally, except on the question of Catholic relief, which he continued to support. Such softening of attitude was not without its reward. On 5 February 1816 Windham's father was promoted to the rank of viscount. The name he chose for his title, Viscount Mount-Earl, was derived from the townland of Monearla on the family estate in Adare.

The promotion had far-reaching implications not only for Richard but also for his son, who would one day succeed to the title. The rise in the family's status made Windham look about his Irish estate with a more critical eye. He concluded that, while his family seat did adequate service as the residence of a baronet, it would not do for a viscount. It was probably at this juncture that the idea of improving Adare House, beyond merely dusting the carpets and providing the walls with a fresh lick of paint, first began to take shape in his mind. The timing of such a project was ideal. While by no means clear of debt, Windham was now on a much stronger footing financially. His building and planting schemes progressed apace and occupied considerably less of his time, leaving him free to pursue other projects. His wife, who not only shared his interest in architecture but had first-hand experience of building works through her father's activities in Dunraven Castle, enthusiastically supported the idea. Moreover, Windham's determination to focus his efforts on his Irish estate, as much as it annoyed his mother-in-law, sent a clear message that it was here and not in Wales or England that he wanted to establish the dynasty he was so anxious to build. Yet, never one to act in haste, Windham mulled the matter over for almost two years before acting. In December 1817 James Pain, a young and promising English architect newly established in Limerick city, was invited to Adare to see what alterations he could make to the house.[39]

Born in Greater London into a family of master builders and architects, James and his brothers Henry and George Richard had all served their apprenticeship with John Nash.[40] Nash, who had begun his career as a builder, was a colourful and contradictory character. Following an embarrassing bankruptcy in his early career, he had sought refuge in his native Wales, where he reinvented himself as an architect. His collaboration with the landscape designer Humphry Repton between 1795 and 1800 brought him not only prominent clients but a reputation as a master of the emerging Gothic style.[41] Nash's picturesque asymmetrical castles quickly gained favour among the landed classes. His return to London, where he reopened his architectural practice in 1796, was followed by a meteoric rise in popularity and culminated in his preferment as architect to the prince regent, the future King George IV, in 1811.

Nash's prominence was of obvious benefit to his apprentices and guaranteed them the patronage of the landed élite hungry for the latest in fashionable architectural designs. Moreover, since his involvement with the prince regent, Nash only rarely accepted private commissions. The few projects that he did take on he was usually too busy to supervise in person, and instead sent his most promising students to do the work for him. James Pain was given an opportunity to prove himself in 1811, when he was sent to Ireland to oversee the construction of Lough Cutra Castle near Gort, Co. Galway, for Colonel Charles Vereker and Shanbally Castle near Clogheen, Co. Tipperary, for Viscount Lismore. His brother George Richard joined him some five years later. By the time Lough Cutra Castle was completed in 1817, the young architects had established a name for themselves and set up an architectural practice in Limerick city. Equally competent in Neo-Classical and Neo-Gothic designs, and with a reputation for being reliable and capable of completing commissions on time and within budget—a rarity among architects of the day—the brothers quickly established themselves as the foremost masters of their craft in the province of Munster. Their thriving practice encompassed a remarkably wide range of buildings, from churches, gaols and court-houses to handsome country seats. George's move to Cork, where he set up his own practice in 1820, did not stop the close partnership. The continued collaboration was advantageous to both parties, since James was better at planning and the business side of things, while George was more skilled as a draughtsman.[42]

In addition to Colonel Vereker and Viscount Lismore, the Pain brothers' early clients included Windham's friend Sir Edward O'Brien of Dromoland, Co. Clare, who in 1813 decided to replace his eighteenth-century mansion with a new family seat. He sought design proposals from prominent architects of the day, including Thomas Hopper and William and Richard Morrison. James Pain also submitted a plan for a rather conventional house of Classical design, which is unlikely to have found favour with the client. Luckily for James, Sir Edward was slow to make up his mind. When George Richard arrived in Ireland, the brothers put together a second proposal, this time for a Gothic Revival castle. Although Sir Edward, who was nothing if not cautious by nature, was still vacillating between his options in 1817, it was this design that eventually won the day.

Shanbally Castle, Clogheen, Co. Tipperary. Watercolour by George Stanley Repton, c. 1810. Photo © National Gallery of Ireland.

In 1817 James and George Richard Pain joined forces with Nicholas and William Hannan, the builders who had worked on minor structural alterations to Adare House in 1811, to design and construct Limerick County Gaol on Mulgrave Street in Limerick city.[43] This, coupled with Sir Edward's activities at Dromoland and their own growing reputation as fashionable new architects, soon brought the brothers to Windham's attention.

The Pain brothers' early proposals for alterations to Adare House do not survive, but something about Windham and Caroline's thinking can be gleaned from their activities at this time. Windham's decision to improve the family home stimulated the couple's general interest in architecture. In 1818, when Caroline accompanied Windham to England for the first time since her father's death, she occupied herself by visiting buildings of note during her husband's absence in the House of Commons. Those she considered the most interesting she revisited with Windham whenever he could remove himself from London. Although such visits were spontaneous and unplanned, made without any particular forethought, they provide an early indication of the direction of the couple's developing tastes.

Charlton Park, Wiltshire, from the west. Painted by Hendrik Frans de Cort, *c.* 1800. © Historic England Archive.

Penshurst Place, Kent. From Neale's *Views of the Seats of Noblemen and Gentlemen in England, Wales, Scotland and Ireland*, vol. 4 (2nd edition, 1828). Courtesy of Special Collections and Archives, Glucksman Library, University of Limerick.

While staying with her father-in-law in Cheltenham in February and March 1818, Caroline befriended Thomas Howard, Viscount Andover, who invited her to the family seat, Charlton Park, to meet his parents, the Duke and Duchess of Suffolk. Charlton Park was one of the finest Jacobean mansions in the country; its oldest western façade, dominated by two massive onion-domed turrets, dated from 1607 and was said to have been designed by Inigo Jones. Inside, one of the most notable features of the house was its remarkable panelled gallery, which extended along the entire length of the western front and contained a fine chimney-piece and a ceiling of richly ornamented stucco work. The duke's substantial estate encompassed the medieval church of St John the Baptist and the beautiful twelfth-century Malmesbury Abbey, built in the late Romanesque style while carrying elements of early Gothic influences in its windows and the shallow pointing of the arches in its nave. Caroline was much taken with the place. She spent several days taking drawings of and copying patterns from the church, abbey and mansion, and later took her husband to see the buildings.

Elizabethan and Jacobean buildings were the dominant house types visited by the couple during the summer of 1818. Among these was the fourteenth-century Penshurst Park near Tonbridge, Kent, one-time home of the great

Elizabethan poet Sir Philip Sidney, which they saw no fewer than three times between late July and early August. It was as much the historical association of the building as its architecture that attracted them. Indeed, while they agreed that the house was extremely old and curious and its large collection of paintings well worth seeing, they felt that the setting lacked any natural beauties to boast of apart from an ancient oak planted at the time of Sidney's birth.[44] In August they travelled to the seventeenth-century Buckhurst Park in East Sussex to view the Elizabethan-style renovations carried out by Arabella, Duchess of Dorset, and her second husband, Lord Whitworth. They also visited Knole, one of the country's largest and most remarkable domestic buildings of medieval origin. The Wyndham Quins at once deemed it the finest they had seen both in style and magnificence, and marvelled at the comfort and well-finished quality of its living rooms. One of the remarkable features of the house was its great early seventeenth-century principal staircase, the newel posts of which were surmounted by gilded carved leopards holding heraldic shields; another was its extensive collection of paintings and family portraits, at which the couple, to their regret, barely had time to glance.[45]

While Gothic detailing and medieval forms clearly appealed to Windham and Caroline from early on, their visits in 1818 reveal an equally strong interest in the clean lines of Classical architecture. In addition, Caroline in particular was attracted to the overall composition and setting of a building rather than any one architectural style in its own right. A good example of this was Hawkstone Hall, an elegant early eighteenth-century Palladian mansion in Shropshire, which Caroline considered well worth seeing even though its setting was poorly chosen in her opinion. What impressed her, however, were the fine grounds on which the building stood. Comprising both natural and man-made elements in highly varied terrain with cliff edges, caves and tunnels against the backdrop of the beautiful Shropshire landscape, the park contained several remarkable eye-catchers: a Gothic arch on top of one hill and a castle on top of another; a grotto approached by an underground passage; a 100ft obelisk with an internal staircase; and a narrow Swiss bridge spanning a steep gorge. Little Edwin had joined his parents on the excursion and shared his mother's fascination. Caroline was not a little pleased to note how her six-year-old son was 'not the least tired, though we walked many miles of extremely hard walking'.[46]

Following this eventful and diverting break, the Wyndham Quins returned to Adare in late September 1818. Some ten weeks later, James Pain arrived with his proposed alterations to the family seat and plans for gate lodges and other ornamental features.[47] The couple spent an entire day with the architect, examining the drawings and altering them according to what they had seen and liked in England. Unfortunately, it was at this point, as Windham and Caroline were preparing to embark on a new and exciting building project, that the wheel of fortune turned once again and threw their plans into disarray.

❖   ❖   ❖

The year 1819 began badly, with Windham embroiled in a political scandal. The county election in Limerick the previous summer had been a bitterly fought contest, and Windham barely managed to hold on to his seat. Following the death of Lord Muskerry in June 1818, Windham also fought hard to secure the now vacant and much-coveted position of *Custos Rotulorum*, or keeper of records, of County Limerick, the highest civil office in the county. One of Windham's first acts in that role was to appoint his close friend Richard Smith to work as his clerk of the peace, whose duties included the maintenance of a register of freeholders eligible to vote. The position, worth £800 a year, had for the previous fifteen years been held by Thomas William Grady of Belmont, Co. Limerick. Windham's reason for dismissing him was that Grady had been appointed at a very young age and as a consequence had never exercised a single function of his office, which instead were performed by a deputy.[48] Grady was not a wealthy man and, aware of the financial implications of the loss of office, Windham saw to it that an annual pension of £200 would be paid in compensation to Grady out of Richard Smith's salary. Supported by Windham's political enemies, Grady at once petitioned the government to initiate a parliamentary inquiry. He claimed that Richard Smith was appointed in his place to combat Windham's diminishing popularity among the local electorate and that the pension offered to Grady had carried the condition of his and his tenants' political support. While initially shocked by this turn of events, Windham and his wife soon 'rejoiced at it, as it would afford Windham an opportunity of clearly refuting all their accusations'.[49] The parliamentary inquiry began in late February 1819 and, following a debate on Grady's petition and Windham's impassioned defence, the matter was resolved in the latter's favour in early April.[50]

Although he had been exonerated, the incident tarnished Windham's political reputation and undermined his already weakened position among the County Limerick electorate. To save embarrassment, he decided not to seek re-election in 1820, using a sudden deterioration in his father's health as an excuse to stand down. In many ways, however, giving up the seat was not such a sacrifice as it might appear. Windham was not comfortable with long absences from his wife, which his political duties had necessitated. Besides, he detested city life. As early as 1811 he complained to Caroline that 'If a Town life did but agree with me as well as a Country one, how happy I should be; for after all my main passion is the House of Commons. But unfortunately it does not. I can bear anything but late hours, they actually destroy me.'[51] Consequently, shaking off the shackle of political duties was ultimately a relief. Writing to his father in April 1820, Windham confessed that 'from the moment I took my resolution to this hour, I have never thought of it but with the greatest satisfaction. I have got rid of a load that tormented me & never felt so much at ease & so happy in my life.'[52]

Another setback with far-reaching consequences was caused by the weather. In April 1815, a volcanic eruption of Mount Tambora in Indonesia ejected an immense quantity of ash into the atmosphere, obscuring sunlight in the process. Temperatures across the globe decreased by about half a degree Celsius as a consequence, and the year 1816 was to become known as 'the year without a summer'. Huge storms, abnormal rainfall and frost in August destroyed crops, and the failure of wheat, oat and potato harvests resulted in famine and outbreaks of typhoid in Britain and Ireland, at the time recovering from food shortages caused by the Napoleonic Wars. In Adare, the Wyndham Quins marvelled at a fall of snow on Easter Sunday in April 1816 and struggled through incessant torrents of rain, which lasted all summer. By October, heavy floods on the estate prevented any further work on Windham's improvements, and much of the winter was spent indoors, as it was too wet to venture out. For the next several years, the havoc wrought on crops by abnormal weather dramatically affected the revenue generated on the estate.[53] To this were added a number of personal setbacks. Caroline longed for more children, but the miscarriage she had suffered in February 1811 revisited her with all too frequent regularity. In October 1819 she suffered a late and severe miscarriage of twins, her seventh loss in eight years. She recovered but slowly from the physical and emotional trauma that had nearly cost her life. In April 1820, Windham suddenly fell ill with a pain in his foot which his wife declared looked suspiciously like gout and indeed turned out to be so.

Maigue River, Adare. Scenic view showing the Franciscan friary in the background. Watercolour by Louisa Payne-Gallwey, *c.* 1833. Courtesy of Lavinia Graham-Vivian.

Windham had barely mended when disturbing rumours began to circulate about an impending financial crisis. Since the end of the Napoleonic Wars in 1815 agricultural prices had plummeted, reaching an all-time low in 1819. The financial depression that followed placed the Irish banking system in jeopardy, as the private banks which dominated the market had neither the resources nor the experience to survive such pressure. Disaster struck on 25 May 1820, when Roche's Bank in Cork, the main city in the province of Munster, collapsed and ceased trading. Alarmed by this turn of events, the remaining three banks in the city—Leslie's, Newenham's and Pike's—also suspended business, leaving Cork in a state of chaos. From there the crisis spread like wildfire. On the very next day, three banks in Limerick city failed to open. By the end of the month, sixteen of the 31 private banks in the country had collapsed, leaving many districts without any banking facilities and causing an almost complete stoppage of all commercial activities across the country.[54]

Windham and his wife followed this unravelling with a mounting sense of dread. Most of their money had been invested in the bank of Maunsell, Kennedy and Company, which for several days stood up to the crisis. The *Limerick Chronicle* soothed its readers by reassuring them that 'Though unusual crowds of peasantry and the labouring classes paraded the streets on Monday much gratification is produced that no riot occurred. The run still continues and, although crowds are in front of the banks, many are drawn there by idle curiosity.'[55] Even before the comment made it into print, however, the bank could withstand the crisis no more. On 29 May, Windham received news of its collapse and rushed to Limerick in a desperate attempt to salvage what he could. It was to no avail. The family's money was gone.

This was one of the darkest moments in Windham's life. The banking crisis had thrown him right back to where he had started and negated the many years of hard work and dedication that he had expended to rejuvenate the family estate. With his political career over, his finances in tatters and rents at an all-time low, Windham's dream of re-establishing his roots in Irish soil seemed at an end. Adare House and its extensive grounds continued to devour money which he no longer possessed. Retrenchment was necessary, but how to manage it without embarrassment? Casting about for options, Windham's thoughts turned to the prospect of seeking a future in Wales. It was an option that his mother-in-law had already proposed in 1817 during their long-winded argument over money. 'How I wish you would all come & spend a year or two with me', she had written to Caroline at the time, 'tho' I cannot flatter myself it could be as agreeable as being in a house of your own, it would be of material advantage … You could at Dunraven, be perfectly master of your time in your own apartments, excepting at dinner but you could breakfast there, if you preferred it … I would render your residence with me as pleasant as I could, if Mr Quin would consent, it certainly is the wisest plan to pursue.'[56]

Windham had rejected the idea in 1817, but three years on in the changed circumstances he viewed it more favourably. The need to focus on the family's Welsh estates would provide him with the perfect excuse for a dignified exit from Ireland, which in turn would considerably reduce his overheads. Having made up his mind, Windham wasted no time in executing the plan. Preparations for the family's removal from Adare began in mid-August 1820. Tools were downed, possessions packed and the house emptied of books, paintings and furniture, leaving the rooms looking desolate and forlorn. Visits were paid to friends in the neighbourhood to exchange farewells. On 2 September the Wyndham Quins, along with a large group of friends, made an excursion to the top of a high hill called the Black Bull in east County

Sunset at sea. Watercolour by Augusta Goold, c. 1830s. Courtesy of the Dunraven family.

Limerick to cast a parting glance on the landscape they had grown to love. 'It was the last time I should see the country in the neighbourhood of Adare', Caroline acknowledged with a heavy heart.[57]

The family's departure took place two days later. At eight o'clock in the morning of 4 September, a large convoy of carriages rolled out through the gates of Adare House and made its way towards Waterford. After a journey of eleven hours by road, the travellers arrived in the coastal settlement of Dunmore, where inclement weather detained them for three days. On the afternoon of 7 September, the winds changed course and a crossing was made possible. An eclipse of the sun took place that morning. Windham and Caroline observed it through pieces of blackened glass and noted how 'the day was much darkened & the atmosphere had a black & unnatural appearance, though the sun was very bright'.[58] It was a fitting echo of their feelings as they gave a last look at the Irish shore, while the ferry pulled away and carried them towards an uncertain future.

CHAPTER
FOUR

Ynyslas

The Wyndham Quins' initial destination in Wales was Dunraven Castle in Glamorgan. Here they spent several months revisiting favourite spots of old, with daylong excursions to St Donat's Castle and leisurely walks on the sands of Southerndown. Caroline tried to adopt a routine similar to her life in Adare by taking an interest in the local school, while Windham made regular journeys to Cheltenham to spend time with his father, who was nearing 70 and showing signs of frailty. The couple visited the church in St Bride's to see a white marble wall monument erected to the memory of Caroline's father and two brothers, and renewed old friendships in the neighbourhood, most notably with the Talbots. They, like the Wyndham Quins, had suffered a relatively recent bereavement with the death of the head of the household, Thomas Mansel Talbot, in 1813. Since then, his widow Mary had remarried. Her second husband, Sir Christopher Cole, had given up a distinguished naval career to manage the considerable Talbot estates and political interests during the minority of Thomas's heir, Christopher, who was only ten years old at the time of his father's death.

The Talbots continued to live at Penrice but owned a second property, Margam Park, some twelve miles north of Dunraven Castle. Originally the site of a Cistercian monastery and subsequently home to the Mansel family, Margam had passed to the Talbots through marriage in the early eighteenth century. Thomas Mansel Talbot, who had inherited the estate in 1758, had little interest in the rambling Tudor house on its grounds and preferred to live at Penrice in the Italianate villa designed for him by Anthony Keck in 1772–3. He did, however, retain an interest in Margam's vast grounds, which were ideal for hunting, and its exceptional and extensive collection of citrus trees. To protect these delicate plants from the ravages of winter weather, he asked Keck to provide him with a design for an orangery. The impressive Neo-Classical structure was built in 1787–90 and, at 327ft, was the longest of its kind in Britain. It not only housed fruit trees but also incorporated pedimented pavilions at either end, one of which served as a library and the other as a statue room. Here Thomas displayed some of the vast collection of sculptures that he had purchased in Rome during his Grand Tour.[1]

As the orangery was being built, Thomas demolished the old Tudor house on the site with a view to replacing it with a more comfortable modern residence. The plan did not materialise in his lifetime, but this did not deter his widow and children from continuing to use the property for pleasure. In September 1820, just two weeks after Windham and Caroline's arrival in South Wales, the Talbots invited them to spend a day at Margam Park. They were shown around the grand orangery, where much was made of a rare aloe plant said to flower once in 100 years and now in bloom. While Caroline confessed in her journal that she and her husband found little to admire in the tall-stalked plant and its deep-clustering yellow blossoms, they were nevertheless charmed by the beauty of the grounds and were glad to rejuvenate the long-standing relationship between the two families.[2]

Southerndown beach, Glamorgan. Watercolour by Louisa Payne-Gallwey, c. 1830s. Courtesy of Lavinia Graham-Vivian.

Margam demesne, Glamorgan, showing orangery, church and chapter house. Watercolour by Thomas Hornor, early nineteenth century. © National Museum Wales.

As pleasant as the reprieve in Dunraven Castle was, it could not last forever. For one thing, Caroline was uncomfortable living there now that John Wick Bennett and not her father was its master; for another, the property was far too expensive to maintain on the couple's diminished income. Even the Bennetts had settled for a house in Cardiff as their main residence and only made occasional use of the castle. Clearwell Court and Llanmihangel were both on long-term leases to tenants, the former to James and Catherine Haffenden, who kept the place in excellent order, and the latter to the old retainer John Franklen, who by now was nearing 90.[3] While no longer acting as steward, he had served the family far too well to be summarily dismissed. A viable solution to the issue of accommodation had to be found, and one that would not expose the family's financial embarrassment nor excessively strain their limited resources.

In late October 1820 the Wyndham Quins set off for an excursion around South Wales which lasted for several weeks. Among the places they visited was the Vale of Neath, some twenty miles north of Dunraven Castle, where they stayed as guests of the Williams family of Aberpergwm House. Its occupants at the time were Rees Williams and his two unmarried sisters, Anne and Jane, who were minding the property during the absence abroad of their eldest brother, William.[4] Accompanied by this hospitable threesome, the couple made several visits to local beauty spots, including the dramatic

Carboniferous limestone promontory known as Dinas Rock and the many caves and waterfalls for which the valley was famous. The beauty and romantic nature of the surrounding scenery greatly impressed the couple, and within weeks of this tour they hit upon the idea of building a cottage-style residence in the Vale of Neath as their new home. By April 1821 a site for the building had been selected in a gentle curve of the River Neath in a place known as Ynyslas (Welsh for green or fertile island), located a short distance to the south-west from Glynneath and directly across the river from Aberpergwm House. What may have increased the appeal of the site to Windham and Caroline was its proximity to the river and to the small St Mary's church a short distance to the east, both elements reminiscent of their home in Adare.

The idea of building a cottage in such an isolated and remote area was not as strange as it might seem, nor indeed was the choice of Ynyslas as the site of the new family home merely the result of a random coincidence of a suitable plot of ground being available in this particular corner of the country. By the early nineteenth century the Vale of Neath was one of the most celebrated beauty spots in South Wales and a much-favoured destination of poets and topographical artists in search of a picturesque thrill. The phenomenon was not unique to Wales but was part of a wider Picturesque movement, an aesthetic ideal first popularised by William Gilpin with the publication of his guidebook *Observations on the River Wye* in 1782 and further developed by Edmund Burke, Richard Payne Knight and Uvedale Price. By the end of the eighteenth century, ruins, old cottages, dramatic landscapes and anything quaint or irregular had become objects of interest. During the Napoleonic Wars, when Continental travel and the *de rigueur* Grand Tour were almost impossible, tourists and artists inspired by the Romantic movement flocked instead to the local countryside and isolated beauty spots in search of aesthetic pleasure. Wales, Scotland and the Lake District were particularly popular as destinations of this Home Tour, as the activity became commonly known, and numerous guides were printed with advice on routes incorporating the best scenic spots and most picturesque ruins.

In Wales, the beautifully wooded hillsides and spectacular waterfalls of the Vale of Neath, coupled with the romantic appeal of Briton Ferry in an attractive coastal setting at the mouth of the river, formed an ideal destination for men like the naturalist Alfred Russel Wallace, who exclaimed during a

Rheola, Vale of Neath, Glamorgan. Watercolour by Thomas Hornor, early nineteenth century. © National Museum Wales.

River Neath, Glamorgan. Watercolour by Thomas Hornor, 1817. © National Museum Wales.

Rheola, Vale of Neath, Glamorgan. Rustic bridge in the grounds. Watercolour by Thomas Hornor, 1817. By permission of Llyfrgell Genedlaethol Cymru/The National Library of Wales.

Hafod, Cardiganshire. Watercolour showing the conservatory and octagonal library designed by Nash, early nineteenth century. Image by Llyfrgell Genedlaethol Cymru/ The National Library of Wales, courtesy of Mrs Anne Robertson.

visit in 1845 that 'I cannot call to mind a single valley that in the same extent of country comprises so much beautiful and picturesque scenery, and so many interesting and special features, as the Vale of Neath'.[5] Virtually every established English artist of the late eighteenth and early nineteenth centuries visited the Neath district to feast on its rich variety of scenes—Paul Sandby, John Varley, Henry Gastineau, William De la Motte and, perhaps most notably, Joseph Mallord William Turner, who toured South Wales as a young man in 1795.[6]

Some enthusiasts took the Romantic ideal a step further and retreated from fashionable society to embrace a more pastoral or natural way of living. The most celebrated icons of this mode of life were Lady Eleanor Butler and Miss Sarah Ponsonby, known as the Ladies of Llangollen, who had eloped from Ireland to live in quiet retirement in the Vale of Llangollen. Caroline had met the two women in 1809 during a month-long tour of North Wales on which her mother had taken her to instruct her on the region's scenic, industrial and architectural highlights. The meeting had touched her deeply. 'Anything so beautiful as their cottage & grounds I never yet saw, everything is on a small scale, but done with so much taste that they quite enchanted me', she recalled in her journal. 'They were extremely civil & attentive to us, & after showing us all the curiosities of which their cottage is replete, we walked with them in their grounds, which show the most beautiful parts of the Vale, & yet are so retired that not a house is to be seen from them. They have built several small buildings which at once combine rusticity, convenience, & elegance, in each there is a small recess for books of which they have an admirable collection. A small meandering stream a tributary of the Dee winds through their grounds which are beautifully wooded. Romance seems to breathe in every leaf I never was so enchanted with anything in my life.'[7]

It was these early nineteenth-century cultural trends that now enabled the Wyndham Quins to economise without embarrassment. A small house in a picturesque valley allowed the couple to minimise daily expenditure, while to the outside world residing in a romantic retreat appeared fashionable and sophisticated.[8] Just how popular such building activities were in this part of the country is demonstrated by the fact that it was here, too, that James and George Richard Pain's teaching master, John Nash, matured as an architect in the 1780s and 1790s.

Nash began as a designer of public buildings, but his absorbingly original style was soon discovered by the Welsh gentry eager to remodel their outdated homes. Nash had an instinctive understanding of the increasingly popular Picturesque aesthetic, which he readily employed in his work. In this regard, even his poor project-management skills and notoriously unreliable cost estimates did little to deter his clients.[9] The most important of these at the time included Uvedale Price, pioneer of the concept of the Picturesque as a mode of landscape, for whom Nash designed a holiday villa known as Castle House in Aberystwyth in 1791–4, and Thomas Johnes, another enthusiast of the Picturesque, who invited Nash to redesign parts of his famous home at Hafod in 1793. Most notably, however, Nash designed a country house in the fashionable cottage style between 1814 and 1818 for his relative and business partner John Edwards. The house, Rheola, stood on the southern bank of the Neath River just four miles downstream from Ynyslas.

❖ ❖ ❖

Windham and Caroline's first visit to Rheola was made in April 1821, soon after they had selected the site of their new home. The owner of Rheola, John Edwards, a prosperous solicitor, was the son of Nash's nephew, John Edwards senior, who had purchased the property. Edwards wished the building, originally a modest farmhouse, to be enlarged and extensively remodelled while retaining its cottage-like appearance.[10] This Nash accomplished by extending the house dramatically to the rear while enhancing its façade with picturesque elements, which included a veranda, a canted end bay, shutters at the first-floor windows and tall chamfered chimneys, thus hiding a substantial country house behind the veneer of a *cottage orné*. The picturesque theme was repeated in the designs of two farm buildings constructed in the vicinity of the house, which incorporated dormer windows, projecting porches and trellised canopies along which flowering plants climbed.

The planting scheme of the grounds further heightened the cottage feel by hiding all but Rheola's compact ornamental front when viewed from the roadside. Instead of a grand drive, the house was approached by a modest gated

Aberystwyth, showing Castle House in the background. Lithograph by William Crane, c. 1840. By permission of Llyfrgell Genedlaethol Cymru/The National Library of Wales.

path, and the rustic air was further heightened by an ornamental alpine bridge, which spanned the brook running alongside the house.[11] The simple and rural setting was captured in a series of drawings made for Edwards by the surveyor and landscape designer Thomas Hornor, who toured Wales between 1816 and 1820 to prepare plans and panoramic views of country estates, presented to clients in handsome leather-bound portfolio albums. The images in the album prepared for Edwards present the house surrounded by gently sloping meadows and long stretches of natural woodland rather than the parkland with exotic specimen trees more commonly associated with estate landscapes.

Windham and Caroline's visit to Rheola sparked their interest in a further exploration of Nash's works in South Wales. This they undertook in September 1821 on a return journey from Llandrindod Wells, where Windham had been recuperating after a short spell of illness. Their first stop was Hafod, where Thomas Johnes had created one of the most important naturalistic Picturesque landscapes of his time. Had Johnes still been alive in 1821, Windham would have found in him a kindred spirit. When he inherited the Hafod estate from his father in 1780, it was in a deplorable condition—the buildings half-ruinous, the grounds mismanaged and the tenants poorly housed. Johnes began a systematic course of estate management by building new cottages for his tenants, offering prizes for good crops, experimenting with sheep- and cattle-breeding and the growing of new crops, and carrying out extensive tree-planting where ground was deemed unsuitable for cropping. In the course of his life, some three million trees were planted on the estate, earning Johnes five Royal Society of Arts medals for his contribution to silviculture.

Influenced by his cousin Richard Payne Knight, Johnes championed the Picturesque concept and utilised it to the full in the design of his plantations at Hafod. The planting was done on an enormous scale, covering some 1,200 acres and combining open pasture with extensive wooded areas. The grounds were bisected by a series of circuitous walks offering a succession of delightful views, some further enhanced by architectural features such as picturesque cottages, rustic bridges and gazebos. In 1786 Johnes demolished the old dwelling house in the heart of the estate and commissioned the Bath architect Thomas Baldwin to design a new and grander edifice. The style chosen for the building was Gothic, which complemented the almost exaggerated picturesqueness of the surrounding grounds. In 1793 John Nash contributed significantly to the design by adding a 165ft conservatory filled with rare and exotic plants, and an octagonal library top-lit by a high cupola, which towered over the house. The asymmetrical form of the building created by these additions was a significant break from the classical regularity of Georgian architecture and opened up for Nash artistic opportunities to master a style which was later to become his trademark. Windham and Caroline were charmed by the appeal of the place. 'The grounds & scenery are romantic beyond all description', Caroline recalled in her journal, '& the house a most beautiful one, filled with fine pictures, marbles & a very fine collection of books ... We drove miles through the grounds, which are wildly romantic & yet highly cultivated, & unite the sublime & beautiful in better harmony than any thing I ever saw.'[12]

From Hafod the couple proceeded to Aberystwyth, where they took possession of rooms at Castle House as guests of its owner, Uvedale Price. The building, designed by Nash in 1791–4 and built in 1795 for Price as a summer retreat, occupied a site adjacent to the evocative ruins of Aberystwyth Castle, then in the possession of Thomas Johnes.[13] It was probably the latter's influence that persuaded the town's burgesses to grant Price a lease in 1788 of a portion of the common land next to the sea on which Castle House was to be built. The aspect was dramatic, commanding on its three sides views of the sea, the coast and the castle ruins. In designing the building, Price insisted that 'I must have not only some of the *windows* but some of the *rooms*' orientated towards these three scenic points to the east, south and west.[14] Nash's solution, a house triangular in plan with an octagonal tower rising from a square base at each of its angles, was simple but ingenious. On the south and east fronts a canted porch was set between the towers, while on the west a semicircular bay with a balcony protected by a hemispherical canopy provided unobstructed views of the sea. Stylistically, the building incorporated Gothic elements but in a restrained fashion.[15] Castle House was built at a time when Price was formulating his theoretical concepts of the Picturesque. Its construction and the dramatic views it offered of the sea churning against the rocks gave him scope to explore and perfect his ideas.[16]

The views afforded by the building were not lost on the Wyndham Quins either. Looking from its windows, they were 'delighted with the sea, whose foaming waves, bathe the terrace walk before the Castle & from the rooms the sea views are very fine'. They were also taken by Aberystwyth Castle and regarded its ruins, standing on rocks projecting into the sea, as one of the finest features in Cardigan Bay. The couple were so pleased that they resolved to stay in Aberystwyth for two days longer than originally planned. When heavy rain prevented further outdoor exploration, they instead filled their time with a private tour of Castle House given by its owner.[17]

Windham and Caroline's trail on the footsteps of John Nash and Uvedale Price reflected their interest in the Picturesque. Caroline in particular was well versed in the concept and throughout her life viewed her surroundings through its lens. The couple's visits formed a concerted effort to grasp the essence of a movement they admired and wished to emulate at Ynyslas within the limits of their purse. Had their finances allowed, the couple might well have desired to commission Nash to design the building. Nash, however, rarely took on private clients following his close association with the prince regent from 1811 onwards. A practical alternative was to work with a less illustrious architect with inspiration drawn from Nash's buildings. With this in mind, the Wyndham Quins turned to William Whittington, an architect and surveyor with offices in the nearby town of Neath. Whittington was an unusual choice, since he made his career primarily as a surveyor of bridges and had little experience in country house design. It is quite possible that it was his convenient proximity to Ynyslas rather than his design skills that weighed in his favour. Without doubt, the Wyndham Quins had a firm idea of what they wanted. A surveyor with good engineering skills to provide working drawings and oversee the building works amply met their needs.

The house built at Ynyslas had much of Rheola in its purview. Although named a cottage, it was in fact a substantial two-storey house. Its asymmetrical façade faced north, overlooking the Neath River, while its east side was dominated by a semicircular end bay with a conical roof, inspired by Rheola's hexagonal projections. Other elements borrowed from Rheola included tall, diagonally set chimneys—a feature much favoured by Nash—and a canopied veranda covered with lead, which had the appearance of billowing fabric when viewed from a distance. To heighten the rustic appearance of Ynyslas, its walls of red brick were left exposed, whereas at Rheola they were given a coating of render. As at Rheola, the utility buildings were discreetly tucked away a short distance from the house, which preserved the compact scale of the building and enhanced the romantic illusion.

Rheola, Vale of Neath, Glamorgan. Watercolour by George Orleans Delamotte, early nineteenth century. © National Museum Wales.

Construction works commenced in April 1821, when a team of workmen laid a road to the building site and marked the outline of the cottage on the ground. The entire family participated with much interest in the latter activity. Another landmark was achieved on 9 May, when the foundation stone was laid with due pomp and ceremony. Windham and Caroline, accompanied by Rees, Anne and Jane Williams, walked in procession to the site, with Edwin and Anna Maria in the front carrying flags, and it was the children who laid the first stone. A musical performance followed, with Caroline on the harp and Jane Williams on the guitar. Afterwards, the merry party removed to the nearby Lamb and Flag Inn for tea and a game of cards. Locals were invited to join in the celebrations with a dance in the club room, which the two children, to their delight, were allowed to watch until midnight.[18]

At the outset, the building construction progressed at pace. By September 1821 it was sufficiently advanced for Caroline to declare the cottage 'by far the prettiest thing I ever saw in my life'.[19] In spite of such initial optimism, construction took longer than anticipated and left the family effectively homeless until the end of 1822. To provide stability for their children, Windham decided that this was a good time for Edwin and Anna Maria to begin their formal education. Edwin, now nine, had in fact already done so, having been placed in a boarding-school run by a Mrs Longford at Kensington in 1818, and only visited his parents sporadically during holidays and when special occasions merited his presence. In early October 1821 Edwin commenced a new chapter in his life, when his father delivered him to Worplesdon in Surrey, where the Reverend Edward Polehampton ran a boarding-school to prepare a small number of boys every year for Eton. Although his mother fretted about this change of circumstance, Edwin by all accounts could not have found himself in a better place. The poet and theologian Isaac Williams, also taught by Polehampton, fondly recalled that 'we had everything that boys would wish for at that age—a garden for each of us, rabbits, donkeys, cricket, and other out-of-door games'.[20] Meanwhile, seven-year-old Anna Maria was entrusted to a Belgian governess, Eliza Bolleau, known to the family as Mademoiselle, and the pair were sent to live with Caroline's mother at Cardiff, with occasional visits to Dunraven Castle.

Their children safely deposited, Windham and Caroline divided their time between Aberpergwm House and the Lamb and Flag Inn, a short walking distance from the Williams estate. This allowed them to monitor the progress of building works at Ynyslas on a daily basis. Rees Williams, a practical and enterprising man, was at the time carrying out extensive improvements on the family estate on behalf of his brother and also took an active interest in building activities at Ynyslas. Meanwhile, Jane Williams developed a rapport with Caroline. Both women were gifted harpists and shared an interest in Welsh music and folklore. In addition, Jane had an exceptional singing voice and was regarded as one of the finest amateur singers of her time.

As 1821 drew to a close, the Wyndham Quins absented themselves from Wales for several months. Building works at Ynyslas had ground to a virtual standstill owing to exceedingly severe weather, 'the storms & wet continuing, the papers full of accidents owing to floods & shipwrecks',[21] and the couple did not wish to impose on the goodwill of their neighbours for too long. Instead, they decided to use the hiatus to acquire suitable furnishings for the cottage. These were best obtained at the auction houses of Gloucester and Cheltenham or in the many well-stocked warehouses of specialist suppliers in London. Furthermore, Windham's father had become increasingly frail, with regular attacks of illness requiring more frequent attendance. Finally, the couple seem to have shared a desire to throw themselves wholeheartedly into a life of culture, replete with art exhibitions, concerts and scenic tours around England. For much of 1822 they lived the Picturesque ideal, fully absorbed in aesthetic pleasure. There was also a practical dimension to such activities, which stemmed from the couple's aspiration to extend and refine their knowledge of architecture and landscape design. This they achieved by visiting both old, well-established and long-celebrated country seats to gain a historical perspective, and new building works undertaken by their peers to gain a better understanding of the latest fashions and innovations. They became architectural magpies, collecting details and features of interest, which gradually deepened their views on architectural composition.

Briton Ferry, Glamorgan. Watercolour by John Smith, 1787. By permission of Llyfrgell Genedlaethol Cymru/The National Library of Wales.

One of the factors that influenced Windham and Caroline's pursuits stemmed from another change in the family's status. In July 1821 the prince regent was crowned George IV in a sumptuous ceremony in London following the death of his father, George III, in January 1820. The king traditionally marked such occasions by coronation honours, which included the elevation of distinguished gentlemen to the peerage. The prime minister, Lord Liverpool, had lobbied the king for an Irish earldom for Windham's father on account of the political embarrassment to which Windham had been subjected in 1819, and to this the king now agreed, albeit with some reluctance.[22] When he gave his approval to the list of coronation honours, however, he felt that Lord Liverpool did not show due deference to his endorsement, appearing to take it for granted. This annoyed him to such a degree that he decided to block all candidates in line for an Irish peerage. The Wyndham Quins were taken aback by the unexpected manner in which the promotion was summarily rejected and regarded it as 'wholly unaccountable both to him [Richard] & all the other Irish Peers that were promised it'.[23] The issue remained unresolved until January 1822, by which time the king had been suitably appeased and Richard's elevation to the earldom was announced in the papers.[24]

In choosing his title, a peer as a rule selected his place of residence or one with which he had a close connection. Richard's choice of Dunraven as his territorial designation speaks volumes about his and his son's decision that the family would settle permanently in Wales and make Dunraven Castle their eventual seat. By the same token, in 1821 Windham gave orders for the old Quin family burial plot in the former St Nicholas's church in Adare to be closed and the closure to be marked by a commemorative stone. He did, however, preserve one link to his Irish home. Now permitted to hold the courtesy rank of viscount, Windham chose Adare as his territorial title.

Although an elevation in rank did not result in a corresponding upsurge in wealth, it did increase Windham and Caroline's social prestige and allowed greater freedom to indulge in country house visits, a pastime which had become a fashionable activity among the genteel classes at the turn of the century. Guidebooks frequently included a mention of the best country seats along scenic routes, and some owners of these properties went so far as to print guidebooks for visitors or provide them with detailed lists of paintings on display. Callers were usually taken round by servants, who freely disclosed, and even boasted of, the cost of choice pieces of furniture or artwork. When the family were absent, no part of the house was out of bounds, giving many a tour an air of voyeurism only thinly disguised as pursuit of culture.[25] As a consequence, not every owner of a ducal residence looked favourably upon tourists, but where a visiting country parson may well have been refused admittance, a viscount was unlikely to have the door closed in his face.

The Wyndham Quins were well connected and could also use social visits as a disguise for house-viewing. It was under this pretext that they visited Holme Lacy in Herefordshire in September 1822. Its part-owner, Mary Burr née Davis, a friend of Windham and Caroline's, had recently inherited her share of the property following the death of Frances Scudamore, Duchess of Norfolk, in 1820. Dating from 1674 and built of brick and sandstone with Bath stone dressings, Holme Lacy was designed by Hugh May and built by master mason Anthony Deane for John, second Viscount Scudamore. It enjoyed a tranquil setting with beautiful but confined views of the surrounding countryside, and its grounds were particularly noted for their long, broad avenues of yew trees and for the beautiful gardens laid out by Alexander Pope in the 1720s. The house was entered through 'an immense hall from whence there are cosy suites of apartments none particularly large'.[26] Some of the finest features of the interior of Holme Lacy were the exceptional wood-carvings of birds, shellfish, fruit and flowers in its principal rooms, executed by the celebrated Anglo-Dutch carver Grinling Gibbons,[27] who originally worked solely on religious objects. Holme Lacy was one of his earliest non-ecclesiastical building ventures and generally considered among his finest country house interiors, second only to Petworth House. Although Windham and Caroline made no particular reference to Gibbons's exquisite craftsmanship, it must have struck a chord with them, sharing as they did an interest in carvings, in both wood and stone.

In Herefordshire the Wyndham Quins also visited Garnons, home of Sir John Geers Cotterell, who, like Mary Burr, was an old friend of the Wyndham family. Cotterell had inherited the property in 1790 and a year later, following his marriage to local heiress Frances Isabella Evans, consulted James Wyatt and Humphry Repton about possible improvements to the house and grounds. Repton visited Garnons in July 1791 to survey the grounds and made a number of ambitious recommendations, most of which were executed. A turnpike road, which passed some 500ft in front of the house, was moved to a new line outside the demesne to create a stretch of uninterrupted parkland. For similar effect, an old canal in front of the house was filled in, while on the southern edge of the park a waterlogged meadow was developed into a water feature to create an illusion of its being part of the Wye River. A series of grass carriage roads were cut through the estate, each culminating in an eye-catching viewpoint, and a new entrance with a rising and curving drive was created to approach the house from the south-east.

James Wyatt had also provided early designs for a new house in the Gothic style in 1791 but, being prone to taking on too many commissions, never provided final drawings. It was not until 1815 that William Atkinson created new designs for a principal residence in the Picturesque style as recommended by Repton and executed its construction, which was completed in 1822. Windham and Caroline were thus among the first to see the house and grounds in their finished state. They were duly impressed by the result and thoroughly enjoyed a walk in the beautiful gardens, 'where all that art can devise for luxury & elegance of taste seemed united', and around the house, 'which is in a castellated style [and] is handsome & extremely well finished the terraces round it are particularly handsome & comfortable, and the whole seems to unite splendour with comfort'. They spent much of the following day walking around the demesne to admire 'beautiful views & scenery, the walks take you through every variety of wood & foliage that can be conceived, & from the heights, we saw the whole of that fertile part of Herefordshire commanded by a succession of finely wooded places belonging to gentlemen of large fortunes'.[28] So pleased were the couple by what they saw that they extended their overnight stay to a three-day visit.

Country houses were not the only building type to attract the couple. Churches and cathedrals, castles and the ruins of medieval monasteries also featured prominently on their itinerary. Gloucester Cathedral, 'a magnificent Pile of building', was a perennial favourite, and in September 1822 the couple had an opportunity to explore the cathedral in Hereford, where they attended the city's annual three-day Music Meeting. The event consisted of a number of choral, vocal and instrumental performances led by Franz Cramer and conducted by John Clarke Whitfield, Professor of Music at Cambridge. The morning concerts were held in Hereford Cathedral and comprised sacred choral repertory, including Handel's *Te Deum* and his ever-popular *Messiah*, deemed by Caroline 'the most sublime composition the mind of man ever produced'.[29] The more secular evening concerts took place in the city's New Shire Hall and consisted of performances of vocal and instrumental music. Windham and his wife attended every performance and in between did some shopping and explored the city's sites. They were particularly intrigued by Hereford Cathedral and its many curiosities. Among these were the tomb of St Ethelbert the King, where miracles were said to occur, and the famous Hereford Mappa Mundi or medieval European map of the world. Caroline, however, failed to be impressed by it. 'The Saxons could know nothing of Geography' was her dry comment. 'Jerusalem is placed in the centre of the world with Europe, Asia and Africa round it.'[30]

Perhaps the most memorable of the couple's visits in 1822 was the excursion they made to the famous thirteenth-century Cistercian abbey at Tintern, deemed the ultimate destination for visitors on the picturesque trail. The ruin and its attractive setting in the Wye Valley had been made famous by the many artists charmed by its grace, most notably J.M.W. Turner, whose watercolour study of the abbey's crossing and chancel was exhibited at the Royal Academy in 1794, and William Wordsworth, whose poem *Lines Written a Few Miles Above Tintern Abbey* was composed during a visit to the Wye Valley in 1798. Until 1829, when a new turnpike road was opened through the valley to provide better access to the abbey, the easiest and most dramatic way to approach it was from the Wye River. This was the method chosen by Windham and Caroline and a group of friends who were travelling with them. The weather was beautifully fine and warm, and 'the woods were just bursting into leaf & by their different budding tints, appeared to singular advantage, & the nightingales & other singing birds regaled us with delicious music all the way'. To prolong the sense of excitement and anticipation, the group stopped at a nearby church to examine the epitaphs on its many headstones before proceeding to the abbey. The couple were overwhelmed by the entire experience. 'We spent an hour wandering about the ruins', Caroline recorded in her journal, 'the first view on opening the doors is quite sublime, the immense height of the Pillars, the arches in the centre being 72 feet high gives the whole an appearance of extreme magnificence the tracery of the windows is likewise very high & tight, & the situation of the ruin

is particularly picturesque.' To her mind, the ruin 'is on a large scale a very close likeness of the Grey Friary at Adare, one being as fine & one cloister in better preservation, but the grandeur of the size of Tintern Abbey makes it pre-eminently fine. The River which is close to it, winds beautifully through the bottom of the Valley & the secluded appearance of the monastery greatly improved by the high & wooded hills that form an amphitheatre round it.'[31]

The setting of Tintern Abbey was not, however, all pastoral beauty. The area surrounding it was not only renowned

Wye River, Monmouth. Image showing a tour boat passing the industrial works at Redbrook on its way to Tintern Abbey. From *The Book of the Wye and the Coast* by Mr and Mrs S. C. Hall (1861). Courtesy of Ruth Waycott.

for its picturesque scenery but was also an important industrial centre which utilised the Wye River as a transportation route. The bucolic southbound river journey from Redbrook to Tintern was punctuated by limekilns, stone quarries, iron foundries and tinworks belching smoke, and pleasure boats vied with sloops and schooners transporting coal and other cargo to and from the factories. Such scenes offended Caroline's sensitivities, particularly the nearby wireworks, which 'entirely in my opinion destroy the illusion of the retirement of the monks, we cannot follow them in their seclusion when the stillness of the air is broken by forge hammers, where no noise should be heard but the singing of birds & the rushing of waters'. When the group walked up the hill on the opposite side of the river to get a better overall idea of the abbey's setting, they were shocked to discover that one side of it was 'surrounded by the filthy cottages of the people from the works, which being tiled with red Pantiles have a peculiarly ugly effect'.[32]

Caroline was not alone in her views; indeed, this juxtaposition between quietude and discord formed a common theme in many a poem written about the place, such as the *Poetical Description of Tintern Abbey* (1793) by the Reverend Duncomb Davis, with its lines 'Here, now no bell calls / Monks to morning prayer, / Daws only chaunt their early matins here; / Black forges smoke, and noisy hammers beat'.[33] Picturesque scenery pockmarked by the effects of the Industrial Revolution was, of course, not limited to Tintern Abbey but a theme that reverberated across the country, not least in Wales, where coalfields, lead-mines and iron manufactories were gaining rapid ground. It spoilt Caroline's enjoyment as early as 1809 on a visit to Valle Crucis Abbey in North Wales, where the beautiful location of the ruins in a steep-sided valley was marred by the establishment of several manufacturing works and a canal cut along the River Dee to service them.[34] In 1812, as Windham and Caroline were making their way to Ireland, they were stunned by the quantity of factories in the neighbourhood of Birmingham, which gave the surrounding countryside the appearance of being wholly in flames.[35] Such was the price of the great Industrial Revolution, the financial benefits of which, however, the Wyndham Quins themselves were soon to reap.

❖ ❖ ❖

The couple's cultural exploits were punctuated by regular visits to the Vale of Neath to monitor the progress of building works at Ynyslas. By late May 1822, they were gratified to find the cottage very much adorned and promising to be a better house than they had expected.[36] Although the building was not yet completed, it was far enough advanced to allow a degree of habitation. This the couple were eager to exploit. Spending the early part of the summer once again as guests of the Williams family at Aberpergwm House, they made almost daily trips to the cottage to drink tea with friends and to dance the night away in its unfinished rooms. Their pastoral summer interlude included several scenic walks and drives to local beauty spots, and an exploration of the Porth yr Ogof caves. During the merry picnic that followed, Caroline entertained the diners with her harp and Jane with her exquisite singing.[37] When haymaking commenced in the middle of June, the women once again gathered their musical instruments and entertained themselves in the style of Marie Antoinette by drinking tea in the hayfield and playing their harps while the haymakers danced.

In the same month the Wyndham Quins befriended the landscape artist George Orleans De la Motte, son of a French refugee and younger brother of the better-known artist William Alfred De la Motte, who worked as drawing master at the Sandhurst Military Academy and had enjoyed the patronage of George III. George De la Motte produced a number of sketches of South Wales between 1816 and 1835, particularly of views around Swansea, Briton Ferry and the Vale of Neath. He spent long periods of 1822 as a guest of the Wyndham Quin family, accompanying them on scenic visits and taking their likenesses. Later in the year, he was employed by the couple to provide daily drawing lessons to their two children. He remained with the family well into 1823.

By December 1822 Ynyslas Cottage was finally nearing completion and preparations to furnish the building commenced. On 6 December a wagonload of furniture arrived from Cardiff and took the family two days to unpack. Three days later, the architect William Whittington supervised the putting up of grates and chimney-pieces, and more furniture arrived on 12 December. Edwin returned from school in the midst of all the bustle and found his mother complaining about everything progressing too slowly.[38] On 30 December, as the linen for the house was being aired, Anna Maria returned from Dunraven Castle with her governess, and the family were once again united.

A house-warming party was held at the cottage on the last day of the year. Every neighbour, rich and poor, was invited to come and dance, with 22 guests in the parlour and 70 downstairs. Rees Williams and Caroline opened the ball with a country dance, in which they were joined by almost all present. They then danced a quadrille in another room. The guests, however, preferred country dances, and it was in this merry way that they hopped and twirled in the New Year. A midnight supper was followed by more dancing, Caroline partnering with her son, who, along with his sister, had a wonderful time and, to their mother's pride, danced very well. The party did not break up until four o'clock in the morning, when the family crept into their beds, thoroughly tired out.[39]

Haymaker taking a break. Watercolour by Louisa Payne-Gallwey, c. 1830s. Courtesy of Lavinia Graham-Vivian.

Although comfortable in their new home, the family's financial troubles were far from over. Throughout 1822, the income derived from their various estates continued to diminish, while the acquisition of land in the Vale of Neath and the building of Ynyslas Cottage had set the couple back by £3,500.[40] Nevertheless, Caroline was determined not to let such matters depress her and looked upon the completion of the house as a significant watershed. Delighted to find herself once more under a roof of her own, she expressed gratitude 'to the giver of all Goodness that he had blessed me once more with a home, which after a life of more than two years of visiting and wandering was particularly comfortable'. She was pleased to note that 'our establishment though small compared to what I had been accustomed to is sufficiently large to enable us to see a few friends and be thoroughly comfortable', and that 'though our elevation in rank did not bring with it any increase of riches we were content though our income certainly diminished rather than increased by the depression of the times'.[41] It was from such thoughts that Caroline took comfort as she and her husband began another year of uncertainty.

Ynyslas Cottage, Vale of Neath, Glamorgan. Watercolour by Percy Williams, *c*. 1820s. Courtesy of the Dunraven family.

Emporiums of Taste

In February 1823 Windham travelled to Ireland for a few weeks to oversee his interests in Adare. Although no longer resident in the country, he nevertheless retained his estates in County Limerick and continued to act as landlord to a great many tenants. In Windham's absence, his land agent, the Reverend Windham Fitzgerald,[1] received the rents and kept accounts. After an absence of nearly three years, however, Windham felt the need to revisit his former home to deal with matters in person. The decision to leave Adare, while necessary, had not been easy and had done nothing to diminish his strong sense of duty towards those dependent on him. If anything, the family's progress in the peerage made it more imperative for Windham to re-establish his connection with the country of his birth, even if the prospect of returning to live there was slim.

Windham was accompanied on the journey by his wife, who longed to see the place again. They travelled to Holyhead, where they boarded the steam packet *Ivanhoe*. The crossing passed without incident, but when the vessel was just a few miles from Howth Harbour a violent storm brewed up and prevented it from landing, leaving the ship and its unfortunate passengers tossing in the sea for twelve hours 'in the most dreadful state of sickness possible'.[2] Windham was none the worse for wear but Caroline, who had no sea legs at all, remained desperately sick for several days. In spite of this, the couple did not break their journey but proceeded in haste to Adare, where an enthusiastic reception awaited them. The entire town was illuminated with bonfires and tar boughs to mark their arrival, and the following day the villagers came in a procession to dance in front of Adare House. For several days, scores of friends and neighbours gathered at the house to welcome the couple, giving them barely enough time to walk around to inspect how the house and gardens had fared in their absence.

Following the initial thrill caused by their return, Windham and Caroline slipped effortlessly into their old way of life. The two months they spent in Adare coincided with the shooting season, and much of their time was occupied by shooting and fishing parties and hunt balls. Nevertheless, their visit also had a more serious dimension. The preceding years had been difficult in Ireland. The failure of the potato crop in the provinces of Munster and Connaught in 1821 and 1822 resulted in severe food shortages in the westernmost counties, including Limerick, leaving more than a million people on the verge of starvation. Food riots and rural unrest became commonplace, and many depended on the money and goods distributed by charitable organisations for their survival. One such organisation was the British and Irish Ladies' Society, which focused its efforts on promoting the welfare of female labourers, arguing that assistance given to men usually only benefited the individual receiving it, while that given to women was passed down to their children and thus benefited the entire family.[3] The organisation had been established in London in 1822 and expanded at a rapid rate. In 1824 it had 254 branches in 29 counties across the British Isles.[4] Limerick city had a district branch, the founding meeting of which was chaired by Caroline in March 1823. A similar association was established in Adare on the first day of April, with Caroline on the committee. The Adare Association re-established her custom of providing the women in the village with spinning-wheels, flax and wool, and ensured the continuance of this practice during her long absences in Wales. Caroline spent several days on what she called 'cabin hunting', travelling up and down the country lanes to prepare a list of the poor in the neighbourhood in need of assistance.

Caroline also renewed her interest in the school that she had established in Adare in 1814. Its first masters, Mr Jones and later Mr Keith from Dublin, had by 1820 been replaced by John Archibald Armstrong, who ran the school during the Wyndham Quins' absence in Wales. John's wife, Catherine Fitzgerald, was Windham's cousin, and when the couple married in 1820 he gave the bride away.[5] While in Adare in 1823, one of Caroline's first actions was to invite James Pain to design a residence for them adjacent to the schoolroom within the grounds of the Augustinian church.[6] The two-storey building, completed in 1825, adjoined the remains of the former gate tower to the north. In its modest Gothic design, it not only emulated the medieval character of the monastery complex but also reflected the style applied to many of the gate lodges within the family estate.

Designing the schoolmaster's house was not the only task given to James Pain in 1823. Windham wished to leave a permanent reminder of the family's close bond with Adare. This he did by asking Pain to execute a new pew for the family in the Augustinian church. Since the Middle Ages, seating arrangements during church service followed a rigid order according to the social status of participants. The gentry pews were located nearest to the altar and designed for additional comfort—the most elaborate examples incorporated a cast-iron fireplace to keep the occupants warm. Gentry pews were strictly private and even in the absence of the family to which they were allocated could not be used by anybody else. During the reconstruction of the Augustinian church, seating arrangements for the family had been part of the overall plan,[7] but the elevation of Windham's father to an earldom allowed for a new design to reflect the family's changed status. Pain supervised the placing of the pew in March, and in May the couple with due reverence 'for the first time sat in Windham's beautiful new seat, which is quite magnificent. Heaven grant us a long life to be in it and a religious mind whenever we enter it.'[8]

Augustinian friary, Adare. Watercolour of women in the cloisters by Louisa Payne-Gallwey, c. 1833. Courtesy of Lavinia Graham-Vivian.

❖ ❖ ❖

While building schemes on a grandiose scale—or, indeed, on any scale—remained beyond Windham's purse, this did not prevent him from cultivating a growing interest in architecture. In July 1823, following their return from Ireland, Windham decided to tour the south-west of England with his wife to view some of the remarkable country houses of the region. Their Vale of Neath neighbours, Anne and Jane Williams, joined them on the tour. Setting off from London, their first destination was not a building but a famous designed landscape garden, Whiteknights Park in Reading, created by George, Marquess of Blandford (later fifth Duke of Marlborough), between 1798 and 1819. An avid plant-collector, Blandford set out to fill his garden with rare and exotic specimens, many of which came to him through Dr Thomas Dancer, curator of the Botanic Garden in Bath, Jamaica. Blandford's park featured three clearly definable areas: the botanic gardens, the woods and the new gardens. He had no overall plan in mind when he created the grounds, instead adding new features in a whimsical fashion as his plant collections grew. He did, however, commission well-known craftsmen and architects for individual projects. The Gothic façade on a chapel in the grounds was created by carver and plasterer Francis Bernasconi; the entrance gates and ornamental bridge were designed by architect Samuel Pepys Cockerell, while artist and architect John Buonarotti Papworth was asked to provide some of the fountains, seats and arbours in which the garden abounded. In 1816 Blandford commissioned the landscape painter Thomas Christopher Hofland and his writer wife Barbara to produce an illustrated guide, *A Descriptive Account of the Mansion and Gardens of White-Knights*, which was privately printed and published in 1819. In the same year, however, Blandford's extravagant lifestyle brought him to the brink of bankruptcy. To clear some of the debts, which amounted to about £600,000, an eleven-day auction was held on the estate. Happily, enough of the garden was left intact for it to remain of considerable horticultural and aesthetic interest to visitors for many years after.[9]

Windham, Caroline and their travelling companions began their tour in the botanic gardens, which in a space of some five and a half acres contained numerous beautifully shaped greenhouses filled with richly perfumed exotic plants. Some

Whiteknights Park, Reading. *A View of Whiteknights from the Park with a Lady Sketching* by Thomas Christopher Hofland. University of Reading Art Collection, UAC/10236.

also contained large cisterns of water for rare aquatic specimens, while others displayed garlands of sweet-scented creepers hanging from timber posts placed in a circle. There were 'all sorts of well imagined seats … concealed or introduced when ornamental, in every part of these buildings', which in Caroline's opinion rendered them 'truly temples of luxury'. Even more attractive were the adjoining American woods. Near the entrance to this area was a stretch of water and on its edge an ornamental cottage for drinking tea, the sight of which revived 'many a tender string' in Caroline's recollection of 'being very like the dear heath house at Adare'. The underwood of the extensive forest consisted entirely of anemone plants, and here and there were trellis walks covered with flowering creepers and culminating in urns, temples and other ornamental eye-catchers. One particular spot in the grounds was to Caroline's mind 'more peculiarly beautiful than the rest'. This was 'a small slope with a stream at the bottom, over it a narrow bridge & at the termination of it a particularly well imagined grotto gives it a sort of retired & tranquil air, which is more than usually soothing & grateful to the feelings'. The visitors also admired the large body of water near the main house and the beautiful shady walks along its banks.[10]

Whiteknights Park, Reading. A view of the spring in the woods. Lithograph by T. F. Hofland. From *A Descriptive Account of the Mansion and Gardens of White-Knights* (1819). University of Reading, Special Collections.

On the following day, the group set off for Wiltshire to visit Wilton, the ancient seat of the Earls of Pembroke. With a ninth-century abbey at its core, the building had a long and complex history involving a number of prominent architects, most notably Inigo Jones and Isaac de Caus. The latter, who also worked on Wilton's famous gardens and introduced one of the first French parterres seen in England, redesigned the south front in severe Palladian style. In 1647, within a few years of its completion, the new south wing was ravaged by fire. Another fire in 1705 resulted in the reconstruction of some of the oldest parts of the house, where rooms were created to display the Arundel marbles collected by the eighth Earl of Pembroke. The house thereafter remained unchanged for almost 100 years, becoming in time a popular tourist destination. Caroline Powys, who toured the house in 1776, was amazed to discover on writing her name in the visitors' book that almost two and a half thousand people had visited the building the year before. She was not, however, the most appreciative of Wilton's visitors. In her opinion, 'to *see*, 'tis certainly one of the finest sights in England, but to reside at, 'tis too grand, too gloomy, and what I style *most magnificently uncomfortable*'. She continued: 'Were I Lord Pembroke, I'd have two superb galleries, one for pictures, the other for statues, busts, &c., of which many here it seems are nowhere else in the world to be met with; they would then appear with advantage, whereas now the whole house gives one an idea of a statuary's shop'.[11]

George, the eleventh earl, had evidently shared Mrs Powys's sentiments. In 1801 he invited James Wyatt, master of both Neo-Classical and Gothic architecture, to modernise the house. Wyatt's alterations, which took eleven years to complete, included a two-storey gallery constructed along the four sides of the building's inner courtyard. The gallery not only served to house the family's collection of classical sculpture but provided better access to the many rooms of the house. This space was entered through a Gothic Hall, where a display of suits of armour immediately drew Windham's attention. From the gallery, the visitors entered a spacious range of sitting rooms with painted ceilings and 'thoroughly well furnished', which 'seem to combine every modern comfort, with ancient magnificence'. They admired a splendid long room with 'many very fine specimens of Vandyke & some very curious family pictures', and walked through a large, handsome library which extended along the side of the mansion. The rooms provided views of the richly wooded park with 'some very fine Cedars of Lebanon' and 'a gay looking flower garden made by the present Countess'. Caroline noted that the 'busts, statues, antiques &c would form amusement for a long time' and concluded that 'this appears a very splendid residence, & one very well worth seeing'.[12]

After Wilton, the unquestionable highlight of the tour was a visit to Fonthill Abbey in Wiltshire. Also known as Beckford's Folly, this was a Gothic Revival house built on a gargantuan scale at the turn of the nineteenth century for William Thomas Beckford, one of the great eccentrics of his day. Reputedly the richest commoner in England, Beckford had inherited the Fonthill estate from his father in 1771 when he was just ten years old, along with numerous sugar plantations in Jamaica and one million pounds in cash. His fortune allowed Beckford to indulge his passion for architecture and to become a consummate collector and patron of art and literature. In 1796 he commissioned James Wyatt to design and construct a Gothic bastion on an unprecedented scale. Wyatt's

Wilton House, Wiltshire. South-east view of house. Watercolour by John Buckler, 1810. Yale Center for British Art, Paul Mellon collection.

Fonthill Abbey, Wiltshire. North-west view of the projected design by James Wyatt, 1798. Yale Center for British Art, Paul Mellon collection.

design comprised an octagonal central area, from which four long wings radiated in a cross-shape, giving the structure a 295ft frontage. The front doors alone were some 35ft in height and opened into a cavernous, cathedral-like hall. The building's most dominating feature, however, was a massive central tower rising to a height of almost 295ft to provide views of the surrounding countryside.

The partnership between Wyatt and Beckford was unfortunate and ill-matched. Wyatt was notorious for accepting more commissions than he could fulfil, affording him little time to supervise projects. Although a brilliant designer, he was also flippant. His initial enthusiasm for a new assignment rapidly waned to indifference, causing projects to be delayed by months, even years. Beckford, on the other hand, was impulsive, impatient and determined to see the project through in the shortest time possible. Five hundred men were employed to work in shifts around the clock on the construction site, and another 450 labourers were lured from the building works at Windsor Castle with promises of increased ale rations. The first part of the house to be built was the colossal central tower. Not only did Beckford keep increasing its height but he also disregarded the structural needs arising from its size and scale and insisted on using 'fast' materials such as timber and cement for its construction instead of stone or brick. Not surprisingly, when the tower reached its full height it collapsed, as it also did on the second attempt. Realising the error of his thinking, Beckford consented to using stone for its construction. This time the structure held but took seven years to complete.

The house, a Gothic landmark structure of its time, was finished in 1813. Here Beckford housed his priceless collections of art and built a 40ft wall around the estate to shield it from prying eyes. He lived completely alone, occupying a single room in the house, and never entertained guests, rousing an insatiable wave of curiosity, gossip and innuendo. In 1822 Beckford lost two of his Jamaican sugar plantations in a legal action and was forced to put Fonthill Abbey and its contents up for sale. The news caused a virtual riot, when thousands of the curious descended upon the nearby village of Hindon to attend the viewings that preceded the auction. 'He is fortunate who finds a vacant chair within twenty miles of Fonthill, the solitude of a private apartment is a luxury which few can hope for', noted *The Times*. 'The beds through the county are (literally) doing double-duty—people who come in from a distance during the night, must wait to go to bed until others get up in the morning ... Not a farmhouse, however

Above: Fonthill Abbey, Wiltshire.

Left: Interior of the great western hall.
From John Rutter's *Delineations of Fonthill Abbey* (1823). Public domain.

humble—not a cottage near Fonthill, but gives shelter to fashion, to beauty, and to rank; ostrich plumes, which, by their very waving, we can trace back to Piccadilly, are seen nodding at a casement window over a depopulated poultry yard.'[13] Some 72,000 copies of the auction catalogue were sold at a guinea apiece and disappointment was intense when the auction was cancelled following the private sale of the property and its contents to John Farquhar for £330,000.[14]

The publication in 1823 of John Rutter's *Delineations of Fonthill Abbey*, which provided a detailed description of the building and its contents with accompanying illustrations, only increased the *frisson* caused by what Windham and Caroline regarded as 'the show place of the age'. Upon arrival, they could barely contain their excitement. 'Our imagination & curiosity were raised to the highest pitch', Caroline recorded in her journal, 'from many parts of these grounds you see the magnificent tower of the Abbey soaring to the clouds, you ascend very steep hills through beautiful woods, & at length arrive at the spot which had long been the object of curiosity and anxiety to all England.' They entered the hall 'resembling a fine cathedral' and ascended the magnificent staircase to admire the enormous galleries furnished with Buhl and Japanese lacquerware, cabinets of gems, collections of books, prints and manuscripts, paintings, cameos and sculpture. Every item was 'the most magnificent of its kind that could be purchased', and 'everything you can look at has a tale attached to it and is an object of interest and curiosity'. The couple admired the carved oak ceilings and Gothic windows of coloured glass, which cast 'the most enchanting light'. They wandered from room to room, 'quite lost with the gorgeous magnificence that surrounded us'.[15] Unable to tear themselves away, they returned the following day for a tour of the grounds and another look at the paintings and display cabinets.

Windham and Caroline were fortunate in the timing of their tour. In December 1825, just two years after their visit, the massive main tower collapsed for its third and final time. An eyewitness who saw the tower fall declared that the sight was very beautiful: 'it first sank perpendicularly and slowly, and then burst and spread over the roofs of the adjoining wings on every side'. The tower 'had come down so silently, crumbling into dust at its fall, that no one heard it. Only the cloud of floating dust told the residents of Fonthill Abbey of the ruin.'[16] By 1858 a small remnant of the north wing was all that survived of Beckford's Folly.

Stourhead, Wiltshire. Watercolour of the gardens by Francis Nicholson, undated. © The Trustees of the British Museum.

The next destination on the couple's itinerary was Stourhead, the celebrated landscape garden created by Henry Hoare, whose father had purchased the property in 1717. The family seat, one of the first in the country to be built in the Palladian style, was, with its clean lines and Classical proportions, the antithesis of the Gothic gloom and extravagance of Fonthill Abbey, just eleven miles away. Designed by the pioneering Scottish architect Colen Campbell, generally regarded as the founder of the Georgian style, it was constructed under the supervision of Nathaniel Ireson between 1721 and 1725. Not all of Campbell's ideas were executed at this time, however; the Palladian wings were not constructed until much later in the eighteenth century to house Sir Richard Colt Hoare's extensive collections of books and paintings, and the handsome portico which completed Campbell's design was only added in 1841, nearly twenty years after the Wyndham Quins' visit.

For all its constrained elegance and beautiful collections of books and paintings, the house paled into insignificance compared to its landscaped grounds, laid out by Henry Hoare between 1741 and 1780. Their focal point, a large ornamental lake, was created by damming a stream feeding the River Stour to flood a small valley in the heart of the Stourhead estate. Instead of utilising the wider landscape beyond the lake, Hoare created a contemplative, inward-looking space by the skilful placement of groves and islands of trees intermingled with Classical temples, bridges and grottoes designed by the Palladian architect Henry Flitcroft. This mixture of artifice and nature was brought together by a pathway that encircled the lake, alternately approaching and moving away from the water, thus producing a series of views from different vantage points and creating elements of surprise for visitors to the park.

Hoare's planting scheme used nothing but trees, and it was not until the early 1800s that his grandson, Sir Richard Colt Hoare, added flowering shrubs of azalea, laurel and rhododendron to further enhance the picturesque nature of the park. With its temples, cascades and magnificent trees, Stourhead became an immediate hit with visitors. Almost 100 years on, when Windham and Caroline toured the grounds over two days, the place had lost none of its charm. While the weather was bad, the visitors were undeterred by rain and explored the park's walks and gardens, ducking into temples and follies to take shelter from heavy downpours. They climbed to the top of King Alfred's Tower to take in the expansive view of the grounds and descended into the grotto and River God's Cave, where they admired 'a sleeping figure of a nymph carved in white marble[17] & apparently surrounded by rocks & water' and 'the figure of a river God passing out of a large Vase a perpetual stream of water'. Close to the lake, they sat in a little cottage to partake of a cold dinner and then walked out again to see the Pantheon, the largest and most iconic of Stourhead's garden buildings. They toured the house and its beautiful specimens of art and drove for miles through beautiful forest scenery before reluctantly leaving the place.[18]

The couple's expedition concluded on 22 July with a visit to Longleat, the home of the Marquess of Bath. The house was commissioned by John Thynne, steward to the first Duke of Somerset, and was begun in 1567 with Robert Smythson as the project's master mason. Smythson, who spent eighteen years perfecting the building, carved much of its external detail, and his influence on the overall design is also believed to have been strong. One of the great Renaissance architects, Smythson was the designer of a number of other Elizabethan masterpieces, most notably Woollaton Hall in Nottingham and Hardwick Hall in Derbyshire. Windham in particular was drawn to this Elizabethan style, its large, mullioned windows and projecting bays and the ornamental gables and groupings of chimneys breaking up the skyline. At Longleat he admired the great baronial hall and the arms and other paraphernalia of the nobility that decorated its walls. The long gallery on the first floor was a disappointment, however, primarily because it remained unfurnished. He agreed with his wife that, considering the room's size and three handsome fireplaces, it 'might be made very splendid'. An extensive park full of game surrounded the house, 'and the whole has quite the appearance of the splendid residence of a great English nobleman'.[19]

The buildings that Windham and Caroline visited were chosen with care. Longleat represented the best of Elizabethan architecture, Stourhead was the epitome of Palladian elegance, Fonthill Abbey in all its extravagance showcased Gothic Revivalism, while Wilton was an amalgamation of all three. What united the buildings was the way in which they combined modern comforts with ancient magnificence. It was this synthesis that was to be of singular importance to the Wyndham Quins when they embarked on their own building project in Adare.

❖   ❖   ❖

Windham spent much of the winter of 1823–4 outdoors with his workmen, creating a new walk on the grounds of Ynyslas Cottage, making a small ornamental bridge and planting trees. Caroline, meanwhile, established flowerbeds near the cottage veranda and filled them with an abundance of plants, which Mary Talbot and her husband, Sir Christopher Cole, sent from the gardens of Penrice in February 1824. Rees Williams continued his improvements at Aberpergwm House, and several visits were made between the properties to inspect and compare the results. Young Edwin, away at school, eagerly absorbed accounts of these activities and wrote to his mother with a note of envy: 'It is very lucky they are painting the house now. I am so glad it is getting on so well. I am longing so for the holy days to come to see it. I should like to see Papa working himself.'[20]

Longleat House, Wiltshire. South-east view. Watercolour by John Buckler, 1805. Yale Center for British Art, Paul Mellon collection.

Such pleasant avocations were a welcome antidote to what was otherwise a tragic and testing year, beset by illness and death. Caroline continued in low spirits caused by an undefined nervous complaint. In January 1824 she suffered yet another miscarriage, which brought Anne Williams to Ynyslas Cottage for several days to nurse her. In mid-March, Windham took ill with a severe attack of gout, which confined him to his bed and prevented him from dining with the rest of the family until April. Just one week after his recovery, the family prepared for Edwin's return from school, chaperoned by Caroline's oldest friend, Catherine Harding. To their dismay, Catherine arrived without Edwin, bearing news of a sudden illness which had prevented the boy from continuing his journey beyond Gloucester. Although Catherine assured them that Edwin had been placed in the care of a competent doctor and was out of immediate danger, his parents remained uneasy and anxiously perused the daily accounts of the young patient, who kept on improving but not sufficiently to travel.

In early May, Windham, Caroline and Anna Maria travelled to Penrice to celebrate Christopher Rice Mansel Talbot's 21st birthday. The celebrations commenced with the firing of cannons, bell-ringing and flying of flags, and continued with a dinner given to Penrice tenants, with several hundred assembled in the barns for a comfortable meal and copious quantities of ale brewed many years before expressly for the day. The celebrations culminated in the firing of 21 cannons on the shore, each answered by a cannon fired from Christopher's yacht *Julia* at anchor in the bay. An extensive fireworks display went on until two o'clock in the morning.[21]

Although Penrice was looking beautiful and the day's entertainment was outstanding, Windham and Caroline's enjoyment was half-hearted, as Edwin continued ill and their minds remained uneasy. After their return from Penrice, the anxious mother could wait no longer and travelled to Gloucester to be by her son's side. During his slow recovery, Edwin was showered with attention by his parents. In late June he received from his father a gift of a toy ship named *The Waterloo*, 'a beautifully made Vessel & most ingeniously contrived'.[22] Later that same evening Caroline, not wanting to be outdone, presented her son with a tool chest. By early July Edwin was well enough to join his mother at Sunday service and to spend a pleasant day at Frampton Lodge, 'sitting by the side of the water in Mr Clifford's park where Edwin enjoyed himself exceedingly fishing, & sailing his little ship'.[23] By mid-July the young patient had left Gloucester and travelled to Dunraven Castle to complete his recuperation.

Briton Ferry, Glamorgan. Watercolour by John Varley, early nineteenth century. By permission of Llyfrgell Genedlaethol Cymru/The National Library of Wales.

Aberpergwm, Vale of Neath. Pen-and-ink sketch of the chapel near Ynyslas. Courtesy of the Dunraven family.

More tragic, however, was the case of Windham's father, now aged 71, whose state of health rapidly deteriorated. In late August 1823 the family received an alarming account of his condition and departed at once for Cheltenham at breakneck speed on a hot and sultry day, only stopping at Pyle for four hours to get some sleep. Fearing the worst, they were much relieved on arrival to find Richard out of immediate danger and getting better. It was clear for all to see, however, that his 'mind was fast sinking under such severe attacks, and the childishness of old age approaching'. Realising that 'Cheltenham or any town where he was exposed to public observations was become improper for him', the couple thought it best to remove Richard to the privacy of Ynyslas Cottage.[24] Over the next two months, Caroline and Windham's sister Harriot took turns to nurse Richard back to sufficient health to enable him to travel. By the end of October he was strong enough to make the slow trip to Ynyslas, where, much to his son's relief, he arrived safely and none the worse for his journey.

For the next eight months Windham assumed all responsibility for his father's care, scarcely leaving his bedside, while Caroline and the children moved to Aberpergwm House to live temporarily with Rees, Anne and Jane Williams. In early August 1824, to break the monotony of their daily routine, Caroline took her children to Briton Ferry for a short seaside holiday. On return to Ynyslas, she learned of the rapid deterioration of her father-in-law. At last, on 24 August, 'Our poor invalid seemed more & more exhausted, & at half past 6 in the Evening, he breathed his last'.[25] Edwin and Anna Maria, who had stayed behind at Briton Ferry, were immediately sent for; on their arrival, they accompanied their father 'to take a last look at their poor dear Grandpapa & to shew them the end of all human advantages both of person & situation and to point out … the superiority of the immortal blessings that attend on the souls of the blessed'.[26] Windham's brother Richard arrived from Cheltenham a few days later, and on the first day of September their father's coffin was carried by eight mostly Irish bearers to be deposited in the vault constructed in the little chapel adjoining Ynyslas Cottage. Caroline watched the sad progression as it left the house: 'never shall I forget my feelings at seeing my poor father in law borne from the Cottage, and taken to his long home. It was indeed a sad dismal day … My dearest husband suffered severely & I could not help feeling relieved that the mournful scene in which he had lately lived, was now closed to him for ever. For this day once passed he could no longer indulge in such extreme grief with the remains of his beloved Parent.'[27] Richard's death marked an important transition for Windham and Caroline, as they took on respectively the mantle of the Earl and Countess of Dunraven.

CHAPTER
SIX

A Noble Mausoleum

F ollowing the death of his father, Windham fell into deep depression from which he found it difficult to emerge. To improve his spirits, his wife removed him from Ynyslas, the recent scene of so much sadness, to Llandrindod Wells immediately after the funeral. Initially, the success of the trip seemed doubtful. The weather, which had been oppressively hot, turned cold and wet, and of the 24 visitors assembled at the spa the couple scarcely knew a soul. Ten days into their visit, however, things took a turn for the better when the Welsh harpist and composer John Parry and his son John Orlando Parry joined the guests. The entertainment they provided at the spa included improvised *eisteddfodau*,[1] musical outdoor excursions and a concert for which Caroline was elected as patroness. Another welcome addition to the party was the historian and antiquary Thomas Price, who arrived at Llandrindod two days after the Parrys. A handsome and genial man, Price was a passionate advocate of the Welsh language and culture and an expert on the Welsh triple harp. An inspired and eloquent speaker, he won numerous prizes for oration at provincial *eisteddfodau*, and a speech that he gave at Llandrindod Wells on the Neath harp was met with great applause from an enthralled audience. The Dunravens took a great liking to Price and invited him to Ynyslas on several subsequent occasions.[2]

Neath, Glamorgan. Engraving of coal works by John Hassell, 1798. By permission of Llyfrgell Genedlaethol Cymru/The National Library of Wales.

At the end of September the Dunravens returned to Ynyslas, where Edwin eagerly awaited his parents to show off a seat which he and his friends had been making under a lime tree near the river with the toolkit his mother had given him during his illness. Such delightful domestic scenes, however, did little to soothe Windham. The painful memories of his father's death at once resurfaced and his spirits plummeted to a state of intense grief and agitation. His wife, increasingly concerned for his well-being, once again removed Windham from the Vale of Neath, taking him first to Dunraven Castle and later to Cheltenham and Gloucester. It was not until mid-November that Windham began to show signs of his old buoyance and Caroline felt confident enough to return to Ynyslas.

As Windham's spirits improved, so did the family's financial situation. At about this time rich deposits of coal were discovered on the Dunraven estate. Mining had formed the industrial backbone of South Wales since Roman times, most notably in the mountainous elevations of its interior and northern parts.[3] By the fifteenth century, small coalmines existed across

Wales, providing fuel for copper- and iron-smelting, but it was not until the end of the sixteenth century that a more expansive and organised coalmining industry developed, particularly around Neath and Swansea. The natural beauty of the landscape in Glamorgan and Monmouthshire was changed irreversibly from the mid-eighteenth century onwards, when extensive coalfields became the source of a lucrative export industry feeding the rapidly growing demands of the Industrial Revolution.

As a result, Windham was heavily involved in business transactions related to the extractive industry throughout 1825 and 1826. Mr Davies of Monmouth spent a day in Ynyslas at the end of May 1825, attending to business with him; in April of the same year Mr Webb and Mr Taylor appeared, and two full days were 'employed by the gentlemen with letting mines'.[4] In April 1826 the Wyndham Quins signed a lease of coal to the Llangennech Coal Company.[5] These and other transactions to permit the mining and transportation of coal and iron ore on their large Glamorgan landholdings dramatically changed the family's prospects. Having been somewhat adrift during his time in Wales, when lack of funds had prevented him from undertaking any meaningful occupation, Windham now had scope to expand his business activities and engage in a more orderly management of his estates. In 1825 he determined to lay out the sum of £21,600 towards the improvement of the Welsh estate, to cancel some of the mortgages encumbering it and to purchase additional land, mainly near Dunraven Castle, to bring in a greater rental income. 'You will find the Estate beginning to recover from its former bad management', he noted with satisfaction to his wife. Shaken by his father's death and increasingly aware of his own mortality, Windham also gave Caroline words of advice on estate management, should she ever find herself in sole charge. He warned against biased advisers and poor judgement, and suggested that 'Mr Webb is a good agent, if kept strictly to his business, which he would otherwise neglect, & you must never dispense with his personal attendance on the Welsh Estates, at the least twice every year. Lord Ilchester has a head and a heart you may safely trust. I advise you to cultivate his friendship and the intimacy of all my Mother's family.'[6]

In spite of his evident interest in improving the Welsh property, Windham decided against making Dunraven Castle his permanent seat and set his heart on returning to Adare. By November 1825, when he travelled to Ireland for the first time since his father's death, both he and his wife knew that their time at Ynyslas was coming to an end. 'We shall probably not be there much more,' Windham wrote to Caroline from Adare. 'It has answered all its purposes & will be an encumbrance to keep. You are happier here than anywhere. We can now afford to keep it up and you shall love here, and any second house we keep shall be in Town [London], where by continuing a prudent & discreet course for two or three years longer, we shall I think be able to have a House & a seat in Parliament, which last I could now afford but I won't separate from you for three or four Months as I then must as I could not take you to Town as yet.'[7]

There was, however, one difficulty that permanent departure from the Vale of Neath posed for Windham. His father's bones remained buried there and from these he could not willingly part. The issue troubled him to such an extent that on Christmas Day he invited James Pain to Adare to discuss an idea he had for 'a noble Mausoleum' to be added to the Augustinian church, which he wanted Pain to design.[8] It was not the first time that Windham had toyed with such a prospect. Just a few months after his wedding, he had expressed to his wife the desire upon his death to 'be laid in that mansion what I purpose making for my remains',[9] but it was not until his father's death that the matter gained a degree of urgency. Commissioning a mausoleum also had a deeper, symbolic meaning. Just as the closure of the family's burial plot in St Nicholas's Church in 1821 had marked the family's departure from Adare, the construction of one in the Augustinian church signalled their return and their determination not to leave again.

The old parish church of St Nicholas, Adare. From *Memorials of Adare Manor* (1865). Courtesy of Special Collections and Archives, Glucksman Library, University of Limerick.

❖   ❖   ❖

The Dunravens returned permanently to Ireland in early April 1826. Their homeward journey was timed to coincide with the birthday celebrations of King George IV, which they planned to attend in Dublin. The couple's passage to the ferry port at Holyhead was shortened and made safer by the new suspension bridge over the Menai Strait, which had been opened some three months earlier to connect the island of Anglesey with mainland Wales. Designed by the Scottish civil engineer Thomas Telford, it was the largest of its kind at the time and, along with Telford's other improvements to the road, reduced the journey time from London to Holyhead by an impressive nine hours.[10] Caroline, who detested ferry crossings, at once declared the bridge the finest work of man she had ever seen, and she and her husband marvelled at the safety and convenience of the gigantic structure.[11] The bridge was without a doubt an engineering wonder: suspended at the height of 98ft to allow for the tall Royal Navy sailing-ships to pass underneath at high water, no scaffolding was allowed in the strait during the seven years of its construction to ensure the unhindered passage of the vessels.

Before crossing the Strait, the Dunravens could not resist a brief detour to Bangor to visit Penrhyn Castle, which was undergoing large-scale alterations by Thomas Hopper, an architect much favoured by George IV. Originally a medieval fortified manor house, the building was remodelled in 1782 by Samuel Wyatt for Richard Pennant, first Baron Penrhyn, who had made a fortune from Jamaican sugar plantations and Welsh slate quarries. Pennant desired Gothic detail on the building to highlight its antiquity, but as Wyatt worked mainly in the Classical style the detailing was so restrained as to be virtually unnoticeable. When Pennant's second cousin, George Dawkins-Pennant, inherited the property in 1808, he at once sought Hopper's services to redesign the entire building in a dramatic Romanesque Revival style. The work commenced in 1820 and took some twenty years to complete, resulting in one of the most celebrated *faux* castles built in Great Britain in the course of the nineteenth century. Although it was far from complete in 1826, the Dunravens considered the style of the building magnificent and spent most of a day exploring its grounds in an open phaeton.[12] Windham retained a strong impression of the visit. In 1836 he asked his solicitor Matthew Barrington, who had reason to visit Bangor, to call to the castle and make a cast of one of its old-style hinges, which he wanted to replicate on some of the doors in Adare.[13]

On arrival in Dublin, the couple found the city busily occupied with parades, concerts and sumptuous balls and dinners to mark the king's birthday, all of which they looked forward to attending with great anticipation. To their bitter disappointment, however, first Windham and then Caroline fell ill with a severe cold and for much of their stay remained too unwell to attend the entertainment. They did, however, manage to make an appearance, if a rather creaky one, at Dublin Castle to attend a ball in St Patrick's Hall, 'where the raised part for the throne was admirably filled by the Lord Lieutenant, & the Marchioness Wellesly [sic], a most elegant & beautiful woman, & the Chancellor in his robes … & all the Court standing in brilliant dresses around them'. Caroline, weak from her bout of illness, was most grateful when 'some of the Peeresses were handed to comfortable chairs in a semicircle from the throne, where I could sit, & enjoy the whole scene … without the least inconvenience from the crowd'.[14]

Penrhyn Castle, Bangor. North-west view. Lithograph by H. Hughes, *c*. 1850. By permission of Llyfrgell Genedlaethol Cymru/The National Library of Wales.

Franciscan friary, Adare. Watercolour by Louisa Payne-Gallwey, *c.* 1833. Courtesy of Lavinia Graham-Vivian.

After this poor start to their return to Ireland, husband and wife were glad to reach the comfort of Adare, where they spent the next ten months boating, gardening, entertaining their neighbours and seeking the perfect moonlit moment among the castle and abbey ruins. Jane Williams from Aberpergwm House arrived for a visit in May, bringing with her Caroline's lifelong friend Catherine Harding. Thomas Price also made an appearance in early July, which resulted in a series of visits to places of antiquarian interest for the distinguished guest. The family circle was completed at the end of July, when Edwin returned from Eton for his summer holidays and the entire village celebrated his arrival with bonfires and illuminations.

In February 1827 Windham and his wife returned briefly to Ynyslas to prepare for their final departure from Wales. Their time was occupied in settling bills and bidding farewell to their neighbours in the Vale of Neath, a task that Caroline in particular performed with a heavy heart. Packing at Ynyslas commenced at the end of April and continued for several days. The architect William Whittington was invited to spend a day with the couple to receive instructions for the upkeep and further improvements to be carried out on the property. On the eve of their departure, John Randall, the new agent of the family's Welsh estates, was given possession of the cottage.

Windham at once resumed his programme of improvements at Adare. During 1826 and 1827 his attention was focused on the demesne, where the family's absence of five years had left its mark. Of particular concern was the Franciscan friary at the northernmost extremity of the estate. While the other two medieval monasteries had been restored and put to use as places of worship, the ruin of the Franciscan building had been neglected. Scores of workmen under Windham's direction spent the summer of 1826 removing ivy, burning weeds and repairing the walls to prevent the structure from deteriorating further. Desmond Castle, the remains of which adjoined the Franciscan friary to the west, had fared rather better and did not require remedial attention. Here a row of trees was planted along the river close to the structure in February 1827. In the same year, 100 brace of pheasants were imported to stock the woods at Boulabally in the southern extremity of the demesne, and a pheasantry was established for their captive rearing and breeding.[15]

Improvements also continued in the village, where the granting of building leases progressed at a slow but steady rate. The most important additions to the town at this time, however, were three sets of thatched cottages built along the south end of the main street. The idea for their construction almost certainly came from a visit made by the Dunravens to Cheltenham in March 1826 to see a row of ornate chalets on the Cirencester road known as Todd's Cottages.[16] This group of seven thatched buildings, also known as the Cranham or Swiss Cottages, was constructed in about 1821 as a summer retreat for a timber merchant named William Todd.[17] The architect is not known, but John Buonarotti Papworth, who was in Cheltenham in the 1820s designing the Montpelier Pump Room and its ornamental gardens, has been suggested.[18] Highly picturesque in their design, the buildings abounded in verandas, Gothic windows and ornamental flowerbeds and became an instant visitor attraction among commuters to Cheltenham, whom Todd accommodated by allowing them to enjoy picnics on his lawn.

The Dunravens were charmed by what they saw, and Caroline provided a detailed description of the cottages in her journal. 'The situation is very pretty',

she enthused. 'The different rooms are in detached buildings the whole filled up with great taste, & much effort particularly the ball room, which is the most delightfully contrived room I ever saw. There are niches with arches made of rustic trees, wound about with Ivy stems, round the whole building, one half of which is fitted up by recesses between the arches, & seats all covered with moss. There were likewise places for refreshments covered with moss, & the rest of the building being left open has a very pretty effect—& the floor being wood & laid on a hollow space has the most delightful spring in it.'[19]

The picturesque charm of these buildings may have reminded Caroline of Merthyr Mawr, a hamlet of thatched cottages some three miles north of Dunraven Castle. The village was home to Sir John Nicholl, a Welsh MP and judge whose only son married one of Thomas Mansel Talbot's daughters. The Nicholls were particular friends of the Wyndhams and the families shared an interest in horticulture. Nicholl had purchased his property in 1804, and two years later demolished the old manor house to make way for a modern dwelling. The grounds were laid out and planted between 1808 and 1809, and Nicholl took an active role in their design. Caroline's early journals record a number of visits to Merthyr Mawr House, during which undoubtedly not only Sir John's improvements but the charm of the adjoining hamlet were much admired and commented on by the Wyndhams. It was only natural for Caroline, so far removed from her paternal home, to recreate an element evocative of it.

Caroline also resumed her interest in the schoolmaster's house adjacent to the Augustinian church, which had been completed in 1825. An ornamental porch was added to the structure in February 1826, and Caroline watched the proceedings with interest.[20] The adjoining schoolhouse, completed some years earlier, was the focus of her attention in October and November, when its interior was redecorated. Caroline personally supervised the mason selected to undertake the works and rolled up her sleeves to paper its walls. With the help of her daughter Anna Maria, she also prepared an ornamental screen for the room.[21]

On one front, however, progress remained stagnant. Although James Pain had duly produced plans for the mausoleum, Windham, despite his initial resolve, did not immediately act on them. The project gained momentary impetus in October 1826, when Windham fell so ill that his life was despaired of and two doctors were rushed to his bedside. Praying for his own survival yet fearing the worst, Windham hastily scribbled this note: 'I purpose next spring building the mausoleum for my father by Mr Pain's plan & in the spot by the church known to him, & then recovering my father's remains to it with decent privacy, from Wales. I wish to repose by his side, & my dear wife with me, should such be her own desire hereafter. Let my funeral be quite private & at the least expense and the coffin carried by my labourers, tenants etc. I leave this memorandum for I am in bad health and possibly may not long survive.'[22] Happily, by mid-December Windham was sufficiently recovered to return to his usual avocations and, perhaps inevitably, the matter of building the mausoleum was once again postponed.

❖ ❖ ❖

While Windham's brush with death did not hasten his determination to complete the mausoleum, it may have shifted his thinking and focused his interest on the family home. Building the mausoleum served as an act of commemoration, a monument to ancestors, while recreating the family seat would instead represent a celebration of life, a positive memorial to the Dunravens and a legacy to be handed down through the generations. Up

Thomastown Castle, County Tipperary. Watercolour by C. H. Mathew (fl. 1836–1851). Private collection.

until 1827, alterations to Adare House were modest and had focused mainly on refreshing the building's exterior appearance and bringing its interiors up to more comfortable standards. Now, in the summer of 1827, James Pain was invited to Adare and asked to prepare plans for structural alterations to the house. Considering Windham and Caroline's interest in the Picturesque and their evident admiration of Nash's work, which they had explored in considerable detail in Wales, their choice of James and George Richard Pain as draughtsmen was understandable. This, however, did not prevent other architects from making representations in the hopes of securing a deal when news of the couple's building plans began to circulate. Among such aspirants was Richard Morrison, who had earned considerable fame as a designer of country houses, including the charming elliptical-fronted villa of Bearforest in Mallow, Co. Cork, and the two Tudor-Gothic masterpieces of Castle Freke, Co. Cork, and Thomastown Castle, Co. Tipperary. He also collaborated from time to time with his exceptionally gifted son, William Vitruvius Morrison, who had produced his first architectural designs—for Ballyheigue Castle, Co. Kerry—at the almost incomprehensibly young age of fifteen.[23] Their collaborative works included a number of exceptional buildings, such as the Classical masterpieces of Ballyfin, Co. Laois, and Fota House, Co. Cork.

Curragh Chase, Co. Limerick. *A Landscape with Curragh Chase, County Limerick* by Jeremiah Hodges Mulcahy. National Gallery of Ireland under the Creative Commons license CC BY 4.0.

Morrison arrived in September 1828 with his wife and son Fielding, who as a clergyman had been invited to Adare to officiate at divine service in the Augustinian church. The Dunravens were by no means strangers to Morrison's work. In 1813 their interest had been aroused by Thomastown Castle, which Morrison had enlarged the year before in the Gothic style for the second Earl of Llandaff and which the Dunravens had visited and admired. The Morrisons were duly invited to dinner at Adare House, and in the evening their guest entertained the family 'with a variety of plans of beautiful houses which he had superintended being a celebrated Architect'.[24] Morrison's polite overtures were equally politely ignored, however, and he was obliged to return home empty-handed.

The Dunravens also followed with considerable interest a parallel building project under way at Curragh Chase, Co. Limerick, home of Sir Aubrey de Vere,[25] some six miles north-west of Adare. Much like Windham, Sir

Aubrey was a responsible and enlightened landlord who supported Catholic Emancipation and spent a great part of his life improving the family estate and resolving financial problems inherited from his father. The family were also known for their interest in theatre and literature, talents which allowed Sir Aubrey's third son, Aubrey Thomas de Vere, to become one of the most distinguished and intellectual poets of his time. The two families shared a close friendship, and visits between Curragh Chase and Adare were frequent and mutually enjoyed.

In about 1828, Sir Aubrey de Vere commissioned the Brighton-based architect Amon Henry Wilds to redesign his family home in the Neo-Classical style.[26] Wilds was a somewhat unusual choice for the task. Originally born in Lewes, East Sussex, he and his carpenter father relocated to Brighton in 1817, as its growing popularity as a holiday resort offered better prospects of employment. In spite of stiff competition, they survived in the business and contributed significantly to the town's Regency-era character. Wilds had an interest in romantic Orientalism and favoured onion domes, richly ornamented pediments and other Indian-style flourishes. In his later career, he demonstrated a strong preference for the equally ornate Italianate style. His trademark motif, which also served as a pun on his unusual first name, was the ammonite pilaster, an Ionic capital decorated with volutes in the spiral shape of an ammonite fossil.[27]

No such whimsical liberties, however, were taken with the drawings presented to Sir Aubrey de Vere. In his design for Curragh Chase, Wilds remained faithful to the original building's elevational composition and simply repeated it on a new eleven-bay north-facing façade. Apart from prominent quoins, five recessed central bays and a curved western end, the new part of the building was entirely void of ornamentation. Its only prominent feature was the wide terrace, which ran along the entire length of the façade to conceal the basement. The austerity of the building suited its remote and ascetic setting, as Sir Aubrey's poet son described in his memoirs many years later. 'One of its approaches', he recalled, 'was three miles long and it passed three lakes, one surrounded by meadows, pastures, and groves, another by woods which had never been planted by man, though perhaps often cut down and successively renewed—a portion of ancient Ireland's "forest primeval." Through those woods my father was never tired of making new drives and walks. The most interesting of these was the "Cave Walk," so called from a deep cave retiring back from a long line of cliff crowned with wood, matted over with ivy, and so perpendicular that it looked like the walls of a castle … With my father, landscape gardening was one mode of taking out the poetry which was so deeply seated within him.'[28]

Windham and Caroline made numerous trips to Curragh Chase in 1828 and 1829, often spending an entire day walking around the gardens and inspecting the improvements at the house. Reciprocal visits were made to Adare House by Sir Aubrey, and on one of these visits in March 1829 he was accompanied by Amos Henry Wilds, whom Caroline regarded highly and considered a fine architect.[29] On that occasion, Wilds spent a day with the Dunravens, resulting in a design proposal for an extension to Adare House. This, however, was not executed, as there had never been any real doubt of the Dunravens' preference for the Pain brothers as their draughtsmen.

❖   ❖   ❖

Despite the contributions of two architects providing professional guidance, planning the new house was a slow process. It was clear from the beginning that the Dunravens were not satisfied with handing over the design of the building entirely to the architects, no matter how accomplished. While the Pains provided the professional framework for planning works to Adare Manor, Windham and Caroline determined the architectural detail with which it was to be embellished, both externally and internally. To that end, between 1827 and 1829 the couple spent countless evenings poring over architectural prints and pattern-books. They also scrutinised sketches and drawings made during their many tours of country houses in England and Wales to determine whether a new house or an extension would be the best way forward and in what architectural style alterations should be effected. Not that there was anything unusual about such hesitancy. Their friend Sir Edward O'Brien of Dromoland Castle wrestled with a similar problem in 1812 before at length concluding that 'such considerable difficulty will attend the adding and linking the old house to the new that I begin to think it would be almost as well to build a new House entirely & to content ourselves with the one we have till we can do it to suit our Purse & wishes in every respect as we are in no hurry about the matter'.[30] Having spent a year making this decision, Sir Edward passed another seven years vacillating between proposals submitted by various architects before also settling on James and George Richard Pain's design in 1819.

While country house-building was traditionally seen as the realm of the male, there is no doubt that, in the case of Adare Manor, Windham's interest in and contribution to its design and construction were, in the early stages at least, equalled if not surpassed by those of his wife. Many of the trips to Curragh Chase were made by Caroline on her own, and she and Sir Aubrey's wife Mary spent many afternoons exchanging building and landscape ideas. When James Pain arrived in Adare at the end of May 1827 to prepare drawings, Caroline accompanied him on the day, even though she was suffering from a heavy cold.[31] Her strong sense of association with the ongoing building activities is also evident in her habit of referring to them in her journal as 'my improvements'. In some ways, this reflected not only her interest in architecture but also her growing sense of belonging and her increasing enchantment with Adare. 'I should be quite content to have very little intercourse with fashionable life— the tranquil & I trust rational life which I pass at Adare is much more suited to my feelings & taste', she mused in January 1828.[32]

Caroline was not the only member of the household to develop a feverish interest in the design process. The couple's teenage son Edwin filled his letters home from the confines of Eton College with endless queries about developments and impatient requests for information, and spent his free time amusing himself 'in making plans for a house of my own invention, which I

The Hall, Shropshire. Front entrance. Watercolour by Miss M. Hanmer, early nineteenth century. Courtesy of the Dunraven family. Drawings like these by friends and family were keenly perused by Windham and Caroline in the early design stages of Adare Manor.

will show you next holydays'.[33] He also took an avid interest in building works at the nearby Windsor Castle, where large-scale reconstruction works had commenced in 1824 under the supervision of Jeffry Wyatville, nephew of the leading architect James Wyatt. The desire to modernise the building had come from George IV on his accession to the throne in 1820, and it was his personal architectural tastes—a mix of Gothic and French Rococo—which determined the design cue adopted by Wyatville. To Edwin's ill-concealed frustration, the construction works were a jealously guarded secret. 'It is quite impossible now for anyone to see the castle', he complained, 'for the King gave orders that no one should go over the new part, until he had seen it himself.' Nevertheless, he promised to bring home 'some prints of the castle if I can get new ones that you may see what sort of thing it is'.[34]

As the couple worked on their plans, improvements within the demesne continued throughout 1828 and 1829. In the deer park a large number of men were employed in creating a horse pond, while in the garden new walls were constructed and a large rockery of alpine plants surrounded by a pond of water lilies was established.[35] A tremendous flood halted activities for a week in the middle of February 1828, when the banks of the Maigue rose so high that Caroline and her daughter Anna Maria were obliged to abandon their horse-drawn carriage in favour of a boat to get to the schoolhouse. 'I am sorry I have missed this great flood in Adare', Edwin wrote with a note of envy from Eton upon hearing the news. 'It would have been such fun, to have been rowing about the fields and about the Demesne.'[36] The Heath House was reroofed and refloored under James Pain's supervision, and in the early part of 1829 new hothouses were constructed and old nettings and rails in the pleasure-grounds were taken down and replaced by ornamental iron palings ordered from England. Beyond the gardens, the planting and removal of unwanted trees continued at a steady pace.[37]

One of the more unusual of James Pain's undertakings at this time was the construction of an ice house, a common feature at country houses before the invention of mechanical freezing. The ice house in Adare consisted of an underground chamber accessed through a short corridor opening into a brick-lined barrel vault. Two solid doors, one at either end of the corridor, controlled access into the chamber and ensured that the interior remained cool at all times. As a further measure of insulation, the vault was covered over by a thick mound of grass-covered earth which was supported on the north side by a rustic retaining wall of rough timber posts.

When completed, the ice house had a whimsical appearance, reminiscent of the lair of a forest creature, an impression which was enhanced by its location on the edge of a small wood immediately south of the walled gardens. Although a simple structure, its construction progressed slowly during the summer of 1828 owing to the effort which was required to dig the chamber in which the ice was to be stored. 'Is the ice house covered with earth yet?' Edwin enquired in mid-October. 'It must take a long time doing.'[38] Towards the end of January 1829, when a hard frost settled in, the process of filling the ice house commenced, with the family eagerly watching the curious sight.[39]

Windsor Castle, Berkshire. *Windsor Castle from Near Brocas Meadows* by William Daniell, 1827. © National Museum Wales.

In 1828 Windham was very much focused on altering and extending rather than replacing the existing house, and considerable effort was expended on the old building to make it more comfortable. During the winter of 1828–9 the house was repainted, the kitchen and bathrooms renovated, and an underground passage to the housekeeper's room constructed.[40] These activities were almost the undoing of Windham's interest in building works, for the cost of the exercise appalled him. 'Mr Pain', he told Edwin, 'has brought over a new Kitchen Grate in London, cost 25 Guineas—one may form some idea what the *real* expense is of building & furnishing a great House by the fact of a common sort of grate costing so much. He is to send over two new water closets & a Marble bath—not the hot bath I think he sayd [*sic*] he could get better in Cork.'[41]

Despite his misgivings over the issue of cost, building plans, perhaps at Caroline's insistence, occupied more and more of Windham's time as the year progressed. Ideas and sketches were circulated among family members for comment, and several proposals discarded as dull or simply unworkable. 'I am very glad Papa is not going to make those rooms where he originally intended', Edwin felt emboldened to write from Eton in October, 'for I always thought they would look bad sticking out to the hall door, and look very patch work.'[42] By the time James Pain's much-awaited first set of proposals arrived on 28 October 1828, nineteen months after his initial visit to measure out the building for alterations, Windham had thrown all caution to the wind and shifted his thinking radically from an upgrading of the old house to the construction of an entirely new one around it. In May 1829 he wrote to Edwin with news and details of his new master-plan. 'Mr Pain came out here to breakfast yesterday. The plans he had sent out some days before. They were not good, & we made many alterations, & laying all our heads together have produced I think very good plans which he is now preparing in Limerick, but they have grown to be very considerable. I remembered your wish for a long room, & we have arranged a most noble Gallery 120 ft long, 18 wide & 22 high, with a coved ceiling, the Gallery being upstairs—lighted by a large window at each end & a lanthern light from the roof in the centre. We shall also have a fine Hall, the roof supported by a large Pillar near the centre. The present staircase must remain, improved, but not very much— we could not help its being rather inferior to the other part, but it signifies

Adare Manor, Adare. Frontispiece to an Ordnance Survey folio of maps, c.1840s, in anticipation of the final design. Courtesy of the Dunraven family.

little.'[43] Windham's ideas would change again over the next number of years. Nevertheless, while the gallery would not sport a lantern light nor the great hall a single supporting pillar in its centre, these two rooms remained firmly fixed in Windham's plans and from the outset grew into the defining elements of Adare Manor.

Edwin rejoiced at the news of the finalisation of working plans for the building. 'I like them very much', he enthused to his mother, '& I think they will be very handsome; for Papa and you have such good taste and judgment; that you would not do anything that was not so. What a splendid room the gallery will be.'[44] Without the drawings to hand at Eton, however, Edwin struggled to work out what exactly his father was planning to do. 'I have been fancying where the gallery is to be, but it is much too great a puzzle for me to guess. I suppose the length of it runs from north to south.'[45] The gallery was in fact proposed to run from east to west, but Edwin's mistake was understandable, since the subject of positioning the new building also puzzled his father. By virtue of its topography, the site on which the old family home stood allowed limited scope for expansion, being located on a narrow strip of

Above: Adare Manor, Adare. Design of the west elevation by James and George Richard Pain, April 1833. Courtesy of the Irish Architectural Archive.

Right: Adare Manor, Adare. Ground-plan of the principal floor by James and George Richard Pain, May 1834. Courtesy of the Irish Architectural Archive.

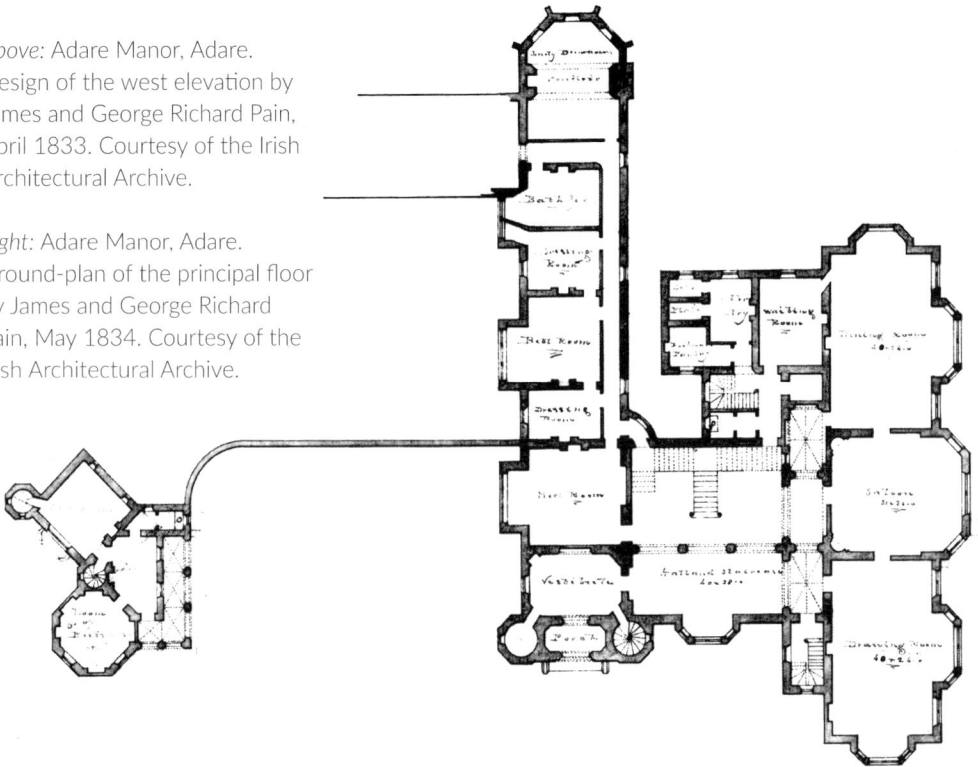

ground bounded by a steeply rising slope to the west and the Maigue River to the east. Windham at length concluded that the best location for the bulk of the new building was in the backyard, north of the old house, even though it meant the relocation of the yard and demolition of several old outbuildings.[46] One of these, a long office known as the Lodge, caused him particular pause, for the structure was well built and made of good materials. Loath to waste it, Windham hit on a positive plan. 'I am preparing to turn the long office to all the uses that can be made of it by building the walls of four cottages *exactly* the same breadth as the office so as to make the old roof answer for them with the windows, floors &c. These things will do very well & come into full play in 4 Labourers Houses, whereas they would have been of very little use here.'[47] A suitable location for the building was found in the village outside an entrance known as Dawson's Gate, which provided access from the estate to Rathkeale Road. By March 1829, Windham told Edwin that 'We are knocking down the old office … at last—it will have bowed its head to the ground before you arrive, and the Cottages made out of its old materials will be finished but not inhabited, not *dry* enough.' Delays associated with the realisation of his plans were to become abhorrent to Windham, causing him to complain that 'Nothing but experience in works could convince people of the time, delays, trouble & expense of various disappointments attendant upon all sorts of works, especially building'.[48]

❖ ❖ ❖

A momentous event affected Ireland in early February 1829, when King George IV made a speech at the opening of Parliament in which he recommended emancipation for the Catholics. The occasion was marked with jubilation in towns and villages across the country, not least in Adare, where bonfires were lit all over the town as villagers gathered to celebrate. Two months later, the passing of the Roman Catholic Relief Act removed the most substantial restrictions placed on Roman Catholics in the United Kingdom and granted them the right to sit in the parliament in Westminster. The campaign had been spearheaded by the Irish lawyer and political leader

Miniature portrait of Windham Henry Wyndham Quin (1829–65), c. 1831. Courtesy of the Dunraven family.

Daniel O'Connell through the establishment of the Catholic Association in 1823. Himself a Catholic, Daniel O'Connell won an election in 1828 but was forbidden from taking his seat in Parliament owing to his religion. His strongest ally in the campaign for Catholic relief was the Duke of Wellington, who threatened to resign as prime minister if the king refused to give royal assent to the Act. The greatest turning-point, however, came when public opinion in Britain began to swing in its favour, leading Home Secretary Sir Robert Peel to concede that civil strife was a greater danger than Catholic Emancipation. The Dunravens, long-time supporters of the cause, rejoiced at the prospect and joined their neighbours in the celebrations.[49]

In the spring of 1829, Windham's wife discovered that she was once again pregnant. Resigning herself to yet another miscarriage, Caroline spent her days in anxious contemplation, from which James Pain's visits brought a welcome diversion. The working plans that Pain produced were never entirely to Windham's satisfaction and required numerous alterations, for which Pain visited Adare on several occasions throughout the summer and autumn of 1829. Edwin, still stuck at Eton, pined to meet the architect, and received news of each visit with mounting desperation, although he noted gallantly that 'I am glad Payne has been again it shews things are getting on'.[50] By no means unsympathetic to his son's feelings, Windham promised to defer Pain's next visit until the start of the school holidays.[51]

Against all odds, Caroline's pregnancy continued. Nevertheless, being by now 39 years old with more miscarriages than she cared to remember, it placed an unprecedented strain on her. Most of her days were spent resting or sitting quietly in the garden, which she had worked so hard to improve and which now proved a source of comfort and solace. 'The weather now was the most beautiful possible', she recalled in May. 'I sat out for hours every day enjoying myself. The singing of the birds, which are so unusually tame at Adare the pheasants & hares all round me, the quantities of Lambs & in short every thing that can render the very quiet life I am obliged to lead engaging, prevented me ever feeling a moments ennui, & my heart was constantly thankful to the almighty Disposer of all events that as it had pleased him to change the usual habits of my life, I should have so little suffering & privation.'[52] In spite of her evident note of cheerfulness, by the time Edwin returned to Adare for his long-awaited holidays in early August his mother's condition had deteriorated to such a degree that she was only able to move about with the help of a wheelchair. On Pain's visit later in the month, the family were obliged to entertain him in Caroline's dressing room to give the expectant mother an opportunity to listen in while the architect talked over the latest set of plans.[53]

Augustinian church, Adare. Family mausoleum shown in the centre of the building. From *Memorials of Adare Manor* (1865). Courtesy of Special Collections and Archives, Glucksman Library, University of Limerick.

As the summer drew to a close, Windham grew increasingly concerned over his wife's condition. In early September he decided that Edwin should remain in Adare and not return to Eton, partly because he knew that the boy's presence would comfort and divert Caroline, and partly because of an underlying and unspoken fear that she might not survive the pregnancy. Once again, it was James Pain's visit in October with an amended set of plans that occupied Caroline's mind for several days and drew her out of her anxious contemplation. The long and apprehensive wait finally came to an end on 2 November, when Caroline went into labour and gave birth to a healthy baby boy.[54] The thriving infant was baptised the following day and named Windham Henry after his father. As news of the happy event spread, local people gathered to celebrate. That evening the entire village was illuminated with blazing bonfires, as people danced in the streets to express their joy at Caroline's safe delivery.[55] As a mark of gratitude for her survival, Caroline commissioned the construction of a fever hospital on Rathkeale Road in 1830. The building was given rent-free to the public on its completion a year later. With eighteen beds in its fever wards, the hospital was funded partly by private subscriptions and partly by parliamentary grants.[56]

In the same year that the fever hospital opened, Windham finally saw to the construction of the long-planned mausoleum, much to the annoyance of his eldest son. 'So the Mausoleum is to be built before the house', Edwin complained to his mother. 'I am afraid Papa's inventive head will discover so many things to be built, that the poor house will stand a bad chance, and the timber and material go to rot in the yard.'[57] These works at the Augustinian church, which coincided with the restoration of its cloisters, were conducted by James Pain. The mausoleum was placed outside the western arm of the cloister quadrant. Its unembellished bulk was softened only by the family coat of arms and a commemorative plaque with the inscription 'This mausoleum was constructed in the year of our Lord 1826, by Windham Henry, Earl of Dunraven, for the remains of his dear father, Richard, first Earl of Dunraven, and for the family of Quin of Adare'. The date on the plaque refers not to the year in which the structure was completed but to that in which it was first conceived. Notwithstanding this anomaly, the mausoleum and fever hospital were two of a number of examples of the way in which the Dunravens utilised architecture to celebrate and commemorate births, deaths, marriages and the safe delivery from calamities.

CHAPTER

SEVEN

Kitchen Gables

Whilst Windham and Caroline readjusted to life with a newborn infant, their two older children took their first steps towards independence. Anna Maria, now a young lady of fifteen, moved to Dublin in early February 1830 to finish her schooling and to be introduced into society. This she did under the guidance of Thomas and Elizabeth Goold, lifelong friends of the Dunravens, who lived in the heart of the city at No. 20 Merrion Square North. The two families were also distantly related through Thomas Goold's mother, Mary Quin, whose father was first cousin to Windham's grandfather. Something of a rogue in his younger days, Thomas had unfortunately squandered much of his inheritance in entertaining and travelling widely. When his money ran out, he sobered and applied himself diligently to the study of law and was called to the Bar in 1791. Although extremely skilled as a lawyer and regarded as one of the great wits of his time, his professional career was hampered by vehement and outspoken opposition to the 1800 Act of Union. This earned him the sobriquet 'honest Irishman',[1] which, it appears, was not intended to be taken as a compliment. Nevertheless, Thomas's strong nationalistic streak did not entirely ruin his career, as in 1832 he was appointed a master of the court of chancery. His wife Elizabeth was the eldest daughter of the Reverend Brinsley Nixon, rector of Painstown, Co. Meath. The couple married in 1803 and had six children: sons Francis, Frederick and Wyndham, and daughters Emily, Caroline and Augusta. The youngest daughter, Augusta, just four years Anna Maria's senior, quickly assumed a proprietorial air towards her and the two girls became close friends.

Also in Dublin in 1830 was Edwin, fresh out of Eton and eager to test his intellectual skills. A studious and academically inclined youth, Edwin had developed an interest in science, particularly astronomy, ever since his parents had given him a telescope to explore the starry expanse above Ynyslas Cottage.[2] A few months short of his eighteenth birthday, Edwin was granted an opportunity to read astronomy as a private pupil of the young but immensely talented William Rowan Hamilton, probably through the influence of the Goold family, with whom Hamilton was on terms of intimacy.[3] A mathematical prodigy, Hamilton had been appointed Professor of Astronomy at Trinity College just three years previously at the age of 22, and during his career he made significant contributions to the study of optics and classical mechanics. Edwin, intellectually gifted and possessed of a restless and inquisitive mind, made an ideal student for Hamilton. The friendship they forged lasted a lifetime, notwithstanding Edwin's later academic pursuits in history and antiquarianism rather than natural sciences.

Edwin's letters from Dublin were filled with news of his studies and social life and requests for news from home, particularly in relation to the building works at Adare, but the young man was kept in a perpetual state of disappointment. 'I have not heard a word about the buildings lately, I mean our own buildings', he complained in April 1830, 'why I thought, Paine had the plans ready and Papa said as soon as he had finished them, they would begin. You must explain to me why they are not commencing.'[4] As spring turned to summer and faded into autumn with no sign of progress, Edwin's frustration increased, made worse by rumour. 'The Duke [of Leinster] told me', he wrote gloomily to his mother, 'that some of our neighbours told him, Papa had been *intending* to build for a long time, and that opinion is very general and not confined to his Grace for no body will believe that he will build till it is begun.'[5]

Miniature portrait of Anna Maria Wyndham Quin, 1829. Courtesy of the Dunraven family.

Mitchelstown Castle, Co. Cork. Watercolour by the Rev. Richard Calvert Jones (1804–77). Private collection.

His parents, however, were in no hurry to progress their building plans for a number of reasons. First and foremost, while there had never been any doubt in their minds about Tudor-Gothic as their preferred style, and although the Pain brothers had been steadily producing proposals to this effect throughout 1829 and 1830, Windham and Caroline had not yet settled on the final layout. The couple's house visits in England and Wales in the early 1820s gave them new and exciting ideas, which they wanted to test with their family and peer groups. This was most likely the reason behind Windham's two-day visit to Mitchelstown Castle, Co. Cork in December 1829 and the reciprocal visit to Adare by its owner, George King, third Earl of Kingston, in January 1830. An extravagant man of excessive tastes, Lord Kingston—or Big George, as he was aptly known—was one of the Pain brothers' most important clients. In 1823 he commissioned them to provide designs for a Gothic castle in anticipation of a visit by George IV, whom he wished to impress. Lord Kingston was no judge of architecture, and his only requirements were that the building had to be larger than any other house in Ireland and that it had to be built quickly.[6] Although not quite the largest of its kind in the country, the scale of Mitchelstown Castle was truly massive. It incorporated an entrance set within a 25ft Tudor arch flanked by octagonal towers that opened into a two-storey entrance hall; a vaulted gallery 93ft long; and enough bedrooms to accommodate up to 100 guests at a time. One visitor to the castle recalled, tongue-in-cheek, that her bedroom was 'of such a size that on a misty night it was difficult to see across it'.[7] The colossal structure was completed in just three years and cost some £100,000 to build—ultimately all in vain, as the anticipated visit by the king did not take place. Although its scale and opulence were not to everyone's taste, Mitchelstown Castle was undoubtedly one of the most successful and talked-about early Gothic Revival castles in Ireland. Lord Kingston's opinion clearly mattered not only to the Dunravens but also to the Pain brothers as a seal of approval from a prominent and evidently satisfied patron.

Another factor that needed to be addressed before the commencement of building works was a practical one. The construction of the new manor house required a significant quantity of cut stone and other building materials, which would need carting to Adare from quarries, sawmills and builders' providers generally. Until 1830, the main entrance to Adare House was located on top of a short but steep hill on the main Cork to Limerick road to the immediate east of the village. The hill was difficult for heavy loads to manoeuvre, as was the sharp right-angled turn required to negotiate the gates. An opportunity to remedy this presented itself in 1830, when the road was upgraded to provide a more efficient mail-coach service between Cork and Limerick. To improve access to his property, Windham agreed to pay for the cost of cutting through rock to level the road and at the same time arranged for a new entrance gateway to be constructed in the village proper. This entrance was placed at a slight angle to the main street, with a large triangular space in front of it for easier vehicular access from both directions. The entire family—except for Edwin, who remained in Dublin—gathered to witness the official opening of the road on 8 October 1830.[8] As was customary, a plaque was erected on the wall adjoining the road to commemorate the family's contribution and to mark the location of the original entrance. The construction of the new entrance, contracted to a stonemason named Thomas Jackson, took somewhat longer and was not completed until 1832.

Another reason for the delay was that there were many other improvements still under way within the estate. 'We have so much to do here & so many things in hand and in places so far asunder that there is little to shew', Windham remarked to his son in May 1830.[9] A new farmyard and gate lodges were being erected, pleasure-grounds improved and field boundaries within the demesne altered to create panoramic views of the surrounding countryside. A large greenhouse was built in 1831 adjacent to the walled garden which bounded the pleasure-grounds to the west, as was a grapery where vines of red and white grapes were cultivated with considerable success. The greenhouse became one of the family's favourite spots, not only for gardening but also as a place where one could while away an hour or two reading a book or entertaining friends to afternoon tea. In the midst of these developments, looking at plans for the house was only one of a number of activities in which Edwin's parents were engaged.

While waiting for events to unfold in Adare, Edwin's attention was drawn to a building project recently commenced by Sir Robert Gore-Booth at Lissadell, Co. Sligo. Edwin's association with the Gore-Booths came about through his growing infatuation with Thomas and Elizabeth Goold's youngest daughter Augusta, whose sister Caroline married Sir Robert in April 1830. Robert's father began a programme of improvements on the Lissadell estate in the late eighteenth

Lissadell, Co. Sligo. Watercolour of the gallery for Sir Robert Gore-Booth's new house. Courtesy of the Dunraven family.

century. This activity was cut short by his sudden death in 1814, when his eldest son and heir was just nine years old. This was not the only tragedy in Robert's life; his first wife, Caroline King, died in January 1828, ten months after the couple's wedding, giving birth to a stillborn daughter. With new love came new enthusiasm, however, and in 1830 Robert selected a site for a new family seat and commissioned the London architect Francis Goodwin to design it.

Goodwin, an architect of churches and other public buildings, later developed an interest in country house design, a role in which he found particular favour in Ireland. Although competent in producing a range of architectural styles, Goodwin's personal preference was for Greek Revival, in which he was heavily influenced by the British architect John Soane. Often seen as the last phase in the development of Neo-Classical architecture, Greek Revivalism was at the height of its popularity in the 1820s and 1830s. It was this style, characterised by a sombre asceticism, that Sir Robert Gore-Booth chose. Nowhere in Ireland can it be found in a more austere form than at Lissadell. Constructed of locally quarried ashlar limestone, the two-storey, nine-bay building stood on elevated ground overlooking Sligo Bay. Notwithstanding meticulous and precisely detailed stonework, the building was virtually unadorned except for giant order Doric pilasters which rose between the bays. Nothing could be in greater contrast to the Gothic ebullience of Adare Manor, yet something about the building captured Edwin's fancy. Following a visit to Lissadell with the Goolds in the spring of 1831, he sent his parents plans of the building to give an idea of the size and disposition of the rooms. One feature that particularly intrigued him was the *porte-cochère*, a porch large enough for carriages to stop under and pass through. 'I must say I like the plan about driving in very much', he enthused, 'for the gates can be shut when a carriage is inside that covered place, and so you would be exposed to no draught or rain or dirt in getting out.' Perhaps in an attempt to entice his parents to get on with their own building plans, Edwin also made sure that further plans and views of Lissadell prepared by Goodwin found their way to Adare.[10]

Left: Adare Manor, Adare. Design of the east elevation by James and George Richard Pain, showing kitchen wing to the right, December 1832. Courtesy of the Irish Architectural Archive.

Right: Adare Manor, Adare. Detail of a drawing showing the front of the kitchen wing. Courtesy of the Dunraven family.

The construction of the new manor house finally got under way in April 1832, when the last of the out-offices behind Adare House were pulled down and James Pain made his way from Limerick to lay out the plans and mark the places on the ground where the foundations were to be dug.[11] The first part of the house to be built was the kitchen wing, which stood at right angles to the rear of the main building. It comprised a tall central block adorned with a clock tower, flanked on either side by lower castellated wings. While starting the project with a kitchen wing and servants' quarters might seem incongruous, it allowed Windham and Caroline to further consider the design of the main house and satisfied their aim of providing for the servants at the earliest possible time. 'Though by dint of furnishing &c we have made our sitting & bed rooms comfortable', Caroline explained to her mother in May 1832, 'we are quite without the numerous old rooms that servants want, & we have really none of the modern comforts below stairs.'[12] The focus on the comfort of servants also speaks of the family's strong sense of duty towards the men and women who worked for them in the house and on the estate, many of whom were regarded almost as family members. When Caroline's personal maid, Anne Buraston, died suddenly in August 1832, Caroline was deeply affected, lamenting 'my dear faithful … maid who lived with me before I was quite grown up & whose attachment and fidelity for 25 years makes her loss quite irreplaceable'.[13]

Above: A Cart and Horses in a Quarry by Joseph Mallord William Turner, *c.* 1798. Photo: © Tate, London 2022.

Below: Labourers with horses and carts. Watercolour by Augusta Goold, *c.* 1830s. Courtesy of the Dunraven family.

While the foundations were being dug, teams of stonemasons were hard at work producing large blocks of hammer-dressed stone, quantities of which were delivered to Adare and stored on site. Unlike many of his peers, Windham was not one to import Portland stone at exorbitant rates from England, favouring native building materials instead. Following two years in search of the finest-quality limestone, he was pleased to discover that local quarries turned out a much better product than he had expected. 'We have not only found one other good Quarry, but several', he noted with evident satisfaction in May 1832, '& are better off now for good stone than any place I ever saw.'[14] To add variety to the external walls, blocks of ashlar were sourced in different colours: grey stone primarily from the townland of Tuogh, red and yellowish red from Dunnaman, and brownish red from Clonagh, all quarries in County Limerick within a few miles' distance from Adare.[15] The stone was meticulously selected, and blocks with white deposits of calcium carbonate (or lime plume, as it was known) were summarily rejected.

Other building materials were also sourced locally. Flagstones for flooring were drawn from a quarry in Bilboa, near the town of Cappamore, Co. Limerick, while, for roofing, hundreds of tons of the beautiful grey-green Killaloe slate, often used on the finest public and private buildings in the country, were ordered from the large quarries operated by the Mining Company of Ireland in County Tipperary. Cartloads of timber boards were delivered by Joseph Roberts from Limerick. 'Building is no joke', Windham remarked to Edwin, 'there is £1000 pound worth of Timber laying on the river bank now, & 250 more waiting to be sent up.'[16] Initially, brick was drawn from Askeaton, Rathkeale and Limerick city, but from the 1840s onwards quantities of it was made to shape and fired on the estate on a large plot of ground established a short distance to the south-west from the walled gardens. The quality of brick burnt here was so good that Windham began selling it, keeping detailed records of quantities sold and payments received.[17]

The Dunravens also saw the building of Adare Manor as being of considerable advantage to the poor in the neighbourhood, since it enabled them to enjoy comforts which 'in the greatest part of this unfortunate country they cannot command'.[18] The masons, carvers and carpenters who built Adare Manor were men and boys from the village of Adare and its immediate neighbourhood, and the house became testament to their

Portrait of Frances Quin *née* Dawson (b. 1729). Courtesy of the Dunraven family. Wife of Windham 'the Drone' Quin, Frances was the driving force behind attracting Palatine families to Adare.

remarkable skills as craftsmen. Many of them were descendants of Palatine families who originated from the Rhineland and were renowned for their thrift and industry and their skills as craftsmen, artisans, masons, weavers and farmers. When religious and political tensions forced these families into a diaspora in the early eighteenth century, the Irish parliament provided a subsidy of £25,000 for their settlement in Ireland to help secure Protestant interest in the country. In the autumn of 1709, a group of 871 families arrived in Dublin, from where they were sent to assigned estates around the country, predominantly in Kerry and Limerick. The greater portion of the colony, 115 families, was settled on the estate of Lord Thomas Southwell in County Limerick between 1710 and 1714.[19] From the 1740s onwards, however, Southwell's high rents resulted in the Palatines moving to nearby settlements such as Adare, where terms were more favourable. By 1808 there were 46 families of Palatine origin on the Quin estate in Adare.[20] It was from the descendants of these diligent and industrious people that a significant portion of the builders of Adare Manor were drawn.

When Edwin asked his father about workmen at the commencement of works in May 1832, Windham told him that 'Our staff consists of the foreman & 24 masons under him. The Stone Cutting is done by contract with Master stone cutters, who employ the hands, & may be 30 or 35 of them at work.' He could not help adding: 'This kind of building is very tedious & immensely expensive, as I am beginning to find *practically*'.[21] A master mason called James Connolly, the son of a cabinet-maker, was given the role of foreman and for the next twenty years steered the building works with exceptional skill. His son Thomas, an apprentice stonemason, worked by his side as James laid the foundations of the mansion. Thomas showed an aptitude for draughtsmanship, and many of the working drawings for masons and carpenters were prepared by him under instruction from Caroline, who had learned the drawing skill from her mother.[22] Other stonemasons included John Crotty with his son, also John; brothers Thomas, Timothy and Edmond Jackson; John Doherty; Michael Donoghue; James Shea; Denis Grady; and Daniel Hourigan. A team of equally remarkable carvers and carpenters also worked on the house, among them Michael and John Creagh, Edmond Dwyer and, from the 1840s onwards, James Connolly, perhaps another son of the gifted master mason.

With such a team of skilled men, building works progressed rapidly throughout 1832. By November the bulk of the kitchen wing was standing, and masons were preparing mouldings for doors and windows and working on the clock turret. Already at this early stage it was obvious that the effort in selecting the best stone had paid off. Caroline felt certain that 'if all is finished to accord with the masonry it will be very handsome—the immense size of the stones, & the beautiful manner in which they are set, gives it a massive look'.[23] Where previously Edwin had expressed annoyance at the lack of building progress, he now feared that matters would advance rather too fast and prevent him from observing enough of the construction works. 'I am very anxious to see the building, I suppose a good deal has been done in my absence', he wrote with a note of concern in October 1832,[24] but by the spring of 1833 his tone had changed and signs of impatience were once again creeping in. 'I should hope the building will get on faster now than it has been doing the last month', he remarked in March. 'I expect to see something by the time I get to Adare or I shall be disappointed.'[25] Edwin could not resist comparing and contrasting the building activities at Adare with those at Lissadell and clearly found in favour of the latter, which took just five years to complete. 'I am sorry to hear they are getting on so slow at the building, I wonder what is the reason', he wrote while visiting Lissadell in March 1833, adding rather pointedly: 'they work away here at such a rate, none ever looks idle, half the rooms and more are plastered, and the ceilings of some done already.'[26]

❖   ❖   ❖

Once begun, building activities at Adare generated great interest in the neighbourhood and attracted curious visitors, some of whom travelled a considerable distance to view the works. In July 1832 Thomas Mullins, third Baron Ventry, and his wife Eliza, who were also engaged in building works at the time, arrived from County Kerry to inspect the premises but found the Dunravens away from home. Undeterred, the couple approached an estate worker, a Mr O'Reagan, who obligingly showed them around the grounds. Mindful of his position, O'Reagan left a written account of the visit for the Dunravens in a beautifully rounded hand but rather halting grammar, unaccustomed as he was to letter-writing. 'My Lord Dunraven', he began, 'I beg leave to let you know that on Sunday last Lord & Ladey Vintry stoped at my House the Requisted I would shuo them the New Building at Adare Abbey as the were Building a New Mantion on their Estate I walked with them and shuod them the Building and when I said that what was Built was offices his Lordship said no more about his Kerry Building he and Lady Ventry was much Delighted at seeing the fine Elms and her Ladyship said that the Building as it now was would make a fine Mansion the were never inside the Demesne of Adare befor and the were greatly awed at what the did see I had a mind to sho them the Pleasure grounds but I di not for fear of doing wrong.'[27]

Adare House, Adare. Sketch of an elm tree by Edwin, 1829. Courtesy of the Dunraven family. These elms were admired by Lord and Lady Ventry on their visit to Adare.

Throughout the construction works, domestic life at Adare House continued on its normal course in spite of the noise, dust and disruption. The Dunravens were a generous and sociable family who enjoyed entertaining, and their door was always open to friends and strangers alike. The poet Aubrey de Vere, one of Edwin's closest friends, recalled their home as 'a gay as well as a friendly and hospitable house; after dinner we had private theatricals, games of all sorts, dances, and, in the daytime, pleasant wanderings beside the beautiful Maigue'.[28]

Edwin's studies in Dublin shifted the family's interest towards scientific pursuits and brought many remarkable guests to Adare in the early 1830s, not least Edwin's tutor, William Rowan Hamilton. His first visit to Adare in September 1830, albeit brief, was long enough for the Dunravens to develop a deep regard for the talented young scientist. The feeling was mutual. Writing to his sister from Adare, Hamilton told her that 'Lady Dunraven … is a charming person, and deserves the fame which she has acquired as such. I like Lord Dunraven too, who came in from his workmen a little before the dinner-hour, which here is four o'clock.'[29] Hamilton was charmed by his visit. 'This evening, before tea, in the twilight', he wrote on 18 September,

149

'we had a delightful boating on the river, along the ruined castle walls which had belonged to the Earl of Desmond, and under arches of a beautifully ivied bridge. Hartopp played the flute and Lady Dunraven her little harp; and a person followed us on the shore, who played very well with the bugle, in the pauses of the other music. You see I have enjoyed my visit.'[30]

Another scientist who entered the family circle through Edwin was the Irish geophysicist Edward Sabine. An army officer by profession, the end of the Napoleonic Wars in 1815 had offered him an opportunity to pursue his interest in science, particularly gravity, geomagnetism, astronomy and ornithology. He participated in two Arctic expeditions, in 1818 with Captain John Ross and in 1819–20 under the command of William Edward Parry, during which he had made observations of the earth's magnetism and gravity. Sabine and his wife Elizabeth, a translator of scientific works, were regular visitors to Adare, always accompanied by Sabine's portable telescope, with which he entertained his hosts by showing them celestial bodies and other objects of interest in the night sky.[31] He also developed a keen interest in the ruins of Desmond Castle, where ivy was being removed from the walls, and spent many hours exploring its dungeons and laying down a plan of the building.[32]

In August 1833 Windham's sister, Lady Harriot Payne-Gallwey, and her three daughters, Fanny, Louisa and Caroline, visited Adare for an extended period. Windham rejoiced to see his sister, whom he had not met for years. Harriot's husband, General Sir William Payne-Gallwey, had died in 1831, since when she had spent much of her time abroad. She brought presents of a set of beautiful alabaster vases and a delicate marble statue of a sleeping baby, purchased in Italy. During Harriot's visit, a number of excursions took place: to Carrigogunnell Castle, where they scrambled about the ruins and partook of picnics of cold meat; to Askeaton Abbey and Castle, where Louisa made several sketches; and a week-long visit to Glin to participate in the 1833 Regatta, which, however, was not a great success owing to torrential rain. The party also amused themselves at home, cutting ivy at Desmond Castle, having tea in the garden and attending a number of scientific lectures and experimentations.

❖   ❖   ❖

Askeaton, Co. Limerick. Askeaton Abbey by Paul Sandby, late eighteenth century. Yale Center for British Art, Paul Mellon collection.

The normal course of life in Adare and across Ireland was disrupted by a cholera epidemic which swept through Europe in the early 1830s. In March 1832, cases of the disease were reported in Belfast and Dublin. Over the next two years the epidemic worked its way across the country, claiming some 50,000 lives.[33] The highly contagious malady reached County Limerick in May 1832. The Dunravens followed its course with mounting horror, as rich and poor were swept away with equal effect. At the end of the month, Caroline recorded that the disease was 'decidedly shewing itself in Limerick, & as usual at first in all towns fatal, & the cases numerous & the people panic struck'.[34] As the root cause of the epidemic remained poorly understood, vapour and mist were blamed for its spread and the family ceased to attend evening lectures, deeming the night air potentially dangerous. Windham, however, remained hopeful that the disease would not extend from the city to the rural areas, and was of a view that building works should continue uninterrupted.

In early September, on their return from a pleasant week as guests of the Knight of Glin at Glin Castle, the Dunravens were shocked to discover that several cases of cholera had been reported in Adare during their absence. The outbreak was limited in extent, however, and once more the family heaved a deep sigh of relief. All seemed well until February 1833, when rumours of new cholera cases in the neighbourhood unexpectedly began to circulate. This time the consequences were tragic. The epidemic broke out in Adare on the night of 20 February with such violence that news of it made it to the London papers, which described the situation in the village as truly frightful.[35] Only for the fever hospital whose construction Caroline had funded three years previously the situation could have been even more calamitous. 'How thankful you must both feel that you built the Hospital which now must be of inestimable value', Augusta Goold observed.[36]

Hearing of the Dunravens' plight of being stuck in the middle of such terrifying scenes, Lady de Vere of Curragh Chase offered her home as a place of refuge. Caroline, on hearing how many new cases had been taken to hospital, accepted the invitation without hesitation and hastened from Adare with her daughter, younger son and the governess. After a week in Curragh Chase, reluctant to impose any longer on the goodwill of her friend yet unwilling to return home, Caroline decided to move her little flock to Limerick city, where no new cases of cholera had been reported. She and her two children established themselves in Lord Limerick's town residence, 'where we found good fires & were thankful to be so snug'.[37] Meanwhile, the epidemic in Adare found its way to the Dunraven estate and wreaked havoc among Windham's workmen. 'The Kitchen Maid had premonitory symptoms, was taken to the Hospital & recovered', Windham wrote to Edwin on 11 March. 'Poor Daley, one of the Master stone cutters died. Whoolahan the Mason, whom you remember moving about selecting cob stones, with rule in hand & halting gait & Nestor the Mason are both dead. Collins another Mason recovered, Connolly the carver also recovered, & Mullins the wheelwright—but his wife died. At first the visitation was terrific, but thank God short. The second night 25 cases poured into the Hospital. Most of the Masons went away. Some probably will never return—there were 22 at work Saturday. Eight remained throughout. However, from one cause or other there has been but little work done for the last three weeks.'[38]

As Adare was once again disease-free, Windham's wife and children packed up their belongings and returned home. Caroline recorded in her journal 'the Gratitude I felt to God at our all being reassembled once more in our own dear sweet home which was happily relieved from the awful scourge which had driven us from it. Our thanks to the Almighty Disposer of all events can never be sufficiently expressed. We enjoyed much our quiet home & being tired went to bed early and Oh! so thankful!!!'[39]

❖   ❖   ❖

In the midst of the confusion caused by cholera, the Dunravens turned to one of their popular pursuits as a potential solution to save them from the worst travails of the epidemic. Boating was a favourite pastime for the family thanks to the tidal Maigue River, which traversed the grounds of Adare House just eleven miles upriver from the Shannon. The ruins of the Franciscan friary and Desmond Castle were enjoyed to best effect from the river, and it was also possible to boat down to the nearby Augustinian church for regular Sunday service. Trips were also taken downstream to the River Shannon, using the tide to best advantage. On one of these trips to visit the FitzGerald family at Glin Castle in the summer of 1832, Windham's attention was caught by the island of Foynes in the Shannon estuary. A spot of natural beauty, it also seemed a safe retreat in the midst of the cholera epidemic. In January 1833, Windham wrote to his London solicitor George Frere and asked him to enquire from the leaseholder, Colonel William Thomas Monsell of Tervoe, Co. Limerick, whether he would be willing to sell his interest in the island. Following lengthy negotiations and

Windham punting on the Maigue River, Adare. Sketch by Lord Monk Kerr, c. 1830s. Courtesy of the Dunraven family.

153

an unsuccessful attempt at haggling—the Colonel would not budge one penny from his original asking price of £2,500—the purchase was eventually completed in September. The Dunravens visited the island in the summer of 1833, choosing to make their way there in a little rowing-boat even though a steam packet service from the mainland provided regular access to the island. The family spent time exploring the place in detail, walking its perimeter and admiring the beautiful views it offered of the estuary. They also examined with great interest Colonel Monsell's fully furnished bathing lodge, which formed part of the purchase along with a coach-house and stables.[40] As soon as the sale of the leasehold was completed, James Pain was invited to accompany the Dunravens to Foynes Island. Over the ensuing months, he provided drawings for the conversion of the bathing lodge into a handsome marine villa.[41]

Maigue River, Adare, showing the Franciscan friary in the distance. Watercolour by Louisa Payne-Gallwey, c. 1833. Courtesy of Lavinia Graham-Vivian.

Another outbreak of cholera in Adare in January 1834 pressed the family into using the island as a longer-term place of shelter from the disease. Arrangements for the move to Foynes House began in March 1834, when a maid was left on the island to clean the dwelling house and to keep it aired.[42] Throughout April, Windham's wife attended a series of auctions to purchase items for the island home, and in mid-May a convoy of carriages set off from Adare to prepare the house for a permanent residence. A week later, Caroline, her three children, Edwin's fiancée Augusta Goold and two servants, Rebecca Downes, and Elizabeth Staunton, made their way to the island and busied themselves with the final touches to the place. Windham joined his family later in the evening and 'was welcomed with flags, a bonfire, two band pipers &c. we had rustic music & dancing, & were very merry, though very tired after the fatigues of the day'.[43]

The summer months on the island were idyllic. The weather for the most part was beautifully sunny and warm and provided perfect conditions for sailing and bathing. In the former activity, the family were frequently accompanied by William Monsell, Colonel Monsell's grandson, who during Windham's purchase negotiations had taken a shine to Anna Maria, now nineteen years old, and become her suitor. His family estate, Tervoe, was located on the western outskirts of Limerick city and was bounded by the Shannon estuary to the north. William, an enthusiastic sailor, became a regular visitor to Foynes, arriving along the river in his smart little yacht and taking the young lady on sailing excursions around the island, with her brother Edwin accompanying the couple as a chaperone. To everyone's surprise, Anna Maria's mother, who preferred rowing-boats owing to her propensity for extreme sea sickness, also ventured on board William's vessel and was delighted to discover that it handled so beautifully that she 'could not have known we were in a ship'.[44]

A favourite boating destination for the family was Cahircon House, a handsome estate belonging to John Bindon Scott, which was located directly across the estuary from Foynes Island. Caroline in particular enjoyed walking the beautiful grounds, taking tea with Mrs Scott and returning home by moonlight, sometimes in her own rowing-boat, sometimes in Mr Scott's yacht *Emerald*. Inland excursions were also made in Mrs Scott's carriage to Kilrush House, where Lady Grace Vandeleur showed off her exceptional gardens,

Shannon estuary. *View of Shannongrove,* County Limerick by Samuel Frederick Brocas (c. 1792–1847). Private collection.

and further afield to Dromoland Castle, where many an hour was spent exploring Sir Edward's improvements. The highlight of the summer's activities was the Shannon Regatta, which ran from late July to early August 1834 and in which Edwin acted as a steward while his mother presented the prizes and prepared a fête on Foynes Island for the contestants.[45] The regatta was organised by the Royal Western Yacht Club, who had elected Windham their president in March 1832.[46] The annual prize for the winner of the Regatta was a silver tureen presented to the club by Windham some months after his election. Worth 200 guineas, it bore the engraved inscription *From Wyndham, Earl of Dunraven, to the Western Yacht Club. 'Keep me who can.'*[47] The winner of the tureen in 1834 was Captain Harrington in his yacht *Comet*.

The family's enjoyment of their island home was overshadowed, however, by a dispute which arose between Windham and Thomas Spring Rice of Mount Trenchard, Co. Clare, head landlord of Foynes Island. Early in 1834, it transpired that Colonel Monsell had failed to attend to Spring Rice's notice to renew his lease, as a consequence of which it had expired. When Windham, realising that he had paid £2,500 for a worthless piece of paper, took steps to renew the lease and change it to his and Edwin's name, Thomas Spring Rice with apparent animosity rejected him without providing a reason for his refusal. Having made several frustrated attempts to negotiate a deal through his solicitors, Windham eventually had no other recourse but to go to court, where the case was decided in his favour.[48]

As the cholera epidemic abated, Windham again became preoccupied with building activities in Adare and only made brief appearances to visit the family on the island. In addition, the weather breaking at the end of the summer also made life increasingly uncomfortable. As October drew to a close the family decided to vacate Foynes House and returned to Adare. While the island remained in the ownership of the Dunravens for years to come, they made no further attempts to live on it after 1834.

CHAPTER

EIGHT

Continental Tours

In May 1833 Edwin came of age. No expense was spared in celebrating his 21st birthday. On 28 May, the entire village was invited to participate in elaborate festivities on the estate. The first guests to arrive were children from the local schools, who gathered in the open glade in front of Adare House at two o'clock in the afternoon, each bringing a plate tied in a napkin to partake of a meal of roast beef, pudding and ale. Later in the day, close friends of the family arrived to attend a more formal celebratory dinner, which commenced at half past four. In the evening, the principal entrance to the demesne was thrown open and a large crowd of people—the estimate of 12,000 suggested by local papers may have been somewhat over-generous—streamed in to join the party and to participate in rural sports. Those daring enough could try their luck at running in a sack race or a donkey race or climbing up a soaped pole. The festivities culminated in splendid fireworks which illuminated the entire town.[1]

Edwin's birthday celebrations were also used to mark another important occasion. Shortly after one o'clock in the afternoon, just before the arrival of the schoolchildren, tradesmen and workmen gathered at Adare House to watch as Caroline, with the assistance of James Pain, laid the first stone of the porch of the new entrance front.[2] The ceremony marked the commencement of the second phase of building activities in Adare, the construction of

Portrait of Edwin as a young man, *c.* 1830s. Courtesy of the Dunraven family.

the gallery wing. It extended from east to west at right angles to the kitchen quarters, to which it was connected at its easternmost or riverside end. Its northern elevation was enlivened by three projecting castellated bays, but the most dominant feature of the gallery range was the turreted entrance at its western end. Copied from the Lupton Tower in the cloisters at Eton College, it was something of a trademark for the Pain brothers, who had used it at Mitchelstown Castle. At Eton the design formed a central feature, but at Adare, as at Mitchelstown, the Pain brothers used it as a corner element, creating the asymmetrical front so greatly favoured in the Gothic Revival. A certain centrality may have been provided by a curtain wall culminating in a hexagonal tower which the Pain brothers designed to project northward from the gallery range to screen the kitchen wing. In the event, however, this part of the design was not constructed.

The turreted entrance led through a narrow porch into a vestibule, beyond which were the family's private quarters. A narrow corridor running the length of the range provided access to the rooms. At the far end of this range, projecting beyond the first floor and designed in the shape of a half-hexagon, was Caroline's private sitting room or boudoir, from which she could enjoy beautiful views upstream and down the Maigue River, which passed within a few feet. Above the private apartments was the spectacular gallery itself, 132ft in length and 26ft 6in. in height. Galleries were a common feature of Elizabethan and Jacobean buildings and were popularised as a country house feature by the Gothic Revival from the mid-eighteenth century onwards. The long gallery was most commonly used to display works of art and sculpture and to entertain large numbers of guests. It could also be used for taking exercise when inclement weather prevented walking outdoors. Indeed, that at Hagley Hall in Worcestershire was almost destroyed by the Lyttelton family's habit of using it for cricket practice.[3] Perhaps the best-known Irish examples include the long picture gallery at Castletown House, Co. Kildare, built in the 1720s, and the beautiful 1830s Ormonde gallery at Kilkenny Castle, Co. Kilkenny. Edwin, who had occasion to visit the latter some 30 years later in 1864, examined the room with a critical and, one suspects, somewhat envious eye; he reluctantly deemed the gallery magnificent but noted with satisfaction that it was 'very cold' and although 'about half as large again as ours … is not near so impressive a room, nor is it used as a living room'.[4]

Eton College, Berkshire. *Eton School Yard* by James Duffield Harding, 1842. Reproduced by permission of the Provost and Fellows of Eton College.

The architectural inspiration behind the gallery at Adare was manifold. Galleries formed a prominent feature at Knole, Corsham Court, Fonthill and Longleat, all houses that Windham and Caroline had visited and admired in the 1820s. Caroline, moreover, was accustomed to long galleries from her childhood at Clearwell Court, where she had been born, and Fonmon Castle, home of her uncle Robert Jones, which she had frequented in her youth. Furthermore, Windham's interest in the evolution of buildings over time played an important part. He sought an amalgam of cohesive yet distinctive elements which suggested forcibly to a reader of the building that this composite structure spanned many centuries. These elements also helped to develop strong parallels between the new dwelling house and the medieval ruins that surrounded it.

The exterior of the gallery wing progressed with speed. By January 1834, Windham was able to report to Edwin that 'We are taking down the scaffolding—& the House looks quite beautiful'.[5] The expense of its construction had also been great, however, and had strained the family's financial resources. Determined to avoid getting into debt, Windham refused to spend money that he did not have. As a consequence, works on the gallery wing exterior were followed by a hiatus during which only the most essential building works were carried out.

In early November 1834, Caroline and her three children travelled to Wales to spend two months at Dunraven Castle with Mr and Mrs Bennett. Caroline was delighted to be reunited with her mother but also took the opportunity to visit the neighbourhood close to her heart. She dined with the family's agent, John Randall, at Ynyslas Cottage, spent a day scrambling about the medieval castle of St Donat's, and paid a visit to Llanmihangel to reflect on the memories of the first days of her marriage. Some of the architectural features of St Donat's and Llanmihangel were later to find their way to Adare Manor, but much more remarkable was the striking similarity between Adare Manor and the house under construction at Margam which Caroline, Edwin and Anna Maria explored in early December. Having come of age in 1824 and taken control of the family estates, Thomas Mansel Talbot's

Adare Manor, Adare. Sketch of the entrance to the gallery wing by Mr St Leger, c. 1841. Courtesy of the Dunraven family.

heir Christopher commissioned the architect Thomas Hopper to design a Gothic Revival building at Margam. A favourite of King George IV, Hopper had also contributed to the works at Windsor Castle. He drafted the plans for Margam between 1827 and 1829, while a site for the house was being cleared. Construction works got under way in 1830. They were supervised by another architect, Edward Haycock, who also contributed to the building's exterior and interior design and prepared plans for stables, terraces and lodges within the estate. Like the Dunravens, Christopher Talbot took a close personal interest in the design process and encouraged his architects to borrow elements of interest from two buildings in particular: Lacock Abbey in Wiltshire, ancestral seat of the Talbot family and home of his cousin, the pioneering photographer William Henry Fox Talbot, and Melbury House in Dorset, the home of his mother's family, the Fox-Strangways. The house at Margam was completed in 1839, although work on the outbuildings, terraces and lodges continued until well into the 1840s. During this time Talbot introduced formal terrace gardens to the west and south elevations, built two new carriageways and redesigned the grounds by damming a marshy valley to the north of the gardens to create an ornamental lake.

The site of the new house was notably chosen to enjoy picturesque views of the ruins of the nearby Margam Abbey and the eighteenth-century orangery constructed by Talbot's father. The building's romantic skyline was characterised by turrets, pinnacles and tall twisting chimneys, and its exterior walls abounded in heraldic shields and carved faces demonstrating Talbot's pride in his ancestry. Like the Dunravens, Talbot utilised local building materials, sourcing sandstone from nearby Pyle and timber from his own estate, and was extremely lucky in securing the services of two exceptionally skilled workmen, a carver named Francis Bray and a mason called Daniel Jackson. The Dunravens were struck by the building's architecture, which Caroline noticed was 'something in the style of our own building', and particularly admired the colossal main staircase of ornately carved stone.[6] Although explicit reference to Margam as a source of inspiration is not made in family correspondence, there are many external similarities between the two buildings and it is most likely that a number of its features were copied by the Dunravens during subsequent visits to the house. There was, however, one particular difference between the Margam and Adare projects: the speed of construction. Although Talbot complained in the summer of 1830 that 'My house shews nothing but vast & substantial foundations of masonry resembling Cyclopean work, though upwards of 120 men have been at work nearly three months', by December 1831 the house was roofed and, 'though I say it, most superbly executed'.[7] By 1834, when the Dunravens visited the building, work was already under way on the interiors; at Adare, in contrast, only the kitchen wing stood completed.

❖ ❖ ❖

The lull in the building works in 1834 enabled the Dunravens to fulfil an ambition that they had been nurturing for quite some time. Although content to live in Adare, Windham and Caroline were increasingly aware that their relative isolation in Ireland put their children at a certain disadvantage. Windham's wife in particular strongly felt that 'this delightful calm should hardly be consistent with our duty, were it perpetrated in such a way that our dear children should see so little of the world, a world in which they will I trust live some years, as the happy servants of their Blessed Lord, and oh that I could teach them to *use the world* without abusing it!'[8]

Following the end of the Napoleonic Wars in 1815, Continental travel had become customary among those with the time and money to do it. Many were curious to see the battle sites that had dominated the news for the best part of twenty years, and an equal number yearned to see for themselves the famous cities, buildings and works of art described in glowing terms in increasingly popular travel books. Some were drawn by a desire for romantic adventure, while others set off for the Continent simply because it was the fashionable thing to do. There were those who travelled abroad to find relief for a physical ailment such as consumption, and those who believed that travel built moral character, improved tolerance and broadened the mind.[9] For the Dunravens, the desire to visit the Continent in the mid-1830s encompassed many of these aspirations. An extended European tour would not only provide their children with a broader world-view but also enable the couple to examine the latest architectural trends on the Continent, to collect ideas to incorporate into their own building plans, and to purchase art and antiques to fill the rooms of their new home.

Paris, France. Tuileries palace and gardens by Gaspard Gobaut, 1847. Source: Bibliothèque nationale de France.

Above: Paris, France. *The Pantheon* by Francois-Étienne Villeret, pre-1866. Public domain.

Below: Paris, France. *An evening with the Duke of Orléans at the Pavillon de Marsan* by Eugène Lami, 1843. Public domain.

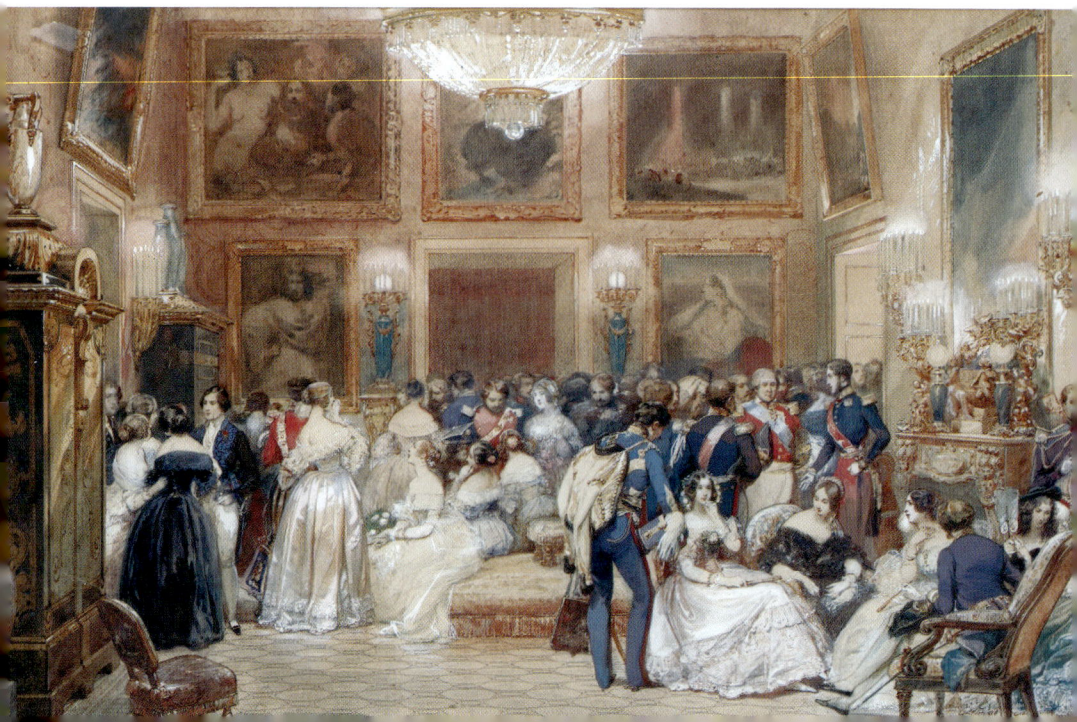

To fulfil these ambitions, the Dunravens made two trips to the Continent in 1835. The first and shorter of these, which took them to Paris, may have been planned as an exploratory tour, since neither Windham nor Caroline had any previous experience of Continental travel. Their journey began in early January 1835 in London, where the family spent several days packing and preparing their carriages. Little Windham, who had just completed his fifth birthday and had rarely been beyond the bounds of his Irish home, was awestruck by the enormous city's heaving traffic and the many gaslights illuminating its streets. On the day of their crossing to France the English Channel was like a millpond, yet Caroline in her customary fashion was violently sick and refused to leave the barouche, preferring to lie inside it on deck while other passengers made themselves comfortable indoors.

Following a brief respite in Boulogne, the family proceeded to Paris, where they took possession of apartments at Hotel Meurice on the rue de Rivoli, immediately opposite the Tuileries Garden. They wasted no time in sampling the city's many attractions, and Caroline in particular was delighted to look about and 'see so many places, about which I had read so much'.[10] One of the first buildings they visited was the Bibliothèque du Roi or Royal Library, with its immense collection of books, manuscripts and antiques. While Caroline was absorbed in ancient coins and Egyptian curiosities, Windham took a more prosaic fancy to the library's finely patterned parquet floor and made a sketch of it. This he later passed to James Pain with instructions to draw a working plan based on it to fit the size of the gallery in Adare.[11]

Over the next several weeks, the family visited the Louvre, Notre Dame, the Pantheon, the Luxembourg Palace and the Botanical Gardens, where they marvelled not only at the beautiful grounds but also at the exotic menagerie of birds and mammals and vast collections of minerals, fossils and corals. They drove to the Champs-Élysées to see the Arc de Triomphe, the construction of which was then nearing completion; spent many hours in the Artillery Museum, delighting in its long, beautifully arranged galleries filled with firearms and suits of armour; and made more than one visit to the Père Lachaise Cemetery to admire its array of exceptional headstones and the fine views of Paris that it commanded. They also had the great fortune to view the private collection of Alexandre du Sommerard, an archaeologist who had spent much of his life collecting medieval artefacts and objects of art, sparing 'neither expense or trouble'. Here they whiled away several hours admiring ivory carvings, armours and furniture, 'all illustrations of the history of France'.[12]

One of the highlights of the family's time in Paris was an invitation to a great ball at the royal palace of Les Tuileries, which they all attended except for Windham, who was suffering from an attack of gout. The grandeur of the palace and the magnificence of the entertainment greatly impressed Caroline, who could only describe it as a realisation of fairy scenes. Seven rooms were thrown open for the ball, the principal of which was lit by 3,000 candles. A sumptuous sit-down meal was provided for the 3,000 guests in several sittings, with a servant behind the chair of every diner. When the Dunravens were introduced to the royal family, Caroline had nothing but compliments. 'The Queen', she considered, 'is a very surprising civil person, & the Princesses peculiarly affable & pleasing & the Duke of Orleans appeared to me to be much the best looking French man in the room.'[13]

In between superlative entertainments, Caroline and Windham spared no effort in utilising the shops of Paris, ordering drapes and choosing a great many curious antiquities for their new house. Windham, however, grew restless and in early March parted from the family to return to Adare. Even though building works at home were at a virtual standstill, he felt obliged 'to be here to see the little things that are doing'.[14] During his absence, Edwin spotted an image of Pegasus, the emblem of the Quin family, at the hotel in which they stayed and sent a sketch of it to his father. Windham was delighted with Edwin's find and deemed the Pegasus 'more spirited than any we have here'.[15]

The family remained in Paris for another month, making excursions to Versailles, Bonaparte's former residence at the Château de Saint-Cloud and the late Empress Josephine's residence at the Château de Malmaison. The final weeks of the Paris trip were marred by illness, however, when first little Windham and then Edwin caught a lingering fever that took weeks to clear. The family returned to London in early April to participate in the birthday celebrations of King William IV, during which both Edwin and Anna Maria were presented at court. In early June Edwin returned to the Continent to attend a series of scientific meetings, while his mother proceeded to Wales with her two other children to pass the summer in the company of her mother at Dunraven Castle.

❖   ❖   ❖

In early September 1835, Windham made his way from Adare to Wales to join his family in preparation for their second and longer excursion to the Continent. Before setting off, however, the Dunravens visited three buildings of interest, all of which were clearly selected with a view to gleaning inspiration for the new building in Adare. The first was Goodrich Court in Monmouth, some ten miles north of Clearwell Court, built between 1828 and 1831 by the antiquarian Sir Samuel Rush Meyrick. Designs for the building were provided by Meyrick's friend and fellow antiquarian Edward Blore, best known for his completion of Buckingham Palace after the dismissal of John Nash in 1829. Blore's interest in Scottish baronial architecture was reflected in the building's numerous turrets, battlements and loopholes. Thomas Roscoe, who visited the house in 1844, enthused that the design of Goodrich Court evoked dreams of Froissart and his chronicles of arms and chivalry,[16] but the enormous building was not to everyone's taste. Some resented its proximity to the ancient ruins of Goodrich Castle, not least William Wordsworth, who was appalled by the way it impaired the solemnity of the scene and longed to have the power 'to blow away Sir Meyrick's impertinent structure and all the possessions it contains'.[17]

Wordsworth's hostility notwithstanding, Meyrick in his own right was Europe's leading scholar in the field of weapons and armour, and he was knighted in 1832 for reorganising the royal collections at Windsor Castle and the Tower of London. He amassed a vast private collection of medieval artefacts and weaponry, which was housed in his London home in Chelsea until his friend Sir Walter Scott convinced him that it would be better displayed in a more authentic setting. Goodrich Court, with its vast array of antiques, was intended as a tourist attraction from the outset. Exhibits were meticulously selected and arranged in the main reception rooms, each of which was individually designed to reflect a specific historical period. Visitors were greeted by Meyrick's servants, who were trained to conduct tours of the various rooms. Goodrich Court became one of the key attractions in the Wye Valley, partly because at that time Sir Walter Scott's historical novels, such as *Rob Roy*, *Ivanhoe* and *Kenilworth*, had done much to popularise the romance of the olden times as an antidote to rapid industrialisation and mercantilism. Enthusiasts of the day expressed this fashionable interest through architecture and interior design. Stately homes across the country were not only redesigned in the Gothic style but also filled with displays of weapons, armour and

Goodrich Court, Herefordshire. Design proposal by Edward Blore, 1828. RIBA Collections.

heraldry to add character and create a sense of medieval authenticity, and even to hint at the owner's noble ancestry, no matter how illusory.[18] Collectors of medieval artefacts and curiosities were facilitated by dealers, some authentic, others inevitably trading in fakes and forgeries. The most prominent dealers could be found in London and of these the best known in the 1830s were Samuel and Henry Pratt, who staged several exhibitions of ancient armour on their premises at 3 Lower Grosvenor Street to draw attention to their stock. The purpose-built gallery that held these displays had been fitted out and designed by the architect and antiquary Lewis Nockalls Cottingham, one of the foremost experts in medieval art and architecture.[19]

Although the Dunravens admired Goodrich Court as most correctly built and executed with considerable taste, the timing of their visit on the eve of their Continental tour was not a mere coincidence, nor the building itself its primary object.[20] The anticipated tour provided Windham with an opportunity to assemble his own collection of armour, and the visit to Goodrich Court was no doubt arranged to seek Meyrick's advice and recommendations for the best items to purchase and the best places in which to find them. Such advice bore evident fruit, for many of the weapons which were later displayed in the great hall at Adare Manor bore close similarity to those at Goodrich Court.

The second building the Dunravens visited was Toddington Manor in Gloucestershire. Its owner, Charles Hanbury-Tracy, was an admirer of Gothic

Revivalism and acted as his own architect but in doing so relied heavily on *Specimens of Gothic Architecture*, published by the French émigré Auguste Charles Pugin, draughtsman for John Nash, between 1821 and 1823.[21] The building consisted of three diagonally connected rectangles, each ranged around an open court, of which the northernmost rectangle, dominated by a great tower, formed the principal building. Windham and Caroline had seen it in its early stages of construction in 1820 during their tour of the Vale of Neath. Fifteen years on, the house was still without its final touches but sufficiently complete to warrant positive comment.[22] Windham was captivated by it. The crocketed pinnacles, sculptured string-courses and numerous carved grotesques and other statues that ornamented its exterior stonework most likely influenced a similar arrangement at Adare Manor. When John Britton published his *Graphic Illustrations with Historical and Descriptive Accounts of Toddington, Gloucestershire, the Seat of Lord Sudeley* in 1840, a copy of the book immediately found its way into Windham's library. Toddington Manor was highly acclaimed for its style and became something of a flagship for Gothic Revivalism in the country. It is notable that in 1836 Hanbury-Tracy was chairman of the commission established to choose the design for the rebuilding of the Houses of Parliament. It is generally believed that Charles Barry, whose proposal was deemed the most suitable out of the 97 entries received, based his design on Toddington Manor to improve his chances of success.

Toddington Manor, Gloucestershire. Garden front by R. Kitton, 1835. RIBA Collections.

Before crossing over to the Continent, the Dunravens also visited Windsor Castle, the remodelling of which Edwin had followed with such frustrated keenness during his Eton days. To the early nineteenth-century observer, Windsor Castle embodied the refinement of the age, which the social élite strove to emulate. The renovations, which remained unfinished at the time of the death of George IV in 1830, cost more than a million pounds and turned the original medieval castle into a Gothic fantasy to give expression to the revival of chivalry and Romanticism that characterised the era. The building was widely admired by its Victorian visitors, although the scale of the renovations left many in doubt as to what was old and what was new. Not that it evidently mattered: the novelist William Harrison Ainsworth praised the king for the restoration of the castle to 'more than its original grandeur', while a guidebook published in 1851 suggested that, 'though sober criticism cannot pronounce Windsor Castle to be by any means a complete and perfectly-studied production of architecture, it is still a noble one, and such as to justify all but the unqualified praise bestowed upon it'. In fact, the guidebook considered that those parts of the castle that had not been renovated looked 'rather too stern and uncouth'.[23] Such blurring of the lines between the past and people's perception of that past was common in the nineteenth century and gave legitimacy to architectural flights of fancy that utilised history in an idealised and improved fashion. The grandeur of Windsor Castle certainly captivated the Dunravens, who could hardly come away from the plethora of beautiful things to see.[24] Here, as at Goodrich Court, the use of arms, armour and heraldry as a form of embellishment resonated strongly with Windham and reaffirmed views and ideas already formed.

◈ ◈ ◈

The Dunravens' second and longer Continental tour, which was intended to take them through the Low Countries and west Germany to the Tyrol and Italy, commenced in late September 1835. The medieval cities and Gothic cathedrals of Belgium and Holland held great appeal for them, as did the magnificent feudal castles in the picturesque river valleys of the Rhine and Neckar. They looked forward to exploring collections of art and armour for their arrangement and effect, and to purchasing wood-carvings, works of art by Dutch masters and lace and textiles from the many manufactories of the region to ornament the rooms of their new house. Italy, of course, was *de rigueur* as a destination for the discerning traveller interested in art and architecture, and Caroline and Anna Maria prepared well for this part of the tour by spending four years learning Italian under the instruction of Signor Sándor Erdődy.

Medieval Gothic was the prevailing theme of the tour from the very beginning. The family admired the 'fine gothic edifice' of the town hall in Ypres and spent two days in Ghent walking around St Bavo's Cathedral and Saint Michael's church.[25] An early highlight was the medieval town of Antwerp, which at the time of their visit was recovering from damage inflicted during the Belgian Revolution of 1830–1. The town was famous for its museum of art, filled with the works of the most celebrated painters of the region, and for its medieval cathedral and churches, all of which the Dunravens visited. They sat through Mass and listened to beautiful organ music at St Andrew's, paid their respects at the tomb of their favourite artist, Peter Paul Rubens, at St James's, and lingered over the richly decorated Baroque interior of St Paul's. This last-mentioned church had undergone a series of interior alterations in 1833, and Windham availed of the opportunity to purchase some of the fixtures and fittings that had been removed in the process. 'Belgium is nearly cleared of carvings by the English market', he wrote to Edwin, who had not joined the family on their tour, 'but I had the luck to find some very fine ones at Antwerp; out of which we can make two great chimney pieces for the Gallery, part of a third, for some other room, & the principal part of ten stalls, such as in our Pew—all in fine brown oak—just taken down in some alterations of the church of (I think St Paul's) but we must not tell that to the Irish Catholics. They cost a great deal of money £120—& £52 duty & Carriage to London.'[26] News of the purchase was received in Ireland with considerable interest and quickly spread. 'Mama tells me you have bought some beautiful carvings', Edwin's fiancée Augusta Goold enthused to Caroline. 'Belgium is the place to get them.'[27]

From Antwerp the family proceeded to Brussels, where they spent a week shopping, sightseeing and visiting a series of exhibitions of art and Belgian manufacture. They departed reluctantly, being 'quite charmed with the gay & smiling appearance of that beautiful little Capital'.[28] They went next to

Cologne, travelling *en route* through Liège, Spa and Aix-la-Chapelle and stopping along the way to pay homage at the battlefield of Waterloo, which had become something of a place of pilgrimage for British tourists. Travelling along the banks of the Meuse, the family marvelled at the beauty of the surrounding scenery, noting how 'such beautiful hillocks, castles perched up on high, & the Hills covered with wood & Vineyards make a lovely landscape'.[29] In Cologne, a day was spent admiring the city's extraordinary cathedral, the construction of which had been halted in 1473 and would not recommence until 1842. Even in its unfinished state, the Dunravens considered the cathedral a 'most beautiful and stupendous building' and a 'perfection of florid Gothic architecture'. What struck them the most was the richly decorated interior. After hours of wandering around, they could hardly tear themselves away from the stalls and beautiful carvings.[30] On their return journey in February 1836, Caroline and Anna Maria revisited the cathedral and spent a further two days copying patterns, many of which were used to decorate the misereres of carved oak framing the long sides of the gallery at Adare Manor. Caroline felt quite overwhelmed 'at being in such a great space, among such a forest of magnificent arches, & looking at the most perfectly beautiful windows I had ever seen'.[31]

Following a reluctant departure from Cologne, the family made their way to Frankfurt, with brief stops along the way at Bonn, Coblenz and Bingen am Rhein, where they toured Rheinstein Castle, a medieval fortification restored by Prince Frederick of Prussia in the 1820s. They were much taken by the castle, which had been rebuilt 'so as to resemble as much as possible the original place, & the rooms are ornamented with armour & every ancient ornament, connecting all the present comfort so as to render it habitable … & the grandeur & yet simplicity of the whole is very striking'. They departed from 'this beautiful specimen of the ancient residence of Chivalry' with great regret.[32]

By the time the Dunravens arrived in Frankfurt, however, the travelling party was in a sorry state. Windham was gouty, and young Windham, who had suffered intestinal problems for much of the tour, became so ill that a doctor was called to his bedside. Worst of all, there was alarming news from Italy that a cholera epidemic, which had made its way there from France in April, was gaining ground and spreading rapidly through the country. With the tragic consequences of the outbreak of the disease in Adare in 1833 still fresh in their minds, the Dunravens decided to cancel the Italian leg of their journey and to make Frankfurt their base

Antwerp, Belgium. *Chancel of the Collegiate Church of St Paul at Antwerp* by David Roberts, 1861. National Galleries of Scotland, gifted by Richard Stanton, 2012.

for the remainder of the tour.[33] The city suited them well, not least because of its religious tolerance and prevailing Lutheran ethos which allowed them to attend church service every Sunday. In architectural terms, the old town immediately became the couple's favourite. Here they walked around and 'admired the old gable ends & varied architecture with arches & towers &c which have such a very picturesque effect at night, some lanes dimly lighted, & others so narrow that the people can shake hands with their opposite neighbours'.[34] They were 'greatly charmed with so perfect a representation of times gone by' and marvelled at the woodwork of the old houses, some of which 'has stood for 2 or 3 hundred years without ever having been painted'.[35]

November was spent visiting the city's museums, art exhibitions and the opera, accepting dinner invitations, copying patterns in the cathedral and celebrating little Windham's sixth birthday. By the middle of the month, the young boy was strong enough to sit by the window and watch horse-drawn sledges driving through the snow past the hotel, an experience which was entirely new to the family. 'The prettiest sledges', Caroline considered, 'are something in the shape of gilt shell, in which a lady is wrapped up in furs. The gentleman who drives being behind, sitting across a little wooden bench, the reins are on each side of her, when the snow is deep they go very fast, & smoothly along.'[36]

While in Frankfurt, Windham, Caroline and Anna Maria made two excursions to explore the scenic Neckar Valley. The first of these was a four-day tour of castles in Darmstadt and Erbach in early December. In Darmstadt their interest was focused on the former residence of the Grand-Duke of Hesse-Darmstadt, which, although abandoned in favour of a new palace built within the town, nevertheless contained a fine collection of paintings. Their main destination, however, was Erbach, where two châteaux attracted their attention. The first was the castle of the Counts of Erbach, noted for its exceptional collection of armoury, housed in a hall specially adapted to the purpose. The Dunravens spent two days examining the collection and on their last night in Erbach dined with Mr Kehler, keeper of the castle's archives, who instructed them in the arrangement of armour and answered questions connected with the castle that particularly interested them. They also drove to the nearby village of Steinbach to see Château Fürstenau, a castle belonging to another branch of the Erbach family. Although the building was nearly deserted, the Dunravens felt that it 'has much in it still to interest a stranger, & contains all the relics of an ancient family, & gives as one the interior of a great feudal family'.[37] Having bought prints of all they had seen, the Dunravens returned to Frankfurt and Caroline immediately wrote to her mother to tell her that 'Lord D. was quite delighted with all he saw, & has learned much that will be useful to him I think in the arrangement of his mansion'.[38]

On 22 December, braving the cold weather, the three travellers set off again for a ten-day excursion to the picturesque towns of the Neckar Valley. For their route of travel they chose the celebrated Bergstrasse or Mountain Road, which connected Darmstadt with Heidelberg along the base of a range of hills bounding the eastern valley of the Rhine. The route was famed for its castles, its vineyards and the general luxuriance of its vegetation, with picturesque villages dotted along the way. Their first destination was Heidelberg and its Renaissance landmark, the ruin of Heidelberg Castle, where they spent the best part of three days exploring the building in detail. The castle fascinated Windham and Caroline because, 'having been added to in so many different ages, it contains specimens of great variety of architecture', although Caroline admitted that 'the old towers, deep moats &c of the older times were to me much the most interesting'.[39]

View of the River Rhine near Bingen, Germany, by Anton Ditzler, *c.* 1835. Public domain.

The family celebrated Christmas Day in Heidelberg by taking a long walk to local beauty spots on the outskirts of the town for glimpses of the castle. After lunch, they 'returned to the Castle to sketch & remained there till the moon rose, & the effect of the snow by moonlight was very beautiful'.[40] It was also in Heidelberg that Caroline was introduced to the German custom of decorating a small fir tree with gilt ornaments, toys, presents and candles for the amusement of children. The practice enchanted her to such a degree that on her return to Ireland she made it a regular part of the Christmas festivities at Adare.

On St Stephen's Day the Dunravens made a long excursion through the Neckar Valley to Neckarsteinach, a town famed for the four early medieval castles which rose from the slopes bounding the Neckar River. 'The views are exquisite', Caroline noted in her journal, 'the rocks so fine, the hills covered with wood, & on the opposite side of the river, a very fine hill with the fortified town of Dilsberg on the summit. We were truly delighted with our scramble which was quite through deep snow. We mounted to the top of every tower we could & did not return home till late.'[41]

The family left Heidelberg again on 28 December, crossing the Neckar River in a ferry to visit Gundelsheim and its imposing Horneck Castle, which, however, did not appeal to them. The building had recently been sold to a merchant who had fitted up its numerous apartments in a modern style, and only the dungeons remained in their original state. Much more satisfying was Wimpfen, where the town's old monastery and adjoining church elicited much admiration, particularly its pulpit hewn out of a single solid piece of stone. Windham and Caroline also admired 'a staircase that is supported without apparently any pillar, some curious old books, among others Luther's Canticles & some fine painted glass', but the finest thing in Caroline's view 'was the roof, which was groined in the most graceful manner I had ever seen, & was much the most perfect roof of the kind I ever saw. The arches were so perfect in their form & altogether I never admired any roof more.'[42]

Continental scene attributed to Samuel Prout (1784–1852). Private collection.

Heidelberg Castle, Germany. *A View of Heidelberg and the River Neckar* by Francois Antoine Bossuet, early nineteenth century. Photo: akg-images.

On the last day of the year the Dunravens made their way to Worms, where the dramatic events of Protestant Reformation had played out in the early 1500s. Making their way to the cathedral, they were initially disappointed with its almost complete lack of ornamentation but were soon captivated by the magical atmosphere of the church. 'They were just beginning to light it up for Evening Service it being New Years Eve', Caroline recalled, 'the high altar was brilliantly illuminated, but the rest of the vast aisles had only an occasional glimmering tallow candle, which seemed even to increase the effect of the size of the building. The first glimmering of twilight through the high windows cast a mysterious light about it, & when the voices all joined with the organ in a fine simple hymn, the effect was very moving.' Retreating to the Swan Inn, the Dunravens watched through the windows the firing of guns and ringing of bells, which lasted until midnight, when the clocks struck twelve and the new year was ushered in with cheers and hurrahs. The tour of the Neckar region drew to a conclusion on 2 January 1836, when the Dunravens returned to Frankfurt laden with patterns for their new building copied from churches and castles along the way.[43]

The family began their homeward journey on 10 February, retracing their steps from Frankfurt through Coblenz, Bonn and Cologne. Two days were spent at Aachen, where Sir Samuel Meyrick had found inspiration for the principal gateway of Goodrich Court, and likewise at Liège, where Caroline spent a morning drawing some of the pillars and grotesque heads in the galleries of the old palace and admiring the curious specimens of old carving which lined its covered interior colonnade.[44] Their next stop was Louvain, where they spent several hours exploring the Town Hall and its Gothic ornaments, 'exquisitely beautiful'. They also visited St Peter's church, where they spent time drawing patterns and copying curious old carvings, although, to their regret, they had not time to do much.[45] More patterns were copied in St Paul's church in Antwerp, where they had purchased carvings at the start of their journey. In the cathedral at Bruges, they remained for several hours drawing the stalls and copying patterns.[46] The tour of the Continent finally drew to an end on 6 March, when the Dunravens crossed over from Calais to Dover. Caroline, as usual, was extremely sick and the family were obliged to stay in Dover overnight to allow her time to recover. Their second night was spent in Sittingbourne, where the family 'found English fare & beds very hard and though the house was most clean & quiet in many things missed the foreign tour'.[47]

The Low Countries provided Windham with a rich store of ideas for the design of his new home. Yet, in spite of the evident interest he showed in medieval buildings during his European tour, it was not his intention to recreate the German Gothic style in Adare. While the patterns of Flemish carvings copied by his wife and daughter found their way into many of the details of the manor, the severe geometrical regularity of German Gothic buildings did not appeal to Windham. Instead, he continued to seek a quintessential English approach, particularly for the great hall. This he found in the Perpendicular Gothic, which flourished in England throughout the fifteenth century and was characterised by vertical linearity, evident in exceptionally large thin-mullioned windows, intricate vaults, and columns comprised of clusters of slender shafts instead of single solid pillars. The style had appealed to him from early on and resulted not only in repeated visits to Westminster Abbey and the cathedrals of Gloucester and Canterbury throughout the 1820s and 1830s but also in the amalgamation in the design of Adare Manor of details from Eton College chapel, all built in or incorporating elements from the Perpendicular Gothic.

Of course, Windham's fascination with the style had deep roots, stemming as it did from his time spent as a student in Oxford. His Alma Mater, Magdalen College, was an especially significant influence. Founded in 1458,

Magdalen College, Oxford. Watercolour by Joseph Mallord William Turner, *c. 1794*.
© The Trustees of the British Museum.

it contained some of the most beautiful medieval buildings in Oxford. The great quadrangle, which formed the main centre of the college, was dominated by the Perpendicular Gothic Great Tower, and its cloisters were adorned by whimsical carved stone creatures. Inside, the walls of its great hall, where dining took place, were covered in seventeenth-century linenfold panelling and early Renaissance carvings. Sunday service was held in the college's magnificent medieval chapel, where odd beasts and medieval scenes dominated the carved misericords, and beautiful eighteenth-century painted glass in soft sepia tones filled the west window. The location of the college in an attractive woodland setting on the banks of the River Cherwell may well have reminded Windham of Adare, where the Maigue River wound its way past the ruins of the medieval castle and abbeys. It was undoubtedly here that Windham's lifelong love of medieval architecture was awakened. It ultimately also brought him into partnership with the master of medieval Gothic architecture, Lewis Nockalls Cottingham, but three turbulent and troubled years were to pass after Windham's return from the Continent before the two men had an opportunity to meet.

Family Matters

T he Dunravens returned to Adare after almost two years' absence in June 1836. As soon as their carriage rolled through the demesne gates in the late afternoon, the family tumbled out, impatient to discover what had been done to the house and gardens in their absence. They were profoundly struck by the beauty of the building and its emerging form, which they considered far superior to any they had previously seen.[1] By now, the exterior of the gallery wing was complete, and the time and care expended in selecting the stone for its construction was paying dividends. The large blocks of hammer-dressed limestone were of different colours, predominantly grey but relieved by occasional blocks in subtle hues of brown, red, pink and yellow. Caroline personally favoured the grey stone, which 'is in my opinion so much handsomer than any other colour'. Looking at the building, she found much to admire in 'the fine massive size of its ornaments', which gave it 'an air of much grandeur & solidity'.[2]

The family's interest was not limited to the progress of their own building. Prior to returning to Ireland, they retraced their steps to Windsor Castle, Toddington Manor and Goodrich Court, undoubtedly at the latter to discuss the armoury and weaponry they had purchased on their tour. Moreover, in the months and years that followed their return from the Continent, the Dunravens continued to pay regular visits to friends and neighbours undertaking building projects of their own to compare designs and to exchange ideas and experiences. Dromoland Castle remained a perennial favourite. By 1836 the old Georgian house had been demolished and the last part of the new castle was nearing completion. Sir Edward did not live to see the house in its finished form. He died in 1837, when the responsibility for completing the building works was passed to his son and successor, Sir Lucius O'Brien.

Six miles north-east of Adare, Eyre Massey, third Baron Clarina, was also building a castellated house in the Gothic style at Elm Park. Designed by James and George Richard Pain, the house with its asymmetrical composition and mixture of round and square towers was similar to Dromoland Castle and incorporated a hall large enough to serve as a ballroom. Finance for the project, which cost some £50,000, came from Massey's Irish-French wife Susan, whose father, Hugh Barton, had made a fortune as a wine merchant. Unlike Windham, Eyre Massey did not waste time considering the finer points of design detail but left such matters to his architects. Building works progressed at a rapid rate: construction began in 1833 and was completed within three years. The Dunravens paid their first visit to see the newly built house, renamed Clarina Castle, in January 1837.

Adare Manor, Adare. Watercolour of the gallery wing and the old house side by side by Miss Philipps, September 1837. Courtesy of the Dunraven family.

Dromoland Castle, Co. Clare. Drawing showing the Georgian mansion and the new castle standing side by side before the demolition of the former. Private collection.

Another building whose construction the Dunravens followed with interest at this time was Glenstal Castle in Murroe, Co. Limerick, commissioned by the wealthy Limerick solicitor Matthew Barrington. Barrington had engaged in preliminary discussions with a number of architects, including James Pain, William O'Hara and Decimus Burton, before settling on a young Englishman called William Bardwell. Bardwell had gained considerable publicity for his Norman Revival-style proposal for the Houses of Parliament during the 1835 design competition. The same style was selected for Glenstal Castle—a rarity among Irish country houses, as the massive scale it required made it largely impractical as a choice for most domestic buildings. While the exterior of the building had the appearance of a twelfth-century English castle, complete with a massive castellated keep and broad round tower, its interior bore all the hallmarks of Celtic Revivalism and was richly decorated with carved oak, Romanesque columns and doorways, and furniture designed in the medieval style. Construction works began in 1836 and progressed slowly.[3] When the Dunravens visited the house some five years later, the only room to have been completed was the library. This, however, was sufficient for them to consider that the castle had all the elements of 'a very fine place'.[4] Whether inspired by Glenstal or not, features of Celtic Revivalism also found their way into Adare Manor, particularly in the vestibule, where marble doorways with singular Celtic Romanesque patterns were put up in November 1839.[5]

Glenstal Castle, Co. Tipperary. Watercolour proposal for the castle, viewed from the south-west. Attributed to its architect, William Bardwell, 1836. Courtesy of Glenstal Abbey.

❖ ❖ ❖

Building activities at Adare in the summer of 1836 were eclipsed by momentous family occasions. In late June, a visibly nervous William Monsell arrived from Tervoe to seek Anna Maria's hand in marriage after two years of courtship. The terrified young man was subjected to a stiff conversation with Windham, who had made numerous calculations regarding William's income and was not at all convinced of the youth's ability to provide his only daughter with the lifestyle to which she was accustomed.[6] The prospective father-in-law eventually relented, probably through gentle persuasion from the bride's mother, who understood better than her husband that there were more ingredients to a happy marriage than a man's earning power. Caroline had no reservations about William. She found him likeable in every respect and regarded his family home as handsome and comfortable.[7] Besides, the proximity of Tervoe to Adare brought her a degree of comfort, apprehensive as she was about the thought of parting with her daughter, who up until then had been her constant companion.

The couple's wedding day on 11 August began with the solemn ceremony of signing the marriage settlement in Windham's dressing room. The bride, dressed in a muslin gown over white satin with a veil of Brussels lace and a wreath of orange flower round her head, was driven through crowds of cheering villagers to the Augustinian church, where the wedding ceremony was performed by the groom's uncle, the Reverend Hunt Johnson. Afterwards, a group of 35 guests returned to Adare House for a lavish *déjeuner* and to see off the newly-weds.

Just seven days later, it was Edwin's turn to walk to the altar with Augusta Goold. The young couple's union was a source of great delight to the Dunravens, who liked Augusta and considered her exceptionally well suited to their son. Even more gratifying to Caroline was Augusta's attachment to Adare, which mirrored Caroline's own sentiment when she first saw Adare as a young wife. 'I am going to *scold* you for thinking I could enjoy anything more than the quiet pleasures of Adare', Augusta wrote to her future mother-in-law in April 1833. 'I am sure you know that I am happier with you than anywhere excepting my own home & had I my own choice I would rather be at Adare than anywhere in the world.'[8]

Conscious of the disparity in the financial standing of the two families, Augusta's father joked that 'If my Daughter does not bring your son a large fortune, she will save him one, for she is the most economical creature in the world'.[9] In spite of such auspicious portents, Windham persistently refused to give his consent for the marriage to proceed until Edwin's 24th birthday, which came to pass in May 1836. What lay at the heart of his reluctance was a concern he harboured regarding his son's over-generous spending habits and penchant for a lavish lifestyle. A cautious man, who abhorred excess in all its manifestations, when Windham finally did consent to the marriage, he determined to safeguard the estate against financial disaster by entailing just £7,000 of his Irish property on Edwin to provide him with an annual income of some £1,500 and retaining the rest of the estate in his own power.[10]

Adare Manor, Adare. The vestibule, showing a Romanesque doorway in the background. Courtesy of Lavinia Graham-Vivian.

Unlike Anna Maria's lavish wedding, Edwin's was a small and more solemn affair. It took place in the drawing room of the bride's home on Merrion Square in Dublin, where a party of 30 friends assembled to witness the occasion. The proceedings began with the signing of the marriage settlement, drawn up by a team of solicitors two days before, and concluded with a ceremony performed by Augusta's brother, the Reverend Frederick Goold. Following a generous wedding breakfast, the young couple set off for an extended honeymoon on the Continent.

The wedding festivities concluded in Adare at the end of August, when Anna Maria's parents organised a grand entertainment to send her and William off on their lengthy honeymoon in Italy. Centre stage was the half-completed gallery, the only room in the house large enough to accommodate the 146 guests who sat down for a meal that day. The Adare military band provided musical entertainment and afterwards the guests wandered outdoors to dance on the green. Later in the evening, as the weather grew damp, the party returned indoors, and merrymaking continued in the hall of the old house. The day proved rather too much for the bridegroom, who came down with such a heavy cold that the newly-weds were forced to postpone their departure by a week.

The bustle of weddings behind them, the Dunravens returned to their usual avocations. Windham threw his energies into supervising the laying out of new walks in the garden, while the masons continued to work on the gallery wing. The first chimney-piece in the gallery was completed in February 1837, and in the same month the space was sufficiently finished to allow Edmond Dwyer and his team of carpenters to commence work on the ceiling. Although the carpenters worked rapidly, Windham had no illusions as to the enormity of their task and estimated that at least a year and a half would be required to finish the interiors.[11]

Eager to share the new building with friends and family, the Dunravens invited the landscape artist Jeremiah Hodges Mulcahy to Adare in October 1836 to paint views of the place for Windham's brother, Richard Quin, who lived in England. A native of Limerick, Mulcahy's classical compositions and his mastery of country scenes had gained him a popular following among the county's landed gentry. The Dunravens probably made his acquaintance through the de Veres of Curragh Chase, views of which Mulcahy painted in 1834. He was a regular visitor to Adare House over the next three years, and his friendship with the Dunravens resulted in further commissions for him, including views of Glin Castle and the Shannon estuary painted for the Knight of Glin.

Above left: Portrait of Anna Maria Wyndham Quin (1814–1855) on her wedding day. Attributed to Richard Rothwell, 1836. By permission of Llyfrgell Genedlaethol Cymru/ The National Library of Wales.

Above right: Augusta Goold (1810–1866), wife of the third Earl of Dunraven, by John Hayter, 1841. Courtesy of the Dunraven family.

Below: Adare Manor, Adare. View of the river front by Jeremiah Hodges Mulcahy, 1837. Courtesy of the Dunraven family.

* * *

The year 1837 dealt the family a series of severe blows. The first of these occurred in early January, when the merchant vessel *Pomeroy*, which set off from London on 22 December, failed to arrive at its destination in Ireland. The ship was carrying a number of valuable items *en route* to Adare. These included paintings that the family had purchased during their tour of the Low Countries, with at least one Rubens among them, and a pair of life-size portraits of Windham and Caroline, commissioned for the gallery at Adare from the leading portrait artist of the time, Thomas Phillips. The couple sat for the portraits in London in May 1835, soon after their return from Paris, and completed the last sitting at the end of March 1836 following the end of their Continental tour. While Windham had chosen to be painted on his own, Caroline was accompanied in the portrait by her youngest child, Windham junior, then five years old.

Mortified by the disappearance of the consignment, Phillips made extensive enquiries into the fate of the vessel. What he managed to unearth confirmed the couple's worst fears. 'I am extremely sorry to inform your Lordship', Phillips wrote to Windham at the end of January 1837, 'that all my enquiries concerning the vessel in which the pictures were sent tend to form that she has foundered at sea. Her owners here think so: they have had no intelligence of her since she sailed & many other vessels have gone & come in the meantime so that I fear my work has gone to the cultivations of the briney realm, instead of helping to furnish the grand apartment at Adair: a change which I by no means approve & exceedingly lament.'[12] Caroline was distraught, not only because of the financial implications—the two portraits had cost the couple £600 to procure—but also because they meant such a great deal to her. 'We had taken such interest in their being painted', she lamented to her mother, '& watched their progress daily, besides I am 2 years older than when they were begun & the child is not of as picturesque an age & what is more, such a likeness as Lord Dunraven, we never can get again.' She admitted that she and Windham had been careless about insurance, 'it never having occurred to us before, to lose anything & receiving things from London every month', but she also laid the blame on the artist, complaining that 'it was very *giddy* of Mr Phillips to send them on … of such a stormy winter'. Her greatest concern, however, was how to replace the portraits: 'here in this corner of the world, how are we to have a painter to do them … [Mr Phillips] is such a perfect gentlemanly old man, he may perhaps when he knows it, offer to do something for us, but I hardly can expect he will.'[13] Her husband, however, had a more sober view of the accident. 'I thank God it pleased him to take the Copies & not the Originals, as we are all three here & in good health'.[14]

In her gloomy prediction that the portraits were irreplaceable Caroline was happily proven wrong. Thomas Phillips took full responsibility for his part in the tragedy and made his way to Adare in August 1837 with one of his daughters to begin a second pair of portraits. Caroline and the two Windhams sat for the pictures for the next eight weeks, a task made difficult by the fact that the autumn was exceptionally cold, which left the artist and his models shivering and glad to have log fires.[15] To break the monotony of the undertaking, the guests were taken on short trips in the neighbourhood, including Carrigogunnell Castle, where Phillips and his daughter made sketches. Another welcome break came in late September, when Augustus O'Brien, a young landowner in County Clare known for his quick wit and cheerful disposition, invited the Dunravens to a party on his estate at Cratloe Woods. It was a delightful day. 'First we had boat races, & we went on board the Paul Pry [Augustus's yacht] to see that, then we had horse, & donkey, & mule races, & then a leaping match, firing at a target & all sorts of fun, we then dined at Mr O'Brien's house in Cratloe Woods, & after dinner had dancing on the green &c. every thing went off delightfully and we were very much charmed to see the affection of the poor warm hearted Irish for their kind young landlord.'[16]

Thomas Phillips concluded the sittings in mid-October and returned to London to finish the portraits. When they were completed, Windham and Caroline found themselves preferring them to the lost originals. Not everyone agreed, however. When the paintings were exhibited in the Royal Academy in 1839, they received a mixed reaction in the popular press. *The Era* was charmed by the portrait of Caroline and her son and the way in which Phillips 'has produced an effect of great splendour of colour; it is full of day-light'.[17] Not so, according to *The Examiner*. 'It happens that we have recently been reading some of his [Phillips's] ingenious speculations respecting the theory of colour', the paper observed, 'and we are really astonished that a gentleman who can write so rationally, should practice so incongruously. By what delusion he can persuade himself into a belief of the harmony of the utterly discordant hues exhibited in this painfully disagreeable picture, we cannot at all imagine.'[18]

✦ ✦ ✦

The crisis brought on by the loss of the portraits was, as Caroline expressed it, a mere flea bite compared to the tragedies that were to follow. The first of these was the sudden death in Wales of Caroline's mother, Anna Maria Bennett, during the influenza epidemic of the winter of 1836–7. She died on 8 February following an apparently short and slight illness, passing away calmly while reading a letter.[19] The news took three days to reach Adare and was a severe blow to her daughter, who was recovering from the effects of the same epidemic, which had left the entire household, servants included, prostrate in bed. Caroline sought solace in her garden, where she spent days on end marking out flowerbeds and 'tried to resign myself to the Divine Will, but could not even pray in comfort'.[20]

Caroline's grief, however, turned into scandalous disbelief when her widowed stepfather, John Wick Bennett, visited Adare in early July and confessed to having clandestinely married Anna Maria's Belgian governess, Eliza Bolleau, only three months after his wife's death. The couple, it seems, had befriended each other during Anna Maria's time with her grandmother in Wales and had continued their relationship behind the family's backs for a number of years. 'The whole affair', Caroline noted with deep distaste, 'is so involved in mystery which I never indeed wish to unravel that it has caused me bitter pain and surprise.'[21] In spite of her personal misgivings, she maintained cordial relations with the Bennetts and could not help feeling a pang of regret when Eliza left the family's service in early October to join her new husband in Wales. 'Her leaving me was accompanied by varied feelings much too conflicted to put down here,' Caroline confessed. 'I sincerely wish her happy, and think she has every prospect of it. After living 20 years with a person habit forms a degree of attachment but on many accounts her conduct lately has been very trying to me.'[22] One can only wonder what her reaction would have been had she known that Eliza and John Bennett had in fact been married on 16 March, only five weeks after her mother's demise.[23]

Mrs Bennett's death brought the entire Welsh estate under Windham's control and increased the family's annual income by £3,000. The future of Dunraven Castle now hung in the balance. The building was for many years used only intermittently by the family and needed extensive repairs. This required an injection of money which Windham was reluctant to provide, as the improvements carried out in Adare were stretching his purse. The family's future, as far as Windham was concerned, lay in Ireland, and he saw little point in expending funds on a rarely used residence in distant Wales. He made the decision to let Dunraven Castle, and the property was advertised in papers to that effect, with or without its 150-acre walled park, during spring 1837.

In early May, Windham experienced symptoms of gout and within days was in dreadful pain and unable to leave his bedroom. What lifted his wife's spirits somewhat was news received from London of Edwin and Augusta's safe return from their extended honeymoon, the latter in the final stages of pregnancy. Just two days later, however, joy turned to tragedy when Augusta gave birth to a stillborn son. Caroline, feeling extremely low, confined herself to her bedroom, complaining of rheumatic pain. Both husband and wife spent much of the month indoors nursing their various ailments, until the return of Anna Maria and William Monsell from their honeymoon in late May. Like her sister-in-law, Anna Maria was heavily pregnant and, much to her mother's relief, appeared to flourish in her condition. The delighted parents were overjoyed at seeing their daughter's smiling face at the breakfast table once more and spent hours showing her the improvements that had taken place during her absence.[24]

Political events dominated the summer of 1837. On 20 June William IV died from heart failure at Windsor Castle, and his eighteen-year-old niece ascended the throne as Queen Victoria. As was customary, the king's death triggered a general election, although it was the last time that a monarch's demise would result in the dissolution of Parliament, as the practice was abolished by the Reform Act of 1867. The Dunravens were thrown headlong into the election campaign when, to their astonishment, a young barrister named John Dorney Harding, secretary of the newly formed Glamorganshire Constitutional and Conservative Society, arrived unexpectedly from Wales in late June to ask Edwin to stand as a Tory candidate for Glamorgan. Edwin, who had arrived in Adare the day before to visit his parents for the first time since his marriage, found himself bundled back into the mail coach to catch the first available steamboat to Wales. The realisation that Edwin had a real chance of winning the seat once held by his grandfather Thomas Wyndham put the entire family into a tremendous bustle. Caroline, unable to think about anything else, at once sat down and wrote seventeen letters to canvass support for her son.[25]

Edwin's decision to accept the candidacy also caused excitement in Wales, where newspapers clamoured to compliment the young nobleman, foremost among them the *Morning Post*. 'To those', the paper declared, 'who are old enough to remember the amiable and deservedly-lamented Mr Wyndham, who for upwards of 20 years sat for Glamorganshire, it will be no slight satisfaction to hear that in the person of his grandson, the heir of the Dunraven property and title, a young and highly-accomplished nobleman, the county will possess a candidate who unites in his own person every requisite qualification for so important a post. Lord Adare is young, unbiassed in politics (with which he has hitherto, from his scientific habits, meddled very little), and of the highest promise. We feel confident that he will be supported by a very large majority of the independent resident proprietors, and by every elector who values the maintenance of the Protestant religion, the stability of the British Constitution, or, what some may think of no less importance, the real and permanent independence of the county.'[26] Nevertheless, Edwin also had his critics. Some considered him 'of too little note or standing in the county to become a candidate'.[27] Others went further, insisting that Edwin's 'ignorance on political matters is frightful'.[28]

The election was aggressively contested. The borough of Glamorgan had two parliamentary seats and there were three candidates vying for them. Edwin, the only Tory candidate, was faced with stiff and experienced competition. His opponents included the liberal Whig and radical sympathiser Josiah John Guest, owner of the large Dowlais ironworks in Merthyr and MP for the borough since 1832, giving rise to slogans such as 'Adare for ever, Guest in the Gutter'; and Windham's second cousin, the moderate Whig Christopher Rice Mansel Talbot of Margam, Glamorgan's largest landowner, who had served as MP for the borough since 1830. Determined not to despair, Edwin's parents spent much of the summer writing canvass letters and anxiously monitoring their son's progress in newspaper reports and in letters from family and friends.

Portrait of Caroline, Countess of Dunraven with her youngest child, Windham Henry Wyndham Quin, with Dunraven Castle in the background. Painted by Thomas Phillips, 1837. By permission of Llyfrgell Genedlaethol Cymru/The National Library of Wales.

In the midst of all the election turmoil Anna Maria went into labour. On 9 July she gave birth to a son, who was privately baptised William. The birth of the child was a welcome respite for the Dunravens, but the lull did not last long. Eleven days later Anna Maria's husband, perhaps motivated by Edwin's campaign in Wales, confirmed his intention to stand as a candidate for Limerick city and the family were pulled into yet another round of canvassing. The day after William's announcement, his newborn son was suddenly seized with violent convulsions, which sent the entire household into a state of alarm. Caroline rushed to her daughter's side but one look at the baby told her that there were no hopes of its survival. After suffering two days of unrelenting seizures, the little boy died close to midnight on 22 July.

In spite of his crushing loss, William was determined to continue his campaign in what was to be a bitterly contested election. A Tory nominee, he was against two candidates supporting the campaign for the repeal of the Acts of Union and suffered not only a humiliating defeat but also significant intimidation. The windows of his committee room on Francis Street in Limerick city were broken by an angry mob days before the election, and his supporters were subjected to such abuse that many were afraid for their lives and forced to abstain from voting. Those who braved the polling booths were greeted by hoots and catcalls and threatened with violence.[29] 'We were all quite relieved, when the business was well over, even though the election were lost', Caroline confessed.[30]

In Wales, however, Edwin's campaign was triumphant. On the day of the election, the young candidate was met on the outskirts of the town of Bridgend by an enormous crowd of people with flags and banners, who drew him out of his carriage and carried him on their shoulders into the polling station. When the news of the final close of the poll arrived in the evening and Edwin's victory was declared, the people were almost frantic with delight.[31] He and the other successful candidate, Christopher Talbot, addressed the jubilant crowds, while in Adare his parents cried tears of joy. Windham suddenly realised the advantage of his property in Wales. To strengthen Edwin's credibility as the representative of the people of Glamorgan, it was imperative that he should establish himself permanently in that county. As a consequence, Dunraven Castle was withdrawn from the market, reroofed and repaired, and presented to Edwin and Augusta as their new home.

The upheavals of 1837 contributed in part to the fact that building works in Adare all but ground to a halt at this time and were not to resume in earnest until the early 1840s. A notable exception was the gallery, the interior of which was largely completed during this period. The rich Tudor Revival style of its exterior was repeated in the internal fittings. Appreciation of the medieval period was one of the leading themes in the construction of the Manor, and the overall appearance of the gallery seems to have been modelled on the plates in Joseph Nash's *Mansions of England in the Olden Time*, a well-thumbed and annotated copy of which could be found in Windham's library.[32] One of the most prominent features of the room was a lavish display of heraldry on a series of stained-glass windows depicting the pedigrees of the Quin, Wyndham and related families, alongside medieval figures of people and animals. Heraldic imagery was central to the fashionable Gothic taste of the time, emphasising as it did the age and status of a particular family. It also provided a subtle allusion to the age of chivalry in the late Middle Ages, thus serving as an indicator of a family's dignity and good breeding.[33] Of course, heraldry could also be abused. Not everyone eager to employ the device had noble pedigrees to boast of and depended instead on sham armorial decoration or made-up family trees proving false descent from a family to which they wanted their origins traced. Others, such as William Beckford, whose home at Fonthill Abbey was awash with bogus heraldry, merely utilised it as a fashionable art form without paying much heed to its layers of symbolic meaning.

The Dunravens, however, took heraldry seriously and turned to the foremost master of the art, the stained-glass artist Thomas Willement, to create the heraldic windows in the gallery at Adare. Willement, appointed heraldic artist to George IV and artist in stained glass to Queen Victoria and author of a number of notable works on heraldry, was one of the first artists of the period to abandon the eighteenth-century habit of painting pictures on glass with coloured enamels. Instead, he turned to the original medieval method of creating stained-glass artwork from individual pieces of coloured glass bound together with strips of lead. Willement's early career

Dunraven Castle, Glamorgan. Watercolour by an unidentified artist, early nineteenth century. Courtesy of the Dunraven family and Special Collections and Archives, Glucksman Library, University of Limerick.

benefited considerably from the growing popularity of Gothic architecture and the immense building activity, both secular and ecclesiastical, which characterised the post-Waterloo era and continued until well into the 1860s. He was patronised by several noted architects of the time, among them Edward Blore, a designer of palaces and country estates on a lavish scale. The two men joined forces on a number of building projects, most notably at Goodrich Court, the castellated mansion built for Sir Samuel Rush Meyrick, which the Dunravens had admired and visited on several occasions. Here Willement created several pieces of stained glass for the windows of the great hall and chapel. Another building in which the Dunravens had witnessed Willement's skill was Penrhyn Castle near Bangor, where he designed two colossal windows for the building's great hall, decorated with signs of the zodiac and the labours of the corresponding months.

While the bulk of Willement's early work was heraldic in character, his later career took him in a predominantly ecclesiastical direction, beginning with the provision of stained-glass windows for St George's Chapel at Windsor Castle in 1840. He was for a time patronised by the ecclesiastical architect Augustus Pugin, for whom he carried out a number of commissions. Pugin soon tired of the association, however, regarding Willement as being only interested in money and refusing to work with him again.[34] The breakup of the partnership did not harm Willement's reputation, and he continued to enjoy the support of influential patrons. Indeed, in 1840 Windham was to complain that 'Willement has not yet finished the glass, he has so much employment, now that his merit is fully known'.[35]

Windham had initially engaged Thomas Willement in 1820 to work on the family pedigree but the financial collapse later that year put a temporary end to their association. It was resumed in 1836, when Willement commenced work on the stained-glass windows for the gallery at Adare. Over the next several years, he produced thirteen large panels, sixteen small ones and eighteen roundels set in thick wooden frames. The first consignment of Willement's glass and fittings arrived in Adare in early November 1839, accompanied by a detailed list of the arms included in the shipment. Windham entertained himself for a day opening the containers and placing the glass and fittings in temporary frames to judge the effect. 'This is by far the finest I ever saw except Cologne', he enthused to his wife, who at the time was visiting friends and relatives in Wales. 'The full length figures of the Duke of Norfolk & Sir John Wyndham addressing him, are most beautiful.' He did, however, discover a mistake in the arms of one of the largest pieces, which was returned to London.[36] A second, more serious issue was identified a week later, when the glass made for the east window turned out to be seven inches too narrow.[37] Nevertheless,

Knole, Kent. The staircase. From Joseph Nash's *Mansions of England in the Olden Time*, vol. 2. Private collection.

such errors did not deter Windham from admiring the overall effect. 'One could run up & down stairs all day to look at it, it is so very beautiful',[38] he wrote. One of his workmen, the young painter, John O'Neill, was equally impressed by the result. 'Oh my Lord, the Gallery will look quite like a Theater', he exclaimed on seeing the stained glass for the first time.[39]

Another feature of the gallery was its wood-carvings. These included a series of carved panels displayed between the windows on the northern wall. Rich in detail, they depicted scenes from the Bible and those copied from Jean Froissart's *Chronicles*, a book which recounted events in western Europe from the deposition of King Edward II in 1326 until 1400. One of the longest prose works of the late Middle Ages, the *Chronicles* were considered to be the most detailed and accurate account of the chivalric culture that characterised fourteenth-century France and England. The twelve-volume work attained immense popularity among the nobility of its time, many of whom commissioned expensively illuminated copies of it. The *Chronicles* enjoyed a revival in nineteenth-century England, when Thomas Johnes of Hafod translated the work into English and published it between 1803 and 1810 in the private press that he had established on his estate. Johnes was not the first translator of the *Chronicles* into English, but his volumes were uniquely illustrated with images selected primarily from a manuscript in the library of St Elizabeth church at Breslau in Prussia.[40] Caroline, whose parents were friendly with Thomas Johnes, not only was familiar with his translation but also owned a complete set.[41]

A team of wood-carvers, including Michael Twomey, Maurice Guerin and James Connolly, a relation of the foreman, worked on the carvings during the winter of 1839–40.[42] 'The old panels are removed in the gallery', Windham told his wife in early February 1840. 'Connelly is now putting the new ones in their place, & the change is admirable, they look remarkably well.'[43] The carvers also prepared a set of coat of arms with carved helmets to range around the ceiling. Their exceptional skill, however, was most evident at the western end of the room, where the set of choir stalls purchased in Antwerp was placed. The carvers replicated it and placed the copy on the opposite wall to the original piece. The only difference between the sets was on the undersides of the misericords or hinged seats. Those of the originals were ornamented with foliate corbels while those of the copy contained carvings of demons and diabolical scenes. The patterns for them were prepared by William Seguier, artist and first keeper of the National Gallery in London, or possibly his brother John, who worked in partnership with him as a picture restorer. Windham was charmed by the results. 'The boys are at work', he reported to his wife, 'carving the bottoms of the seats of the stalls there, for which Seguier drew the patterns & most comical they look. The boys are greatly improved in their bold stile [*sic*] of carving.'[44] As a final touch, the pair of Flemish oak panels dating from 1491 and decorated with scenes from the lives of the Virgin Mary and St Germanus, bishop of Paris, which Windham had purchased in Antwerp were converted not into a chimney-piece, as he had originally intended, but into a double door for the gallery.[45]

The work produced by Windham's wood-carvers was of singular quality. William Monsell reflected on the skill of these men when delivering the inaugural address of the Limerick Trades' Literary Institute in November 1851. 'As an instance of the taste and power of the Irish', the *Freeman's Journal* reported, 'he would mention that a short time ago he showed some beautiful stalls of carved oak which are placed in the gallery at Adare Manor, to an intelligent friend of his from England. One of these screens or stalls was made at Antwerp; the other was copied from that which was made at Antwerp, a city so celebrated for its carvings, and was made in the village of Adare. His friend judged the stall which was made at Antwerp was made at Adare and that which was made at Adare was made at Antwerp.'[46]

Dunraven coat of arms supported by a wolf and a raven. Courtesy of the Dunraven family and Special Collections and Archives, Glucksman Library, University of Limerick.

Thomas Willement's illustration to accompany the poem *Lay of the Last Minstrel* in a presentation book of the poems of Sir Walter Scott for the prince regent, 1817. Private collection. Courtesy of Bonhams.

The interior of the gallery was nearing completion in February 1840, when the carpenters finished off the floor.[47] The stained-glass windows, however, were not completed until the late summer, when the corrected pieces arrived from London and the entire family were back in Adare to witness the unpacking. The gallery was patently the family's pride and joy, though its enormous scale brought its own challenge: 'the gallery looks almost like a Cathedral', Windham mused in the late autumn of 1839. 'I do not know how we shall ever fill it.'[48]

A Dabbler in Architecture

From 1837 onwards, Windham's gout, from which he had suffered intermittently since 1829, grew increasingly severe. His wife inadvertently stumbled on the cause of the problem when she noted that the illness 'always happens … when anyone comes',[1] but neither she nor Windham seem to have associated the attacks with the rich food and wine shared with visiting friends. A particularly low point came in early February 1838, when Windham developed a pain in his hands so crippling as to confine him to his bed for a number of weeks. 'My penmanship shows that the Gout still holds a high position on my hand & more impregnable than Navy Island', he wrote with evident frustration in the middle of this episode.[2] His recovery was slowed by exceptionally cold weather, which detained the family indoors and limited their opportunities for exercise to walking around in the gallery. The severe weather conditions culminated in a tremendous storm of snow and wind, which tore through Adare in mid-February and decimated the demesne. The family could only watch in helpless horror as some of their finest old trees were torn up by the roots or shattered to pieces. 'I never witnessed such devastation', Caroline told John Bennett, '& some old favourites were laid low whose shade we shall sadly miss I fear.'[3]

Portrait of Queen Victoria. Watercolour by John James Chalon (1778–1854). Yale Center for British Art, Paul Mellon collection.

After a brief reprieve, Windham's symptoms returned in early May, and by the end of the month he was once again too ill to leave his bed. Meanwhile, his wife developed rheumatic pains in her head and, in the hopes of relieving their symptoms, the ailing couple decided to make their way to a spa at Miltown Malbay in County Clare. Their departure from Adare at the end of June coincided with Queen Victoria's coronation at Westminster Abbey, and the couple stopped in Limerick city to take part in celebratory festivities there. Owing to budgetary constraints in government, Prime Minister Lord Melbourne denied the queen the traditional medieval banquet, and the coronation became known as the penny crowning. In Limerick, however, there was no shortage of revelry, and the city bustled with performing bands, the peeling of the cathedral bells, handsomely illuminated public buildings and the ceremonial firing of rifles by the local militia, all of which Windham and Caroline watched with interest.

The Dunravens broke their journey at Dromoland Castle, where a large and merry party was gathered to enjoy an evening of good food and music. The rich meal laid out for the guests had inevitable consequences, and the couple were forced to cut short their stay and rush to the spa as fast as their carriage would take them for fear that the rapid worsening of symptoms would render Windham incapable of travel. Although their hotel was extremely comfortable, Windham remained in excruciating pain for almost two weeks until warm baths relieved the symptoms. By mid-July he was well enough to join his wife on an excursion to the Cliffs of Moher, but the pleasure was short-lived, as his symptoms returned with a vengeance the very next day. Defeated, the couple decided to return home. An uplifting surprise awaited them in Adare, when the first sight they saw on driving up the avenue was a nursemaid walking out with Edwin and Augusta's new baby, who had been born in Wales in May. Her christening was celebrated in Adare on 2 August, when she was baptised Caroline Adelaide. To mark the day, all the schoolchildren in the neighbourhood were invited to tea and games in the grounds of Adare House, and in the evening the family walked down to the village to see fireworks and illuminations prepared by its residents. The couple were particularly glad to have among the guests Anna Maria and William Monsell, who had returned from the Continent, where they had travelled in order to recover from the death of their first-born child. Caroline noted, however, with a hint of concern that her daughter was '*exceedingly* thin, & evidently what the world calls a *serious* character—as unlike what her Mama was at her age, as anything you can fancy'.[4]

Anna Maria's return set off a flurry of building and renovating activity at her home in Tervoe, which continued throughout the summer and in which her mother took an active part. A new terrace was laid out and the entire house was freshly painted and papered. The furniture was taken out and dusted, the linen washed, and new books and china bought for the drawing and other rooms. The two small libraries in the house were thrown into a single sun-filled one with two fireplaces and an abundance of books. The new library was connected to a music room, which contained an organ and a magnificent piano on which the composer and virtuoso pianist Sigismond Thalberg had played during a concert tour in Ireland. A large house-warming party was held at Tervoe on Anna Maria's birthday in November, with a boat race, fireworks and a large dinner laid out for the tenants and labourers of the estate. The festivities culminated in dancing, in which the Dunravens joined with the workmen.

Portrait of Anna Maria Wyndham Quin, *c.* 1830s. Courtesy of the Dunraven family.

Since the upturn in the family's finances in the late 1820s, Windham had harboured a desire to return to politics. As an Irish peer, he would have been able to canvass for a seat in the House of Commons but only as a representative of a constituency in Great Britain. While a seat as a representative of a Welsh constituency might have been within his grasp, Windham wanted nothing to do with local politics, which he considered a disagreeable business. Rather than risk the humiliation of a failed and potentially violent election campaign, Windham chose the more discreet route of attempting to secure a place in the House of Lords. There were two means by which this could be achieved. The first was to gain an English peerage. Since peerages were conferred at the behest of ministers, Windham wrote to the prime minister, Lord Grey, on the subject, but the correspondence did not have the desired result. A further opportunity in this regard arose in 1833, however, when rumours began to circulate that Standish O'Grady, Viscount Guillamore, whose eldest son held a seat in the House of Commons as a representative of County Limerick, was dangerously ill. In the event of his death, his son would succeed to the title and as a consequence lose his seat. Sensing that a by-election was likely, Windham pushed his eldest son to canvass for the vacancy. Should he succeed in gaining it, Edwin would be in a position to press the ministers for an English peerage for his father, just as Windham had done to gain an Irish one for his own father. 'Let us get our Peerage if possible, then give up your seat if you like', he proposed, although he also advised Edwin to keep such thoughts to himself so as not to ruin his odds.[5] Much to Windham's disappointment, reports of Lord Guillamore's precarious state of health turned out to be unfounded and the by-election never materialised.

The second option available to Windham was to become an Irish representative peer. While peers of Great Britain or, after 1801, of the United Kingdom enjoyed an automatic right to sit in the House of Lords, the same privilege did not extend to Scottish or Irish peers. Instead, they were allowed to elect 16 and 28 representatives, respectively, from among their number. The Scottish peers were only permitted to serve for the duration of one parliament or a maximum of seven years, but the Irish ones sat for life. The reason for such limits stemmed from a desire to prevent any potential for

Houses of Parliament, London. The House of Lords in 1809 by Thomas Rowlandson and John Bluck after Auguste Charles Pugin. Yale Center for British Art, Paul Mellon collection.

domination by Scottish or Irish peers in the House of Lords, as the latter group alone comprised some 200 individuals and formed the largest single peerage in the kingdom. For a peer to be singled out from such a number added an attractive dimension to the role. 'The representative Peerage', Windham observed, 'is not per se, an object to stir my ambition, but to be sought out, or thought of by the great body of Conservative Peers adds to it quite a new value & most attractively … If they desire me to be one of their representatives, it is the highest compliment they could possibly pay me.'[6]

On 30 July 1839, the sudden death of Richard Bingham, second Earl of Lucan, gave Windham his opportunity. He had first expressed interest in becoming a representative peer in the early autumn of 1838, when he had sought Sir Robert Peel's support for a vacancy. Although Peel was sympathetic to the idea, as prime minister of a Tory government he found Windham's political background problematic, since Windham had begun his career as a Whig and his Tory credentials rested largely on the fact that his son, who now held a seat in the House of Commons, had voted consistently with Peel. In many other ways, however, Windham was an ideal candidate, steadfast in his opinions and popular with his peers. In the event, after some clever political manoeuvring by the Duke of Wellington, with whom the decision ultimately rested, Windham was unanimously elected to replace Lord Lucan in September 1839.[7] He assumed his seat on the Conservative bench in the House of Lords when the appointment was formalised at the opening of Parliament in January 1840.

The election brought considerable changes to the Dunraven family. Having enjoyed several years of relative quietude in Ireland, Windham was again obliged to divide his time between Adare and London. As both he and his wife disliked long spells of separation, and as Caroline had an aversion to living in London, the decision was made to relocate to Wales and to live at Dunraven Castle with Edwin and Augusta for the duration of the parliamentary season of 1840. Although the arrangement was not ideal, it had several advantages. It enabled Caroline to spend time with her grandchildren—a second granddaughter, Augusta Emily, had been born in Wales in August 1839—and to manage the family's Welsh and English properties, all of which needed repair. In addition, construction works at Adare had reached the stage where the old dwelling house was being demolished by degrees, and a temporary relocation to Wales was a convenient solution to problems caused by dust and noise. Above all else, Dunraven Castle was much closer to London than Adare and made it possible for the couple to meet more frequently, particularly since the introduction of rail transport. Caroline had her first taste of rail travel in Dublin in August 1839 when, departing for Wales, she journeyed from Dublin to Kingstown Harbour on the country's first railway line, which had been opened in 1834. Prone to severe travel sickness, she was curious to try the motion of it, and found to her surprise that 'I liked it very much—& altogether bore the expedition to Kingston better than I expected'.[8]

Preparatory sketch by Isaac Shaw of the opening of the Liverpool and Manchester Railway on 15 September 1830. Yale Center for British Art, Paul Mellon collection.

The emerging railway system was also to revolutionise Windham's pursuit of his architectural interests. Since his return to Ireland after the Continental tour, he had taken an increasingly prominent part in the design of Adare House, casting aside James Pain's plans and experimenting with ideas of his own. Although the architecture of Germany and the Low Countries had acted as an important trigger of renewed enthusiasm for Windham, it was not a style he wished to replicate in Adare. Instead, he turned with greater focus to English medieval architecture, a theme which had captivated both him and his wife throughout their married lives. In 1841 he became a member of the Oxford Society for Promoting the Study of Gothic Architecture, founded in 1839 to encourage the use of the archaeologically correct Gothic style in church design.[9] Edward Blore, Thomas Willement and Lewis Nockalls Cottingham were among the society's honorary members. The sharpened focus of Windham's architectural interests was also reflected in his library in

Adare, which contained an eclectic mix of illustrated volumes on cathedral churches and antiquities of England and Wales, architectural pattern-books, works on Classical architecture (including Ware's *Four Books of Andrea Palladio's Architecture*), and books on castles and châteaux bought during the tour of the Low Countries. To these were added from the mid-1830s a series of newly published books devoted to English medieval domestic architecture. In addition to Joseph Nash's *Mansions of England in the Olden Time* (1839), they included John Sell Cotman's two-volume *Specimens of Architectural Remains in Various Counties in England but Principally in Norfolk* (1838) and Henry Shaw's *Details of Elizabethan Architecture*. The latter, published in 1839, consisted of 60 full-page copperplate engravings of ornamental details copied from the best examples of Elizabethan architecture in England, among them Haddon Hall, Gilling Castle, Montacute House, Hardwick Hall, Hatfield House and Blickling Hall. In similar fashion, Charles James Richardson's *Observations on the Architecture of England During the Reigns of Queen Elizabeth and King James I* (1837) contained plans, elevations and ornamental details copied mainly at Claverton Manor in Somerset, Duke's House in Bradford on Avon and Holland House in Kensington, London. Richardson also provided three short essays to accompany the plates, one of them dedicated to the manor house, which, he writes, 'generally forms in every situation the most picturesque and interesting object in the landscape. The peaceful residence of the lords of the soil has a more captivating character than could be boasted by the proud castle which preceded it; yet, like that, it is connected with historical records or local tradition worthy of inquiry, and attractive from various associations.'[10] Perhaps inspired by Richardson's words, it was at about this time, in 1840, that the Dunravens changed the name of Adare House to Adare Manor.[11]

The mere reading of books, however, was not enough to satisfy Windham's interest. He wished to observe and compare, and to view buildings in their original setting in order to gain a better understanding of what constituted authentic medieval style and atmosphere. Like an architectural magpie, he was eager to collect details that intrigued him and to use them in combination to create his own unique style of design. His election as a representative peer, which placed him in London for several months of the year, combined with the emergence of the rail network system, which provided rapid transport to

Windsor Castle, Berkshire. The lower ward with St George's chapel on the left by Joseph Nash, 1846. Royal Collection Trust / © Her Majesty Queen Elizabeth II 2021.

remote parts of the country, provided Windham with unprecedented access to buildings of interest. In March 1840 he embarked on a tour in search of old English country seats. This was no random journey but a carefully planned expedition to seek inspiration from some of the country's most iconic stately homes: Windsor Castle, Warwick Castle, Alton Towers, Haddon Hall, Chatsworth House and Hardwick Hall.

Windham's tour began at Paddington Station on 23 March 1840. Although by now familiar with rail travel, he could but marvel at the speed of his journey to Windsor. 'I … reached Slough by the Great Western Railroad in 38 minutes', he recounted the events of the day to his wife, '& Windsor by the omnibus in 20 more, so that I was standing by the coffee room fire, two minutes under the hour … Certainly railroads are inconceivable things, & the Great Western is very superior to the Birmingham & Liverpool, both in the convenience of the carriages and the speed.'[12] Even though this was his third visit to Windsor Castle, Windham went round and round the building and left with great reluctance. Two parts of the castle in particular drew his attention: St George's Chapel, considered one of the most beautiful examples of Perpendicular Gothic in the country, and those parts of the castle remodelled by Jeffry Wyatville, whom Windham considered a great architect. It is easy to see the two elements that intrigued him the most: the authentic late medieval Gothic architecture and its reinterpretation in the nineteenth-century context.

Although Windham's visit was brief, it held considerable symbolic significance. The royal residence embodied 800 years of British history. It served as a marker against which all other buildings in the country were measured and, as such, set the tone for the rest of Windham's tour. The buildings that followed it were the ancestral homes of earls, dukes and princes, representatives of some of the oldest and most powerful families in England. Their palaces served as their owners' pedigrees, each generation contributing a new layer of brick and mortar. This sense of continuity was something close to Windham's heart. When he came of age and his father expressed his deep regret over the heavy burden of debt that he had placed on his son's young shoulders, Windham had confidently promised to raise the family back to prominence.[13] What he saw when observing these magnificent buildings was not the past but the future, the legacy that he would leave for his descendants to enjoy and look upon a thousand years hence. When choosing a style for his house, Windham did not settle for a single unified theme. Instead, he sought medieval authenticity and combined stylistically pure elements from different centuries to create a patchwork of history, the illusion of a house not twenty but 800 years in the making.

From Windsor, Windham caught another train and headed north to visit Warwick Castle. His first stop, however, was in the medieval city of Coventry, where his wife had urged him to see one of her favourite edifices, St Mary's guildhall. A half-timbered structure constructed of red sandstone in the 1340s and enlarged and embellished in the fifteenth century, the building's most notable feature was its great hall. Although built for commercial and civic purposes, it bore a striking resemblance to a church, with its ornate ceiling of carved angels and remarkable stained-glass windows created by the city's famed medieval glazier John Thornton. Windham admired the room as being very handsome but what struck him the most was the large oriel window in the corner of the great hall, which, he decided, would be of use to him.[14]

Warwick Castle, Warwick. Painting by Francis Harding, c. 1764. Yale Center for British Art, Paul Mellon collection.

Leaving Coventry for Warwick, Windham arrived before sunset to walk under the river front of the castle and to 'look up on what can have been but little altered from the days of the Barons'.[15] 'It is very fine', he concluded, 'almost sublime—no one front at Windsor at all to compare with that part— but the other part at the inside in the court is nothing remarkable & has probably been much altered & added to.' Located on a sandstone bluff at a bend of the River Avon, Warwick Castle was built as a military defence to safeguard the midlands against rebels. Begun in 1068, its fortifications were meticulously planned and built on a lavish scale during the fourteenth century. By 1604 the castle had fallen into ruin and was given by James I to Sir Fulke Greville, who converted it into a country house. The riverside façade, which Windham admired, contained the central portion of the castle. It incorporated the original fourteenth-century great hall and state rooms, and extended on the courtyard side to accommodate a range of additional rooms.[16]

Early the following morning, Windham returned to the castle to see the interiors, although to his regret not many rooms were shown, as the family were at home and visitors were not allowed free range of the building. The castle had been fitted with hot-air stoves in 1830, and the evident comfort of the interior struck a chord with Windham. 'They are fine rooms & very handsome & very warm with hot air, & very comfortable, with a noble view down upon the river at a great depth below.' What he looked forward to seeing the most was the medieval great hall with its seventeenth-century wainscoting, but here he was to be disappointed. The wainscoting consisted of large panels, unornamented except for plain bolection moulding, and the rest of the interior had undergone a series of alterations in 1830–1. These affected the floor, which was newly covered with Venetian red and white marble, and the ceiling, which was taken down and replaced with one designed by the young and upcoming architect Ambrose Poynter, who was making a name for himself by his unique style of Palladianism fused with Tudor Gothic elements. 'The hall is a very fine one', Windham conceded, 'but I saw nothing that would suit us.' In fact, he could not help a hint of smugness creeping in when he considered that there 'are many fine portraits at Warwick, but the armour not to compare with ours'. By the time Windham left Warwick Castle, he was glad to do so. 'I should not like to live there, the town does not, most of it, belong to Lord Warwick and is also pretty radical, & I think the contrast must force itself upon his mind between all that & the power & station of the former Lords of old. Still it is a glorious place and I believe he has a large estate joining it on one side.'[17]

Windham's next stop was Alton Towers, home of the Talbot family, Earls of Shrewsbury, and the only building on Windham's list that could not claim a long and distinguished past. Originally a modest hunting lodge of Classical design known as Alveton Lodge, the house was doubled in size in the early nineteenth century by Charles Talbot, fifteenth Earl of Shrewsbury, and converted into a Gothic country estate, which was renamed Alton Abbey. A number of noted architects, among them Thomas Hopper, William Hollins and Thomas Allason, contributed to the building's design, which incorporated a long gallery and a Catholic chapel that also served as the parish church.[18] In addition to the house, Charles transformed the surrounding farmland into one of the most exotic and spectacular gardens of the time, complete with several water features, a range of conservatories and other ornamental buildings, and dense plantations of heather, conifers and rhododendrons. The gardens were opened to the public in 1839.

When Charles died in 1827, his nephew John, who succeeded as the sixteenth earl, further extended the house between 1824 and 1840, building a central vaulted room from which formally aligned rooms were extended to

Alton Abbey, Staffordshire. View from the park after Thomas Allason, 1819. © The Trustees of the British Museum.

create a long single view from one end of the building to the other, similar to the style adopted by William Beckford at Fonthill Abbey. These alterations almost doubled the size of the house and provided elegant galleries for John's extensive collection of paintings, sculpture and armoury. The house was renamed Alton Towers in 1832 to reflect its fanciful and distinctively vertical profile. Five years later, Augustus Welby Northmore Pugin was employed and given a lavish budget to decorate the interior. Although the design of the building was not entirely to Pugin's taste, he used his creative genius to give it one of the finest Gothic interiors, complete with exquisite carvings, vaulted ceilings, beautifully detailed doors and panelling and delicate stained-glass windows executed by Thomas Willement. Windham could hardly tear himself away. 'The house may well be called Towers—there are plenty of them, in the very worst stile [*sic*] of the Modern Gothic—but the inside is well worth going a long way to see', he assured Caroline. 'There is an immense collection of armour, marbles, & pictures, in galleries lighted from above, & very badly managed, & too low. Another gallery is now building & may be better, but many of the rooms are delightful, with their pillars, arches, Oriels, stained glass, beautiful flock papers, curious ceilings & I know not what, all done by Willement, whose taste is admirable. You know Lord Shrewsbury is a Roman Catholic. The chapel is admirable very large, & immensely high, with beautiful windows executed by Willement & a gorgeous altar.' The gardens, however, perplexed him. He concluded that 'Lord Shrewsbury's taste is inconceivable. It is difficult to judge which he favours most, young fir trees, or Chinese Pagodas. The grounds seem very extensive & the gardens and pleasure grounds immense, but I was so horrified with the very outset that I would not go any further … to go outside & look about was sickening.'[19]

If Alton Towers exemplified the best in modern architecture that money could buy, Windham's next stop, Haddon Hall, represented a building of exceptional antiquity as one of the finest surviving examples of a medieval manor house in England. Originally owned by William Peverel, illegitimate son of William the Conqueror, Haddon Hall passed to the Vernon family in 1170. Except for the so-called Peverel tower and part of the chapel which already existed at the time, the construction of the manor house was carried out by the Vernons at various stages between the thirteenth and sixteenth centuries. In 1563 the property passed to the Manners family, who used Haddon Hall but seldom. As a consequence, the building remained in its unaltered condition throughout the eighteenth and nineteenth centuries. With its many towers and rich array of gargoyles and grotesques, it was subject to much romantic interest and influenced writers and artists such as Ann Radcliffe, Sir Walter Scott and J.M.W. Turner, who made several sketches of the place in the early nineteenth century.

Parts of Haddon Hall bore a remarkable similarity to St Donat's, a medieval castle in the Vale of Glamorgan built in the course of the fourteenth and sixteenth centuries by the Stradling family. Located some six miles south of Dunraven Castle, St Donat's was a popular destination with the Wyndhams, who enjoyed exploring its then-uninhabited rooms and picnicking on its grassy slopes overlooking the Bristol Channel. Windham noted the similarity at once and felt almost guilty about his preference for Haddon Hall. 'Oh such a glorious old place, putting me very much in mind of St Donat's, but I grieve to say, as I love St Donat's so much, there is no comparison at all as to beauty. They are much of the same age, but Haddon is more than twice as large, having *two* court yards, surrounded by the buildings of such beautiful old stile, such graceful irregularity, I would go again & again and again to it if I could. The rooms are not good, though numerous, not so good as the drawing room & dining room at St Donat's, but the gallery is much better. It is without furniture, or inhabitants for the last hundred & sixty years, as the cottager who shews it avers, but it is in good repair & the roof &c properly attended to … There hangs in the hall a portrait of an old huntsman of the Vernon time & it was his descendants who shewed it to me and the house. The chapel windows were ones full of stained glass which they said was nearly all stolen one night about 70 years ago.'[20] On his return to London, Windham was fortunate to pick up a copy of Samuel Rayner's *History and Antiquities of Haddon Hall* (first published in 1836), which he hoped would give his wife an idea of the place.

Haddon Hall, Derbyshire. Painting by Henry Lark Pratt (1805–1873). Courtesy of Buxton Museum & Art Gallery.

Just six miles north-east of Haddon Hall was Windham's next destination, Chatsworth House, home to the Cavendish family since 1549 and generally regarded as the finest private dwelling in England. The contrast between it and Haddon Hall could not have been greater. Originally built by Bess of Hardwick in the 1550s and 1560s, Chatsworth was enlarged and partly reconstructed at the end of the seventeenth century by William Cavendish, fourth Earl of Devonshire, who demolished the south front to make way for new family quarters and lavish state apartments. Raised to a dukedom in 1694 for helping William of Orange to claim the English throne, William could not resist the urge for further building works and remodelled the east front, which incorporated a remarkable painted hall and long gallery. The reconstruction of the west and north fronts followed between 1699 and 1707. The grounds were also developed into formal gardens, which incorporated a magnificent cascade designed by the French hydraulic engineer Monsieur Grillet. The formal gardens were later swept away by Lancelot 'Capability' Brown and replaced with his trademark naturalistic look.

At the time of Windham's visit in 1840, Chatsworth was the home of William Cavendish, sixth Duke of Devonshire, also known as the Bachelor Duke. He converted the long gallery into a library to house his extensive collection of books, commissioned Jeffry Wyatville to design a new north wing and hired as his head gardener a young man called Joseph Paxton. Paxton's best-known achievement at Chatsworth was the construction of the great conservatory, which, when completed in 1841, was the largest glasshouse in the world. It also formed the blueprint for the Crystal Palace, which Paxton later built in Hyde Park for the Great Exhibition of 1851.

In spite of its opulence, Chatsworth was not to everyone's taste. Owing to its proximity to Haddon Hall, visitors could not help comparing the two buildings, and not always in Chatsworth's favour. 'It is well to see Chatsworth and Haddon Hall in the same day', wrote the American author Lydia Sigourney during her tour of Derbyshire in October 1840. 'The contrast of their features deepens the impression which each leaves on the mind. The overwhelming splendor of one prepares you to relish and to reverence the silent, mournful majesty of the other.'[21] Windham's opinion followed a similar line of thought. 'It looks like a French Palace, with all that unbounded expense can give it, but if that gave it ten times more I could not admire it. No fine trees near the house, & very cold climate. The house inside very fine & grand & I dare say very comfortable, but I do not feel the least interest or pleasure in that sort of stile, & would not accept it on the condition of living there six months in the year. Many fine pictures & marbles by Canova, very well arranged in a sort of gallery opening into a conservatory occupied principally by a few palms & pines that cannot live in our climate out of a house.'

Chatsworth House, Derbyshire. *The Conservatory* by William Callow, 1843. Royal Collection Trust / © Her Majesty Queen Elizabeth II 2021.

Paxton's great conservatory also found little favour with Windham. 'You may judge the size by the fact of a carriage road going through the middle', he described the structure to his wife. 'It is 300 feet long, about 160 wide & 120 high … & looking something like a vast balloon, & I saw them measuring the ground for two great wings to be added to it. It was said & I should think truly to be the largest space covered in by glass in Europe, which I think more creditable to the sense of the sovereigns of Europe than of the Duke of Devonshire. It is rounded at the ends & as I thought a very absurd thing altogether.'[22]

Windham's final stop on his tour of old English buildings was Hardwick Hall, some eighteen miles south-east of Chatsworth and also the property of the Dukes of Devonshire. It was in fact not one building but two, an old hall begun by Bess of Hardwick in 1585 to provide an escape from her unhappy fourth marriage to George Talbot, sixth Earl of Shrewsbury, and a new hall begun in 1590 following George's death while the old hall was still under construction. Although a mere five years separated the two buildings, the contrast in their architectural form could not have been greater. Designed by Robert Smythson, one of England's first architects, who had learnt his trade as a master mason at Longleat, the new hall explored two entirely new concepts: symmetry and a generous quantity of glass. The great size of its windows even gave rise to the popular local jibe of 'Hardwick Hall, more glass than wall'. The building represented a distinctly English take on Renaissance architecture: enormously large to demonstrate the wealth and status of its owner, with corner towers rising well above the roofline, large mullioned windows and a skyline ornamented with balustrades and decorative openwork. In direct contrast to its Georgian counterparts, the ceiling and window height of Hardwick Hall increased from bottom to top, the servants occupying the ground floor while the top floor was reserved for entertaining on a grand scale, allowing the guests to enjoy panoramic aerial views of the surrounding countryside.

Bess of Hardwick remained at Hardwick Hall for the remainder of her life and filled the building with a unique collection of paintings, furniture, tapestries and needlework. When she died in 1607, the two halls passed to her son, William Cavendish, from her second marriage. He and his descendants made Chatsworth their main residence, while Hardwick Hall was used as

Hardwick Hall, Derbyshire. North view. Watercolour by John Buckler, 1813. Yale Center for British Art, Paul Mellon collection.

an occasional hunting lodge and dowager house. The old hall fell gradually into dereliction and was partly dismantled, while the new hall remained in a semi-neglected state but managed to retain its original form, which was much to Windham's liking. 'Much has fallen, but part is still roofed … It is an enormous specimen of Elizabeth's time & taste, immense rooms with windows large beyond imagination & vast gallery 160 feet long they said, covered with portraits, many of them very curious, & strange stale beds in the bed rooms, & acres of tapistry [sic] & needle work. A noble park, and such oaks. No comparison a finer situation than Chatsworth.'[23]

Windham returned to London full of enthusiasm. 'I wish you could have been with me during this tour', he wrote to his wife, 'it would have amused you very much. It has not cost me any thing like what living in London would. Rail roads are magical things about four hours & a half from here to London, which is 92 miles.'[24]

⧫ ⧫ ⧫

Adare Manor, Adare. James and George Richard Pain's proposal for the south front, May 1834. Courtesy of the Irish Architectural Archive. This design failed to satisfy Windham.

The ideas that Windham had collected during his tour were put to good use when the building works at Adare were reactivated in 1840 with the construction of the south front and the great hall. As Windham was no architect, he required a good draughtsman to give form to his vision. James Pain would have been the obvious choice, but by 1840 the relationship between the two men had become strained. In fact, cracks had begun to appear as early as 1833, when Windham complained about Pain's long absences in London, which at one point forced the masons to lay down tools for want of work.[25] Windham was also dissatisfied with Pain's drawings, disliking his alterations and discovering mistakes in his plans.

In April 1835 Windham once again had reason to complain, this time as a consequence of the sketch of the floor of the Royal Library which he had made while in Paris and which he had given to James Pain to work into a plan to suit the gallery. 'He made his usual mess of it', Windham told Edwin with an evident note of irritation, '& then I gave it to George who is a practical & clever man, & today he finished it all out correctly, to the size of the Gallery, & very handsome it will be.'[26] Just three months later, Edwin wrote to his mother to tell her that 'Pain is worse than ever he has made two blunders in the staircase of the tower', adding that 'Papa looks well and is in good spirits nothing annoys him but Pain & he certainly is a great bore'.[27] What grated with Windham most of all, however, was not James Pain's shortcomings as a draughtsman but his apparent lack of taste and his inability to understand Windham's design concepts, particularly when it came to the detail of finishing and decorating. 'Mr Pain with gentlemanly qualities, & skill in some things, has no knowledge of, & no taste whatever in *Tudor* architecture & makes a shocking mess of it & of every part & detail left to his management—& this embarrasses & perplexes me exceedingly.' It was a disappointment for Windham to realise that his own taste in Tudor architecture was more cultivated than that of his architect.[28]

Things were not to improve. George Richard Pain, the more gifted and creative of the two brothers and the one whose taste and ability Windham implicitly trusted, died suddenly in December 1838 at the age of 46. James subsequently suffered a series of humiliating professional setbacks while supervising the construction of Thomond Bridge in Limerick city, the worst of which was the collapse of one of its arches in June 1839. Such events, allied with Windham's personal misgivings about Pain's suitability, steeled his resolve to discontinue his association with Pain. When construction works at Adare recommenced in 1840 and no request was issued to the architect to come and supervise the works, Pain grew increasingly alarmed. In February 1842 he felt compelled to enquire after the matter and to salvage what was left of his professional integrity. 'Within these few days I have been spoken to by several gentlemen', he wrote enquiringly to Windham, 'who mentioned that your Lordship was about to recommence the building at Adare and asked if I was employed or if I had any differences with your Lordship. To this I replied as I feel, that I never had had any differences with your Lordship and was also unconscious of any thing having occurred that should cause the withdrawing of your Lordship's countenance from me. These conversations have made me feel particularly uneasy which causes me thus to intrude myself on your Lordship to request the favour, if any thing I have done, or omitted to do, has been the cause of offending your Lordship, of your being so good as to inform me that I may exonerate myself and stand as I believe I heretofore did, on your Lordship's good opinion.'[29]

Windham's dismissal of Pain was tactful and courteous. He reassured the architect that, 'If any body fancies we have had any difference, or that you ever did anything to offend me I am happy to say that such a gratuitous assumption is utterly unfounded. I did not cease to employ you professionally for the purpose of placing myself in any other professional hands. Building is my amusement, & I am a dabbler in architecture, & I have now for some years been carrying on the new works here entirely from my own design, & without any professional assistance whatever. I feel great respect and regard for you & am yours very truly Dunraven.'[30]

Windham was not, of course, entirely honest in his reply. His interest in medieval Gothic and his desire to locate an architect more attuned to his personal vision had brought him into the sphere of Lewis Nockalls Cottingham, a highly respected architect and pioneer in the study of medieval Gothic architecture, and it was to Cottingham that he now turned for architectural drawings for the unfinished south front. Originally trained in the classical eighteenth-century architectural tradition, Cottingham had been strongly influenced in his early career by the antiquary and draughtsman John Carter, one of the first promoters in England of the revival of Gothic architecture. Carter instilled in his pupil a passion for the scholarly study of medieval art and opened the way for him as a distinguished conservator, collector and designer of medieval architecture. Cottingham, in his time, published several volumes of working drawings of medieval buildings, Gothic ornaments and decorative metalwork, which were eagerly absorbed by the young Augustus Welby Northmore Pugin. It was from Cottingham that Pugin learned the importance of copying not merely Gothic ornamental forms but also their structure by studying and understanding the modes of construction used by medieval masons. Both men put great weight on historically correct restoration work, in which personal preferences or flights of fancy had no place.[31] While Pugin ultimately moved away from this strict historicism and the restrained and sensitive modes of restoration, Cottingham remained faithful to this approach throughout his career.[32] He was well respected by his patrons, most notably William Brougham, second Baron Brougham, who regarded Cottingham as 'far better than Pugin, who is of the florid Church style, and Barry, whose Houses of Parliament turn out like conservatories'.[33]

Much of Cottingham's success stemmed from a vast collection of medieval artefacts and architectural fragments that he rescued from demolished buildings and used as a resource for his designs. The artefacts were housed in chronological order in a series of rooms at his home at 43 Waterloo Bridge Road. The place became known as the Museum of Medieval Antiquities and was openly available for visitors to view and study. The collection contained some 31,000 individual items, ranging from architectural details cast from churches and cathedrals in England and Europe to panelling, chimney-pieces, windows and entire ceilings from demolished domestic buildings. There were also vast rooms filled with furniture, paintings and monumental sculpture.[34] The museum allowed Cottingham to instruct his patrons on the subject of medieval interiors with tangible examples and to actively promote a knowledge and understanding of medieval architecture.

Cottingham also incorporated medieval fragments into the interiors that he designed, most notably at Snelston Hall in Derbyshire, which he created for the wealthy attorney John Harrington between 1827 and 1837. This practice of utilising authentic medieval fragments was popular and widespread among builders of country seats throughout the 1830s and 1840s. Pugin incorporated Flemish carvings into the gallery at Scarisbrick Hall, while at Toddington Manor Charles Hanbury-Tracy used richly stained medieval glass purchased from monasteries in Switzerland, Germany and Holland.[35] Nowhere, however, was this device utilised more than at Abbotsford, built by Sir Walter Scott near Melrose in Scotland. Its walls incorporated stones from the region's ruined abbeys and castles, and many of its windows, chimney-pieces and doorways were taken or copied from medieval buildings. Scott, who was not only a popular author but also a leading influence both in antiquarian circles and in the revival of medieval taste, was friendly with Cottingham, and it is likely that Abbotsford benefited from this friendship. Moreover, the depth of historical detail in Scott's *Waverley* novels may well have been based on information generously supplied by the architect.[36]

As a result of his unquestioned integrity as a medievalist, Cottingham enjoyed an unrivalled professional standing among the architects of the day. His patrons treated him not as a servant but as a respected authority to whom they turned for instruction and advice. Cottingham's clients were primarily drawn from the aristocratic circles, the landed gentry and the wealthy professional classes, and were often well-travelled men with a deep-seated interest in the study and preservation of Gothic architecture or a fascination with heraldry, armour and genealogy.[37] Many, such as the Earl of

Snelston Hall, Derbyshire. Entrance front. Watercolour by L. N. Cottingham, 1827. Courtesy of Derbyshire Record Office.

Snelston Hall, Derbyshire. Design for bookcases by L. N. Cottingham, c. 1827. Courtesy of Derbyshire Record Office.

Dunraven and Charles Hanbury-Tracy of Toddington Manor, acted as their own architects or, like Samuel Meyrick of Goodrich Court, controlled and contributed to the design process with firm ideas of their own, and sought Cottingham's assistance to give their plans the authenticity they craved which pattern-books alone could not produce.

Windham's interest in Cottingham was long-standing. At least one of Cottingham's books, *Plans, Elevations, Sections, Details and Views of the Magnificent Chapel of King Henry the Seventh at Westminster Abbey Church*, published in 1822, found its way into his library. In July 1835, when his frustration with James Pain was at its height, Windham wrote to Cottingham to ask whether he could come to Adare and provide drawings for the gallery ceiling. To Windham's deep regret, 'the expense was such I was obliged to give it up'.[38] Edwin, unaware of this setback, developed a low opinion of the architect and complained to his mother that 'The gallery ceiling cannot be commenced until next year, as Cottingham has sent over no plans'.[39]

Nevertheless, Windham's temporary financial privations did not diminish his admiration for Cottingham's work. In 1836, following their return from the tour of the Low Countries, Windham and his wife visited Oxford, where the main focus of their interest was the restoration of the interior of the chapel of Magdalen College, Windham's Alma Mater, completed the year before by Cottingham, who had won a competition to remodel it in 1829. He stripped away most of the chapel's eighteenth- and nineteenth-century alterations, remade the ceiling put in by James Wyatt in the 1790s, and erected a new stone organ screen decorated with carved angels playing musical instruments. The result did much to boost interest in Gothic Revivalism in the country and was widely utilised by architects such as Blore and Pugin, the latter of whom considered it to be 'one of the most beautiful examples of modern design I have ever seen and executed in both wood and stone in the best manner'.[40] Windham also had an opportunity to admire Cottingham's work elsewhere during his 1840 tour, when he stopped to look around the thirteenth-century St Oswald's church on his way to his lodgings in Ashbourne in Derbyshire. The building was undergoing repairs and Windham was so taken by the quality of restoration that he could not help asking one of the workmen for the name of the architect; 'my wonder ceased', he wrote to his wife, 'when they told me Mr Cottingham'.[41]

On the last day of March 1840, Windham made his way to 43 Waterloo Bridge Road to meet Cottingham and Thomas Willement. The three men spent most of the morning arranging Windham's plans for Adare and putting them in a tangible form.[42] The plans related to the south front of Adare Manor, which was to contain the main reception rooms of the building and which, when completed, would engulf the existing Georgian family home, which up to now had stood cheek by jowl with the new gallery wing. The initial discussions led to a second meeting with Cottingham on 4 April. 'I was most of the day yesterday with Mr Cottingham & like him much', Windham told his wife. 'He entered clearly into my ideas and is to draw out the elevations, & all the details, but I was obliged to write to Adare for the exact thickness of the walls, size of the rooms and many such things, without which he could not begin to draw.'[43]

❖   ❖   ❖

Windham and Cottingham modified the elevations proposed by James and George Richard Pain but remained more or less faithful to their floor plan, which in turn had utilised the blueprint of the old Georgian family home. This consisted of a range of three south-facing reception rooms—a drawing room, saloon and dining-room—running on a west–east axis. To the north of this range was a large central hall, behind which was a small study, where Windham conducted his business. The three reception rooms presented a Classical symmetrical façade, with the front wall of the centrally located saloon and the floors above it projecting boldly forward to form a pedimented two-bay breakfront. Windham and Cottingham's new plan broke this symmetry by enlarging the drawing room southwards, bringing its front wall level with that of the adjoining saloon. This new elevation was to incorporate two oriel windows, a large one for the drawing room and a smaller one for the saloon. 'I decided upon that when I saw the Oriel in St Mary's Hall at Coventry', Windham explained to Caroline, '& it happens to be just what Cottingham likes.'[44] The drawing room was also extended to the west. The new end-point incorporated an octagonal projection, the interior of which featured 'an arch

& there will be no break where the Saloon is, as the drawing room new would will be taicilt pair with it — So that the oriel will be as on the thickness of the walls, the window part projecting — The dining room will be altered thus — you will move the door to the center of Arches where the two dotts are — & part of the present wall taken down to the front & a great projection & fire place 2d where the dotted line

Letter containing sketches of Windham's first design ideas for the south front of Adare Manor. Courtesy of the Dunraven family and Special Collections and Archives, Glucksman Library, University of Limerick.

springing from corbels which will enable the roof to be different from the rest of the room & that part may be arranged for musical instruments'.[45] Windham had also intended to further enlarge the drawing room by throwing it into one with the adjoining saloon but, to humour his wife, 'as you fancy keeping the saloon for a second room, I decided to do so'.[46]

The south wall of the dining room, which adjoined the saloon to the east, would remain unaltered except for its far end, which incorporated 'a great projection & 2nd fire place'. Windham enthused that 'in fact that will be *the* room, with windows to the south for sun & the east & west for views'. Inside the dining room, he planned to have a music gallery to rest on two arches over the door leading to the saloon, but this idea was later abandoned. The 'great projection' was also reduced in size and, to maximise the effect of sunlight, a long south-facing colonnade was built to run the length of the dining room wall. In designing the new south face of the building, Windham first experimented with pointed windows but concluded that while they 'look pretty on paper … they are too church like for a dwelling house'. He also 'found it impossible to make the front regular' as per the Pain brothers' original design, but this did not overly bother him; in fact, he felt that 'it will be much handsomer as it is now planned'.[47] To unify the asymmetrical front, Cottingham designed an open-work parapet to run the length of the façade, spelling out the first line of Psalm 127, 'Except the Lord build the house their labour is but lost that build it'.

The focal point of the house, of course, would be the great hall. This space served as a bridge between the gallery and kitchen wings to the north and the range of reception rooms to the south. Pain originally designed this as a space within which a central dominant bifurcated staircase provided access to the gallery to the north and bedrooms to the south. Windham now changed the layout. Two colonnades, retained from the Pain brothers' original plan, traversed the room, one from north to south to divide the room along two thirds of its width, the other from east to west to run parallel to the south wall. However, the staircase was now moved from its central position to the south-eastern corner of the hall, into a space between the second colonnade and the south wall. The effective hiding of the staircase, coupled with the spectacular height and graceful proportions of the octagonal pillars and pointed arches of the colonnades, created a space reminiscent not of a medieval hall but of a vast medieval abbey or cathedral. Caroline's touch is evident in this space,

R I V E R   M A I G U E

River Garden

Lower

L   L   L   Q

K

L   L   L

KITCHEN   COURT

GALLERY

TERRACE

G

D

H

C

C

B

F

A

E

E

PLAN OF THE OLD MANOR HOUSE.

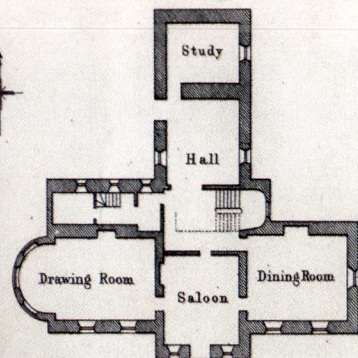

Study

Hall

Drawing Room

Saloon

Dining Room

SCALE.

Adare Manor, Adare. Plan of the ground floor. From *Memorials of Adare Manor* (1865). Courtesy of Special Collections and Archives, Glucksman Library, University of Limerick.

for she was a great admirer of skilled stonework and on her many visits it was the Gothic arch that elicited her most appreciative commentary. She admired the fine interior pillars at Salisbury Cathedral, 'which with their immense height & gothic arches gives it a light, & very elegant appearance'.[48] At Notre Dame she was forcibly struck by 'the singular beauty of the long line of arches'[49] that ran uninterrupted from one end of the interior to the other, but her greatest admiration was reserved for Cologne Cathedral, 'that most beautiful and stupendous building' whose 'pillars are the most beautiful I ever saw, they are immensely high, & go off in such high & graceful arches, that they give one an idea of all perfection of florid Gothic architecture'.[50] The cathedral-like feel of the great hall at Adare was further enhanced by Willement's stained-glass windows, the rich wainscoting of its walls, made from oak trees grown in the deer park,[51] and in later years by the construction of the colossal Telford organ in its south-west corner.

Cottingham also designed several items of furniture for Adare Manor. These included most notably six oak throne chairs with blind tracery on the backs and with their arms and legs carved with heraldic beasts, and a set of three oak bookcases with stepped columns and ogival arches, which in their design closely resembled those created by Cottingham some years earlier for Snelston Hall. Windham also asked Cottingham to design frames for Thomas Phillips's pair of portraits, which he wanted to 'put up in fixed frames inserted in great carved work up to the ceiling' in the gallery.[52] Here, however, Cottingham disappointed him. When Windham inspected the design some days later, he discovered to his dismay that it was 'quite different from what I directed and not suited at all, & not suited to us, & now he must draw a fresh one'. Indeed, Cottingham's slowness and his inclination to run with his own rather than his client's ideas tested Windham's nerves in spite of his profound admiration for the architect. 'He can have nothing ready before the end of next week', he complained to his wife in May 1840, 'and so far it is not without use that I am kept in town, for I find I cannot trust him at all unless I am constantly superintending.' Windham, however, did not remain idle while waiting for Cottingham's designs. He commissioned engravings of a bronze chimney-piece for Adare Manor (ultimately not constructed) and purchased 'all sorts of things for the kitchen', which 'are to be engraved with the coronet & letter D, as a check to stealing'.[53]

❖   ❖   ❖

Building works at Adare Manor in the early 1840s were primarily focused on the great hall, the construction of which necessitated large-scale demolition of the old house interior. A gabled section connecting the gallery wing to the old house had already been built, outside and to the west of the hallway of the old house. As part of James and George Richard Pain's original design, it incorporated three tiers of windows to accommodate three floors, which Cottingham modified to two by extending the double space of the great hall to the western façade. As this wall could not be altered without tearing it down, it was left unchanged and provided an element of surprise to visitors entering the building and expecting a single-storey hall. Demolition of the old building began in November 1839, when the wall at the back of Windham's study was broken through. Two large iron chests kept in the study were hauled out and dragged through a temporary passage into Windham's new dressing room, where they were placed by the side of the fireplace to enable him to attend to his business without interruption.[54] Breaking through the back wall was not an easy task, for this was one of the walls of the old tower that formed the core of Adare House, and as hard as solid rock.[55]

Gutting of the old building continued in the spring of 1840, when the hall next to Windham's former study was taken down, with his wife performing the ceremonial removal of the first stone.[56] As the new manor was built piecemeal, connecting its various parts in a seamless fashion was problematic, and not all the solutions adopted were successful. Access to and from the kitchen wing provided the greatest challenge for servants. They were obliged to come through the family's private quarters beneath the gallery to access not only the main house but also the first floor of the kitchen wing. To solve this problem, a tall and slender castellated octagonal tower, copied from the chapel tower at Haddon Hall, was constructed adjacent to the kitchen wing to house a spiral staircase.[57] The top of the tower, which served a purely ornamental purpose, was decorated with tall lancet windows and with eight fantastical grotesques and other figures carved out of stone projecting from the corners of its eight sides. These and other elaborate grey limestone carvings of plants, human figures and mythical beasts that proliferated on

Haddon Hall, Derbyshire. Watercolour of a tower at Haddon Hall by Joseph Mallord
William Turner, 1794. Courtesy of the Indianapolis Museum of Modern Art. The tower
was copied by Windham and used at Adare Manor.

the walls of Adare Manor were for the most part based on sketches and patterns that Caroline and Anna Maria had copied from churches and castles during their tour of the Low Countries but were also influenced by some English buildings, most notably Haddon Hall, and Toddington Manor. The working drawings of stonework were prepared by Thomas Connolly under instructions from Caroline.[58]

Another difficulty arose when the main staircase was moved from its central position to the furthest point of the great hall, cutting off access to the gallery. In this case the ruins of Heidelberg Castle in the Neckar Valley, which the Dunravens visited in December 1835, provided Windham with inspiration. There, an arched tunnel-like passage, apparently formed in the thickness of the walls, had captivated his interest. This he recreated in Adare Manor to lead from the first landing of the staircase to the gallery. Concealed from view of the great hall, the hidden stairwell provided a singularly quaint and picturesque effect for the unsuspecting visitor.[59]

Access was not the only problem that dogged the new house. The enormous size of the rooms made heating difficult, even with a forest of tall and handsome chimneys ornamented with beautiful patterns. Caroline's bedroom was particularly uncomfortable, and in February 1840 its grate was enlarged to throw out more heat. The gallery likewise was practically glacial, especially during the winter months. To remedy the problem, Windham had a large stove put up in the central chimney-piece. This, however, he feared would be too hot but, 'if so, it will answer for the great hall, which will be cold enough for anything'.[60] Heating problems afflicted the house for the next decade, causing a warping of floorboards and panelling. This was remedied only when Edwin took over the building project after the death of his father in 1850.

In spite of such issues, the Dunravens derived almost childlike joy from their building project. Windham revelled in purchasing items for his beautiful house. 'I have bought two old portraits for the gallery', he told Caroline in the spring of 1840, 'one full length of James the 1st rather a fine portrait, the other, two full length figures in the same picture of Sir Reginald Mohun & his wife hand in hand, of the time of either Elizabeth or James 1st. Nothing looks so well in old places as old portraits & old glass, we have plenty of each.'[61] From his brother Richard he received a gift of a pair of tusks of an elephant killed by their nephew Captain Philip Payne-Gallwey, and these Windham intended to display in the great hall along with a profusion of flowers, because 'the more flower stands & flowers can be put into the hall the better'.[62]

Before it could be filled with flowers, however, the great hall needed to be completed. For the interior touches, the Dunravens, encouraged by their son Edwin, turned to Augustus Welby Northmore Pugin, but not until a series of dramatic upheavals shook the family to the core and threatened once again the progress of building works.

Adare Manor, Adare. Minstrel's gallery. Watercolour by Louisa Payne-Gallwey, *c.* 1850. Courtesy of Lavinia Graham-Vivian. Note the concealed staircase lit by pointed windows copied from Heidelberg Castle.

CHAPTER
ELEVEN

Progress Through Adversity

The early 1840s bore little evidence of the calamities that the decade would bring. Under the ever-growing edifice of Adare Manor, the normal routine of life with its ups and downs continued uninterrupted. Friends were entertained to lunch and dinner in whichever room happened to be free from the presence of masons, carpenters and mountains of sawdust, or treated to picnics on the lawn or the grassy slopes of Desmond Castle. On fine days, boating on the Maigue remained a favourite pastime. When the weather was inclement, diversions were found indoors in the form of musical soirées or theatricals, in which the servants participated as a willing and appreciative audience. Some forms of entertainment were rather more daring. On one occasion, when the Dunravens were sneezing and blowing in the throes of an influenza epidemic and disinclined to venture outdoors to pursue the thrills of the shooting season, the men of the family painted a target for a match of pistol-shooting indoors. Caroline, too, decided to join in the fun and 'fired twice but could hit nothing'.[1] One can only wonder where her stray bullets may have landed.

There were also additions to the family. In November 1840, Edwin and Augusta arrived from Wales with their two little daughters in advance of the birth of their third child. Augusta's pregnancy was a difficult one, and she spent most of December in bed in the care of a doctor and a team of nurses, and frightened her in-laws with several false alarms of premature labour. In January, when the Maigue burst its banks and the flood waters rose so high that travel was impossible, the family was left housebound without the aid of a doctor. In the end all went well, and on 12 February 1841 Augusta gave birth to a much-longed-for son. The news of the happy event caused such an accumulation of letters of congratulation that by way of reply the family were forced to print bulletins and send them around. The future fourth earl was christened Windham Thomas on 17 October 1841 in Adare and the occasion was marked by two days of festivities. The entertainment on the first day was hampered by incessant rain and the guests took shelter in the barn and granary, where local schoolchildren were treated to dinner. In the evening, the bravest of participants defied the ongoing downpour and ventured outdoors to witness a brilliant exhibition of fireworks. The party continued in the house, where fires were lit and tea made to warm guests. A band of pipers played for those who wished to dance. On the second day, a dance was organised for the servants in the housekeeper's suite of rooms and a supper laid out in the kitchen. The Dunravens and their guests dined in the saloon before joining the staff in their gaieties. The dancing continued until three o'clock in the morning and 'all about the house wherever you went the sounds of cheers & merriment resounded'.[2]

Three more children were born to Augusta and Edwin over the next few years: Mary Frances in 1844, Edith in 1846 and Emily Anna in 1848. When Edith was born, Edwin, evidently piqued by the number of women surrounding him, wrote to his mother hoping that 'no one will be more disappointed than I am about the stranger's sex: I feel that all is so completely in God's hand, & that he sends us what is best, that really I am almost indifferent—if given a choice, one would naturally prefer the other'.[3] In Tervoe, Anna Maria and William Monsell also rejoiced in the birth of a baby son in March 1841. The child was christened William on Easter Monday, with his grandparents and Archdeacon William Wray Maunsell as sponsors. As the only grandchild living near Adare, young William became the apple of his grandmother's eye and a comforting substitute for her youngest son Windham, who at the time of his nephew's birth was eleven years old and preparing to leave Adare to begin his schooling at Eton. Windham's birthday on 2 November was always a day of great festivity, and every year the domestic staff postponed their annual Hallowe'en party for two nights to combine the two celebrations. In 1841, when Windham turned twelve and Eton loomed large on the horizon, a special effort was made, and his birthday was passed boisterously in playing snap apple and other party games and dancing late into the night to the tune of a piper. Windham's parents, however, witnessed these cheerful scenes with a tinge of sadness. Not only did they know that 'it would … probably be long ere the dear boy passed another birthday with us', but Windham's father 'also proposes altering the house next year so that we also felt our last revelry in the old kitchen had taken place'.[4]

Cards at the Manor. Sketch by Mrs R. Wingfield, August 1846. Courtesy of the Dunraven family.

Young Windham's departure for Eton on 26 January 1842 coincided with one of the worst storms ever to hit Ireland. It began at three o'clock in the morning and swept across the county like a tornado, blowing down chimneys, ripping off roofs and showering streets with mortar and breaking glass. In Adare village, the wind stripped virtually every roof of its slates, leaving not a single house untouched. Demesnes throughout counties Limerick and Clare suffered extensive damage. At Adare Manor alone, the wind uprooted between 600 and 700 mature trees, mutilating the fine avenues and stripping the estate of its finest specimen trees.[5] The family spent much of the day watching the storm from their windows while packing up Windham's trunk. By four o'clock the winds had abated sufficiently for the schoolboy to begin his journey to England. Caroline spent a sleepless night worrying about her son's sea crossing and watching over her husband, who was showing signs of yet another attack of gout.[6] While young Windham, to his parents' relief, made the journey to Eton without injury, his father remained on a downward spiral of illness, with only brief periods of respite.

❖ ❖ ❖

The last guests to enjoy hospitality at Adare Manor before large-scale works demolished the remains of the old Georgian house were Charles Lennox Kerr, his wife Charlotte Hanmer and their two young daughters in February 1843. Not only were the Kerrs among the Dunravens' favourite friends but the two families were also connected through marriage. Charlotte's mother, Arabella Bucknall, was Caroline's cousin and also one of her closest friends. Charles, a younger son of the sixth Marquess of Lothian, had proposed to Charlotte in Adare while they were both staying as guests of the Dunravens in the spring of 1839. Both Windham and Caroline took a great liking to Charles, who was an exceptionally charming and amiable character. During his 1839 visit, the family organised an impromptu jig-dancing evening with their servants, during which Charles and Caroline's maid, Rebecca Downes, kept up a jig for 35 minutes without stopping while Caroline provided the music.[7]

Entertainment during the 1843 visit was somewhat less vigorous but no less enjoyable. The Kerrs' leave-taking towards the end of the month was a melancholy event, as the Dunravens knew that they were the last company the family would ever have in the old house.[8] Windham's plan was to have the bulk of the building pulled down during the parliamentary season of 1843, which he and Caroline intended to spend in London to avoid the dust and clamour of demolition. In late February the rooms in the old house were cleared of furniture and artefacts, and numerous other preparations were made in anticipation of a lengthy stay in England.

Portrait of Windham Henry Wyndham Quin, 1 May 1836. Courtesy of the Dunraven family.

Stormy seas. Watercolour by Augusta Goold, *c.* 1830s. Courtesy of the Dunraven family.

The couple's date of departure was set for 6 March, but as the day drew closer Caroline's maid suddenly fell so ill that travel was out of the question. No sooner did Rebecca Downes show signs of recovery than Windham developed gout, which rapidly escalated and showed every prospect of a long fit. The disorder, which had first manifested itself in 1820, did not become a persistent problem until the autumn of 1835, and even then Windham as a rule was able to continue his building works and to enjoy shooting and fishing in spite of the increasing frequency of attacks. From the early 1840s onwards, however, the disorder became so debilitating as to render him incapable of pursuing his daily activities for weeks or even months on end. In 1843, when the couple's carriage finally rolled through the gates of Adare Manor a full month after the intended date of departure, Caroline observed with a note of optimism that 'Windham seemed very much better, & though one hand continued painful yet we hoped it was the last lingering of the gout'.[9] In this hope they were to be bitterly disappointed.

The couple broke their journey in Dublin as guests of Thomas and Elizabeth Goold. Within two days of their arrival Windham's gout flared up again, and this time with such violence that he was obliged to see a doctor. Sir Philip Crampton, a surgeon with a successful medical practice in Dublin, duly arrived and put Windham on a new regime of medication, but with little apparent effect. A serious relapse in mid-May prompted Dr Crampton to recommend a change of air, and Caroline at once set off for the nearby seaside resort of Kingstown[10] to seek suitable accommodation. Unable to find a private house with a bedroom on the ground floor, she settled for apartments at a hotel on the northern edge of the town. The fresh air and sunny weather brought momentary relief to Windham's condition. Within a few days of his arrival, he was well enough to move about in a wheelchair lent to him by the doctor. This cheered his wife, even though she was shocked by his 'pallid cheeks & thin form, the active light limbs now so changed, actually distorted by pain & swellings, & the whole appearance one of a person who had gone through much'.[11]

On 8 June the illness took another vicious turn and rendered Windham incapable of moving or feeding himself for several days. As weeks passed without a marked improvement, the couple abandoned their hopes of ever reaching England. In early July they returned to Adare, even though Windham had the gout in both feet and was ill equipped to endure the homeward journey.[12] In August, when he was still ailing, the Dunravens travelled to the popular seaside resort of Kilkee in the hopes that sea air might provide some relief. This remedy at last appeared to work, perhaps as a consequence of a change of diet from meat to fish. By the time the couple returned home in early September, Windham was able to move about quite easily. His wife was overjoyed with his recovery, and both were relieved to be back in Adare. 'I never saw any thing to equal the beauty of the trees, gardens, &c', Caroline rejoiced, 'we enjoyed our return so very much—I ran about every where to look about me, & was delighted to see so much done—and laid down most thankful to be at home again.'[13]

Windham's long illness in 1843 marked the start of a downward spiral in the family's fortunes. The first serious blow came in October 1843, when Windham's only brother Richard died after a long illness in England, aged just 53. Further sorrow followed in 1845, first in May, when Richard's widow Amelia Quin died, and again in December, when Windham's sister and last surviving sibling, Lady Harriot Payne-Gallwey, passed away. With a shudder,

Caroline realised that 'her death leaves Lord Dunraven the survivor of all his family, that generation seems past—what warnings do these events leave on our brains, & show that our turn must soon come'.[14]

Tragedy of a different kind hit the family in April 1844, when a raging fire destroyed a number of outbuildings and several tons of straw in the farmyard at the Manor. The fire was first detected by Caroline when she was returning home from a dinner party late one evening and noticed a strange glow illuminating part of the demesne. She immediately thought of the house, with her husband and young son in it, but on driving up the avenue as fast as the horses would go she found, to her relief, all safe within its walls and that the fire emanated from the top of the nearby hill. As Windham was in bed incapacitated by yet another crippling attack of gout, it was left to Caroline to alert the servants and rush to the village to seek assistance.

Adare Manor, Adare. Drawing of house and demesne by Lady Harriot Payne-Gallwey, 1830s. Courtesy of the Dunraven family.

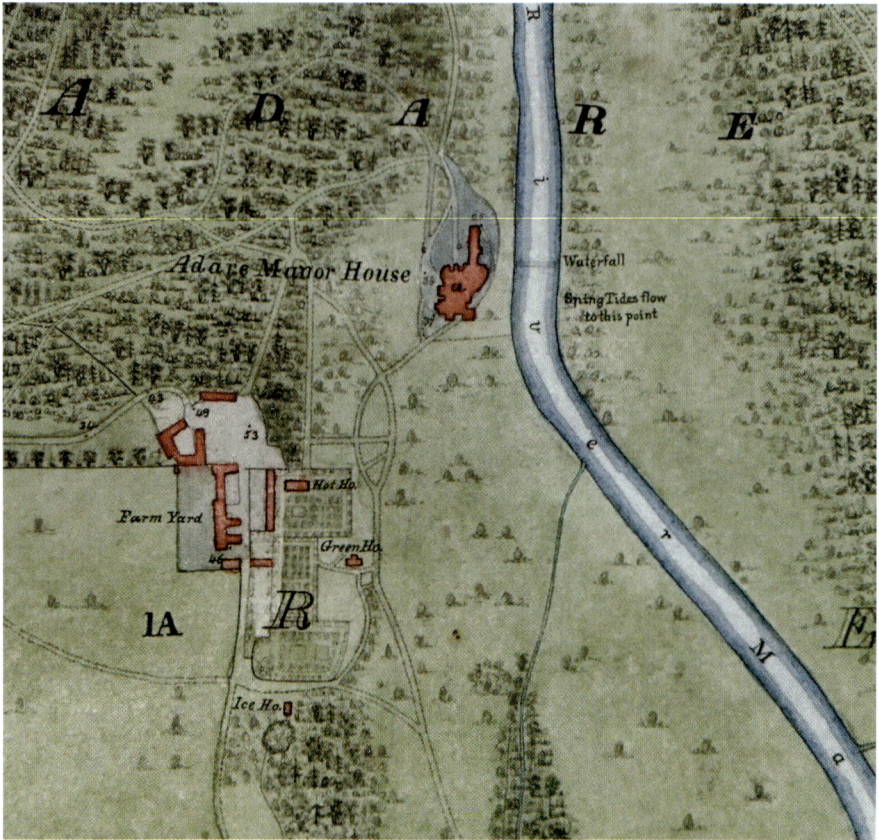

Adare Manor, Adare. Map showing the farm buildings set on fire in 1844. Courtesy of the Dunraven family.

For five hours a heaving crowd of men and women battled the flames. Men quickly organised themselves into four groups to save the surrounding buildings, with the head gardener, Andrew Coghlan, watching over the garden houses, John Doody the stables, Tom Twomey the granaries and James Connolly the houses where the building materials were stored. Women formed chains to supply each group with water and worked so indefatigably that to Caroline they seemed to possess 'almost supernatural strength'. The groups worked steadily and methodically through the night, and by five o'clock in the morning the flames had been subdued and nothing burnt except for some cart houses and a thatched barn with a quantity of straw.[15]

The day after the fire, the Dunravens were shocked to learn from the local police that the fire had been started maliciously. The investigation that followed the incident unearthed a plot by James O'Regan, Mary Burns and Thomas Looney to burn the Dunravens' stables, then lay the blame for the atrocity on ten innocent people and collect a large reward for informing against them.[16] When a few days later a window in the Protestant church accidentally shattered during Sunday service, some newspapers quickly embellished the story by claiming that the perpetrators had also attempted to blow up the church with gunpowder placed under the Dunravens' pew.[17] News of this so-called 'Adare Conspiracy' caused such pandemonium in the village that when the police arrived to make the arrests it was all they could do to protect the perpetrators from a crowd of enraged people ready to tear them apart. Four days after the fire, a delegation of local residents presented the Dunravens with an address demonstrating their respect for and loyalty to the family. Windham considered the attachment shown to them during the upheaval as one of the most gratifying events of his life and reciprocated by publishing an open letter of thanks in the *Freeman's Journal*.

The year 1845 was without a doubt the family's *annus horribilis*. It began ominously on 3 January with the death of William Mortell, their devoted butler of 29 years' service, who had been seized with apoplexy on St Stephen's Day. The shock brought on Windham's gout, and it was not until the middle of March that his condition began to improve. Caroline, too, was ill with a persistent chest infection, which showed little sign of abating. In mid-March the couple received news that their youngest child had been taken dangerously ill with a lung complaint at Bristol while on his way home from Eton. Although far from well themselves, the alarmed parents at once set off for England. To their immense relief, they found young Windham much recovered, albeit very thin and pale. The strain of the journey and anxiety over his son's safety precipitated Windham's gout, however, and left him grievously ill for a fortnight. In early April the two patients were finally well enough to travel to London, and the three months the family spent in the city provided a happy interlude.

On 6 July, only one day after their return to Adare, Windham and Caroline received news from Tervoe that their grandson William Monsell, now four years old, had fallen ill with scarlet fever, an epidemic of which was making its way through County Limerick. Young Windham, who had gone to Tervoe to spend a few days with his sister, was sent back at once by the doctor, and the anxious grandparents were forbidden from hastening to the little patient's side for fear of spreading the infection to their own household. Anna Maria spent every waking moment watching, soothing and praying over the little boy. Initially the child appeared to be on the mend. This, coupled with the fact that the epidemic in Limerick had generally been mild, gave the family in Adare good hopes of his survival. It was not to be. On 11 July they received news of William's death and a request from his father for Caroline to come to the aid of her devastated daughter. Two weeks later, the afflicted parents set off for the Continent for the second time to recover from the loss of a child. Meanwhile, Caroline fell grievously ill in Adare, hovering 'in a constant stupor or dreaminess' for ten days.[18] It was not until the end of August that she was sufficiently recovered to resume her daily routine.

To the personal tragedies that the family faced in 1845 were added the horrors which began to unfold in September of that year, when news of disease in the country's potato crop was first reported. Heavy rains in early November did much to worsen the damage, leaving 'all hearts quaking about the Potatoes'.[19] Although the Dunravens inspected the crops of some of their tenant farmers and found them better than expected, the relief was temporary. By early February 1846, typhus brought on by starvation was running rampant. The Dunravens at once made the decision to remain in Ireland for the entire year with a view to 'spending all our money here to assist our own poor as much as possible'.[20] Windham's gout abated sufficiently to enable him to chair meetings of various relief committees, the purpose of which was to provide employment opportunities for those in need, while his wife and daughter visited the sick and the poor, handing out food, coal and clothes and providing the women of the village with flax and wool for spinning and weaving to help them generate much-needed income. As the year progressed and the need for food became more pressing, the Dunravens set up a soup kitchen in Adare and paid for a consignment of half a ton of Indian meal, which they distributed in the village during the winter of 1846–7.

Not everyone appreciated their efforts, however: in April 1846 the *Morning Chronicle* published an exaggerated account of the scale of distress in Adare, which it blamed squarely on the Dunravens. The article derided Caroline's efforts to provide flax for spinning for the women of the village and attacked Windham for building 'a castle in the old style, which will rival in magnificence nearly any seat of any of our English nobility', while the labourers in his employment were paid a pittance, forcing them to exist in untold misery.[21] The article greatly embittered Caroline, who felt 'deeply pained and wounded that after having passed more than 30 years here, & spending a large income every day among the poor here, that they should have appeared so ungrateful'. It was cold comfort for her to learn that the author of the article had promised to remunerate the people he interviewed 'according to the emergency of their wants & … it encouraged the people to conceal what they received from us, in order to make their case as pitiable as possible'.[22]

The harshness of the winter of 1846–7 killed thousands, and by now even relatively prosperous towns were beginning to struggle with the numbers of the starving pouring in from rural areas. The British government, reluctant to

Rural scene. Watercolour by Augusta Goold, *c.* 1830s. Courtesy of the Dunraven family.

create a system of habitual dependency, began to withdraw its support, insisting that landlords should share in the burden and take greater responsibility for the problem. Many, like the Dunravens, did so by reducing or cancelling rents, providing employment schemes and distributing food, but equally many remained disinterested or even used the tragedy as an opportunity to evict unwanted tenants. The *laissez-faire* nature of Victorian economics meant that although other food crops like wheat and turnips were unaffected they would not be directed to the hungry but continued to be exported out of the country. Even consignments of American maize ordered by Prime Minister Sir Robert Peel could not be handed out for free, as this would interfere negatively with the markets. Instead, it was sold or offered to the poor in exchange for employment through a scheme of public works. These works frequently consisted of road-building and other forms of hard and often pointless labour for which the starving were ill fitted, besides which the scheme was rolled out so slowly that men desperate for sustenance began to resort to riots and violence. In May 1847 a band of distressed men attacked several houses in Adare in search of food and weapons, then proceeded to the Earl of Dunraven's demesne, where they held a meeting and threatened to kill and plunder if not given employment. A company of the 59th Regiment of Foot from Limerick city was billeted in Adare for several months to contain this and other famine riots, many of which were directed at landlords and their agents.[23] The desperate situation weighed heavily on Caroline, who felt that 'the wants of the people seem so far beyond what any one individual could do for them that really the reflexion is a sad one that individual Charity is really but a drop of water in the Ocean & that for one that is really relieved you hear of Dozens equally in want that you cannot relieve … & beyond the feel that a sacred duty is to be fulfilled by administering to their relief, & therefore employing our talents according to the will of Him who Granted them to us, one has no other stimulant to exertion'.[24]

By 1849, one and a half million people had emigrated and 800,000 had died from starvation, typhus, dysentery or cholera. Countless priests and doctors who had treated the dying were among the victims. In Adare alone, four medical practitioners died from famine fever in 1849, among them a much-liked dispensary doctor, George McKay.[25] The dramatic reduction in population size was poignantly brought home to the Dunravens in October 1849, when they travelled from Adare to Rathkeale to pay visits in the neighbourhood. It being fair day in both towns, 'we … thought the roads would be crowded—but such is the depressed state of the country that neither at Adare Fair or Rathkeale did we meet pigs or any thing to indicate any stir or bustle'.[26]

The Famine also sounded the death-knell for many Irish estates, whose owners bankrupted themselves in a desperate attempt to help the needy. What saved the Dunravens was the financial support from Wales, but even this was pushed to the limit. 'I hope every thing is going on better in Glamorganshire than here for money is more difficult to get than ever', Caroline wrote in November 1849 to John Randall, agent of the family's Welsh estates; 'all the landed proprietors seem *smashed* one after another—no one can tell where it is to end. It is very sad. Lord Dunraven is thank God well & in good spirits, his prudence tells more for we are not *smashed*—but every shilling seems of consequence.'[27]

❖ ❖ ❖

In the event, and notwithstanding the naysayers, the determination of the Dunraven family to carry on with the building works at the Manor provided a lifeline for the local populace during the Famine years, as did the practice established by Caroline as early as 1823 of providing local women with spinning-wheels, flax and wool.[28] The house continued to employ great numbers of men as masons, carvers, carpenters and bricklayers, while local women were trained to execute a variety of ornamental fabrics from patterns supplied by Thomas Willement, which were used to upholster the furniture made for the gallery.[29] Work on the house between 1843 and 1849, while fitful and carried out in a piecemeal fashion without a fixed plan, progressed on three fronts—furnishing the gallery, completing the interior of the great hall and proceeding with the construction of the Cottingham-designed south front. As Windham by now was almost perpetually ill with gout and so crippled by it as to find the use of his hands and feet difficult, he relied increasingly on his wife and eldest son for assistance when dealing with builders. The preparation of drawings for carvers fell almost entirely on Caroline and Thomas Connolly, the stonemason, while Edwin assumed an occasional supervisory role. Edwin's prolonged absences in Wales and England limited his usefulness, however, and resulted primarily in a string of frustrated letters in which he beseeched his parents to 'tell me more about the building, as for what is really doing, & at what rate it proceeds'.[30]

By the mid-1840s the gallery had neared completion and was ready for furnishing. The second pair of portraits by Thomas Phillips were put in place, mounted together in a single gilt frame suspended over the large central fireplace on the north wall. Many more paintings were hung on the gallery walls, bookcases were filled with books, and sofas and chairs arranged in tasteful little islands along the length of the room. In September 1844 the gallery was ready to receive morning visitors for the first time, and a great many guests arrived to admire the handsome room.

Beyond the gallery, the Manor continued to change shape during this time. By now, so much of the old Georgian house had been gutted that living arrangements within the building became problematic. Apart from Windham and Caroline's private quarters in the gallery wing, there was scarcely a bedroom in the house, and even Edwin and his family were forced to forgo their usual Christmas celebrations at Adare Manor in 1843, as there was simply nowhere in the house to accommodate them. In September 1844 the gallery was converted into a temporary dining room to allow the family to entertain their guests while the old dining room was being remodelled.[31] The arrangement proved highly successful and large-scale Sunday lunches after church service became part and parcel of life at Adare Manor. The gallery, however, was too large and too awkwardly situated to be used as a permanent dining room. This problem was solved when Caroline's sitting room beneath the gallery, conveniently close to the kitchen, was turned into a dining area. The sitting room furniture was moved into the old saloon, now transformed into a spacious library, and at long last 'we all felt as if we had room to move & breathe'.[32] New bedrooms were also nearing completion, and much of October 1847 was spent in fitting them up for the first guests.

In March 1848 the Dunravens made their only visit to England during the Famine years. Much of it was dedicated to buying furniture and other goods for the Manor. Substantial purchasing was done at Messrs Shoolbred & Company on Tottenham Court Road, one of the first great department stores in London, which incorporated a haberdashery, a carpet warehouse and a large stock of textiles, including wool, silk and linen. Here Windham and Caroline spent two long days selecting rugs, curtains and other soft furnishings for the house, including carpets for the gallery as the finishing touch.[33] When the large shipment of furniture and textiles arrived a few months later, the family had a great job unpacking the boxes and putting up the fittings. The new servants' hall in the basement below the great hall was used for the first time to celebrate young Windham's twentieth birthday, with all the local schoolchildren invited to the house for entertainment. 'The new hall is a beautiful room for Music', Caroline noted with satisfaction, '& we sung the Grace & also the God Save the Queen with great effect—the numerous little voices returning through the arches of that beautiful room had a lovely effect & the whole scene was to me most interesting.'[34]

The refurbishing of the dining room was completed in September 1849. The family spent an eventful day 'arranging furniture &c preparatory to moving into the new dining room or rather the old dining room made larger—we enjoyed ourselves there very much, & … had a very cozy dinner there for the first time for eight years'.[35] Stemming from the slow progress of construction works, one of the elements that characterised life in the ever-changing building was the family's eagerness and determination to use new parts of the house as soon as it was safe to do so, whether completed or not. Furniture was moved about and pictures and curtains hung to create impromptu spaces for entertainment, and the ongoing building works and half-finished masonry with which guests were surrounded undoubtedly provided an amusing topic of conversation for many social gatherings. When young Windham was appointed as a cornet in the 13th Light Dragoons, the family celebrated the occasion with a party for 82 guests, who 'sat down to dinner in the dear old dining room where we had not dined for many years—it was in an unfinished state but still held us very comfortably'.[36] After a cheerful meal, the equally unfinished great hall was lit up for dancing, which continued until half past one in the morning. The colonnade adjoining the dining room to the south was also in regular use as a place for the local children to gather for Sunday school.[37]

In many respects, the gradual dismantling of the old house was an affecting experience. It was not only walls of stone and mortar but also lives lived and memories created within those walls that slowly crumbled away, never to be captured again. A poignant farewell was bidden by Caroline and her daughter in March 1846, on what would have been the fifth birthday of Anna Maria's second son. The two women 'paid a visit to the room in which her darling had been born & it was a most pleasing though sad remembrance of past days, we took our last look of that room, which was the only one left of the old house. What sad & happy associations it recalled particularly to my dear child—we lingered there as with an old friend & returned to the world again with softened but relieved feeling.'[38]

◆   ◆   ◆

As the interior of the new house took shape, the Dunravens turned to yet another architect to provide designs for fireplaces, ceramic tiles, wallpaper and other interior details. The man of choice was Augustus Welby Northmore Pugin, who had inherited a profound love of medieval architecture from his French father, Auguste Charles Pugin, an architectural draughtsman for John Nash

Adare Manor, Adare. Watercolour of the gallery by Louisa Payne-Gallwey, *c.* 1850.
Courtesy of Lavinia Graham-Vivian.

and illustrator of numerous books on Gothic design. From early childhood, Pugin spent much of his life observing and drawing buildings both on the Continent and in Britain. In 1836 he published a controversial manifesto, *Contrasts*, in which he argued that architecture reflected the state of society. He scorned the pretentious Neo-Classical Regency style by contrasting it with beautiful examples of medieval architecture. A Catholic convert, Pugin went as far as to claim that only a Roman Catholic society could produce a truly Gothic style of architecture. In another manifesto, *The True Principles of Pointed or Christian Architecture* (1841), he outlined his two cornerstones of design: that 'there should be no features about a building which are not necessary for convenience, construction, or propriety'; and that 'all ornament should consist of enrichment of the essential construction of the building'.[39]

In the early part of his career, Pugin worked for established architects such as James Gillespie Graham and Charles Barry to create Gothic interior decoration and furnishings for their buildings. The decorative arts always remained close to his heart. When he began his career as an independent architect in 1837, he worked closely with notable manufacturers to give life to his decorative designs—initially with stained-glass artists Thomas Willement and William Warrington, and later with John Hardman the Younger of Birmingham for metalwork and stained glass, Herbert Minton for ceramic tiles and John Gregory Crace for decorative painting, wallpapers and furniture. His principal builder was George Myers, who executed Pugin's most important commissions.

Pugin's Catholicism was a deterrent to some but it also gained him a number of important patrons, most notably John Talbot, sixteenth Earl of Shrewsbury, a wealthy Catholic landowner, who allowed Pugin free expression of his aesthetic views, first with the interior of Alton Towers and later with the construction of the Roman Catholic church of St Giles in Cheadle. As Pugin's reputation grew, so did his workload. Throughout the early 1840s he was inundated with commissions for ecclesiastical buildings, particularly from Ireland, where the passing of the Catholic Emancipation Act of 1829 opened the way to greater religious tolerance, manifested in an abundance of church construction across the country. He also contributed to the design of the Palace of Westminster in London. As a young draughtsman, Pugin had drawn Charles Barry's winning entry for the building's design competition in the autumn of 1835, and some nine years into construction Barry turned to Pugin for assistance with interior fittings and exterior details. The interior of the House of Lords, which opened in 1847, was widely admired, and Pugin's Elizabeth Tower, better known as Big Ben, eventually became the city's most iconic landmark. Such was the influence of the joint efforts of Barry and Pugin on the Houses of Parliament that its construction effectively led to Gothic Revival becoming the mainstream national style.[40]

Pugin also did much to popularise the style and philosophy of Gothic Revivalism. Edwin was an impassioned follower of Pugin's architectural doctrines. On a visit to Munich in the autumn of 1847, he expressed disappointment in the city because 'there is no true taste for gothic: they have only built one church in that style … It is quite a different effect & one which is at variance with true gothic principles.'[41] It was not only Pugin's architectural viewpoints but also his Catholic faith that resonated with the future earl. In fact, Edwin's growing interest in Catholicism worried his mother. Recording with some alarm that her son 'has been surrounded by false teachers', she spent anxious nights praying 'that he may escape the errors of Romanism to which creed he seems much disposed'.[42]

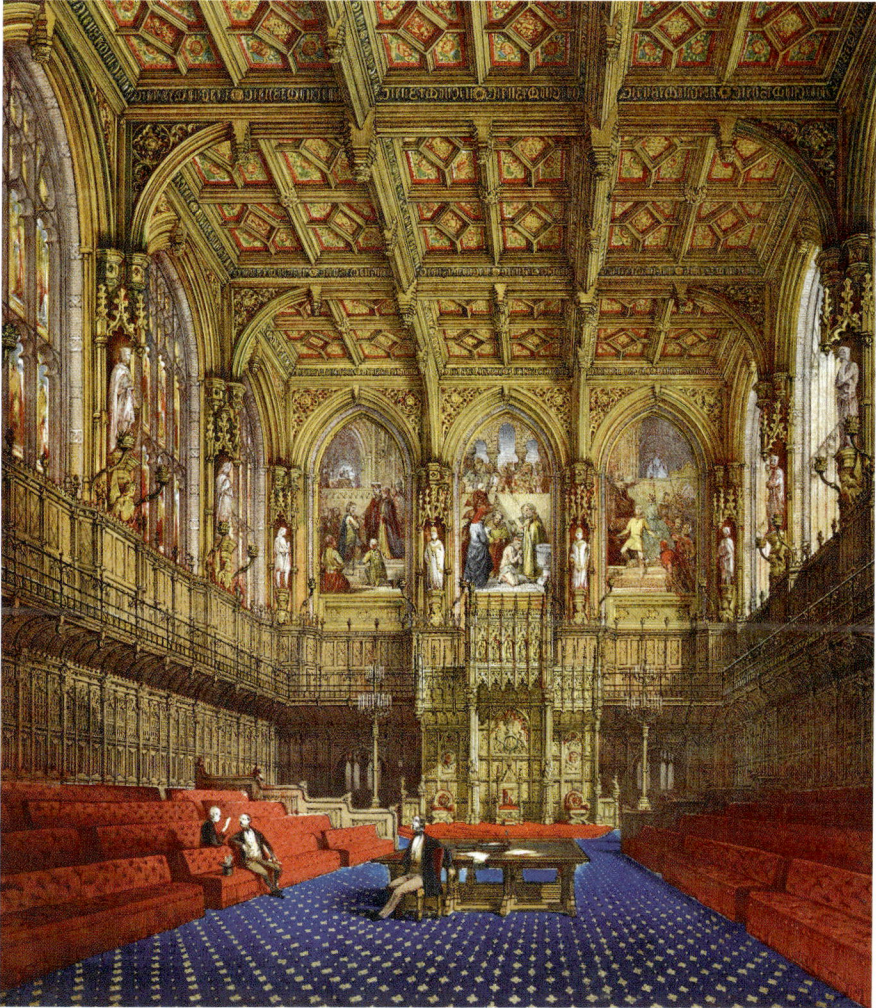

House of Lords, Houses of Parliament, Palace of Westminster, London. Watercolour of the chamber looking to the Royal Throne, designed by Sir Charles Barry and A. W. N. Pugin. RIBA Collections.

Adare Manor, Adare. Proposal for a chimney-piece to drawing room by A. W. N. Pugin, 1846. Courtesy of the Dunraven family.

Edwin's first meeting with Pugin most likely took place in April 1845, when he and William Monsell travelled to England as guests of Ambrose Phillipps of Grace Dieu Manor in Leicestershire, a wealthy landowner and, as a Catholic convert, one of the leading lights of Catholic revival in England.[43] On their meeting, the rapport between Edwin and his host was immediate, while Phillipps went so far as to regard the day that commenced their friendship 'as one of the happiest and most fortunate of my life'.[44] Pugin was a personal friend of Phillipps and also his architect, having enlarged a chapel on the grounds of Grace Dieu in 1839 and built another about a mile from the house three years later. At around the time of Edwin's visit, Pugin was preparing plans for the addition of an east wing and stable court gateway for Phillipps. Edwin's interest in Pugin was evident in his and William's itinerary, which included tours of local country houses and Catholic churches, many of which bore Pugin's mark. 'I am glad you liked Alton', Phillipps noted with satisfaction, 'and I am sure Cheadle Church must have pleased you, it is certainly Pugin's best work and it will be a real ornament to England worthy of comparison with any even of the Old Parochial Churches.'[45]

Within three months of his visit to Grace Dieu, Edwin was making arrangements to bring Pugin to Adare to provide designs for the library, the dining room, the great hall and the terrace adjacent to the house. Pugin at the time was preparing his first plans for the expansion of St Patrick's Roman Catholic College in Maynooth, Co. Dublin, towards which the British government had provided a grant of £30,000. He was scheduled to visit Ireland later in the year, but bringing him to Adare proved more difficult than Edwin had anticipated. During his career, Pugin produced thousands upon thousands of designs and was constantly on the move. Between May and October of 1845 alone, when the Dunravens were hoping to receive him in Adare, he not only drew plans for Grace Dieu Manor and St Patrick's College, but also produced designs for the House of Lords, created designs for three churches, set up his own glassworks and spent three weeks on a tour of Germany to study architecture.[46] Edwin could barely keep up with this mercurial schedule. Hopes of a meeting in the summer were dashed when Pugin 'wrote to say he could not come before the end of August, or after the end of September'.[47] Edwin made two further attempts to bring the architect to Adare before the year's end, but on both occasions had only disappointment to offer his parents. 'It is provoking about Pugin, but how can it be helped. He would not of course break up all his arrangements to go to Adare. I hope he will move early in the spring.'[48]

In the spring of 1846, the prospects of having Pugin in Adare improved when he was once more beckoned to Ireland by the dean of St Patrick's College. Pugin had distanced himself from the project when his initial proposals for the seminary were rejected by the Board of Works as too expensive. The dean, anxious to get the building works under way, was determined to entice him back with the promise that 'We have £30,000; let us begin with that sum, and when exhausted, Providence will not be wanting'.[49] Separate arrangements were made for Edwin to accompany him to Ireland in mid-April, but on the appointed day the elusive architect failed to turn up.[50] A new date was scheduled for the end of the month. As in a comedy of errors, timing went astray again, and on this occasion the entire household at Adare Manor was thrown into chaos when Pugin appeared unexpectedly on their doorstep without Edwin. However, 'after a few hours had elapsed we all understood each other better & found him very clever & agreeable'. Edwin made his way to Adare the following day and 'he & Mr Pugin & Lord Dunraven had great talks and planning about the building'. Later in the afternoon, Pugin was taken to Tervoe to meet William and Anna Maria Monsell, who commissioned from him a memorial cross to be placed on the grave of their son. After another night in Adare, Pugin departed on the morning of 30 April.[51]

Unlike Cottingham, who kept the Dunravens waiting for months—even years—for proposals, Pugin wasted no time in this regard. The first drawings for the great hall, library and dining room arrived in Adare with due haste just three weeks after his visit. His proposals for the hall included designs for the staircase, patterns for ceiling panels and carved wooden panels for the walls and the minstrel's gallery, designs for a large fireplace and patterns for stained-glass windows and fireplace grate, tiles and firedogs. In addition to drawings, Pugin produced scale models of several decorative features and strongly advised Windham to 'have a *model made of the staircase* in wood about 1" to a foot', because 'it will repay the expense by the ensued facility the joiners will have in executing the real work after they have done it'.[52]

The proposals for the hall were reviewed in detail by the Dunravens but not immediately acted upon. His parents' dithering quickly got on Edwin's nerves.

'You ask me what Pugin is about?', he wrote to his mother from London with barely contained irritation in June 1846. 'He called yesterday & asked me a more natural question what you were about! You have every drawing for the Hall so that there is nothing to do but make the men work as fast as they will … You have more work cut out than your men will do in a year I should think, therefore Pugin can do no more at present.'[53] As summer turned to autumn and work in the hall remained at a standstill, Edwin's frustration flared up once again. 'I cannot at all see why the Hall ceiling cannot be begun without Pugin's presence; the working drawings are at Adare are they not?, & what more can be wanted.' Aware of the curt tone of his letter, he hastened to assure his mother that 'No one … could wish to see the building expedited more than I do, for your sake chiefly: there is no effort or sacrifice I would not make for that purpose, any thing to contribute to your happiness is dear to me & you have been long enough in the uncomfortable state'.[54] In the end, work on the interior decoration of the great hall did not get under way until January 1848, by which time Edwin had resigned himself to never seeing the room completed. 'I am so very glad the Hall is being gone on with', he commented dryly, 'this is a great point, & will be very delightful next winter: if really finished.'[55]

Drawings and estimates for fitting out the library and dining room were completed in January 1847. They included designs for fireplaces, bookcases, wood panelling for walls and ceilings, an ornamental screen and stained-glass windows for the dining room, and patterns for tiles for laying in the open colonnade which adjoined the dining room. Pugin's estimate for the work was £2,689 for the two rooms combined—'a great deal of money', he acknowledged, 'but I think the estimate very fair & reasonable for the quantity & quality of the work to be done'.[56] Throughout his involvement in Adare, Pugin was aware of the mounting cost and made various suggestions as to how this could be kept down. When he designed the hinges for the hall doors, he sent the full-sized drawings to Adare and advised Windham to give them to one of the local blacksmiths instead of having the hinges made in England and sent to Adare.[57] Conversely, when it came to the library and dining room fittings, he proposed to execute them in England and have them sent over ready for being fixed, because 'if the work was carried on under my own eye, the expense would not be so great as for supplying models & certain joinings'.[58] Whether it was the cost or the detail of Pugin's designs, the Dunravens were not overly enthusiastic about his proposals for the dining room. Nevertheless, the architect remained hopeful 'of seeing the design I have made for your Lordship executed yet. I can assure you that the dining room would not be surpassed by any modern work. I feel assured you would have it done if you could foresee the effect that would be produced.'[59] Ultimately, however, little of his proposal was executed.

The Dunravens entertained hopes of a second visit by Pugin to Adare in 1846, but the architect's immense workload continued to present a problem. 'I should not think of going to Killarney without taking Adare on my way,' Pugin assured his clients, 'but I do not think that I can go there for the present. I have been sent for suddenly to Dublin relative to the Maynooth affair but must return as soon as possible on account of the House of Lords fittings which are pressing forward with all possible speed.'[60] Another attempt to invite Pugin to Adare was made in 1847 but again without success. Instead, Windham, Edwin and William Monsell visited him at his home in Ramsgate while in London in May 1848.[61]

In the end, Edwin's admiration for Pugin was not unequivocally shared by his parents. Although reasons for this remain obscure, dissatisfaction with delays is unlikely to have played a role, even though Edwin appeared to think so. 'I could not avoid a smile at your remark about Pugin', Edwin wrote to his mother in September 1846, 'of all men on earth to accuse of not working: as if any man of his age has worked as hard, & as successfully. I cannot think that he is to blame for delays'.[62] Pugin's proposals may have been at odds with Windham's own ideas or his personal and well-defined taste, which he had carefully cultivated over two decades. It may also be that Windham's reticence stemmed not from any personal reservation towards the architect but from financial constraints caused by efforts to ameliorate the effects of the Famine. Windham was a man of principle and one of his leading tenets was never to spend money he didn't have. Pugin's ideas may well have appealed to him, but budgetary constraints obliged him to postpone their completion. In the event, few of Pugin's proposals except for the interior of the great hall were executed, and most of that not until the 1850s, when Edwin succeeded his father.

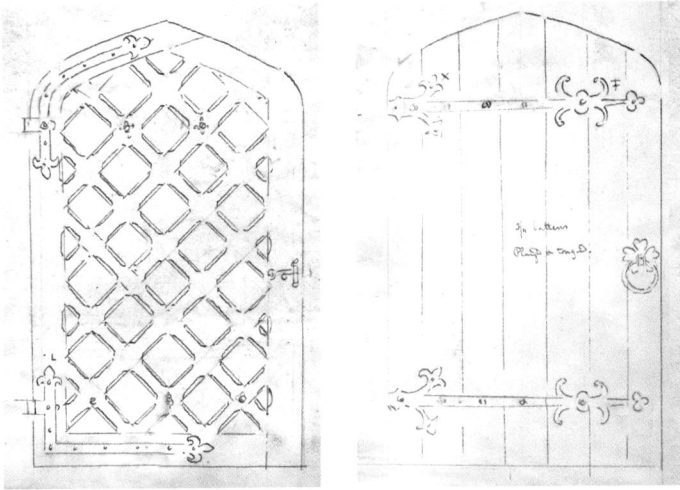

Adare Manor, Adare. Design (inside and outside) of the entrance hall door by A. W. N. Pugin, 1846. Courtesy of the Dunraven family.

There was, however, one feature that Pugin designed for the manor that was executed without hesitation. This was a panelled case for a magnificent organ built into the south-western corner of the great hall and one of the most striking features of the house. The old Adare House also contained an organ in its drawing room, but this is likely to have been a small portable chest or box instrument. The idea that such a musical apparatus would form part of the fabric of the building was first mooted by Edwin in the early 1830s following a series of visits to Lissadell, Co. Sligo, where a Gothic chamber organ in the music room had caught his interest. Designed by the Hull Company of Dublin in 1812, the instrument, pumped by bellows situated in the basement, was moved from the original family home and incorporated into the new house during construction. Edwin's suggestion appealed to his parents—particularly his mother, with her strong interest in music—and by 1833 the prospect of having one specially constructed for the house was a regular topic of conversation.

The gallery was initially considered to be the most suitable room to house the instrument. Its precise location, however, was hotly debated. Windham and Caroline preferred to have it on the long side of the room, where they felt it would be better heard, while Edwin wished to see it placed at the end, where it would look more decorative. He also wanted to proceed with the purchase at once.[63] His father, however, was less enthusiastic, as the gallery remained unfinished. 'It would not be prudent to buy an Organ now', he insisted. 'We should not know where to keep it; we have no fit place to put it in; It is liable to damage—also before we could use it, some improvement may chance to be made in such Instruments.'[64] His argument won the day and the matter was temporarily dropped.

The idea was resurrected in 1844. By then the great hall provided the best location for the organ, since Cottingham's decision to enlarge the room gave scope for creating an instrument of substantial proportions. The task of assembling it was given to the famous Dublin organ-builder William Telford, who arrived in Adare in early October to take measurements of the great hall. As with all building activities in Adare, the progress of work was painfully slow. A year after his initial visit, Telford notified Edwin that he expected the instrument to be ready by September.[65] This estimate, however, proved to be wildly optimistic, and it was not until the very end of 1848 that the organ finally neared completion. In December of that year, Edwin travelled to Dublin to see the instrument. 'The great pedal pipes look grand', he reported to his parents. 'I am only sorry they will not be visible, but they must be stowed away in the background. The bright tin pipes in the front have a very good effect.'[66]

The instrument finally arrived in Adare in late January 1849, followed three days later by its builder to assist with the assembly. The organ was placed on a platform over two small arches opposite the entrance, framed by the panelled case designed by Pugin. Assembling and fine-tuning the instrument took several weeks and attracted many curious onlookers, including Lady de Vere, who came from Curragh Chase and spent an entire day lying on a sofa in the hall listening to the proceedings. The instrument also held centre stage during the celebrations of the eighth birthday of Edwin's son Windham Thomas in February. The party was held in the gallery but, to Caroline's delight, 'Mr Telford arranged part of the Organ so that we could hear its beautiful sounds. Though not near completed we enjoyed it as it came pealing through the slide in the Gallery door & were delighted that the first time it was played on here was on Windham's birthday, as it marked the time, & was an event we had long looked forward to.'[67]

Adare Manor, Adare. Nut and bolt flange, designed by A. W. N. Pugin, 1846. Courtesy of the Dunraven family.

Adare Manor, Adare. Detail of A. W. N. Pugin's design for the overmantel of the dining room fireplace, 1846. Courtesy of the Dunraven family.

Adare Manor, Adare. Sketch for the dining room ceiling plasterwork by A. W. N. Pugin, 1846. Courtesy of the Dunraven family.

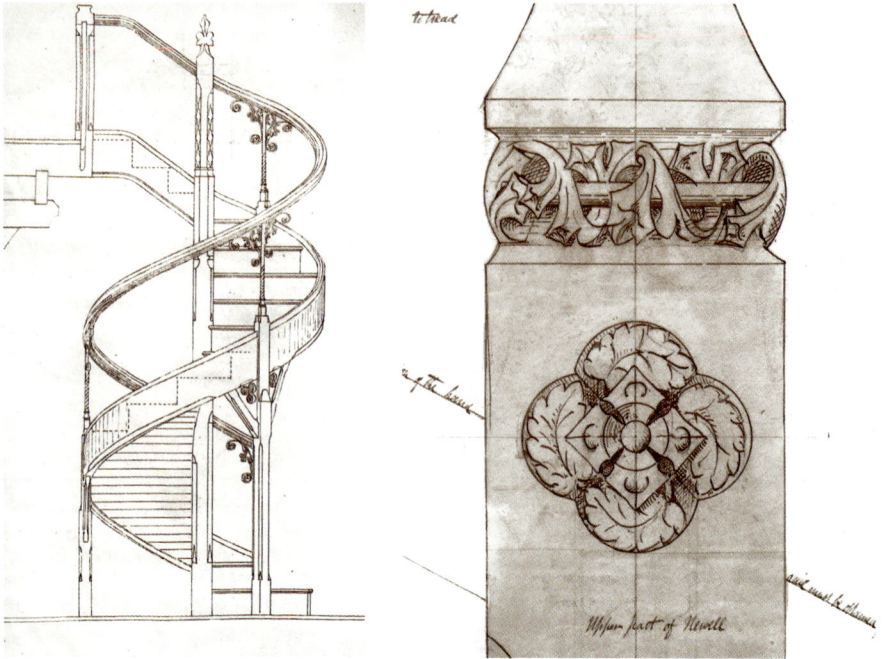

Adare Manor, Adare. *Above left:* Design of staircase to the organ gallery by P. C. Hardwick, early 1850s. Courtesy of the Dunraven family. *Above right:* Details of woodwork to circular staircase to organ gallery by P. C. Hardwick, early 1850s. *Below:* Adare Manor, Adare. Details of metalwork to circular staircase of organ gallery by P. C. Hardwick, December 1852. Courtesy of the Dunraven family.

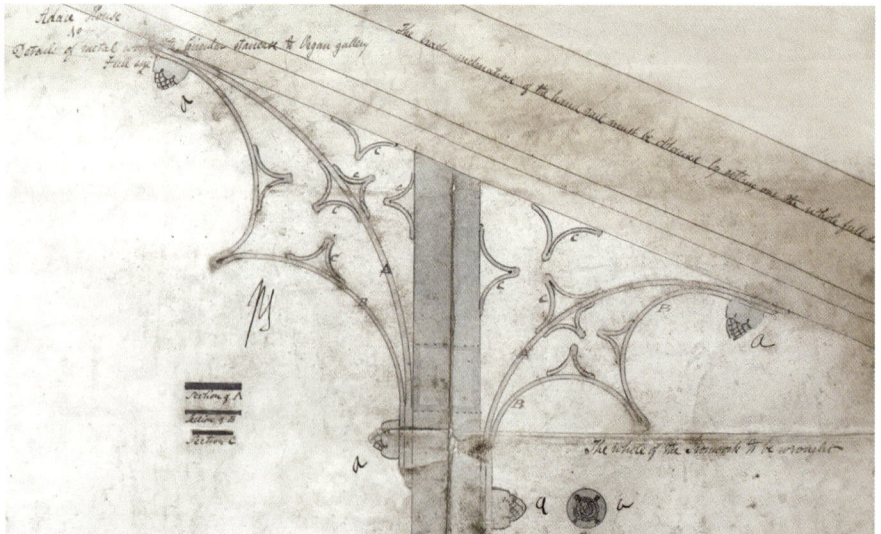

When William Telford finally departed, Caroline felt less sure of her skills and sought regular lessons from George Frederick Handel Rogers, the vicar choral of Limerick. To share the organ with a wider audience, the Dunravens planned to hold a musical festival at Adare Manor in March 1849. A great deal of practising followed but, to Caroline's disappointment, her husband, who had been complaining of gout since Christmas, became so ill that a decision was made first to postpone the festival until after Easter and then to abandon it altogether, as Windham was showing no signs of improvement.

In 1851, when Edwin took over the building works from his father, he decided to take down the original instrument and replace it with an even larger one. This was partly because the organ was frequently out of order and needed regular repairs, and partly as a result of the commencement of the construction of the Pugin-designed staircase, which changed the internal proportions of the great hall and, in Edwin's view, risked dwarfing the organ.[68] Edwin's decision also coincided with new developments in organ-building technology, which he explored at the Great Exhibition of 1851. Among the several large organs on display was one built by Henry Willis, the music of which could be heard above the mêlée of the Crystal Palace. The instrument revolutionised the art of organ-building. It incorporated a newly invented Barker lever, a pneumatic system which enabled the organist to produce sound by a light touch of the keys. Prior to its application, the action of each key required several pounds' worth of pressure, which rapidly exhausted even the strongest of players. Enthused by what he had seen, Edwin at once determined to redesign the organ at Adare to incorporate the Barker lever.[69]

The old instrument was taken down in July 1851, and the assembly of the new one, again built by Telford, commenced in February 1852. When completed, it was one of the largest chamber organs in the United Kingdom, consisting of 2,353 pipes and 44 stops, many of which had been procured by Edwin in Paris from the celebrated organ-builder Aristide Cavaillé-Coll.[70] The completion of this behemoth was not without its difficulties. First, the maker of the metal pipes, Mr Crombie, who had travelled from Dublin to work on the instrument, suddenly ran away without offering a word of explanation. 'We were all rather alarmed', Edwin later told his mother, 'as he had been in very low spirits; however on the following Saturday he turned up in Dublin, having walked the whole way. This will cause 10 days additional delay, but no additional expense.'[71] Installing the stops and finding the right combinations took months of trial and error, as did tuning the instrument. 'I wish to make the organ as complete as I can for Augusta', was Edwin's reasoning in the face of increasing delays.[72] It was not until September 1855 that he could write that the 'organ is nearly finished, & will be exquisite'.[73]

The organs, old and new, were a focal point of life in Adare Manor, where their magnificent sound accompanied every family celebration. Writing to his mother in November 1849, Edwin hoped that 'we shall all live to see the day when you will play a duet on it, with your grandchildren. Fancy Windham & you playing a duet the day he comes of age. But one ought not perhaps to look so far forward.'[74] Regrettably, the next occasion to be marked in Adare Manor was not a birthday but a funeral.

Adare Manor, Adare. The great hall and the Telford organ. From *Memorials of Adare Manor* (1865). Courtesy of Special Collections and Archives, Glucksman Library, University of Limerick.

Deaths and Duties

B y 1850 Windham's fire was spent. Years of escalating illness had crippled his body, and the strain of steering his family and tenants through the terrible years of the Famine had exhausted his energy. Although not bankrupt, the family's finances were stretched to the limit, and building works at Adare had all but ground to a halt, leaving the south front only half-completed. The unfinished state of the manor house was a source of concern to Edwin, who wrote to his father on the subject in May 1850. 'I have never heard what you have done about the building. I almost dread hearing that you have deferred doing any thing towards completing the South Front. I assure you I often think of this. I have a great desire that you should do it. I have always indulged in the idea that at all events Adare would be an exception to the general rule about Irish houses in matters that nothing can be properly finished, or if finished, he who does it is ruined. I hope you will think over the matter & make an effort to commence. Whether done in one, two, or three years makes but little difference so that a beginning be made, & that it may not be said afterwards, oh even Lord Dunraven could not complete his house, which he took so many years about: let it rather be: "he alone built his House & lived in it however he took so many years about it".'[1]

Windham was touched by his son's concern over the fate of the manor and reassured him of his determination to see the project through, but, as ever, on his own terms. 'I hope to take down the old House', he wrote back to Edwin, '& propose for going on, but I will never do anything imprudent for the sake of building a House. I early in life saw through the sophistry by which others supported and have since grievously suffered for that folly. Where are Lord Gort & Lord Kingston now, with their fine Houses. What would the Dunraven Estate have become but for me, & your Mother's inimitable self denial.'[2] True to his word, Windham gave the order for the demolition of the last remains of the old house in July 1850.[3] It would be his last contribution to the building.

Windham's final months were spent in London, where he attended to his parliamentary duties for the first time since the start of the Famine, and at Dunraven Castle, where he and his wife had not been for many years. The welcome they received there from their Welsh tenants and neighbours was so genial that they felt almost sorry to return to Ireland. In late July, three weeks after his return to Adare, Windham complained of a choking sensation in his throat. Two local doctors, John Worrall and William Griffin, spent several days at his bedside but could do little to alleviate his discomfort. Caroline, by now 'more alarmed than I liked to own to myself', sent an urgent message to Dublin to seek the assistance of Sir Philip Crampton, who at once travelled to Adare.[4] For several days, prayers for Windham's recovery were offered in the Protestant and Catholic churches, but his disorder gained ground. In early August a second surgeon, the pioneering Dr William Stokes of the Meath Hospital, travelled from Dublin to examine Windham and ordered a tracheotomy to be performed. The operation was carried out by Dr Robert Gelston from Limerick, who by inserting a silver tube into Windham's airway instantly relieved his difficulty of breathing. Grateful for this brief respite, Windham, now unable to speak, signalled for pen and paper and wrote down his last words: 'I want to sleep *really* and go to bed, and be *alive* and safe next morning'.[5] He died peacefully and 'in so blessed a state of mind that death seemed to have no sting' on the morning of 6 August. Caroline, numbed by the loss of her husband of 40 years, sought comfort from Windham's final moments. 'Oh the last time I ever saw him alive, his smile was so lovely that I have it always before me when alone, the remembrance of it is the one great balm of my life.'[6]

Portrait of Windham in his later years, c. 1840s. Courtesy of the Dunraven family.

Windham's body lay in repose at Adare Manor for three days, in a coffin of three cases: the inner, in which his body was placed, was made of Spanish mahogany and upholstered with white satin; the middle was made of lead; and the outer was of Irish oak, covered with black silk velvet and decorated with a gilt breastplate on which the Dunraven arms were emblazoned. More than 4,000 people, from labourers to peers, gathered to witness the funeral. When the moment came to convey the coffin to the Augustinian church, Windham's tenants asked to be allowed to carry it on their shoulders. A cortège of 1,600 men in black scarves and hatbands followed the bearers, while thousands of others thronged the road and surrounded the church to catch a glimpse of Windham's final journey.[7] As upper-class women did not generally attend funerals, Caroline hid in her bedroom and listened to the commotion outside as 'my darling one was carried away to the resting place he had prepared in the Mausoleum, and I was indeed a widow!'[8]

Adare Manor, Adare. Watercolour by Louisa Payne-Gallwey, 1837. Courtesy of the Dunraven family.

Windham was a popular landlord and his passing was regretted well beyond his immediate family circle. His obituaries were quick to recognise the building of Adare Manor as his most enduring legacy and unanimously praised his beautiful mansion as 'one of the most striking monuments of architectural taste in this country'.[9] Windham did not forget those who had helped him in its construction. In his will, he bequeathed a year's wages to those of his domestic servants who at the time of his death had been living with him for four years or more, and left legacies of £50 to James Connolly, the foreman of masons employed in Adare, and to Maurice Guerin, foreman of carpenters.[10]

❖   ❖   ❖

Windham's death brought significant changes to the family dynamics, with his eldest son Edwin succeeding to the estates and title as the third Earl of Dunraven. As personalities, the two men could hardly have been more different. While Windham was a singularly practical man possessed of sharp business instincts and limited interest in abstract reflection, Edwin was a restless intellectual torn between his equally strong scientific and esoteric leanings. Where Windham's circle of friends was dominated by fellow peers and landowners, Edwin sought the company of scientists and thinkers, counting among his friends the antiquary George Petrie, the poet Aubrey de Vere and the French historian Charles Montalembert, who dedicated a volume of his *Les Moines d'Occident* to Edwin. What separated father and son perhaps more than anything else, however, was their attitudes towards money. As a prudent and parsimonious man driven by a desire to raise his family to greatness and comfort, it was a profound disappointment for Windham to realise that his eldest son did not share this ethos, choosing instead to live extravagantly and getting into financial difficulties from which his father was forced to rescue him more than once during his lifetime.[11] Just two years before his death, thinking about Edwin and Augusta, Windham acknowledged with sad reflection that the vision for the family's future towards which he had so painstakingly worked might ultimately come to nothing: 'out of landed property alone, unaided by commerce or by a profession, enough is not yielded to enable one generation to raise the family greatly and firmly, as I wished to do', he wrote to his solicitor, Matthew Barrington. 'It requires the concurrence of two generations, and I little thought my successor would begin to undermine what I had built up with such self-denial. It is with great pain I see them following a course where they will sink step by step, till their little boy will be the sacrifice, doomed like so many sons of fine London ladies to cut off entails and pay for their parents' recklessness.'[12] Although time proved Windham's prediction to be unduly pessimistic, for many years after his death money remained a bitter bone of contention between Edwin and Caroline.

While Windham and Edwin did share an abiding interest in architecture, here, too, the men had their differences. Windham's pursuit of the perfect architectural form for Adare Manor was intelligent but not intellectual and, in the words of his grandson, was undertaken 'as much for something to do as for any other reason'.[13] The search for ideas and inspiration meant as much to Windham as the end result, and architectural purity as a concept was never so strict as not to be capable of yielding to cheerful ebullience and flights of fancy. Edwin's approach, on the other hand, was characteristically academic and rested firmly on Pugin's concept of true principles. Whether intentionally or not, Edwin's insistence on architectural purity occasionally came dangerously close to resembling snobbery, as did his undoubtedly genuine and heartfelt pride in the family home. In the summer of 1843, when the Duke and Duchess of Leinster of Carton House, Co. Kildare, visited Adare Manor and expressed their admiration for the place, Edwin took their praise for granted, merely observing that the couple's 'ecclesiastical & general historical associations would naturally give them our interest in the place, in addition to which its own intrinsic merits would convey'. He could not help adding the snub that there 'is nothing very striking about Carton: a pretty good piece of water, a beautifully situated cottage, & the house large & handsome'.[14] He was equally dismissive of Glenstal. 'I can quite fancy the new hall at Adare being all that you describe', he wrote to his mother in 1844. 'I like a room that is out of the common way, provided it be not fanciful, as Mr Barrington's round room appears to be.'[15] It is quite likely, however, that the sense of superiority that Edwin expressed was not an indication of inherent snobbishness on his part but stemmed from the simple fact that, in Edwin's own words, 'Adare *rather* spoils one for other houses'.[16]

Adare Manor, Adare. Edwin's children playing battledore and shuttlecock in the great hall. Drawing by Louisa Payne-Gallwey, c. 1850. Courtesy of the Dunraven family.

The most significant event that followed in the wake of Windham's death was Edwin's conversion to Roman Catholicism. The roots of his change of faith were linked to the emergence of Tractarianism, a movement opposed to increased secularism and rationalism in the church and governmental involvement in ecclesiastical life, seeking instead the separation of Church and State, a return to the beliefs of early Christianity and the reintroduction of Catholic liturgy within the Church of England. The philosophy was outlined in a series of pamphlets known as the *Tracts of the Times*, published between 1833 and 1841, which gave the movement its name. Its leaders— John Henry Newman, Richard Hurrell Froude, John Keble and Edward Pusey—were all fellows of Oriel College, Oxford, which gave Tractarianism its alternative name, the Oxford Movement. Edwin, his father and his brother-in-law William Monsell had shared an interest in the movement. As early as 1838, and inspired by its tracts, they considered the idea of establishing a school that would encourage social and religious cohesion and foster a sense of national identity by providing the sons of landlords with an education focused on Celtic Irish history, the Irish language and the importance of the early Irish church.[17] The founding philosophy of the school, St Columba's College, was formulated at Adare Manor during the winter of 1840–1 with the assistance of the English divine and author Dr William Sewell, the Irish scholar James Henthorn Todd, and MP and landowner Augustus O'Brien of Cratloe Woods. Initially, the school was to be located at Tervoe House, but the plan was abandoned in 1843 in favour of a short lease of Stackallan House in County Meath. Because St Columba's ran on the principles of the Oxford Movement it was suspected of papist leanings, but in spite of such reservations it managed to attract enough of a following to make the venture a success.

By 1845, Edwin's fraternisation with prominent Catholics such as Pugin, Ambrose Phillipps and John Henry Newman left no one in doubt about his strong Catholic leanings. The reputational damage that this would do to St Columba's College worried William Sewell to such an extent that he was left with no choice but to ask Edwin to step down as one of the governors of the school.[18] Over the next four years, several of Edwin's friends converted to the Catholic faith, including the brothers Stephen, Aubrey and Vere de Vere of Curragh Chase. What came as the biggest shock of all, however, was the radical transformation of Edwin's brother-in-law William Monsell, whose early political career was defined by his profound hostility toward 'popery'. He was received into the Roman Catholic Church in December 1850 at Grace Dieu Manor, with his wife by his side.[19] Newspapers made much of Anna Maria's presence at the ceremony, and the *Limerick Reporter* went as far as to suggest that she, too, had 'become reconciled to the church'.[20] While this was not the case, Anna Maria took her husband's decision with surprising calmness, and firmly defended it to other family members stunned by the turn of events. 'We are now a divided family,' Caroline lamented in January 1851, 'oh how do I miss the dear head which had kept us so united.'[21] William had clearly decided to bide his time until his father-in-law's death before taking the radical step. Although known for his favourable disposition towards his Catholic neighbours, it is not certain that Windham's benevolence would have extended to welcoming a Catholic son-in-law under his roof.

Edwin's own conversion did not take place until 1855, primarily owing to his wife Augusta's violent objection. Nevertheless, their son noted in his memoirs that Edwin 'must have been far on his way there long before, for my earliest recollections are of some impalpable difference existing between my father and mother'. This difference eventually expanded into a full-blown animosity when Edwin insisted on bringing up his only son as a Catholic. Augusta was having none of it. 'My mother', the fourth earl recollected, 'being an equally sincere and ardent Protestant, exercised all her will, and a very strong one, against my conversion', leaving the young boy 'bothered and worried and exhorted by one side and the other.' To resolve the dispute once and for all, Edwin packed his son off to Rome, where he was placed in a Roman Catholic school and prevented, albeit unsuccessfully, from writing to or receiving letters from his mother. Considering the harshness of his experience, Windham Thomas emerged remarkably unscathed, never losing his affection for either parent, the only casualty of his early upbringing being his religious faith. 'Consider the controversy that I was so early plunged into. Told on the one hand that Roman Catholicism was the sure road to indescribable physical agony, and on the other that it offered the only certain means of escape! The inevitable consequence was indifference, hardening into disbelief in anything.'[22]

Edwin's Catholic conversion turned out to be an almost insurmountable impediment in his marriage. By 1853, two years before Edwin's reception into the Catholic Church, communication between husband and wife on the subject of religion was so strained that they resorted to using Edwin's mother as a go-between, both outlining their points of view to Caroline and instructing her to pass them on to the other party. By 1856 Edwin and Augusta were living more or less separate lives, the former immersing himself in building works in Adare while the latter threw herself into charitable works and chaperoned her daughters in London during their first ventures into society as young adults. Their twentieth wedding anniversary was spent apart, with Augusta receiving an angry letter from her husband accusing her of being the misery of his life for her resolute opposition to the Church of Rome.[23] The more piously Catholic Edwin became, the more staunchly Augusta expressed her devotion to Protestantism. The rancour that grew between them gradually extended beyond the religious divide, until it permeated almost every aspect of their married lives. 'Augusta is better than I have seen her for ever so long', Edwin wrote to his mother in a bitter frame of mind in 1856. 'It certainly is very marvellous the way her illnesses seem to come just when they are advantageous to her wishes, & when that ceases she becomes well again. How do you explain this? Lady Cremorne would call it a special mercy of Providence, brought about for the benefit of my angelic wife as she calls her. We are getting on very well as she has everything her own way at present.'[24]

Franciscan friary, Adare, showing women and children in the cloisters. Watercolour by Louisa Payne-Gallwey, c. 1830s. Courtesy of Lavinia Graham-Vivian.

The domestic estrangement that resulted from Edwin's Catholicism was the great tragedy of his life. Shunned by his family, his post-conversion years were plagued by loneliness and disillusionment. Yet he would not veer from his chosen path but sought practical outlets for expressing his faith through the promotion of religious education and the improvement of the lot of the Irish Catholic. He tried to explain to his mother the motivations that moved him and pleaded for her understanding. 'I have lost the spring of life, my home is embittered to me; my family alienated from me, & what have I left, but a duty to perform, or rather two: one, as I told you, to enlarge my parish catholic church, that my poor people may at least be able to enter & *kneel* in the House of God during service. This I must do, cente qui cente: I have money left me which will go a good way for this end. My other duty is to try & improve the condition of my tenantry. Do not let me be a blank in the family; see how much my father did; but could you see how much remains you would feel with me, that to live in a Palace while so many of your dependants are in little better than hovels is very very painful.'[25]

With his lifelong interest in architecture, it was inevitable that Edwin's faith should find expression in stone. His most notable contributions to Adare, apart from finishing the work that his father had begun at Adare Manor, were the conversion of the former fever hospital on Rathkeale Road into a school and monastery for the teaching order of the Christian Brothers, and the restoration of the Trinitarian church and

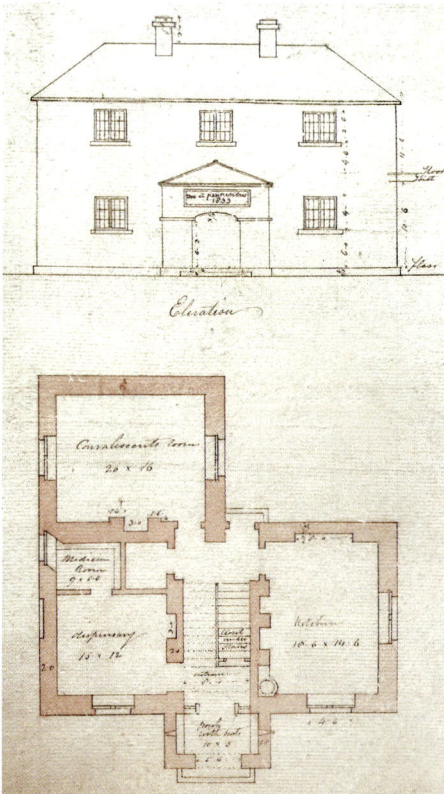

Fever hospital, Adare. Elevation and ground-plan, *c.* 1850. Courtesy of the Dunraven family.

its expansion to incorporate a school and convent for another teaching order, the Sisters of Mercy. His reasons for such lavish gestures of benevolence were simple and reflected his earlier interest in the founding of St Columba's College. 'This is the most important of all', he reasoned with his mother, 'for what can be so necessary for the people as a religious education? In founding one of these schools, one does all that one can do, relying on God to give His blessings to our efforts to ameliorate the condition of our poor people.'[26] So strong were Edwin's feelings on this subject that, instead of progressing the completion of Adare Manor as a priority, he advanced the three schemes in parallel. In the end, the two schools and churches were finished years before the family home received its final touches.

Christian Brothers' monastery, Adare. Designs for altars by P. C. Hardwick, 1852. Courtesy of the Dunraven family.

Unlike his father, Edwin had little inclination to experiment with designs of his own and preferred to seek the services of a good architect to oversee the three projects. Cottingham, with his vast experience in the conservation of medieval buildings, would have been the obvious choice, but he had died from heart disease in 1847. Even had Cottingham been alive, it is unlikely that he would have been enticed to come and work in remote Ireland, or that Edwin would have had the patience for the extreme slowness the architect had so amply demonstrated in Windham's day. Another natural choice, and one that must have held great appeal for Edwin, was Pugin. Although he provided designs for vases, curtains, candlesticks, crucifixes and tabernacles for the Trinitarian church,[27] by 1850 Pugin was already profoundly ill, with only two years left to live, having, in his doctor's words, 'worked one hundred years in forty'.[28]

Instead, Edwin turned to the young and gifted London-based architect Philip Charles Hardwick. Born in Westminster, Hardwick was the fourth generation of one of the most successful architectural families in Britain and had begun his training in Edward Blore's office. His first Irish commission was to provide drawings for St Columba's College following its move from Stackallan House to Rathfarnham, Co. Dublin, in 1849. His association with Edwin pre-dated this commission, however, and arose from their shared interest and involvement in the Oxford Movement, although Hardwick was more moderate in his approach than Edwin and never entertained the prospect of conversion. He 'would rather work on for the revival & restoration of every Catholic practice in our own Church than seek for myself what *might* be a kind of peace in Rome', while at the same time acknowledging that 'much delight and warm feelings of happiness are expressed by those who have left us'.[29] Hardwick's sympathetic attitude and non-judgemental views on religious conversion were no doubt a deciding factor for Edwin in making up his mind.

Hardwick distinguished himself predominantly as a designer of public buildings such as banks, schools and railway termini, but he was also popular in aristocratic circles for his asymmetrical Gothic country houses. Windham, too, had admired the young architect's taste, another factor which weighed heavily in Hardwick's favour when it came time for Edwin to make his choice.[30] Religious faith and paternal approval were not, however, perhaps the best of reasons for selecting an architect and, while the two men were good friends, their professional relationship was not always a comfortable one. Edwin's views were often at odds with Hardwick's recommendations and their differences of opinion raised many a storm, which the architect, known for his charm and amiability, always diplomatically navigated. While Hardwick's work tended to be stylistically correct yet rather cold and impersonal, Edwin nevertheless managed to find it too florid. 'I wish he would design more simply', was a frequent complaint in his correspondence.[31]

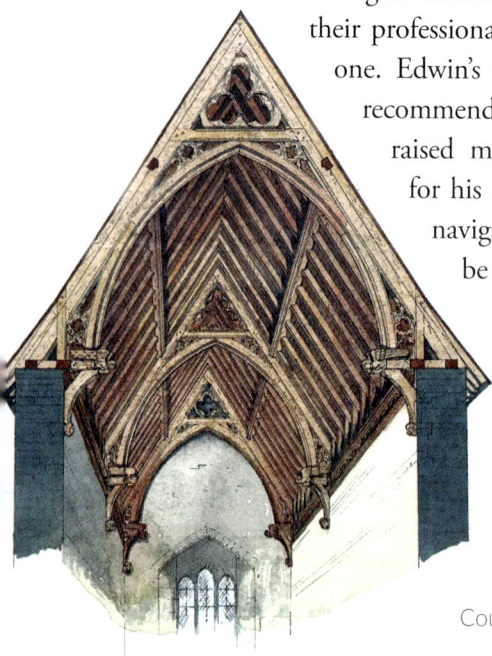

Trinitarian church, Adare. Sketch of the new roof to the chancel by P. C. Hardwick, 1850s. Courtesy of the Dunraven family.

Front and Side elevations ⅔ Inch Scale

Trinitarian church, Adare. Sketch of the nave door lock by P. C. Hardwick, 1850s.
Courtesy of the Dunraven family.

Between 1850 and 1856, Hardwick produced drawings for the completion of the south front of Adare Manor, the conversion of the fever hospital and the expansion of the Trinitarian church. The conversion of the hospital into a monastery was a relatively straightforward affair. Existing rooms were subdivided into monastic cells and a new wing was added to contain a kitchen and oratory. Building works commenced in July 1853, and the Christian Brothers took up residence in April 1854. A far more ambitious undertaking was the restoration of the Trinitarian church and its cloisters, of which only fragments survived, and the reconstruction of the latter into a school and convent for the Sisters of Mercy. To accommodate a large congregation, the original church, restored by Edwin's father some 40 years earlier, was converted into an aisle. A large new nave was added to the north, where the cloister garth had formerly stood. To balance the discrepancy in size between the nave and the aisle, the latter was lengthened and its chancel rebuilt to incorporate a Lady Chapel. The combination of the large, projecting nave and smaller recessed aisle gave the east front of the church

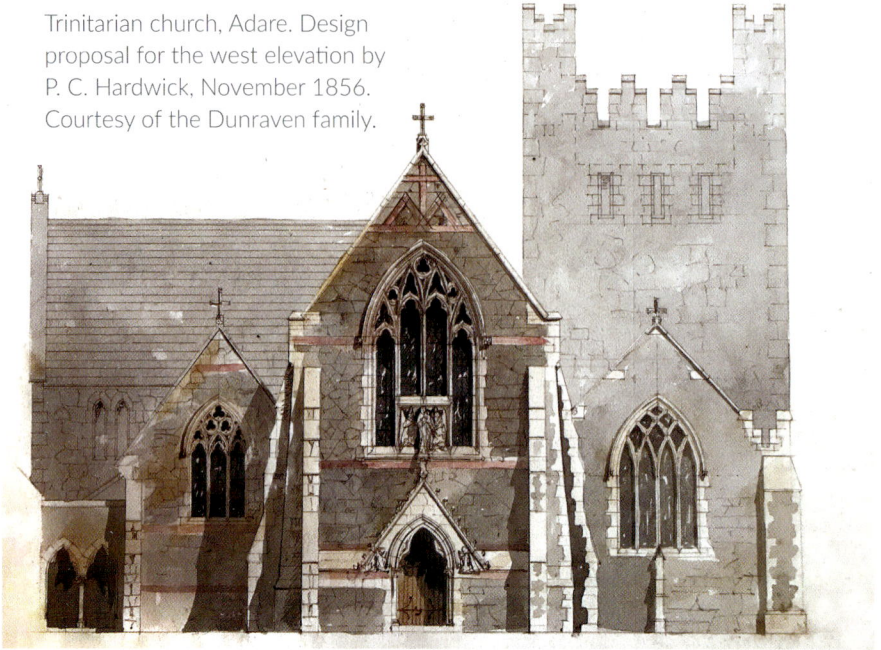

Trinitarian church, Adare. Design proposal for the west elevation by P. C. Hardwick, November 1856. Courtesy of the Dunraven family.

Trinitarian church, Adare. Design proposal for the east elevation by P. C. Hardwick, November 1856. Courtesy of the Dunraven family.

a greatly varied outline. The picturesque effect was further enhanced by the addition of a large stained-glass window by John Hardman, representing the Magi offering their gifts. In contrast, the west elevation appeared rather flat. Hardwick proposed to improve its appearance by the addition of bands of red limestone, which he considered a good method of enriching a plain front with local material without adding to the cost of the work.[32] The plan, however, did not seem to appeal to Edwin and was never executed.

When work on the Trinitarian church commenced in August 1851, the building contract was granted to a mason called Nagle, a young man whom Edwin found intelligent and respectable and who came highly recommended. Although efficient and capable, Nagle was not without his foibles. Part of his contract specified his entitlement to any old materials from those parts of the building that had to be dismantled, and this encouraged him to lay claim to the old altar in the church. Edwin was appalled by his antics, but Hardwick remained unperturbed. 'Nagle has not the slightest ground for claiming the old altar', he assured Edwin. 'He might as well take the confessionals, to which indeed he might be welcome; but the altar he shall not have. The specification refers to "the old materials of that part of the church to *be pulled down*". I have written to Mr Nagle & asked him if he has pulled down the Tower that he lays claim to anything placed within it!'[33] The incident greatly embarrassed Edwin, who feared that Hardwick 'will entertain but a low opinion of Irish honesty, & practicability of dealing with; but he says it is what he hears from all builders &c. who have to do with them'.[34]

Although works in the Trinitarian church were not completed until 1856, the Sisters of Mercy took possession of their new convent in April 1854, on the same day that the Christian Brothers moved into their monastery. The schools run by these two teaching orders opened their doors on the same day, and hundreds of children were enrolled as pupils. Edwin's generosity of spirit was widely praised in the newspapers, and the *Freeman's Journal* went so far as to claim that 'the change that has taken place, even in the external appearance and conduct of the children of Adare since the Christian Brothers and Sisters of Mercy came there, is very striking and remarkable. Instead of being often seen idling and ill-conducted in the streets and elsewhere, at school hours they are diligent, and at all other times they may be noticed gentle and orderly.'[35]

Trinitarian church, Adare. Hardwick's original design concept, *c.* 1852. Courtesy of the Dunraven family.

❖ ❖ ❖

Edwin was not Hardwick's only client in the Dunraven family. His widowed mother also wished to honour her husband's memory by restoring the Augustinian church, in the cloisters of which his body rested, and asked Hardwick to oversee the project. The interior of the building was restored between 1852 and 1854 according to Hardwick's drawings. A vestry was also added to the north wall of the chancel. In addition, Caroline invited William Telford to build an organ for the church and commissioned several stained-glass windows from John Hardman to commemorate her husband and other late members of the family. Owing to its proximity to the Maigue River, the Augustinian church was prone to flooding and, when restoration work commenced, measures were taken to protect the building from further water damage. Mr Nagle was given the charge of constructing a drainage system and built an embankment that curved around the church between it and the river. Work began in May 1852 and progressed rapidly; by late June, Edwin was glad to report to his mother that the embankment was mostly finished and would not look as ugly as he had feared.[36]

Caroline's desire to restore the Augustinian church acted as a counterbalance to her son's wish to enlarge the Trinitarian church. Using the same means, Edwin sought to honour and benefit an entire community while his mother desired to establish a lasting memorial to a beloved husband. In their own way, both had the same goal: to create an enduring presence in the village, a daily reminder of the family in its very fabric. For Caroline, the act was all the more poignant, since the loss of her husband wrought irrevocable changes in her life. Edwin's succession as the third earl elevated his wife

Trinitarian church, Adare. Design for a carving under the west window by P. C. Hardwick, 1850s. Courtesy of the Dunraven family.

Augusta to the role of countess and brought Caroline's reign to an end. Although able to retain her title with the prefix of dowager, Caroline was expected to move from her husband's home to make room for a new generation and to allow her son to take control of the family estate. For many widows this was a difficult step to take, let alone for a woman who had lived in Adare for close to 40 years and who was now asked to leave behind the house which she and her husband had built together. However, Caroline, ever true to the duties of her station, put away her personal feelings of loss and calmly accepted her lot. Although she could have remained in Adare and settled in a comfortable house within the village, she decided to return to Wales and make Dunraven Castle her home.[37]

Before departing for Wales in 1851, Caroline once again turned to Hardwick and asked him to design a drinking fountain to be erected beside the Trinitarian church

Drinking fountain, Adare. Watercolour by Louisa Payne-Gallwey, c. 1850. Courtesy of Lavinia Graham-Vivian.

as a parting gift to the people of Adare. Hardwick designed the fountain in the shape of a tapered column mounted by a Celtic cross, the plinth of which bore the inscription: 'In grateful memory of the zeal shown by the people of this village in quenching a fire at the offices of Adare Manor on the 18th April 1844. This supply of water was brought and fountain erected by Caroline Countess of Dunraven. Lord Prosper Thou Our Handy Work 1855'. As the inscription indicates, the fountain took much longer to complete than originally envisaged. The delay was caused by a difficulty in locating a suitable water source to feed the fountain. It was not until June 1853 that Edwin had good news to impart to his mother: 'we find there is fall enough from Clenagh spring, to bring the water by pipes, & we have a little stream constantly flowing, & the water is beautiful'.[38] The spring, however, was half a mile distant from the spot selected for the fountain, and the construction of the conduit to carry the water proved much more expensive than anticipated. Edwin was shocked to discover that the pipes alone would cost at least £150. 'I don't know what to do', he wrote despairingly to his mother,[39] but Caroline permitted the project to go ahead and the fountain was completed two years later.[40]

❖ ❖ ❖

It may well be said that, during her time in Adare, Caroline's contribution to the building of Adare Manor was overshadowed by her husband's collaboration with prominent architects of the day and the intense personal interest he developed in refining the house in the 1840s. Yet there can be no doubt of her influence, particularly in the early stages, when James and George Richard Pain worked on their first drawings. In more ways than one, Caroline's surroundings and her early experiences prepared her for just such an undertaking and made her an ideal partner for Windham. She grew up in the very heartland of the Picturesque movement, dividing her time as a child between the Wye Valley, famed for its outstanding natural beauty, and the dramatic coastline of Dunraven Bay at a time when the exquisite Welsh landscape had not yet been marred by the effects of the Industrial Revolution. Her careful cultivation of the terms 'beautiful' and 'sublime' in her journals speaks of a more than skin-deep understanding of the Picturesque theory. In this, and in her interest in architecture, she was moulded and encouraged by her mother. Together, the two women visited local beauty spots and in 1809 embarked on an extended tour of North Wales to explore its scenery, buildings and industrial developments. From her mother Caroline also learnt architectural draughtsmanship, a skill which she later put to good use in Adare. Meanwhile, her father's renovation works at Dunraven Castle in 1802–5 not only sparked her interest in building activities at an early age but also prepared her for the ever-present dust and din of construction works and the uncomfortable living conditions in unfinished rooms that formed part of her daily life in Adare for almost twenty years.

Windham's interest in medieval Gothic was most likely triggered, or at least certainly influenced, by Caroline. In spite of its great age, Adare House, with its symmetrical and pedimented façade, outwardly at least bore all the hallmarks of a Classical house, whereas the buildings in Caroline's frame of reference—Clearwell Court, Dunraven Castle, Llanmihangel, Fonmon Castle and St Donat's—were demonstrably and unashamedly medieval. Their halls and galleries, pointed windows and castellations were as familiar to her as the thatched cottages in the nearby hamlet of Merthyr Mawr, and both elements were later transposed to Adare. The idea to build may not have come from Caroline but the direction taken by the building works was without doubt inspired by her tastes and background.

Caroline's departure from Adare did not diminish her interest in building works. During the 1850s and 1860s she undertook large-scale remodelling works at Dunraven Castle, and likewise renovated and improved the grounds at Clearwell Court. In 1866, when Edwin replaced the organ in the great hall, the old one was sent to and installed in the latter house. The renovation works at Clearwell were carried out under the supervision of John Middleton, an architect who had built up a successful business in Cheltenham as a designer of churches. Middleton's professional association with Caroline blossomed further in 1863, when he designed a church for her in the French Gothic style, richly ornamented with carvings and coloured stone.[41] An orchard adjacent to Clearwell Court was selected as the location, and the foundation stone of St Peter's church was laid by Caroline in a ceremony presided over by the bishop of Salisbury on St Peter's Day in 1863.[42] The church was opened in 1866 but not formally completed until 1869, when the Adare organ from Clearwell Court was put in, along with a clock and bells. 'I confess it cost me a penny', Caroline admitted, 'but is there anything too good for a church?'[43]

In August 1867 Caroline again contacted Middleton, this time with a plan to construct a cottage hospital in Clearwell. Cottage hospitals were rural operations that provided a small number of beds for routine medical care and assistance in emergencies to save patients a long trip to a larger hospital. That built by Caroline contained seven beds and was specifically meant for people with limited financial means resident in the parish of Clearwell.[44] It was opened in November 1869 and the ceremony was attended by Caroline, who drank a glass of wine to its success. Within hours, a patient called

George Grindall was brought in, and Caroline expressed her gratitude 'to the Almighty for enabling us to begin this interesting work'.[45]

For much of her remaining life, Caroline divided her time between her two homes—Dunraven Castle in the summer and Clearwell Court, as the warmer and more comfortable of the properties, in the winter. She also made occasional appearances in Adare, which were always met with great rejoicing. Her feelings about Adare Manor were mixed, however. Having spent decades building the house, she was not entirely satisfied with Edwin's improvements. During a visit to Ireland in 1856, she couldn't help noting that 'a general want of taste seemed to pervade everything'.[46] She was also disturbed by the rift between her son and his wife over their religious differences, which to her mind destroyed the peace she had always associated with the house. Her visits to Ireland became increasingly rare, and after 1863 they ceased altogether.

Clerks of Works

A t the time of Windham's death in 1850 Adare Manor remained incomplete. Of the Cottingham-designed south front, only the eastern half incorporating the library and dining room was built, while nothing yet existed of the large drawing room and the bedrooms above it. Acutely aware of the unfinished state of his family home, Windham on his deathbed expressed to his wife an urgent wish that the house should be completed. He gave her directions on how it should be done and urged her to ask him for more, but in her distraught state Caroline could barely speak and many important questions were left unasked and unanswered.[1] She was, however, determined 'to go on with the building as it was the thing he wished, & felt that I still could do his will which had been so much the object of my life that I felt as if I could hardly exist without something to do for him'.[2] In name it was her son who oversaw the building works, but it was for the most part Caroline's money that paid for it.

Although Cottingham had provided sketches for the entire south front, these were of limited use, as the architect had died without providing detailed drawings or instructions on execution. Edwin forwarded Cottingham's drafts to Hardwick and directed him to use them as a basis for a full set of designs for the unfinished portion of the house. Hardwick began the task by paying a visit to Adare to view and measure the site. His first visit took place just six weeks after Windham's death. Caroline, notwithstanding the fact that she was in deep mourning, took an active part in the process.[3]

The project commenced badly. When Hardwick's new drawings arrived in Adare in early November, they were found to be inaccurate in terms of scale and position. Edwin went to great lengths to point out the architect's error and Hardwick promptly apologised. He explained that the mistake had arisen from the fact that 'I had to make the best of several [plans], all of which differed from each other and as it now appears from the building itself'. He expressed the hope that 'my new plan will be more nearly what you desire than the first … I am sorry it should have given you so much trouble in criticising errors, which that has occasioned.'[4] While Hardwick remained faithful to Cottingham's footprint overall, he employed a different mode of elevational detailing, which gave rise to heated correspondence between patron and architect. For the next several months designs passed back and forth, as every detail was scrutinised, queried and debated.

One of the biggest challenges facing Hardwick stemmed from the fact that the eastern portion of the south front had been completed, which meant that certain design elements could not be altered. This, of course, did not prevent Hardwick from doing precisely that. The exterior base moulding, for instance, was remodelled to highlight the divide between the two parts of the south front, though Hardwick emphasised that in designing it 'I do not wish to make *too great* a difference between the old and the new'.[5] Other elements were less yielding, however, most notably the openwork inscription 'Except the Lord build the house their labour is but lost that build it', which Cottingham had devised to run the full length of the parapet and of which the last eight words were *in situ*. Hardwick incorporated the missing words into the new design but not without apparent difficulty, as individual letters were squeezed together unlike their earlier counterparts. Part of the problem was caused by a proposed large bay window on the south face of the drawing room. This extended to the parapet and partially hid it from view. The window had been part of Windham's original plan, but its exact position remained subject to debate. Edwin's desire to place it off-centre found little favour with Hardwick. In his opinion, 'it should either be precisely in the centre or at one end. In these very large rooms I have frequently noticed the good effect of oriels either in one position or the other; but they never look

Adare Manor, Adare. P. C. Hardwick's proposal for the south front, *c.* 1850. Courtesy of the Dunraven family.

well placed so very irregularly as you suggest. Besides this norm for replacing the oriel in its first position, I think it will give us a far better arrangement on the bedroom floor.'⁶ After some deliberation, Edwin conceded the point.

Another debate revolved around a small extension to the drawing room at its western extremity in place of an old bay window. Windham's original idea was to construct the extension in the shape of a semi-octagon, but he later decided upon a simple rectangle. Edwin did not like the notion of this small space. In his opinion, it robbed the drawing room of the beautiful view the bay window had afforded and was 'neither one thing nor the other'.⁷ Hardwick, however, saw no difficulty in utilising the space as a billiard room. To accommodate Edwin's wish for a more spacious drawing room, the opening in the wall between the two rooms was made as wide as possible to create the impression that they formed a single space.[8] To counter the loss of view, Hardwick added a large, mullioned window to the west wall. Above this, he designed a fine oriel window to dominate the west gable. Edwin was slow to warm to this feature, partly as he considered the design too elaborate, and partly because he feared it too complex for his masons to execute. Hardwick disagreed. 'The west oriel will not be at all intricate, although the plan may at first sight look complicated. I assure you in England we have to deal with masons infinitely less skilful than those at Adare.'[9] It is fortunate that Edwin decided to follow Hardwick's recommendation, for the oriel window with its finely carved stone detailing was one of the most striking features of Hardwick's otherwise restrained designs.

A more intractable issue concerned the positioning of the so-called Wyndham Tower. The tower motif, with a high mansard roof and elaborate wrought-iron roof frame, which gave it a distinct French air, was something of a trademark for Hardwick, who first utilised it at Aldermaston Court in Berkshire, built for Daniel Higford Davall Burr between 1848 and 1851. In fact, Aldermaston Court served as an important blueprint for Hardwick's contribution to Adare Manor overall. The architect supplied Edwin with lithographs of the building in 1850, noting that 'I wish I could shew you the original, which seems to please its possessor very well'.[10] At Aldermaston, a four-storey tower served as the central feature, while at Adare Manor Hardwick's choice was to place it in a less dominant position at the junction of the great hall and the southern range. While he was convinced from the outset of the placement, it remained a moot point for months. The design of the tower was also a source of some controversy, and not for the first time Edwin's interference tested Hardwick's patience. 'The tower is already *eighteen* feet square, and I don't quite understand what is meant in your letter when you say you wish it increased to 16 feet', he wrote with rare tetchiness in January 1851.[11] This debate delayed the start of the building process by several weeks and it was not until Augusta lost her patience that 'the little difficulty there seemed to be in determining the exact position of the Tower' was settled.[12] In mid-February 1851, Hardwick finally pronounced that 'The whole work is now so much studied that I trust no further delay will take place'.[13] Soon after, patron and architect signed off on a set of final design drawings, which allowed building works to commence.

Adare Manor, Adare. Design for the oriel window on the western wall of the south front by P. C. Hardwick, *c.* 1850. Courtesy of the Dunraven family.

Aldermaston Court, Berkshire. East front by P. C. Hardwick, 1849. © The Trustees of the British Museum.

Work on the foundations of the new wing began in January 1851 under the supervision of James Connolly, the old foreman who remained in charge of the builders at Adare Manor. Despite the mason's increasing frailty, Hardwick had implicit faith in his experience and judgement. Forwarding the drawings of the foundations to Edwin, he noted that 'I have not shown any *concrete* under the walls—if it is found necessary from the condition of the ground I think I may trust to Connolly's judgement to use it—unless the foundation is found to be full of loose sand & water it is not often used when the building material is so large and of such hard quality as the stone found at Adare'.[14] Uncertain about the exact height of the existing basement, Hardwick did not specify its dimensions but left it for Connolly to ensure that the new one would end up being the correct size. Some of Hardwick's letters were addressed directly to the foreman. In them he provided detailed instructions on how to determine the exact thickness of the walls to be built and encouraged Connolly to 'write to me always when you are in want of any information or drawings, or when you find drawings incomplete'.[15]

Preparation of the foundations was hindered, however, by adverse weather conditions through the winter and early spring of 1851. 'The weather has been, & continues to be miserable for building', Edwin complained to his mother towards the end of March. 'I am sure more progress will be made next week: but I am sure the work will not be up to the level of the ground before June. Today we have been treated to violent hail showers, & most every day.'[16] Such delays would hardly have mattered to Windham, who regarded building as a hobby and a pleasant diversion, but Edwin, who saw the completion of Adare Manor as a duty and an obligation among many vying for his attention, was frustrated by delay. Two days after his complaint about the weather, Edwin fumed again. 'The masons are by way of being hard at work, but really at the end of the day, I can scarcely see anything done. It is very annoying.'[17] Augusta did her best to put up with her husband's moods but could not help remarking to her mother-in-law that it was a pity that Edwin was not more like his father. She complained that Edwin 'would dispute for hours theoretically on the love of God, but to restrain his expressions of resentment or annoyance he considers a trifle'.[18]

Bad weather was not the only problem testing Edwin's patience. At the time of his father's death, Adare Manor employed 54 skilled workmen— masons, carpenters, painters, slaters, plasterers, carvers and sawyers—and 129 general labourers, all with James Connolly as foreman.[19] Owing to his age, Connolly found the management of such a large workforce increasingly difficult, and workmen took advantage of his diminishing authority by doing as little as possible.[20] His dated working methods also irritated Edwin, who constantly complained that the old foreman 'has no conception of the method of work; he never had it, & has no natural talent for it'.[21] Hardwick did his best to encourage Connolly to keep a tighter rein on his workmen but his gentle words of persuasion did little to remedy the

Adare Manor, Adare. Proposal for the Wyndham Tower by P. C. Hardwick, March 1851. Courtesy of the Dunraven family.

Augt 1851. (155)

Nº	Name	No.	No. in family		Wages	Work			
+ 1	Maurice Guerin	3	8	avenue	2.6	Carpenter	d		
+ 2	James Connolly	1	4	Village	2.6		d		Foreman
+ 3	John O'Neill	1	5	Village	2.0	Painter	o		
+ 4	Peter Keenan	1	7	Village	2	Slater	o		
+ 5	Abm Mullens	2	9	avenue	1.6	Carp.	d		
+ 6	Thomas OBrien	1	2	Village	1.4½	Do	d	o	
+ 7	William Slattery	1	4	Village	2.0	Smith	d		
+ 8	John Bourke	2	7			Saddler	o	o	
9	Mic Mollony	1	2		1.6	Plasterer	o	o	1
+ 10	Mic Toomey	1	3		10½	Carman	d		Bk
+ 11	James Connolly	1	3		1.6	Do	d	7	
+ 12	James McNamara	2	8	avenue	2.0	Mason	d		
+ 13	Wm McNamara			Do	2.0	Do	d	7	5 6 12
+ 14	Patrick Collens	1	8	Bo. St.	2.0	Do	d		
+ 15	John Collens	1	1	Vill.	2.0	Do	d		13 & 14
16	John Fitzgerald	1	2	Avenue	2.0	Do	d	o	
+ 17	John Dundon	4	9	Vill.	2.0	Do	d		
+ 18	Mic Dundon			Do	2.0	Do	d	7	Sf 17
+ 19	John Connolly	1	3	Do	2.0	Do	d		Sf 2
+ 20	James Grady	1	2	Bo. St.	2.0	Do	d		
+ 21	Wm Mollony	1		Vill.	2.0	Do	d	7	Sf 9
22	Thos Connolly	1	4	Bo. St.	2.0	Do	o		Sf 2
+ 23	Denis Guerin			avenue	1.6	Carpenter	d	7	Sf 1
+ 24	Maurice Guerin			Do	1.6		d	7	Do
+ 25	Thomas Bourke	1	3	Village	1.6	Tricker	o	o	
+ 26	Wm Danihar	2	6	Graig.	1.2	Un. Gard.	d	7	
+ 27	Thomas Dundon	2	6	Bo. St.	1.0	Sawyer	d		
+ 28	Jas Morrissey	1	6	avenue	1.0	Do	d		
+ 29	Wm Hawley	2	6	Bo. St.	1.0	Quarry	d		
+ 30	Patrick Connor	1	2	avenue	1.0	Hathler	d	o	
31	Patrick Doody	1	4	Vill.		Slab	d		
+ 32	Dundons Boy			vill.	.10	Ap. Mason	d	7	S 6 17
+ 33	Mullens Boy				.10	Ap. Carp.	d	7	Sf 5
+ 34	Richd Toomy	2	7	Lodge	.10	Und. Stew	d		
+ 35	Micheal Ryan	1	4	Vill.	.10	Gard.	d		
+ 36	William Duite	1	3	Lodge	10	L.	d		
+ 37	Mich Toomy	2	5	Bo. St.	10	Gard.	d		
+ 38	Wm Shouldine	1	6	Lodge	10	L.	d	o	

List of workmen at Adare Manor in August 1851. Courtesy of the Dunraven family and Special Collections and Archives, Glucksman Library, University of Limerick.

situation. Even Edwin had to acknowledge that altering Connolly's habits at his time of life would be impossible.[22] As a result, the head carpenter Maurice Guerin, whom Edwin regarded as the only man in the entire place who worked sufficiently quickly, ended up bearing much of the responsibility for supervising workmen on top of his own duties, and was almost pulled to pieces with everything he was given to do.[23]

To find a more permanent solution, Edwin looked for a new man to take charge of the joiners and carpenters to allow Guerin to concentrate on his duties as foreman. Initially he met with little success. Hardwick also took an interest in the search. 'I have been making enquiries in London', he told Edwin in October 1850, 'but have not yet been able to find a man who will answer your purpose. I am now going to write to Pugin about it—he may know a Houses of Parliament man who would be accustomed to that kind of work.'[24] He did, however, warn Edwin that 'no *good* joiner will go to Ireland for 5 shillings a day. A good workman gets at least that sum in regular work in London.'[25]

Hardwick's perseverance eventually bore fruit in February 1851. 'I believe I have at last found a man who would go to Adare on moderate terms to take charge of the joiners', he wrote, 'his trade is that of a carver and he is so good a workman that I should never have thought of suggesting to him to take such a situation; but he applied to me to know if I knew of any *permanent* work, as he was anxious to have *regular* employment and wages. If you please I will send him to you on one of the days you are in London.'[26] The new man, Storey by name, met with Edwin's approval, but it was several months before he made his way to Adare. In the meantime, bad weather and low morale continued to plague progress, and the foundations rose at the rate of just eighteen to twenty inches per week. By Edwin's estimation, '6 masons here, may do what 4 would do under proper system & control', costing £100 a year extra in terms of labour. 'I am greatly vexed about the way the building goes on', he erupted. 'I would far rather *leave Adare* for a year than be a witness to the way the work is conducted.'[27] Soon after this outburst, however, things began to improve. The weather turned warm and sunny, the number of masons working on the foundations was increased from five to eleven, and by mid-April stonecutters began the preparation of blocks of ashlar for the exterior walls in anticipation of the foundation reaching ground level by June.[28]

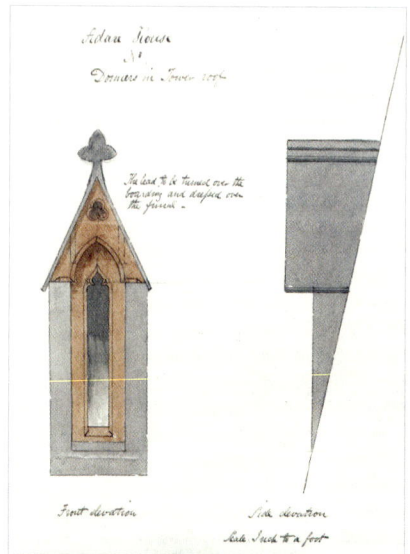

Adare Manor, Adare. *Above left:* Working drawing of the cresting to the roof of the Wyndham Tower by P. C. Hardwick, 1850s. *Above right:* Front and side elevations of dormers in the roof of the Wyndham Tower by P. C. Hardwick, 1850s. *Below left:* Elevation showing the positioning of the dormers on the roof of the Wyndham Tower by P. C. Hardwick, 1850s. *Below right:* Working drawing of the finial on the west gable of the south front by P. C. Hardwick, December 1852. Courtesy of the Dunraven family.

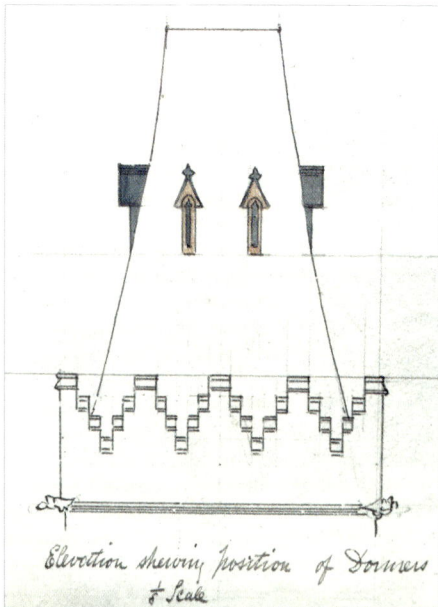

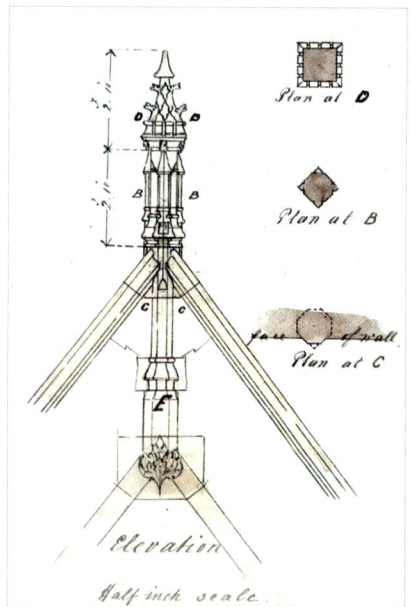

Things improved further with Storey's arrival. His first task was to arrange for a new workshop for the carpenters, something Edwin had for years attempted to persuade his father to do without success. The carvings and carpentry work at Adare Manor were suffering from splitting and warping as a consequence of the lack of proper dry sheds, as Edwin reminded his father shortly before the latter's death: 'Pugin, if you remember said at once it is impossible your wood work & carvings can fit well when executed in such places, & even Guerin & others have told me they cannot help it, their work is all spoiled by it: they should have rooms floored, plenty of light, so that they might have the doors shut, or what is better a good stove … What a difference would there be had one good joiner been secured, & dry sheds, & how trifling the difference of expense.'[29] With Storey's arrival, the problem was finally resolved, as was the lack of speed. The new foreman put carpenters through their paces, often making them work until late into the evening. Edwin was gratified by such efficiency and described Storey as someone who 'understands his business thoroughly'.[30]

Edwin's praise turned out to be premature. Within weeks of his arrival in Adare, Storey caused Hardwick to raise an eyebrow with a request to procure him a small book on carpentry. 'I never heard of foremen or clerks of the works, under one of which denominations I suppose Storey classes himself, being allowed *books*', Hardwick told Edwin with ill-concealed amazement. 'They almost always *have* them but they are their own … He might as reasonably ask for *tools*.'[31] Very soon other problems emerged. Storey failed to provide Hardwick with measurements of interior details when requested and developed a habit of meddling in everything.[32] By the end of the year Guerin was back in charge of the carpenters.

❖   ❖   ❖

A much greater issue than the peccadilloes of individual workmen was to affect building works. During the Famine, thousands of men and women left the country to seek a better life across the Atlantic. The annual rate of emigration reached its peak in 1847 and continued at a rate of some 200,000 people for another five years before it waned. Some landlords actively encouraged emigration by offering to pay their tenants' fares in order to remove the weak and destitute and to concentrate landownership in fewer and more capable hands. In time, this resulted in a general expectation that financial assistance would be provided to all who wished to emigrate, which in turn forced landlords such as Edwin, who were fundamentally opposed to the practice, to go along with it. 'I think it is a bad plan to give money to these young men to go out to America', Edwin reasoned, 'it is a bad example.' To limit the negative effects of emigration, his solution was to preferentially remove large families and men of indifferent character while persuading young and able-bodied men to remain.[33]

The emigration issue put Edwin in a difficult position not only in terms of farming but also with building works. Skilled workmen were increasingly hard to find, as most had left the country in search of better opportunities abroad. Those prepared to remain did so on expectation of higher wages, a demand which Edwin found impossible to meet. By mid-June 1851, securing workmen was a serious issue. 'We have now but 8 masons & 2 apprentices, who will come & stay with us at our wages, which are 2s, whereas masons get 2.6 everywhere & are in great demand at present … Our only check is that with us they are sure of constant work; but if they came to me tomorrow & said we will not work under 2s 6d what could we do, as no other could be got? It was much easier to manage these things some time ago.'[34]

Dissatisfied with Edwin's inability to offer better terms, his masons and stonecutters retaliated by slowing down the work. To Edwin's bitter disappointment, throughout the summer of 1851 the walls of the new wing 'do not rise 1 foot per week, which makes me see clearly that there is no chance of the work being finished by the autumn of next year. There is the same laziness & indolence in their work, which is simply useless to attempt to alter under present arrangements.'[35] The difficulty was compounded by an inadequate supply of cut stones, occasioned by neglect on the part of Hannigan the quarryman, which caused the masonry to progress even more slowly. 'The … tower is getting up but the S & west joint is only to the level of the bottom of the windows', Edwin complained to his mother at the end of August, although he consoled himself with the fact that 'what is done is sufficient I think to show that it will look handsome, which is our first object.'[36]

Adare Manor, Adare. Outside and inside of the external door by P. C. Hardwick, July 1852. Courtesy of the Dunraven family. A separate sketch was provided for the iron hinges.

The American mania, as Edwin termed the phenomenon, continued to cause serious strife throughout the summer of 1851, beginning in March, when the first of the masons left Adare Manor. In the same month, one of James Connolly's sons threatened to follow suit when he was told that Edwin had called him an idler and was only prevented from departing by his pleading father. Another mason, named Sheahan, decided to leave in April and worked hard at encouraging others to join him but, much to Edwin's relief, did not succeed. By April, 33 men and women had emigrated or announced their imminent departure and more followed in July, when a group of masons decided to down tools and leave the country.[37] 'I was quite right in predicting the coming move about the masons', Edwin reported glumly to his mother. 'I had this choice, to refuse them, which would have ended by them dropping off, leaving us to pay other masons 2.6—or at once agreeing to raise them & telling them I would not keep idlers.' In desperation, he pleaded with his mother, who had enjoyed great popularity among the workmen in Adare, to write to them: 'say that upon my representation of their ways having given them the usual wages, you will agree to raise them; that you have not been satisfied with their rate of work, & that you will expect more to be done, now, without which, you must get other men—something to this effect but in your own nice way. The rise must be permanent, for you cannot & will not get masons under 2s 6d, such is the rush from this country.'[38]

The remarkable dowager countess did more than just write a letter. In October 1851, she packed her bags and made her way from Wales to take charge of the building works during Edwin and Augusta's absence in Kerry and Sligo between January and April 1852. A much-liked figure in Adare, locals had entertained high hopes of Caroline's return ever since her departure, and news of her impending visit caused feverish excitement. 'I need hardly say that everybody asks after you', Edwin joked to his mother, 'in so much that I have thought of pasting a paper round my hat, or on my back, to this effect: "My Mother is well, & will be here please God, in July".'[39] Caroline's arrival caused great cheer in Adare and, according to several newspapers, was hailed with congratulations high and low on the estate.[40]

Caroline's familiarity with the house and its workmen and her long experience of building works did not prevent her son from showering her with instructions during his absence and insisting upon regular reports from her on the progress of works.[41] Distrustful of his mother's ability to deal with workmen, he provided detailed directions on how to handle various individuals, including the painter, John O'Neill. 'If by the time you get this Neile has not put in the window to the side, you had better at once send to know why he has not, & also see that he *at once* paints the other side window (near the organ) the stone colour. By the end of this week he ought to have the whole of the lower windows. You will have to be at him almost daily: it is the only thing of consequence, to get those windows all right before Augusta arrives, which please God she will do before the end of next week, putting in the panes, & the painting.'[42] Edwin need not have worried. In fact, in time he was forced to admit to his mother that 'you are far the best Clerk of the Works at Adare. You do get things on somehow.'[43]

Difficulties of a different kind beset Edwin in 1852. In spite of the new and comfortably warm workshop established for the carpenters, fittings inside the house continued to cause trouble. This time the problem was the result of a purchase of bad timber which Edwin confessed 'was cheaper to buy … but for near 3 weeks 4, 3, or 2 men have been daily at work stopping cracks in the wood, & it will not be ready to put up for a fortnight'.[44] Chastened by his mistake, Edwin ordered a large consignment of seasoned timber, 'much of which will not be used for 2 or 3 years … but I get discount by paying at once'. The timing of the purchase was disastrous, as it coincided with an epidemic of cattle distemper in the demesne. The disease caused a loss of £100 worth of animals and forced Edwin to stop construction works for a month, 'for I could not otherwise keep within the £200 a month on account of the immense timber bills'.[45]

The greatest tragedy of the year, however, was the gradual fading of James Connolly. By August 1852 he was so unwell that he was forced to temporarily resign as foreman and hand over the reins to his eldest son. Thomas proved a much better foreman than his father, and under his supervision the workmen kept busy and building works progressed steadily. Some of his demands, however, gave Edwin some pause. 'He actually asks for port wine with which he is supplied regularly! What people the Irish are.'[46] A far more serious breach of conduct was revealed in September, when Edwin to his shock discovered that 'young Conolly has been cheating us for several months, in the way of taking on stones for his own contracts. He knows that I have been informed of this, & therefore there can be no longer any concealment. I shall have an investigation on Monday & if convicted of course he must be dismissed.' Yet letting

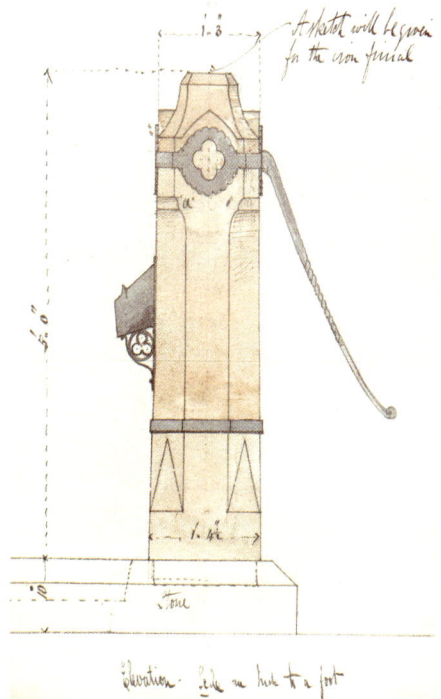

Adare Manor, Adare. Working drawing for a pump by P. C. Hardwick, 1850s. Courtesy of the Dunraven family. A separate sketch was provided for the iron finial on top.

go of Thomas would cause a serious problem. 'Who then is to superintend the building? Mr Hardwick knows of no one who would come without an extravagant price, & if even he did, as we are going away one could not leave the work in the hands of a stranger.'[47]

Thomas Connolly's conduct was investigated more closely in the presence of the family solicitor, Matthew Barrington, in early October, when it became evident that he had taken at least 40 stones from the estate. How to deal with the theft remained an issue, particularly since both Edwin and his solicitor were anxious to spare James Connolly, now grievously ill, the shock and humiliation of his son's dismissal. After some consideration, it was decided that the way to get over the difficulty was to make Thomas pay for the stones. 'Any further proceedings', Edwin reasoned, 'must have ended by his dismissal besides implicating his father, who was the person really to blame, & who showed such weakness or negligence in allowing such fraud under his very nose, that one had rather not think about it.'[48] Although Thomas was allowed to retain his job at Adare Manor, Edwin no longer trusted him in a supervisory role. At the end of October, when Edwin left Adare for three weeks, he put a temporary halt on building works rather than leave Thomas Connolly in charge.[49]

By November 1852 it became clear that James Connolly would not be returning to his job at the Manor. When Edwin learnt the seriousness of Connolly's condition from the local doctor, any resentment that he may have felt towards the mason melted away. Throughout December, Edwin visited Connolly at his home, and kept his mother up to date about his condition. 'He does not look so ill as I expected', Edwin reported on 11 December, 'but I fear his case is hopeless. He speaks with great interest about the building, & at the same time perfectly resigned to the will of God.'[50] Three days later, just as Augusta was preparing to pay him a morning visit, the old stonemason passed away.[51] On 15 December Edwin attended his funeral. 'Conolly's funeral took place yesterday afternoon', he described the occasion to his mother, 'but so late that it was moon light before they reached the church yard. Mr Beere & I walked there together, with the people. The effect of the old revived church & the castle tower, the tall trees, thrown into relief by the pale light of the river, & accompanied by the wild lament of the relatives, was very chilling. The fabric which he reared with such solidity & such skill may endure for ages, but where is he who raised it: what a brief span & all is over.'[52]

Adare Manor,
Adare. Sketch
of proposed
wall panels
in the billiard
room by P. C.
Hardwick,
1850s.
Courtesy of
the Dunraven
family.

The profound void left by James Connolly's death was felt by every member of the Dunraven family. Augusta could not help thinking how 'the dear old man's whole existence was in the building & he seemed as great a fixture as the very stones—his familiar face & look & walk all seem so identified with the noise of the Masons I can scarcely believe they are all working as usual & he gone'.[53] To mark the family's respect for Connolly's outstanding contribution, Edwin proposed to erect a tribute to his memory, to which his mother readily agreed. The tribute took the shape of a memorial tablet designed by Hardwick with the inscription: 'In memory of James Conolly of Adare, mason and faithful servant of the Earl of Dunraven, and builder of this house from A.D. 1831 till his death in 1852'. The placement of the tablet caused some debate. 'We talked, if you remember', Hardwick reminded Edwin in March 1854, 'of the *south* front of the house & I think it would look best on either the dining room gable or on the south wall of the library. Wherever it is it should be below the string over the ground floor windows & near the quoins of the building; that it may not seem a mere *architectural ornament*.'[54] Eventually, a suitable place for the tablet was found on the east front, facing the Maigue River.

Finishing the exterior took almost six years and required one more spell by Caroline as a clerk of works in 1853 to keep the workmen on the straight and narrow. The walls of the south front finally reached their full height in September 1852, allowing for the cornice and coping to be carved and the missing words from Cottingham's openwork parapet to be added by stonemasons Edmond Jackson and Nicholas Bible.[55] Estimates for stone dressings to windows and doorways were sought from other masons and tasks allocated to those offering the most competitive prices, although Hardwick often complained about the absurdity of the estimates. 'I cannot understand the enormous discrepancy in the estimates for the doorway', he was forced to write to Edwin in 1851, 'it shows singular ignorance in the art of making estimates. O'Malley's is so very much below the others that it would be right to ask him if he is ready to do the work for that sum & to ascertain if he has made any mistake or omission. There is too much difference in the estimates for the window: but it is not so flagrant as the other. I suppose there are two John Kirbys living in Queen St Limerick as there are two estimates dated on the same day and place, the hand writing and the amounts only differing.'[56]

In spite of such complications, the building progressed steadily until July 1856, when Edwin told his mother that the 'scaffolding is down & the building looks very handsome. I hope some of the attic rooms will be habitable this autumn.'[57]

CHAPTER
FOURTEEN

Finishing Touches

W ork on the interior of Adare Manor continued throughout the 1850s and for much of the 1860s. In addition to finishing the new rooms, Edwin redecorated many of the interior spaces built by his father, some of which were by now more than twenty years old and in need of a freshening touch. The open colonnade on the south front was glazed in and quickly became one of Augusta's favourite places, where she lay on the sofa for hours reading novels and basking in the warmth while recovering from an illness caused by a weak heart.[1] Large-scale changes were made to the great hall, where the construction of the Pugin-designed staircase began in 1851 and took some three years to complete. Its positioning in the south-eastern corner of the room caused a degree of difficulty, as limited space increased the risk of making the stairs appear too hemmed-in. To minimise such an effect, Hardwick recommended that 'I would certainly not repeat a stone balustrade on the south side. The panelling should be continued down with a newel at the bottom like the others. It would be as well to keep the newel up—perhaps on the second or even third step, round them off if the newel is on the bottom step, so as to stop it.'[2] The newel posts were decorated with carved ravens bearing the Wyndham coat of arms, which Pugin had designed. A master version of the raven was prepared by Pugin's favourite interior decorator, John Gregory Crace, who produced many of Pugin's fittings for the Palace of Westminster and was later commissioned to decorate the Waterloo Chamber at Windsor Castle for Queen Victoria. Crace charged Pugin six pounds and ten shillings for carving, and one pound and sixteen shillings for painting and illuminating the ornament.[3] It was sent to Adare Manor, where multiple copies were replicated by wood-carvers John Dowling and James Connolly and painted by John O'Neill. Crace also designed several paper hangings and borders in Gothic patterns for various rooms in the house in 1859, and four years later provided an estimate for oak bookcases and doors for Edwin.[4]

Hardwick continued to produce detailed drawings for interior features such as doors, fireplaces and wall panelling between 1851 and 1854, utilising where possible Pugin's sketches from the 1840s. Where these were not available, Hardwick applied Pugin's overall design concept. For example, the door between the library and dining room was copied from Pugin's design for the dining room screen.[5] Fireplaces proved problematic, for most of Pugin's drawings remained sketchy and incomplete and had to be extensively reworked. In the end, two fireplaces based on Pugin's designs were executed, one in the great hall and the other in the library. The second fireplace in the library was Hardwick's own design. As Edwin's tastes often differed considerably from his, the architect decided to take no chances and provided two designs, one with a castellated front and one without. 'I like the first best', Hardwick admitted, 'but knowing your objection to that sort of enrichment, I thought it better to leave the other side plain—will you give instructing [*sic*] for whichever you like to have executed?'[6] Some of the chimney-pieces were ornamented with ceramic tiles designed by Pugin and made by Herbert Minton, son of the founder of the noted

Bilton Grange, Warwickshire. Sketched perspective of the hall and staircase at by A.W.N. Pugin, 1849. RIBA Collections. A similar arrangement was adopted at Adare Manor.

ceramics manufacturing company and one of Pugin's closest associates in the execution of his decorative schemes. Perhaps owing to a heavy workload, Minton took his time with the order, causing Edwin to complain.[7]

Much thought was expended on the best location for each chimney-piece. A particularly handsome one based on a design copied during the family's stay in Belgium and originally intended for one of the bedrooms Edwin felt was better placed in one of the principal reception rooms.[8] He also decided to replace an old fireplace in the dining room with a new one designed by Hardwick. Having completed his drawings, however, the architect was so pleased with the result that he felt it would be better to leave the old chimney-piece in the dining room and place the new one in the drawing room. He suggested that 'If this is made in alabaster, it will be

Adare Manor, Adare. Sketch of a carved raven for the newel posts at Adare Manor, attributed to A.W.N. Pugin, *c.* 1846. Courtesy of the Dunraven family.

more appropriate for the room and make a variety with the red marble, of which so much is already used'. He also advised Edwin to place Pugin's great hall chimney-piece in the billiard room and have a new one for the hall of a better character.[9] Edwin disagreed, and new fireplaces in red marble were made for both the dining room and the billiard room, albeit not until 1860.[10] Edwin also decided to remove the grates from the three fireplaces in the gallery, presumably for a more authentic medieval effect, but the experiment was not a success. Augusta, who considered the gallery her hobby and pride, rather caustically remarked that 'on a day when happily there is no smoke the effect is beautiful'. After losing his patience with putting out fires, Edwin had the grates reinstated.[11]

◈   ◈   ◈

Several pieces of furniture in Adare Manor were custom-made for the house. A number of these were designed by Edward Welby Pugin, the architect's eldest son, who a few short years after his father's death took over the family business although barely in his twenties. Edward attained considerable popularity with his distinctive design style, which was more original and more personal than that of his father. Having inherited his father's driven personality and tendency to overwork, Edward designed more than 100 churches in addition to scores of other buildings and miscellaneous works before dying from an injudicious use of chloral hydrate, used for the treatment of insomnia, at the age of 41. Edwin spent several hours in Edward's company in London in March 1853, and six months later received the first designs from the architect, which included working drawings for a wardrobe and several looking-glasses.[12] In January 1856 Edward unexpectedly visited Adare Manor, which both surprised and pleased Edwin. 'Fancy young Pugin coming here on Friday. He remains a myth. We all liked him so much. He admired the hall immensely, the SE part & Hardwick's Towers; he criticized the drawing room window, & other things in Hardwick's work, but the Tower he was most struck with … He was in raptures with the place particularly Desmond Castle.'[13] Edward Pugin's designs were executed in 1855 by Henry Owens, an upholsterer and cabinet-maker with premises on Mallow Street in Limerick. Owens's furniture, not all of which was designed by Pugin, was intended for the many bedrooms at Adare Manor and included dressing-tables, chests of drawers, washstands, cane-bottomed bedroom chairs, bedstands and wardrobes. He also supplied the house with hair mattresses and several pounds of feathers for stuffing bolsters and pillows.[14]

Adare Manor, Adare. Sketch for a chimney-piece in the great hall by P. C. Hardwick, *c.* 1854. Courtesy of the Dunraven family.

In 1856 building works at Adare Manor were temporarily suspended, as the issue of foreman remained unresolved. Since Storey's dismissal in 1854, a Mr Merripew had assumed the responsibility for supervising workmen but proved equally unsatisfactory and was dismissed at the end of 1856. At the same time, the number of workmen in the house was significantly reduced and only the wood-carvers Maurice Guerin, James Connolly and Michael Twomey were retained to finish some of the interior detailing, along with two stonecutters to work on the chimney-pieces. Edwin hoped that such measures 'will save expense, save great trouble & annoyance, & will not really delay the new building a week'.[15] In August 1857 a new clerk of works, Henry Gathercole, took on the supervision of the construction works at Adare Manor. His efficiency and carefulness satisfied not only Hardwick but also the usually difficult-to-please Edwin, who felt that under Gathercole's watchful eye it was now possible 'to go on with the shutters of the new rooms, & the floors & ceilings, so that by next summer the rooms will be in a certain state of completeness, & can then be left'.[16] Hardwick duly prepared an estimate for finishing the main reception rooms, predicting that finishing the ceilings, preparing and laying the floors, making the doors and chimney-pieces and glazing the windows ought not to exceed £450.[17] Mostly thanks to the new foreman, work on the interior progressed at a rapid rate over the next two years. Ceilings were decorated, floors laid and planed, doors and shutters made and hung, and walls painted and papered. John Hardman sent a consignment of finely detailed brass fittings—doorknobs, escutcheons, mortice locks, bell-pulls and shutter knobs—for the bedrooms, gallery and drawing room, and the painter John O'Neill busied himself with Crace's wall hangings.[18]

❖   ❖   ❖

One important issue regarding the interior which Edwin was anxious to resolve was heating. This, or rather its lack, had been a bone of contention between Edwin and his father throughout the 1840s. Windham, for whatever reason, demonstrated considerable reluctance to procure a heating system until the

cavernous size of the new rooms made it necessary to install an apparatus of some kind. In February 1846, he invited John Sylvester of the heating and engineering firm Sylvester & Company of London to Adare to arrange a plan for warming and ventilating the house.[19] The heating system adopted was probably something akin to Strutt's Cockle Stove, which consisted of a coal furnace into which cold air was drawn from outside. The heated air collected in a brick chamber, from which it was directed into the house by means of a duct. Charles Sylvester, founder of Sylvester & Company, had adapted and improved the stove and marketed it with some success to warm halls, staircases and passages.[20]

The stove was finished in the autumn of 1847 but Windham, not really wanting to have it in the house, did not send for it. The apparatus sat in the company's stores until Edwin lost patience and gave instructions for its transportation to Ireland.[21] The stove was installed in the great hall, from where heat was directed into other parts of the house. 'Your account of the warm air is delightful', Edwin responded to his mother's enthusiastic reports during what was an exceptionally cold winter. 'I wish it would penetrate to the Tower Room, which is the coldest room I ever inhabited.'[22] Soon, however, Edwin discovered that his father had left the gallery without a supply of heat, even though Sylvester's system had been designed to make provision for it. Instead, Windham insisted that the hot air rising from the great hall would in itself be sufficient to heat the room. This infuriated Edwin, as the gallery was badly marred by the warping of woodwork, which he blamed squarely on the cold and damp air that persisted in the room. 'I am sorry you do not make a plan for the warm air to get to the gallery', he wrote to his father in a temper, 'it is so uncomfortable in cold weather that even Mama was driven out, last winter, tho she tried to remain as long as she could.' As Edwin predicted, the warm air of the hall never reached the gallery; instead, the cold air in the gallery penetrated the hall, 'which is certainly very useful in keeping down the temperature of that room', as Edwin tartly noted.[23]

Windham stood his ground, pointing out that tearing up the gallery to conduct the heat to its upper end, where it was most wanted, was a serious undertaking and one that he was not prepared to consider.[24] There the matter rested until after Windham's death. In 1853 Edwin finally took matters into his own hands and installed a new heating system to serve the entire house.

The results were much admired by Edward Pugin, who during his visit to Adare Manor in 1856 remarked that he had never been in a house so beautifully warmed.[25]

It was not only the heating but also the lighting of the enormous house that needed to be addressed. Throughout the 1860s Edwin struggled with want of illumination in the building. In 1868 he contacted the owners of several stately homes to seek advice on the best method to adopt and recommendations for a suitable contractor.[26] From the replies he received it was evident that many great Irish properties were lit by gas. Based on the suggestions of James Talbot, fourth Baron Talbot de Malahide of Malahide Castle, Edwin awarded the contract to provide Adare Manor with gas lighting to Edmundson & Company of Dublin. As was his wont, he opted for an extensive system capable of burning some 300 lights, not only in every room, stairwell and passageway of the house but also in the adjoining newly built stables.[27]

Adare Manor, Adare. Half elevation of a fireplace by Edward Pugin, 1856. Courtesy of the Dunraven family.

The installation took over a year to complete, but by November 1869 work on the ground floor was far enough advanced to enable Edwin to test the lights. 'We are—or at all events I am—like a child turning on & off the gas, & producing all sorts of pretty effects. When you walk about the Hall you see little groups of three stars in different positions. The Gallery looks so dim with the old lamps ... the house looked like a Fairy Palace the night of the Ball.'[28]

Although the bulk of the interior had been completed by 1860, much remained to be done. Final touches to the house were applied as time and money allowed in the course of the next ten years. Indeed, Edwin had resigned himself to the fact that 'I shall never live to see Adare House finished; I mean really finished & furnished', yet this did not unduly depress him. In bringing the house close to completion, Edwin's duty to his parents had been fulfilled, even if the end result was not quite what he had envisaged, as he explained in a letter to his mother. 'My wish has been to complete the building in a way worthy of the master mind who left a monument of taste & skill unrivalled in these days. What work of modern architecture (domestic) have you seen to equal Adare? I trust in what we have done we have not marred that which we found; that it is surly cannot be denied, but that seems a necessary consequence of the style my dear Father adopted.'[29]

❖ ❖ ❖

Work on the demesne continued apace. The parkland that enveloped Adare Manor was the result of an assiduous planting programme carried out by six generations of the Quin family. Edwin, who shared his forefathers' interest in arboriculture, continued the work throughout the 1850s and 1860s, although his early endeavours in this regard almost resulted in a falling out with his mother. On one occasion, having spent a day pruning trees and removing dead stumps, Edwin sat down to describe the day's events. 'One delightful result of cutting trees is', he observed, 'that it makes me take such a much greater interest in them, & one gets quite fond of particular trees, & views, which one had hardly noticed before.'[30] His innocent comment was misunderstood by Caroline, who at once charged her son with cutting down fine old trees and changing the character of the place. The unfounded accusation deeply offended Edwin,[31] but the dispute was eventually amicably resolved. Whenever the issue of trees was broached again, however, Edwin limited his comments to planting rather than thinning activities.

Edwin's main interest was focused on Mount William at the eastern edge of the demesne, where the beeches planted by his great-great-grandfather had reached their full growth and the oaks and chestnuts planted by his father were thriving. In addition to thinning and pruning the existing trees, Edwin planted a further 40 acres of woodland at Mount William in 1865 to fulfil his father's original plans. 'How glad he would have been to know, long ago, that I should ever take such a great interest in improving & beautifying the place he was so fond of', Edwin mused.[32] Three years later, over twenty men were employed to plant tree belts at Castle Roberts in the south-eastern extremity of the demesne. A new drive was also created to run along the eastern boundary of the demesne from Castle Roberts to its north-western corner, where a new Gothic gate lodge, known as the Lantern Lodge owing to its unusual hexagonal shape, was constructed in 1869.[33]

Adare Manor, Adare. Design for a door leading from the great hall to the drawing room by P. C. Hardwick, 1850s. Courtesy of the Dunraven family.

Edwin's arboreal activities suffered a setback during the winter of 1867–8, when a thick grey lichen spread through the plantations, covering the branches of trees like thick snow and injuring all the oaks his father had planted.[34] Edwin attempted to solve the problem by draining the parkland, but the lichen continued its relentless invasion. 'I believe the whole place will be ruined', Edwin despaired, 'every sort of tree is becoming attacked; we shall have no large trees; the growth is stopped by this terrible thing; then the small branches rot off ... I fear nothing can be done to arrest the progress of the plague. It is quite melancholy to see beautiful young trees attacked.'[35] Desperate to find a cure, Edwin wrote to the Royal Horticultural Society in London, who discussed his problem during their monthly meeting in late February 1868. From a sample Edwin had supplied, Miles Joseph Berkeley, editor of the society's journal, identified the lichen as oak moss and suggested that draining, which Edwin had already tried without success, should eliminate the problem.[36] As lichens in themselves are harmless but tend to grow on trees which are not healthy, it is likely that the oak moss at Adare Manor was not the cause of Edwin's problems but rather the result of an aging tree population too densely planted and struggling for sunlight and water.

❖   ❖   ❖

As the exterior of Adare Manor neared completion in 1854, Edwin turned his attention to the grounds immediately adjacent to the building. Although Pugin had provided plans for the treatment of the ground between the River Maigue and the east face of the house, these had not been executed, nor were any plans in place for landscaping the grounds visible from the main reception rooms in the south front. In his attempt to remedy the situation, Edwin was faced with two problems, the first of which was Hardwick's reluctance to undertake the work owing to his father's increasing frailty. Philip Hardwick was suffering from a spinal complaint which by 1854 affected his lower limbs, rendering him helpless for extended periods of time. Hardwick, who was deeply attached to his father, assumed the main responsibility of caring for him and regretted to inform Edwin that it was quite impossible for him to travel to Ireland and leave his father without assistance.[37] Edwin's reaction to Hardwick's domestic privations was unfortunately less than charitable: 'fancy my *humor* at receiving a letter from Hardwick to say that in the present state of his Father's health it is quite impossible to have him except for what requires his absolute attention ... neither, from what he says do I see any chance of his coming over! ... Patience, patience, patience!!!'[38]

Edwin's second problem was money. Financing the completion of the manor had since his father's death been a source of bitter contention between Edwin and his mother, who initially had determined to pay for it out of her own purse. Her own building activities in Wales, however, and other financial commitments quickly made her reconsider the matter. In 1851 she suggested that the money—£1,200 a year to be spent over four years—should instead be taken out of the rents of the Irish estate. This infuriated Edwin, whose finances were already at breaking point as a consequence of the after-effects of the Famine, the reduction of rents and the several annuities that he was obliged to pay. 'I am better to have given up the building altogether than complete it out of my poor remnants', he contended, and pointed out rather tartly how far larger her fortune was than his. 'It is no use acting upon a fancy that I have what I have not', he added, 'all my books and accounts are open to your inspection whenever you like. The only real way for us to get on comfortably is to pull together, & assist each other to carry on in the way most beneficial to our properties & our dependents & ourselves, but certainly I do hope most earnestly that you will not find it necessary to employ my money for the completion of the building.'[39] Caroline relented and subsequently provided Edwin with a building fund, which varied from £100 to £200 a month.

By the end of 1854, however, the new wing had cost more than £9,200 and was nowhere near completion.[40] When Edwin approached his mother with a request that £2,000 a year out of the income of the Welsh estates be expended on further building works in Adare, Caroline's temper was roused. She insisted that the house should not have cost more than £5,000 to complete and accused her son of living like a duke. 'How can you say that I have made the house too large to live in', Edwin retorted. 'My Father built a magnificent house far too large for my single fortune ... & then you turn round upon me & blame me!' He admitted having lately been living beyond his means, but only because 'To live cheaply in this huge house is impossible, therefore one had better not live here at all'.[41]

Adare Manor, Adare. Drawing for bookcases in the drawing room by P. C. Hardwick after Pugin, *c.* 1854. Courtesy of the Dunraven family.

The financial impasse halted Edwin's plans to proceed with the landscaping of the terrace gardens. He sought estimates from builders based on drawings prepared by Hardwick's colleague Mr Thomas, but they were so high that Edwin could not undertake the works without borrowing a good deal of money and was forced to abandon the plan.[42] This deeply disheartened him, particularly since the garden project had been intended as a diversion for his wife Augusta, whose health, frail at the best of times owing to a congenital heart condition, was gradually deteriorating. Annual complicated pregnancies,

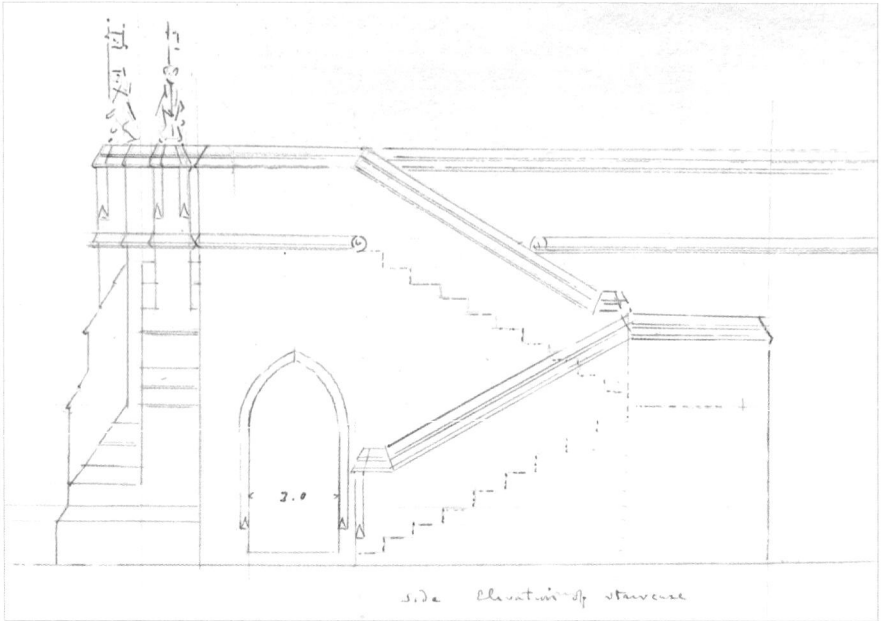

Adare Manor, Adare. *Above*: Side elevation of staircase to the viewing terrace by A. W. N. Pugin, 1846. *Below*: Details of parapet coping to the viewing terrace by A. W. N. Pugin, 1846. Courtesy of the Dunraven family.

many of which ended in late miscarriages or stillbirths, had taken their toll, and to this physical strain was added an emotional one as a consequence of a series of tragedies which beset the family in quick succession between 1853 and 1855. The first of these was the death, probably from meningitis, of the couple's fifteen-year-old daughter Caroline in July 1853. In spite of the doctor's best efforts, the illness progressed relentlessly and the girl's stricken parents could do nothing but stand by and watch 'our very first born, very beautiful child sinking, sinking, sinking, gradually breathing more & more gently until at last the moment came, when one could not tell whether or not time had been exchanged for eternity'.[43]

Augusta's next tragedy was the loss of her mother, who died at her home in Dublin in May 1854. This was followed by a virtual avalanche of heartbreak, including the deaths of Augusta's unmarried brother Wyndham Goold from a stroke at his residence in London in November of the same year, her uncle Valentine Goold in December, and her eldest sister Caroline Gore-Booth in

January 1855 after a long and lingering illness. The wave of deaths that had removed so many members of Augusta's family also swept away Edwin's 40-year-old sister Anna Maria Monsell. She died from consumption in early January 1855 at St Leonards-on-Sea, where she had travelled with her mother in the hope of improving her failing health. Her remains were brought to Tervoe, where she was laid to rest in the Monsell family vault close to her two infant sons.[44] Her death was a particularly heavy blow for Edwin. Anna Maria was the only one of his relatives who remained sympathetic to and defended the family's Catholic converts, and her death meant the loss of an important ally and a mediator between Edwin and the rest of the family.

The enormity of her many losses stunned Augusta. 'I find it is a dreadful effort to do anything', she wrote to her mother-in-law two weeks after the death of her sister, '& would be

Portrait of Anna Maria Monsell née Wyndham Quin, c. 1840s. Courtesy of the Dunraven family.

thankful to go to bed for a month & to be told I might spend the remainder of my life there & never be asked to go out of the place.'[45] Edwin was alarmed to note how severely the repeated shocks had worsened his wife's condition and regretted deeply that he could not provide her with the interest and occupation which laying out the gardens would have given her.[46] What deepened Edwin's tragedy further was that when the terrace gardens finally progressed in 1857 his Catholic conversion had driven Augusta away, and the task of creating the gardens became yet another solitary duty to perform. His one consolation was that his mother, who nurtured a considerable interest in the terrace gardens, offered to contribute to the cost of construction.

Owing to Hardwick's disinclination to prepare drawings for the project, Edwin approached the English landscape gardener William Andrews Nesfield in the hopes of securing his services. Following a successful career in the army, Nesfield had eked out a living as a watercolourist but later found his true vocation as a landscape architect. Having gained his first commission in 1836, he rapidly became so popular 'that his opinion is now sought for by gentlemen of taste in every part of the country'.[47] During his long and successful career, Nesfield worked on more than 260 country estates across Britain and designed a number of parks, including London's Regent Park and the arboretum at Kew Gardens. His heavy workload may have prevented him from accepting Edwin's commission, for Hardwick continued to offer his colleague Mr Thomas for the job. Although Edwin acknowledged that 'he is I fancy next best to Nesfield', he also confessed that 'I have more confidence in Hardwick's own taste. Perhaps between them (as they work together) they might hit off the best plan.'[48] Eventually a compromise was reached and Hardwick agreed to design the riverside terrace. He also prepared a rough plan for the ornamental parterre, which was sent for Nesfield to appraise and amend. The working drawings, which gave the details of planting and thickness of the box hedge, were made out by Nesfield's clerk and returned to Hardwick.[49]

Completing the garden front took nearly two years and required several amendments to the original drawings, partly because of structural problems encountered along the way and partly because once again patron and architect failed to agree over design details. Hardwick's first set of drawings, completed in 1856, did not satisfy Edwin, who against the architect's advice considerably enlarged the plan. Realising his mistake, he later reduced the

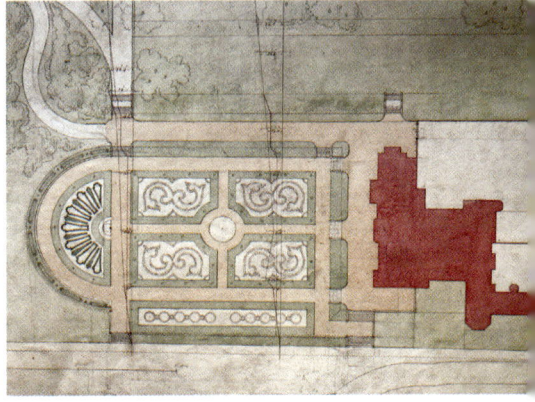

Adare Manor, Adare. *Above left:* Early proposal by P. C. Hardwick for a simple parterre, with a fountain and a 'border to be arranged in flower-beds', 1857. *Above right:* An advanced proposal for the parterre, with ornamental box planting, 1857. *Below:* Plan for laying out the parterre, *c.* 1857. Courtesy of the Dunraven family.

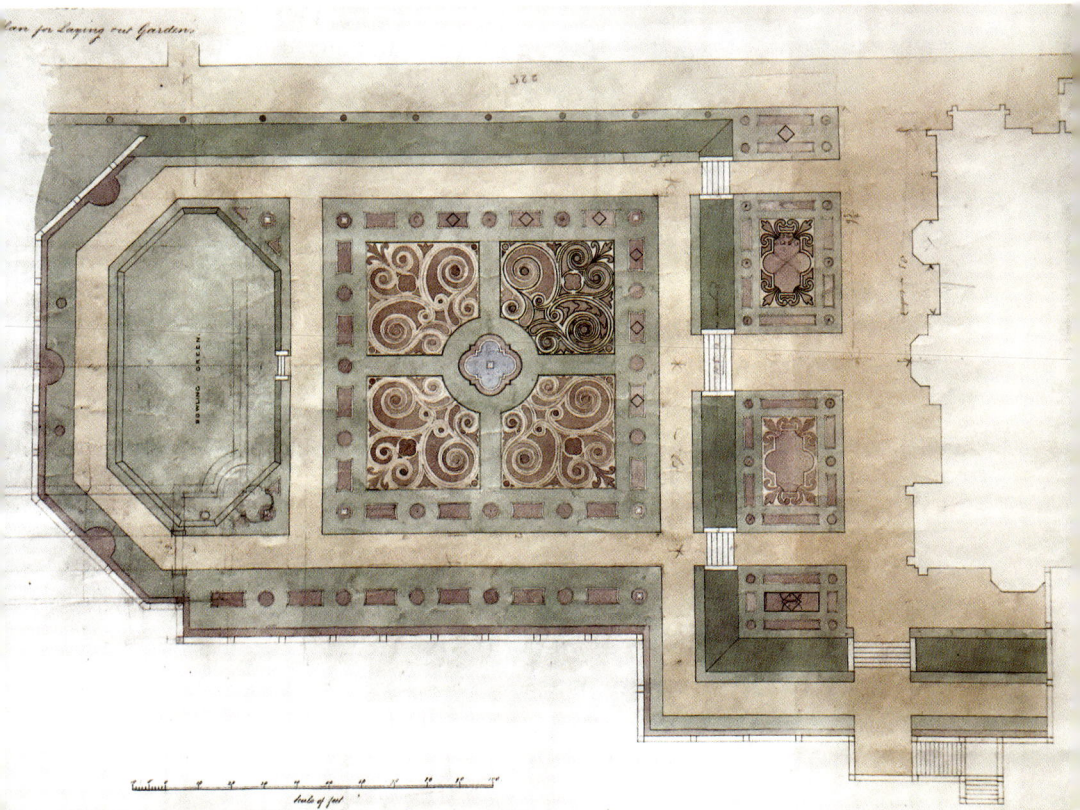

size a good deal but not until much valuable time had been wasted.[50] Another argument revolved around a flight of steps at the southernmost end of the garden, which Hardwick had proposed in his original drawing but Edwin had rejected. Two years on, Edwin changed his mind but by then Hardwick had cooled to the idea.[51]

Work on the gardens got under way in April 1857 to the cost of just under £800. Edward was pleased to note that the price, which included boat landings and the rebuilding of the river wall, was less than two thirds of what it would have been the year before.[52] By February 1858 the gardens were far enough advanced for Hardwick to judge the outcome. 'I think the general effect of the gardens is very good', he considered with some satisfaction. 'The improvement to the house [is] considerable, & when seen from the opposite side of the river the Terrace appears to me very satisfactory both in *proportion* to the building & play of lines.'[53] No sooner had he written these words than a problem presented itself in the form of John Duggan, one of the contractors hired to work on the riverside wall and boat landing. Hardwick had never liked Duggan, who was inclined to be troublesome, or the quality of his work, which he found unsatisfactory. Consequently, the builder was dismissed at Hardwick's request in February 1858.[54] Duggan promptly presented Hardwick with his bill, which the architect found exorbitant and flatly refused to settle. This resulted in a bitter argument between the two men, the only solution to which was to seek arbitration. Hardwick selected as his representative the Dublin-based architect John McCurdy, with whom he had worked in connection with St Columba's College, while Duggan sought support from James Pain. To this Hardwick objected, because in his view it was improper 'to submit the question of the accounts at Adare to any gentleman practicing in Limerick as an Architect'.[55] Duggan vigorously defended his case. 'I did not object to the appointment of Mr McCurdy on your part', he pointed out, 'and if we are to have an arbitration surely it cannot be expected that … you should dictate who I am to select.'[56] The matter was eventually resolved, but not without considerable embarrassment on the part of William Spaight, manager of Francis Spaight & Sons Limited, timber merchants in Limerick city, who originally recommended Duggan for the job. 'While I live I never will recommend another contractor', Spaight wrote to Hardwick by way of an apology.[57]

❖ ❖ ❖

Only a handful of masons and carvers were retained to work on the interior detail during the 1860s. Edwin found the task of letting men go unpleasant, made all the more painful by the fact that families in Adare depended heavily on work provided by the Dunravens. Unaware of Edwin's intentions, the workmen and tradesmen in Adare gathered at his front door on New Year's Eve in 1863 and presented him with an address of thanks amidst loud cheers. Edwin reciprocated by providing the assembled crowd with beer, but the knowledge of what the unsuspecting men would soon face weighed heavily on his heart. 'Poor fellows I felt sad when I thought from 20 to 30 of them would soon be out of work, including the old masons who have been working here from before the new house was begun.'[58]

Adare Manor, Adare. Detail of a painting showing the riverside terrace and boat landing. Private collection.

Dreading the task ahead of him, Edwin dragged his feet for another two months until early March 1864, when he finally let the axe fall. 'I never did so painful a thing as dismissing the labourers here', he confessed to his mother, 'several of them have been at work all their lives. Between Estate & Demesne, 30 are already put off, & there are to be 30 more reduced. All the things to be done by borrowed money are finished except the buildings, until next winter's planting. Poor people I wonder what they will do: there will be great temporary distress here. The making a selection is odious, for the number always employed is so much larger than what can possibly be done now that the pressure will be very severe.'[59] To ease his conscience, Edwin spent much time in December 1864 on providing the villagers with fuel for their fires. 'I have been out marking trees', he told his mother, 'to provide the people with fuel, & have come in tired & my feet icy cold. Every day we are employing carts & horses of mine carrying loads of tops & branches to the cottage … Oh the cold of rooms & passages, & the shiverings of the poor people.'[60] It was a tradition that he was to continue for the rest of his life.

CHAPTER FIFTEEN

Quae Sursum Volo Videre

During the latter part of his life, when building works no longer dominated his days, Edwin developed a reputation as a prominent antiquary and emerged as one of the pioneers of the new science of archaeology in Ireland. Much of his initial interest was directed towards the medieval remains on his estate in Adare. Between 1863 and 1864 he cleared the ivy from Desmond Castle, made structural repairs to the walls and carried out extensive archaeological excavations on the site. His mother viewed these activities with her usual jaundiced eye, concerned that the removal of vegetation could damage the building. Edwin assured her that such fears were unfounded. 'I don't think I shall destroy any walls by removing the ivy; it is sad to see the way it has injured them, particularly the tops ... I might become poetical on this subject so I must descend into the mud of the moat, where we have been finding old shoes, burnt wood, & other odds & ends but nothing of much value.'[1] Edwin also carried out exhaustive surveys of the town's other medieval ruins and of those in its immediate neighbourhood, and compiled his observations into an illustrated book, *Memorials of Adare Manor*, copies of which were privately printed in Oxford in 1865.

Augustinian church, Adare. Sketch of a plaque to the memory of Caroline's housekeeper, Charlotte Sullivan, to be placed in the cloisters, 1851. Courtesy of the Dunraven family.

Memorials also served a more personal purpose for the Dunraven family. From the very start, marking and commemorating people and events formed an integral part of their building activities. Every gate lodge and cottage they constructed was provided with a date plaque. Stained-glass windows and other memorials to family members adorned the churches they restored, and commemorative stone tablets in honour of loyal servants were placed in the cloisters of the Augustinian church. P.C. Hardwick was asked to design a tribute not only to the foreman James Connolly but also to Edwin's parents for their work on Adare Manor. While the first plaque caused a dispute between Edwin and Hardwick over its positioning, it was the wording of the second plaque that resulted in an outright disagreement. 'I really must again beg you to consider the wording of the inscription', Hardwick pleaded in March 1851, 'the termination seems to me to provoke so much criticism—could it not terminate with "owing", entirely omitting "shilling" or perhaps better with the words in the order "*without owing selling or borrowing*". I am sure I shall have one day to cut away the "*shilling*" if it is now added.'[2] In the end, a compromise was reached with the wording 'This goodly house was erected by Windham Henry Earl of Dunraven and Caroline his Countess without borrowing selling or leaving a debt'. The plaque was placed on the south wall of Adare Manor in May 1852.[3]

It was not only Windham's prudence that the Dunravens wished to celebrate. *Memorials* was dedicated to his memory, and Caroline contributed to the book a chapter containing a detailed description of the house he had built and notes on its building history. Edwin added the flattering but misleading comment that 'the greater portion of the building, and that the boldest in conception and most picturesque in effect, was designed by an amateur, not a single drawing having been furnished by an architect'.[4] His efforts to deflect attention from the suite of architects who had worked on the building and given form to Windham's ideas had the desired effect. The sentiment quickly passed into popular lore and became widely accepted, ensuring Windham's lasting if somewhat misguided reputation as an Irish architect earl.

Over time, Edwin's antiquarian interests extended far beyond Adare. He counted among his closest friends the Irish artist and antiquary George Petrie, whose writings on early Irish architecture formed the cornerstones of Irish archaeology, and Dr William Stokes, who had looked after Windham in the last days of his illness and who shared Edwin's interest in Irish antiquities. Edwin was a co-founder of the Irish Archaeological Society in 1840 and the Celtic Society in 1845, both of which were established to publish early Irish records and scholarly works on Irish antiquities, and took a personal interest in the production of many of their publications. A prominent member of several distinguished archaeological societies, Edwin was a popular guide on

Adare Manor, Adare. Design of a bay window by P.C. Hardwick incorporating a plaque paying tribute to Edwin's parents, 1851. Courtesy of the Dunraven family.

antiquarian excursions both in Ireland and Wales, not only because of the breadth and depth of his knowledge but also because 'he brought his knowledge to bear without the least assumption of superiority, and with a vast deal of fun and humour, and never a trace of harshness or ill-nature'.[5]

When George Petrie died in 1866, Edwin formed a committee to oversee the sale of his collections and the publication of his unfinished manuscripts. One manuscript in particular, on the subject of Irish ecclesiastical architecture, caught his interest to such an extent that he eventually decided to take personal responsibility for its completion. For the next four summers, between 1866 and 1869, Edwin travelled all across Ireland in search of ecclesiastical remains. His son, the fourth Earl of Dunraven, remarked that, 'with the exception of Tory Island in the County of Donegal, I don't think that there is a single island or barony in Ireland containing anything of architectural value which escaped his notice'.[6] Dr William Stokes and his daughter Margaret often accompanied Edwin on these excursions, and it was Margaret who completed the book after Edwin's death in 1871. Published in two volumes between 1875 and 1877 with 125 mostly photographic illustrations, *Notes on Irish Architecture* was hailed as a masterpiece and marked a sea change in the way archaeological monuments were depicted in pictorial publications.

A scene in County Kerry. Watercolour by Louisa Payne-Gallwey, *c.* 1850s. Courtesy of Lavinia Graham-Vivian.

Sneem, Co. Kerry. Design for St Michael's church by P. C. Hardwick, *c.* 1863. Courtesy of the Dunraven family.

As an admirer of fine scenery and the beauties of nature, Edwin was particularly drawn to County Kerry, where he made frequent excursions, often as a guest of the Herbert family of Muckross House near Killarney or as a visitor to Derryquin Castle in Sneem, home of James Franklin Bland. In 1851 he braved the elements to visit the ancient monastic site on the distant island of Skellig Michael with the Revd Dr Richard Hastings Graves. 'We had a capital day for the Skellig', he described the event to his mother, 'which is indeed a surprising place, both in respect of an ancient Irish Monastery of the 6, 7 or 8th century—a wonderful monument of antiquity; perched on the edge of the precipices, at 600 above the sea, then the cliffs & rock are very grand & quite fantastic in their appearance.'[7] Some days earlier, the two men had discovered several fine ogham stones in a good state of preservation.[8] It was most likely as a result of this journey that three such stones made their way to Adare Manor, where they were erected in a small wood to accompany two other ogham stones given to Edwin as a present by the Westropp family of Attyflin Park near Patrickswell, Co. Limerick.[9]

Such was Edwin's infatuation with Kerry that in 1855 he rented the private island of Garnish in the Kenmare River near Sneem from James Franklin Bland and there created an idyllic summer retreat designed by Denis William Murphy.[10] It was not his only architectural contribution to Sneem. Dismayed by the condition of the local Catholic church, Edwin paid for the construction of a new church, for which Hardwick prepared the drawings. The old structure was demolished in 1861 and the new one constructed between 1863 and 1865 on a plot of ground donated by Bland.

◈   ◈   ◈

While Edwin immersed himself in archaeological pursuits, his mother, now well into her 70s, continued to commute between Clearwell Court and Dunraven Castle to oversee construction works at both locations. Beyond these properties she rarely ventured. Her last trip to Adare took place in the summer of 1863, when a grand fête was held on the estate, attended by the Limerick Choral Society and 500 Catholic children from the two schools that Edwin had established in Adare. The visit raised mixed feelings in her, particularly since it coincided with the anniversary of Windham's death. Finding herself once more in the rooms she had built and shared with her husband, Caroline could not help dwelling on the past. The sadness that these memories evoked almost overpowered her, and followed her everywhere.[11] In August, shortly before her return to Wales, Caroline paid a visit to Foynes Island, where she had not been since the family's brief sojourn in 1834. 'I found the trees much grown & the place looking very pretty, but our dear Cottage where I had passed so many happy days was in ruins—the site of it alone remained, it was sad to see how the Cottage & those who had formed my happiness there were no longer to be seen—Is not this a passing world?'[12]

One source of constant joy in Caroline's life was her youngest son, Windham. A captain in the Grenadier Guards, he retired from the army during the Crimean War, when a severe attack of malaria permanently impaired his health. He settled in Wales and married Caroline Tyler, daughter of Vice-Admiral Sir George Tyler of Cottrell Park near Cardiff, in 1856. To secure Windham's future, his mother began a complicated legal procedure to enable him to inherit Clearwell Court, which, along with all other family property, was to pass to Edwin after her death. This she eventually accomplished by purchasing the reversion of the property from her eldest son and paying him a large annuity besides by way of compensation. The agreement was signed in March 1863 and gave Caroline a renewed sense of purpose, as she and her younger son undertook to improve the house and grounds. Windham also took an interest in St Peter's church, which Caroline was then building at Clearwell, and expressed a wish to be involved in its construction. Knowing his mother's love of stained glass, Windham ordered a set of memorial windows for the church, depicting the figures of St Peter, St Mary Magdalene, St John and the Virgin Mary.[13]

In 1864 Windham developed a recurring chest pain. Despite undertaking a course of medical treatment prescribed by Dr Charles James Blasius Williams, a leading specialist in diseases of the chest, he began a gradual but inevitable decline. In May 1865, accompanied by his wife and mother, Windham travelled to Folkestone in the hopes that sea air might produce a cure. By now, however, his condition was hopeless, and his female companions could do little besides take turns to watch over the fading patient. Windham died on 24 October while sitting in his wheelchair by the window, watching the waves. His body was removed to Dunraven Castle and interred at St Bride's cemetery.

Windham's death devastated his mother. Returning to Clearwell Court, 'I … walked about the place, & saw all the improvements made for the special use of my darling child, had he been spared to me—but the grave closed over him yesterday—& so I had outlived him & he was taken from this world that he had a brighter inheritance—I cannot doubt, but what is Clearwell without him to me?'[14] It was with equal desolation that she witnessed the unpacking of Windham's stained-glass windows and attended the consecration of the church in April 1866.

Tragedies rarely visited the Dunraven family singly. In September 1866 Augusta, who had come to Wales to arrange for her eldest surviving daughter's marriage, began to feel unwell. Only too aware of Augusta's weak heart, Caroline urged her daughter-in-law to see a doctor. On the recommendation of the physician who examined her, Augusta abandoned the wedding preparations and placed herself under the care of a heart specialist in London.

In late October, alarmed by reports of her condition, Caroline rushed to her side and was shocked to find 'dear Edwin most anxious & unwell, & Augusta lying on the sofa in the back drawing room very weak & emaciated'.[15] As weeks rolled by, Augusta appeared to rally a little, but on 22 November she died quietly while sitting in her chair.[16]

Augusta's death was keenly felt not only by her friends but also by the local population in the neighbourhood of Adare, who had benefited from her generosity and her ceaseless efforts to improve the lot of the poor. One of Augusta's most important contributions had been the establishment of an industrial school at Croom, Co. Limerick, in 1855 to provide girls with an opportunity to learn a useful trade. Their proudest moment came in 1857, when the school received an order from Queen Victoria for a supply of Irish lace and embroidery to form part of her eldest daughter's trousseau on her marriage to the future German Emperor Frederick III.[17] As a mark of their respect, Augusta's friends and admirers decided to erect a memorial to her in the Augustinian church. Edwin was deeply hurt when he discovered that the inscription would include 'some paragraph about Augusta's views of Protestantism'. He appealed to his mother and son to try and put a stop to it, because 'it is not only most painful to me, but prevents any Catholics joining in the memorial; making it a complete party thing; just what I expected they would do, if allowed … What a country Ireland is.'[18] In the end, whether through Caroline's efforts or by a common consensus, the sponsors of the memorial agreed upon the suitably neutral wording 'erected by her attached and admiring friends in acknowledgment of her unwearied efforts not only in this church and parish but wherever her influence extended to promote God's glory and the welfare of her fellow-men by the pious and beneficent use of her many talents'.

❖ ❖ ❖

Edwin's three eldest children married in quick succession. His daughter Augusta's wedding to Arthur Vivian, delayed as a consequence of her mother's illness and death, took place at St Peter's Church in Clearwell in a quiet ceremony in March 1867. Mary married Arthur Hugh Smith Barry of Fota House, Co. Cork, at Dunraven Castle in August 1868. The first wedding ceremony to be held in that house since Caroline's own almost 60 years earlier, it was the cause of great celebration in the neighbourhood. Windham Thomas, Edwin's only son, also married quietly in London in late April 1869. His bride Florence was the daughter of Charles and Charlotte Kerr, the couple much liked by the Dunravens, and the match was a source of joy to both families. What pleased Edwin even more was the timing of the occasion, which presented him with a convenient excuse to refuse the proposed visit of Queen Victoria's third son, Prince Arthur, to Adare Manor at the end of April. Edwin considered it 'rather a bore to have to spend at least £100 or perhaps more to have the honour of receiving that hopeful youth for a couple of nights'.[19]

The weddings marked a gradual dispersal of the family and foreshadowed a deepening of Edwin's sense of loneliness and isolation, made more pronounced by the prolonged absences of Edith and Emily, his two remaining unmarried daughters. Separated from his mother by distance and from many of his former friends by his devout adherence to the Catholic faith, Edwin drifted aimlessly from place to place seeking comfort and solace but finding it nowhere. 'Were I as good, as dear, & as healthy as you have been through life', he remarked to his mother, 'I might perhaps wish to live to a good old age; but somehow I am very careless about it. Were my two girls married, I fancy I should be quite indifferent in the matter.'[20] The death of his wife in 1866 had been a blow from which Edwin found it difficult to recover. The rift that his religious conversion had created in their marriage had not lessened his affection for his wife, nor wiped away the familiarity and closeness created by 30 years of shared life. In spite of their differences and bitter arguments over religion, Augusta had remained Edwin's bedrock, and the void created by her death now became almost insurmountable. 'How I miss my darling one', Edwin wrote two years after her death on his arrival in Adare from Wales, 'when one returns the blank is dully present to one.'[21] Adare Manor, built for a dynasty, was now the home of a solitary man entombed in its cavernous rooms. Even in company Edwin remained fundamentally alone. When friends and family gathered at the Manor in 1868 to celebrate Christmas and filled the house with music and song, all he could think of was Augusta: 'how one feels the absence of prevailing genius, in this most particularly, & indeed, if one wanted

Portrait of Countess Caroline as a widow by James Rannie Swinton, 1851. Courtesy of the Dunraven family.

reminding, that grand organ, now always mute, ever bears its daily testimony to the sad change. Some times when I look at it I can hardly help fancying that the glorious sounds will burst forth, & all be as it was—but no, silence will continue, & sadness will remain.'[22]

Edwin's morbid reverie was eventually broken by a move which was as unexpected as it was perhaps inevitable: a new marriage. His second wife, Anne Lambert, was from a long-standing Catholic and politically influential family in County Wexford. Her mother's uncle, John Hyacinth Talbot, was the first Catholic MP for the county after Catholic Emancipation in 1829, and both her father and her brother subsequently held seats in the House of Commons. Moreover, Anne's maternal aunt, Maria Theresa Talbot, married John, sixteenth Earl of Shrewsbury, of Alton Towers, a prominent Catholic and an early patron of Pugin. It was through this patronage that Pugin was first introduced to Ireland, when John Hyacinth Talbot commissioned him to design the church of the Assumption in Bree, Co. Wexford.

Edwin's unexpected announcement of his engagement in December 1869 unsettled his mother, but she received Edwin with her usual affectionate manner in January 1870 as he was travelling through Wales on his way to the nuptials in London. In spite of Caroline's initial joy at seeing her son, the three-day visit turned into something of a trial, as Edwin 'could talk of nothing but his approaching happiness'.[23] The wedding took place on 27 January in the Roman Catholic church of Our Lady of the Assumption on Warwick Street in London. As Caroline was too frail to attend the wedding, the newly-weds made their way to Clearwell immediately after the ceremony to introduce Anne to her mother-in-law. Initially, Caroline was pleased with her son's choice of wife and charmed to see him so happy. When frosty weather and a cutting east wind confined the family indoors, however, the relationship between the two women became strained. To relieve the ennui, Caroline attempted to amuse Anne by showing her views of Adare, in which the young lady took not the slightest interest. All Anne wished to do was to play cards, which in turn bored Caroline.[24] It was with ill-disguised relief that she waved the couple goodbye as they departed for their honeymoon in Rome.

Franciscan friary, Adare. Distant view of Adare Manor with Windham Thomas Wyndham Quin in the foreground. Watercolour by Louisa Payne-Gallwey, January 1850. Courtesy of the Dunraven family.

❖ ❖ ❖

During her final years, Caroline rarely ventured beyond Dunraven Castle and Clearwell Court. One of her last longer outings took place in September 1867, when she travelled by train to pay a visit to Ynyslas Cottage in the Vale of Neath. The house was now occupied by her old friends and former neighbours Jane and Anne Williams, who gave her a warm welcome. After her first night in the house, Caroline 'awoke with much delight at seeing the beautiful scenery which at first had induced [us] to build there, the place looked perfectly lovely with the mountain mists, & though not a clear day, it was very becoming'. Her only source of annoyance was the disturbance caused by the passing of the trains on the Vale of Neath railway line, which had been built to run close to the cottage.[25]

In early January 1868, Caroline caught a severe cold from which she found it difficult to recover. A month later, another attack of illness left her so weak that her doctor advised her to keep perfectly quiet and confine herself to the ground floor of Clearwell Court to avoid the fatigue of stairs. Charlotte Kerr arrived from Scotland to nurse her and, although initially put out by having to leave her old comfortable quarters, Caroline soon saw the benefit of having her bedroom on the same floor as her sitting room. Even in her weakened condition, Caroline pursued her building works in the village with considerable interest and John Middleton continued his regular visits, bringing plans and drawings for her approval.

On Christmas Eve 1868, Caroline was taken ill in the night and spent most of her Christmas in bed. On St Stephen's Day she developed symptoms of jaundice. Her state of health ebbed and flowed until late spring, when she began a temporary recovery, and by July 1869 she was strong enough to make her final journey to Dunraven Castle. During this visit, Edwin, as president of the Cambrian Archaeological Association, led a four-day archaeological tour to Bridgend. The doors of Dunraven Castle were thrown open to the group and Caroline was able to make an appearance and to welcome the visitors 'with that happy blending of dignity and kindness which upon her sat so naturally and became her so well'. The visitors were treated to lunch at the castle, after which a toast was proposed to 'Auld Lang Syne', to which

Dunraven Castle, Glamorgan. Watercolour by Louisa Payne-Gallwey, *c.* 1830s. Courtesy of Lavinia Graham-Vivian.

Edwin heartily responded on his mother's behalf. Although the participants gathered round the table had no way of knowing it, they were witnessing the last time that either mother or son would appear in public.[26]

Caroline returned to Clearwell Court in late October and, although seized with fresh attacks of illness, continued her building works with John Middleton, who kept up his fortnightly visits throughout the winter and early spring. In late March 1870 Caroline suffered a stroke. She died two days after her 80th birthday on 26 May, drawing her last breath in the same house where she had drawn her first. News of her death was received less with surprise than with deep regret. Her obituary noted that she 'was not only the centre of a happy home, but the connecting link between the present generation and one which has passed away', and added that 'much of the prosperity of the district over which her care extended was due to her enlightened views of the relation which ought to exist between the owner of the soil and those who cultivate it'.[27]

Four days after her death, Caroline's body was removed to Adare to be laid to rest in the family mausoleum. The cortège from Clearwell Court was followed by a procession of tenants and shopkeepers to the edge of the village. In every doorway, residents gathered to show their respect for the venerable countess on her final journey home. 'There are few of the rising generation in the village', noted the *Western Mail*, 'but she has patted on the head and has spoken kindly words to. Even the middle-aged of Clearwell, in many cases, can remember the same kindly notice; indeed, there is scarcely an inhabitant whom the late Countess did not personally know. Her memory will, therefore, be long cherished, and her name held in reverence.'[28]

Caroline's remains arrived in Adare Manor on 31 May, and once again the walls of the great hall were draped in mourning to mark the passing of a family member. Thousands of people poured into Adare to attend the funeral. On the morning of 2 June, Caroline's coffin, covered with roses gathered from the gardens of the Manor, was carried on the shoulders of her tenants to the Augustinian church, where she was laid to rest beside her husband.[29] On the same day, the shops in Bridgend closed their doors and business was suspended as local residents made their way to church, where a special service was conducted in Caroline's memory.[30]

In her will, Caroline left numerous legacies to friends, relatives, servants and charities. She bequeathed £100 to the poor of Clearwell and the same amount to the cottage hospital that she had established in the village. She also set up a fund of shares worth £1,000, the interest of which was to be used to pay the salary of the teachers at St Peter's National School, which she had built at Clearwell. To Edwin she left the rent of her estates together with family plate, books, pictures and furniture at Dunraven Castle, but the residue of her property she left to her son Windham's eldest child and her favourite grandchild, Windham Henry Wyndham Quin, who was to succeed to the family title as the fifth Earl of Dunraven in 1926.[31]

Edwin did not long survive his mother. He had for some time been suffering from signs of pulmonary disease, which gradually worsened during 1871. In September of that year, on the advice of his doctor, Edwin and his wife made their way to the spa town of Great Malvern, Worcestershire, to elicit a cure from the mineral waters of its springs. Edwin remained despondent, however, and entertained faint hope of his survival, caring little whether he lived or died. The only thing that continued to spark his interest were the ongoing building works at Adare Manor. His steward, John Doherty, kept meticulous accounts of building activities and kept Edwin abreast of developments during his absence by means of correspondence. On 9 September he wrote to Edwin to tell him that 'the bricklayer has taken the bricks out of the fireplaces and today has commenced to set the tiles in the library, the ceilings of the dining and billiard rooms are finished the rubbish was cleared out yesterday, none of the wainscot is put up in the dining room but I understand that a good deal of it is ready'.[32] The prediction Edwin had made some ten years previously that he would never see Adare Manor really finished and furnished came true in the late evening of 6 October 1871, when he died at Great Malvern in the presence of a Catholic priest. John Doherty's final entry in the account books had been made just one day before.

A chalk sketch of castle ruins by Edwin, *c.* 1830s. Courtesy of the Dunraven family.

Adare Manor. View from the south-east. From *Memorials of Adare Manor* (1865).
Courtesy of Special Collections and Archives, Glucksman Library, University of Limerick

Edwin's contribution to Adare and beyond was considerable. He had brought to completion the house his parents had spent 30 years planning and building, restored two churches and built two schools in the village, and through architectural and agricultural improvement provided almost constant employment to those dependent upon him. His intellectual pursuits had opened the way to a more scholarly view of archaeology, and his liberal politics, combined with his deep religious conviction, contributed in no small measure to the furthering of the rights of Irish Catholics to education and freedom of worship. Both spiritually and temporally, Edwin always aimed upwards to improve, to refine, to advance. His obituary noted the peculiar aptness of the family motto, *Quae sursum volo videre*—'I wish to look at what is above'—and observed that Edwin 'lived, always entertaining views which were elevated, and he died turning his eyes in gentle confidence towards the throne of God'.[33] There was, however, a price to pay for such single-minded devotion. A man of deep intellect, Edwin never quite found his place in the world but spent his life in restless pursuit of unattainable ideals. Moreover, his religious conversion, although stemming from a deeply felt desire to return to the true faith of his forefathers, created a rift that threatened the very foundations of his life,

Edwin's shield of arms. Courtesy of the Dunraven family and Special Collections and Archives, Glucksman Library, University of Limerick.

driving away his wife and children and creating a coolness between him and the mother he adored. Yet it was a rift that time gradually diminished and death finally repaired, as Edwin's remains, after a Catholic funeral Mass, were carried on the shoulders of his tenants across the medieval bridge in Adare to the family vault and deposited beside those of his parents.

The legacy that Edwin left behind was perhaps best captured by his closest and lifelong friend, the poet Aubrey de Vere, whose childhood memories of a house filled with music and laughter contrasted sharply with the silence that followed Edwin's death. Aware of the sense of failure and disappointment that had plagued Edwin during the later years of his life, in his elegy de Vere restored to his friend his rightful place among his home and his people.

EDWIN, EARL OF DUNRAVEN

Once more I pace thy pillared halls,
And hear the organ echoes sigh
In blissful death on storied walls:
But where art thou? not here; nor nigh.

Once more the rapt spring-breezes send
A flash o'er yonder winding flood,
And with the garden's fragrance blend
A fresher breath from lawn and wood.

Friend! where art thou? Thy works reply;
The lowly School; the high-arched Fane.
Who loves his kind can never die;
Who serves his God, with God shall reign.[34]

Abbreviations

AG	Augusta Goold, later Augusta Wyndham Quin, Countess of Dunraven, wife of the third Earl of Dunraven
AMW	Anna Maria Wyndham (née Ashby), later Bennett, Caroline Wyndham's mother
CE	Charlotte Edwin (née Jones), Caroline Wyndham's grandmother
CW	Caroline Wyndham, later Caroline Wyndham Quin, Countess of Dunraven, wife of the second Earl of Dunraven
EWQ	Edwin Richard Wyndham Quin, later third Earl of Dunraven
NLWDER	National Library of Wales, Dunraven Estate Records
PCH	Philip Charles Hardwick
TW	Thomas Wyndham, Caroline Wyndham's father
ULDP	University of Limerick, Dunraven Papers
VRQ	Valentine Richard Quin, later first Earl of Dunraven
WHQ	Windham Henry Quin, later Windham Henry Wyndham Quin, second Earl of Dunraven

Endnotes

Preface

1 The Special Collections and Archives Department, Glucksman Library, University of Limerick, holds the papers relating to the family's Irish estate, and the National Library of Wales in Aberystwyth those relating to their Welsh and English properties. In addition, the Glamorgan Archives in Cardiff hold correspondence of the Randall family of solicitors in Bridgend, Glamorganshire, who for much of the nineteenth century acted as agents to the Dunravens. Some material, including architectural drawings, remains at the time of writing in the personal possession of the Dunraven family.

2 M. Bence-Jones, *A Guide to Irish Country Houses* (1978), p. 2.

3 WHQ to VRQ, 6 March 1810, ULDP, D/3196/B/1H.

4 *Recollections of Aubrey de Vere* (1897), p. 26.

Chapter 1 – A Welsh Heiress

1 Ingamells 1997, 792; Young 1780, II, 141.

2 Martin 1998, 21; Anon. 1942, 81.

3 Martin 2004, 59.

4 Thady Quin to Sir John Kirwan, 1 March 1714, ULDP, D/3196/I/7/2.

5 For leases obtained by the Quin family over the centuries, see ULDP, D/3196/K/3/1–61.

6 For agreements concerning the paying off of Windham Quin's debts, see ULDP, D/3196/A/11.

7 VRQ to WHQ, 4 November 1799, ULDP, D/3196/C/1/2.

8 VRQ to WHQ, 7 April 1799, ULDP, D/3196/C/1/1.

9 WHQ to Francis Goold, 17 July 1835, ULDP, uncatalogued item.

10 Baggs and Jurica 1996 (https://www.british-history.ac.uk/vch/glos/vol5/pp195-231, accessed 10 October 2022).

11 Rudder 1779, 569; Crisp 1902, 149.

12 Will of John Wyndham of Clearwell,10 December 1724 (https://www.ancestry.co.uk, accessed 10 October 2022).

13 Baggs and Jurica 1996.

14 Rowan 1970, 149; Colvin 2008, 706–7.

15 Baggs and Jurica 1996.

16 Grose 1775, 109.

17 Swift 1705, 214.

18 Thomas 1997, 26–7.

19 *Ibid.*, 27.

20 Quoted in J. Brooke, 'Edwin (formerly Wyndham), Charles' (http://www.historyofparliamentonline.org/, accessed 10 October 2022).

21 Quoted in Rees 1964–5, 243.

22 R.G. Thorne, 'Wyndham, Thomas' (http://www.historyofparliamentonline.org, accessed 10 October 2022).

23 For more on Fonmon Castle, see Thomas 1999, 63–82.

24 CE to AMW, undated but *c.* 1787–8, ULDP, D/3196/D/3/2.

25 CE to AMW, undated but *c.* 1792, ULDP, D/3196/D/3/2.

26 TW to AMW, 15 August 1793, ULDP, D/3196/D/3/4.

27 Grose 1786, 81–2; Hopkins 1963, 163–4.

28 Hopkins 1963, 163.

29 Quoted in Suggett 1995, 37.

30 Dunraven 1926, 50–1; C.H. Nicholas, 'Dunraven Park' https://coflein.gov.uk/media/17/588/cpg249.pdf, accessed 10 October 2022, 3–4.
31 Dunraven 1926, 51; undated note at the end of TW's 1802 diary, ULDP, D/3196/D/1/12.
32 CW to CE, 4 June 1803, ULDP, D/3196/D/2/38.
33 CW to CE, 3 October 1803, ULDP, D/3196/D/2/41.
34 CW to CE, 25 August 1804, ULDP, D/3196/D/2/43.

35 Undated note at the start of TW's 1806 diary, ULDP, D/3196/D/1/15.
36 Rees 1964–5, 240.
37 Dunraven 1926, 42.
38 *Ibid.*, 44.
39 Guernsey 1857, 296.
40 Printed notes at the end of TW's 1795 diary, ULDP, D/3196/D/1/8.
41 Thomas 1987, 133.
42 Rees 1964–5, 248.
43 Thorne 1986, 499.
44 See, for example, Martin 1998, 217, 243.

Chapter 2 – Adare House

1 CW's journal, 4 June 1808, ULDP, D/3196/E/2/1.
2 Unidentified writer to VRQ, 19 July 1810, ULDP, D/3196/B/1/9.
3 Earl of Balcarres to CE, 17 July 1809, ULDP, D/3196/D/2/57.
4 CE to Earl of Balcarres, 20 July 1809, ULDP, D/3196/D/2/58.
5 CW's journal, 13 and 15 July 1808, ULDP, D/3196/E/2/2.
6 WHQ to VRQ, 6 March 1810, ULDP, D/3196/B/1H.
7 *Ibid.*
8 TW to CE, 17 May 1810, ULDP, D/3196/D/2/86.
9 CW's journal, 27 August–26 November 1810 passim, ULDP, D/3196/E/2/7.
10 CW's journal, 27 December 1810, ULDP, D/3196/E/2/8.
11 Evans 1938, 298.
12 Marriage settlement of Windham Quin and Caroline Wyndham, NLWDER2/308; WHQ to TW, *c.* May 1810, ULDP, D/3196/E/3/2. The Irish pound was valued a few pence below the sterling pound until 1826, when it was brought into line with sterling and ceased to exist as a separate denomination.
13 Malcomson 2006, 202.
14 WHQ to Sir Matthew Barrington, 14 June 1848, ULDP, D/3196/C/12.
15 WHQ to VRQ, 6 March 1810,

ULDP, D/3196/B/1H.
16 Assignment between VRQ and WHQ, 21 April 1811, ULDP, D/3196/B/3.
17 Derrick 1767, II, 3.
18 Will of Valentine Quin, 12 March 1743, ULDP, D/3196/K/1/4.
19 Young 1780, II, 140.
20 Ilchester and Stavordale 1902, I, 315; Dunraven 1865, 147.
21 Dunraven 1865, 147, 159.
22 Holmes 1801, 82.
23 WHQ to CW, 17 March 1811, ULDP, D/3196/E/3/23.
24 Coghlan 1836, 450; WHQ to CW, 4 April 1811, ULDP, D/3196/E/3/36.
25 Extracts from the journals of Susan O'Brien, 1794, 1801 and 1810, and from a letter from Elizabeth Talbot to Harriot Strangways, 27 May 1799, quoted in Martin 2004, 32.
26 WHQ to CW, 26 March 1811, ULDP, D/3196/E/3/26.
27 WHQ to CW, 2 April 1811, ULDP, D/3196/E/3/33.
28 WHQ to CW, 26 March 1811, ULDP, D/3196/E/3/26.
29 WHQ to CW, 4 April 1811, ULDP, D/3196/E/3/37.
30 CW's journal, 15 April 1812, ULDP, D/3196/E/2/10.
31 Earl of Balcarres to CE, 17 December 1811, ULDP, D/3196/D/2/91.

Chapter 3 – All My Beautiful Territories

1 CW's journal, 22 July 1812, ULDP, D/3196/E/2/10.

2 CW's journal, 22 and 25 July 1812, ULDP, D/3196/E/2/10.

3 Dunraven 1865, 158.

4 *Ibid.*, 160.

5 Coghlan 1836, 451–2.

6 VRQ to WHQ, 20 September 1813, ULDP, D/3196/C/1/8.

7 CW's journal, 25 October–18 November 1816 passim, ULDP, D/3196/E/2/14; Coghlan 1836, 451.

8 Dunraven 1865, 65.

9 *Ibid.*, 70.

10 WHQ to CW, 10 April 1811, ULDP, D/3196/E/3/41.

11 Dunraven 1865, 3.

12 Anon. 1823a, 283.

13 CW's reflections, January 1817, ULDP, D/3196/E/1/1.

14 Dunraven 1865, 159.

15 *Ibid.*, 2; *Lancaster Gazette and General Advertiser*, 28 January 1815.

16 CW's journal, 13 August 1813, 27 and 29 September 1813, ULDP, D/3196/E/2/11; also note CW's comments on Askeaton made on 14 October 1815, ULDP, D/3196/E/2/13.

17 Her previous husbands were George Atkinson L'Estrange (d. 1773) and Colonel Arthur Blennerhassett (d. 1799).

18 Memo by VRQ, 26 August 1819, ULDP, D/3196/B/6E.

19 Emma Evans to CE, 8 December 1813, ULDP, D/3196/D/2/115.

20 CW's journal, 8 November 1814, ULDP, D/3196/E/2/12.

21 Dunraven 1926, 43.

22 CW's reflections, January 1815, ULDP, D/3196/E/1/1.

23 CW's journal, undated but written between 22 November and 19 December 1814, ULDP, D/3196/E/2/12.

24 AMW to CW, 5 August [1816?], ULDP, D/3196/E/4/6.

25 *Ibid.*

26 AMW to CW, 25 February 1817, ULDP, D/3196/E/4/10.

27 AMW to CW, 19 December [1815?], ULDP, D/3196/E/4/2.

28 *Ibid.*; and 21 July 1816, ULDP, D/3196/E/4/5.

29 AMW to CW, 5 August 1816, ULDP, D/3196/E/4/6. Pin-money was an allowance usually granted by a husband to his wife to buy clothing and manage the household; it

was considered the wife's personal property and provided women with a small safety net at a time when they had few legal rights.

30 Coghlan 1836, 451–2.

31 AMW to CW, 5 August [1816?], ULDP, D/3196/E/4/6; and 4 February 1817, ULDP, D/3196/E/4/8.

32 WHQ to CW, 15 February 1819, ULDP, D/3196/E/3/49.

33 AMW to CW, 21 February 1819, ULDP, D/3196/E/4/9.

34 CW's journal, 1 and 23 July 1818, ULDP, D/3196/E/2/16; and CW's reflections, January 1819, ULDP, D/3196/E/1/1.

35 AMW to CW, 17 July 1818, ULDP, D/3196/E/4/12.

36 P.J. Jupp, 'Quin, Windham Henry' (http://www.historyofparliamentonline.org, accessed 10 October 2022).

37 The review was published in several instalments in the *Freeman's Journal*; Windham Quin's name appeared in the instalment published on 20 August 1774. Also see Kelly and Dymoke 2004, 199; Large 1958, 39.

38 Wilson and Mackley 2000, 15.

39 CW's journal, 22 December 1817, ULDP, D/3196/E/2/16.

40 For more on James Pain and his contribution to Adare Manor, see Lee 2005, esp. 208–18.

41 Colvin 2008, 766.

42 Anon. 1911, 772.

43 'Hannan, Nicholas' (http://www.dia.ie/architects/, accessed 10 October 2022.

44 CW's journal, 27 July and 6 and 12 August 1818, ULDP, D/3196/E/2/16.

45 CW's journal, 13 August 1818, ULDP, D/3196/E/2/16.

46 CW's journal, 31 August 1818, ULDP, D/3196/E/2/16.

47 CW's journal, 11 December 1818, ULDP, D/3196/E/2/17.

48 *Reports from Committees of the House of Commons* (1819), vol. 5, p. 39; *Parliamentary Debates* (1819), col. 622.

49 CW's journal, 9 February 1819, ULDP, D/3196/E/2/18.

50 Burney 1825, 824–5.

51 WHQ to CW, 13 April 1811, ULDP, D/3196/E/4/44.

52 WHQ to VRQ, 16 April 1820,
ULDP, D/3196/B/1/11.

53 CW's reflections, 2 January 1822,
ULDP, D/3196/E/1/1.

54 Hall 1949, 127–8, 133; Ollerenshaw 1987, 9.

55 *Limerick Chronicle*, 31 May 1820.

56 AMW to CW, 25 February 1817,
ULDP, D/3196/E/4/10.

57 CW's journal, 2 September 1820,
ULDP, D/3196/E/2/19.

58 CW's journal, 7 September 1820,
ULDP, D/3196/E/2/19.

Chapter 4 – Ynyslas

1 D. Robinson, 'Margam Park'
(https://www.countrylife.co.uk/
architecture/margam-park-and-
castle-a-landscape-and-buildings-
with-an-incredible-tale-spanning-
millennia -225344, accessed
10 October 2022).

2 CW's journal, 27 September 1820,
ULDP, D/3196/E/2/19.

3 Thomas 1997, 29–32.

4 For the Williams family of
Aberpergwm House, see Belcham,
n.d. [1992].

5 Wallace 1905, I, 248.

6 Jenkins 1963, 46–8.

7 CW's journal, 19 October 1809,
ULDP, D/3196/E/2/5A.

8 CW's reflections, 2 January 1822,
ULDP, D/3196/E/1/1.

9 A good example of Nash's haphazard
costings can be found at Corsham
Court in Wiltshire, where his initial
estimate for redesigning the house in the
Gothic style was £5,647. The final bill
stood at £25,500.

10 Jenkins 1978.

11 For a more detailed treatment of the design
of Rheola see Suggett 1995, 92–101.

12 CW's journal, 25 September 1821,
ULDP, D/3196/E/2/21.

13 Prichard 1824, 11–12.

14 Quoted in Watkins and Cowell 2006, 68.

15 Suggett 1995, 69–71.

16 Watkins and Cowell 2012, 104.

17 CW's journal, 26 and 28 September 1821,
ULDP, D/3196/E/2/21.

18 CW's journal, 9 May 1821,
ULDP, D/3196/E/2/21.

19 CW's journal, 1 October 1821,
ULDP, D/3196/E/2/21.

20 Provost 1891, 2.

21 CW's reflections, 2 January 1822,
ULDP, D/3196/E/1/1.

22 Aspinall 1947, 84.

23 CW's reflections, 2 January 1822,
ULDP, D/3196/E/1/1.

24 See, for instance, *Morning Post*,
14 January 1822.

25 Wilson and Mackley 2000, 80–2.

26 CW's journal, 13 September 1822,
ULDP, D/3196/E/2/23.

27 Beard 2015, 52.

28 CW's journal, 13 and 14 September 1822,
ULDP, D/3196/E/2/23.

29 CW's journal, 6 February 1818,
ULDP, D/3196/E/2/16.

29 CW's journal, 11 September 1822,
ULDP, D/3193/E/2/23.

30 CW's journal, 9 September 1822,
ULDP, D/3193/E/2/23.

31 CW's journal, 1 May 1822,
ULDP, D/3196/E/2/22.

32 All comments relating to Tintern Abbey
are from CW's journal, 1 May 1822,
ULDP, D/3196/E/2/22.

33 Davis 1793, 48.

34 CW's journal, 19 October 1809,
ULDP, D/3196/E/2/5A.

35 CW's journal, 3 July 1812,
ULDP, D/3196/E/2/10.

36 CW's journal, 25 May 1822,
ULDP, D/3196/E/2/22.

37 CW's journal, 13 June 1822,
ULDP, D/3196/E/2/22.

38 CW's journal, 20 December 1822,
ULDP, D/3196/E/2/24.

39 CW's journal, 31 December 1822,
ULDP, D/3196/E/2/24.

40 'An account of some of the Money
expended by me Lord Dunraven,
in improving the income to be derived
by my good wife out [of] her Welsh
estates', [January 1825],
ULDP, D/3196/E/3/62.

41 CW's reflections, January 1823,
ULDP, D/3196/E/1/1.

Chapter 5 – Emporiums of Taste

1   The Reverend Windham Fitzgerald was also Windham's first cousin, the former's mother being sister to the latter's father.
2   CW's journal, 23 February 1823, ULDP, D/3196/E/2/24.
3   Anon. 1823b, 159.
4   Luddy 1995, 183.
5   CW's journal, 22 May 1820, ULDP, D/3196/E/2/23.
6   CW's journal, 8 March 1823, ULDP, D/3196/E/2/24.
7   In a letter to his wife on 6 April 1811, Windham noted: 'They commenced roofing-in the church today. I have decreed that nothing shall be done about the pew till the building is more advanced and you are here to judge for yourself', ULDP, D/3196/E/3/37.
8   CW's journal, 4 May 1823, ULDP, D/3196/E/2/25.
9   Information relating to Whiteknights Gardens taken from Cooke 1992. The estate was broken up into leaseholds in the 1860s, and eventually sold to Reading University. Although the estate remains for the most part intact, very little of its historic garden survives.
10 CW's journal, 17 July 1823, ULDP, D/3196/E/2/25.
11 Climenson 1899, 165–6.
12 CW's journal, 19 July 1823, ULDP, D/3196/2/25.
13 *The Times*, 30 September 1822.
14 Melville 1910, 314.
15 CW's journal, 19 July 1823, ULDP, D/3196/2/25.
16 Walters 1897, 146.
17 It was in fact made from lead.
18 CW's journal, 22 July 1823, ULDP, D/3196/2/25.
19 *Ibid.*
20 EWQ to CW, 9 November 1823, ULDP, D/3196/E/7/3.
21 CW's journal, 10 May 1824, ULDP, D/3196/E/2/27.
22 CW's journal, 28 June 1824, ULDP, D/3196/E/2/27.
23 CW's journal, 5 July 1824, ULDP, D/3196/E/2/27.
24 CW's reflections, January 1824, ULDP, D/3196/E/1/1.
25 CW's journal, 24 August 1824, ULDP, D/3196/E/2/27.
26 *Ibid.*
27 CW's journal, 1 September 1824, ULDP, D/3196/E/2/27.

Chapter 6 – A Noble Mausoleum

1   Eisteddfod (pl. eisteddfodau) is a competitive festival of the arts popular in Wales.
2   CW's journal, 4–24 September 1824, ULDP, D/3196/E/2/27.
3   Nicholas 1874, 2.
4   CW's journal, 9 April 1825, ULDP, D/3196/E/2/27.
5   Lease dated 7 April 1826, NLWDER, File 67.
6   WHQ to CW, 2 January 1825, ULDP, D/3196/E/3/61–62.
7   WHQ to CW, 24 December 1825, ULDP, D/3196/E/3/66.
8   *Ibid.*
9   WHQ to CW, 12 April 1811, ULDP, D/3196/E/3/43.
10 Rolt 1958, 110–26.
11 CW's journal, 13 April 1826, ULDP, D/3196/E/2/29.
12 CW's journal, 12 April 1826, ULDP, D/3196/E/2/29.
13 Matthew Barrington to WHQ, 6 September 1836, ULDP, D/3196/C/12.
14 CW's journal, 25 April 1826, ULDP, D/3196/E/2/29.
15 Blackwood 1828, 48.
16 CW's journal, 12 March 1826, ULDP, D/3196/E/2/28.
17 Herbert 1981.
18 Temple 1996, 137.
19 CW's journal, 12 March 1826, ULDP, D/3196/E/2/28.
20 CW's journal, 9 February 1827, ULDP, D/3196/E/2/30.
21 CW's journal, 8 October and 5, 8–9, 13 and 21 November 1827, ULDP, D/3196/E/2/30.
22 Note by WHQ, 28 October 1826, ULDP, D/3196/E/3/63.
23 Morrison 1844, 3.

24 CW's journal, 21 September 1828, ULDP, D/3196/E/2/31.

25 Born Aubrey Hunt (1788–1846), he changed his surname to de Vere in 1832 in reference to his Earl of Oxford ancestors. At the same time, he changed the name of the family seat from Curragh to Curragh Chase. He succeeded his father Sir Vere Hunt as second baronet in 1818.

26 *Brighton Gazette*, 16 April 1829.

27 For an account of Amos Henry Wilds and his career see Berry 2012. The ammonite pilaster had originally been devised by the architect George Dance the Younger and had also been used by John Nash, but Wilds adopted the design idiom and made it his own.

28 De Vere 1897, 34–5.

29 CW's journal, 12 March 1829, ULDP, D/3196/E/2/32.

30 Quoted in O'Brien 1991, 105.

31 CW's journal, 31 May 1827, ULDP, D/3196/E/2/30.

32 CW's reflections, January 1828, ULDP, D/3196/E/1/1.

33 EWQ to CW, 18 May 1828, ULDP, D/3196/E/7/8.

34 *Ibid.*

35 CW's journal, 12, 24 and 29 November 1828, ULDP, D/3196/E/2/31; Coghlan 1836, 451. Horse ponds were long and shallow stretches of water, often build adjacent to roads, which allowed horses to be driven in one end and out the other in order to have their legs washed.

36 EWQ to CW, 2 March 1828, ULDP, D/3196/E/7/7.

37 CW's journal, 8 and 14 January 1829, ULDP, D/3196/E/2/31; EWQ to CW, 16 November 1828, ULDP, D/3196/E/7/8.

38 EWQ to CW, 19 October 1828, ULDP, D/3196/E/7/8.

39 CW's journal, 22 and 23 January 1829, ULDP, D/3196/E/2/31.

40 CW's journal, 1 and 30 September 1828, ULDP, D/3196/E/2/31.

41 WHQ to EWQ, 21 February 1829, ULDP, uncatalogued item.

42 EWQ to CW, 19 October 1828, ULDP, D/3196/E/7/8.

43 WHQ to EWQ, 28 May 1829, ULDP, uncatalogued item.

44 EWQ to CW, 7 June 1829, ULDP, D/3196/E/7/10.

45 EWQ to CW, 14 June 1829, ULDP, D/3196/E/7/10.

46 WHQ to EWQ, 18 November 1828, ULDP, uncatalogued item.

47 WHQ to EWQ, 21 February 1829, ULDP, uncatalogued item.

48 WHQ to EWQ, 13 March 1829, ULDP, uncatalogued item.

49 Even with the passing of the Roman Catholic Relief Act, Catholic Emancipation in Ireland remained imperfect; for example, it was not until the Universities Tests Act of 1871 that Roman Catholics were allowed access to university education.

50 EWQ to CW, 12 July 1829, ULDP, D/3196/E/7/10.

51 EWQ to CW, 5 July 1829, ULDP, D/3196/E/7/10.

52 CW's journal, 17 May 1829, ULDP, D/3196/E/2/32.

53 CW's journal, 25 August 1829, ULDP, D/3196/E/2/32.

54 CW's journal, 2 November 1829, ULDP, D/3196/E/2/32.

55 CW's journal, 3 November 1829, ULDP, D/3196/E/2/32.

56 *Parliamentary Gazetteer of Ireland*, vol. 1 (1846), 12; Dunraven 1865, 6.

57 EWQ to CW, 20 March 1831, ULDP, D/3196/E/7/13.

Chapter 7 – Kitchen Gables

1 L.C. Sanders, 'Goold, Thomas (1766–1846)' (http://www.oxforddnb.com, accessed 10 October 2022).

2 WHQ to EWQ, 13 March 1829, ULDP, uncatalogued item.

3 Graves 1882, I, 318.

4 EWQ to CW, 24 April 1830, ULDP, D/3196/E/7/12.

5 EWQ to CW, 16 November 1830, ULDP, D/3196/E/7/12.

6 De Vere 1897, 53.

7 Quoted in Robertson 1960, 90.

8 CW's journal, 8 October 1830, ULDP, uncatalogued item; WHQ to EWQ, 8 October 1830, ULDP, uncatalogued item.

9 WHQ to EWQ, 8 May 1830,
ULDP, uncatalogued item.

10 EWQ to CW, 9 May 1831,
ULDP, D/3196/E/7/13.

11 CW's journal, 9, 17 and 28 April 1832,
ULDP, uncatalogued item.

12 CW to AMW, 21 May 1832,
ULDP, D/3196/D/3/24.

13 CW's reflections, January 1833,
ULDP, D/3196/E/1/1.

14 WHQ to EWQ, 14 May 1832,
ULDP, uncatalogued item.

15 Dunraven 1865, 7.

16 WHQ to EWQ, 28 May 1832,
ULDP, uncatalogued item.

17 Account books kept of building works,
ULDP, D/3196/J/3A/1–6; and bills for
ironwork, brick, plumbing work and Killaloe
slate, ULDP, D/3196/J/4/1–16.

18 CW's reflections, January 1833,
ULDP, D/3196/E/1/1.

19 Hick 1989, 124.

20 Dunraven 1865, 251–2.

21 WHQ to EWQ, 14 May 1832,
ULDP, uncatalogued item.

22 *Second Report of the Royal Commissioners on
Technical Instruction* (London, 1884), IV, 28.

23 CW to AMW, 21 November 1832,
ULDP, D/3196/D/3/23.

24 EWQ to CW, 27 October 1832,
ULDP, D/3196/E/7/14.

25 EWQ to CW, 22 March 1833,
ULDP, D/3196/E/7/14.

26 EWQ to CW, 29 March 1833,
ULDP, D/3196/E/7/14.

27 J. O'Reagan to WHQ, 18 July 1833,
ULDP, D/3196/J/3/2.

28 De Vere 1897, 22.

29 Graves 1882, I, 391–2.

30 *Ibid.*, 392. 'Hartopp' was Edward
Bourchier Hartopp (1808–84), Edwin's
friend at Eton College, who shared
Hamilton's interest in science.

31 See, for example, CW's journal, 17
November 1833, ULDP, D/3196/E/2/36.

32 CW's journal, 15 March 1834,
ULDP, D/3196/E/2/36.

33 Fenning 2003, 77.

34 CW's journal, 30 May 1832,
ULDP, uncatalogued item.

35 See, for example, *Morning Post*, 27 February
1833; also see CW's journal, 20 February
1830, ULDP, uncatalogued item.

36 AG to CW, 28 February 1833,
ULDP, D/3196/E/7/11.

37 CW's journal, 28 February 1833,
ULDP, uncatalogued item.

38 WHQ to EWQ, 11 March 1833,
ULDP, uncatalogued item.

39 CW's journal, 12 March 1833,
ULDP, uncatalogued item.

40 CW's journal, 12 July 1833,
ULDP, D/3196/E/2/36.

41 CWs journal, 7 October 1833 and 28 July
1834, ULDP, D/3196/E/2/36; Lewis 1837, II,
635.

42 CW's journal, 22 March 1834,
ULDP, D/3196/E/2/36.

43 CW's journal, 23 May 1834,
ULDP, D/3196/E/2/36.

44 CW's journal, 28 May 1834,
ULDP, D/3196/E/2/36.

45 *Cork Constitution*, 5 August 1834.

46 *Tipperary Free Press*, 28 March 1832.

47 *Freeman's Journal*, 31 December 1832.

48 For material relating to Foynes Island
and the dispute surrounding the lease
see ULDP, D/3196/C/14.

Chapter 8 – Continental Tours

1 *Dublin Evening Packet and Correspondent*,
1 June 1833.

2 CW's journal, 28 May 1833, ULDP,
uncatalogued item; *Dublin Evening Packet
and Correspondent*, 1 June 1833.

3 Hagley Hall, 'The Long Gallery'
(http://www.hagleyhall.com/,
accessed 10 October 2022).

4 EWQ to CW, 16 and 20 December 1864,
ULDP, D/3196/E/9/1 and 7.

5 WHQ to EWQ, 23 January 1834,
ULDP, uncatalogued item.

6 CW's journal, 2 December 1834,
ULDP, D/3196/E/2/37.

7 The correspondence of William Henry Fox
Talbot: Christopher Rice Mansel Talbot
to William Henry Fox Talbot, 14 July 1830
and 14 December 1831 (https://foxtalbot.
dmu.ac.uk/letters/letters.html, accessed
10 October 2022).

8 CW's reflections, January 1835,
  ULDP, D/3196/E/1/1.
9 Mullen and Munson 2010, 1–19.
10 CW's journal, 20 January 1835,
  ULDP, D/3196/E/2/37.
11 WHQ to EWQ, 9 April 1835,
  ULDP, uncatalogued item.
12 CW's journal, 30 January 1835,
  ULDP, D/3196/E/2/37.
13 CW's journal, 25 February 1835,
  ULDP, D/3196/E/2/37.
14 WHQ to EWQ, 1 July 1835,
  ULDP, uncatalogued item.
15 WHQ to EWQ, 9 April 1835,
  ULDP, uncatalogued item.
16 Roscoe 1844, 100.
17 Grosart 1876, III, 18.
18 Harris and Banham 1984,
  66–7.
19 Westgarth 2009, 19.
20 CW's journal, 5 September 1835,
  ULDP, D/3196/E/2/38.
21 Kingsley 1992, 250.
22 CW's journal, 7 September 1835,
  ULDP, D/3196/E/2/38.
23 Ainsworth 1843, 164–5;
  Knight 1851, 8.
24 CW's journal, 14 September 1835,
  ULDP, D/3196/E/2/38.
25 CW's journal, 22–23 September 1835,
  ULDP, D/3196/E/2/38.
26 WHQ to EWQ, 30 November 1835,
  ULDP, uncatalogued item.
27 AG in a letter from EWQ to
  CW, 7 November 1835,
  ULDP, D/3196/E/7/17.
28 CW's journal, 28 September 1835,
  ULDP, D/3196/E/2/38.

29 CW's journal, 6 October 1835,
  ULDP, D/3196/E/2/38.
30 CW's journal, 14 October 1835,
  ULDP, D/3196/E/2/38.
31 CW's journal, 18 February 1836,
  ULDP, D/3196/E/2/39.
32 CW's journal, 22 October 1835,
  ULDP, D/3196/E/2/38.
33 CW's reflections, January 1836,
  ULDP, D/3196/E/1/1.
34 CW's journal, 10 November 1835,
  ULDP, D/3196/E/2/38.
35 CW to AMW, 5 December 1835,
  ULDP, D/3196/D/3/43.
36 CW's journal, 13 November 1835,
  ULDP, D/3196/E/2/38.
37 CW's journal, 10 December 1835,
  ULDP, D/3196/E/2/38.
38 CW to AMW, 14 December 1835,
  ULDP, D/3196/D/3/44.
39 CW's journal, 23 December 1835,
  ULDP, D/3196/E/2/38.
40 CW's journal, 25 December 1835,
  ULDP, D/3196/E/2/38.
41 CW's journal, 26 December 1835,
  ULDP, D/3196/E/2/38.
42 CW's journal, 29 December 1835,
  ULDP, D/3196/E/2/38.
43 CW's reflections, January 1836,
  ULDP, D/3196/E/1/1.
44 CW's journal, 24 February 1836,
  ULDP, D/3196/E/2/39.
45 CW's journal, 25 February 1836,
  ULDP, D/3196/E/2/39.
46 CW's journal, 2 March 1836,
  ULDP, D/3196/E/2/39.
47 CW's journal, 8 March 1836,
  ULDP, D/3196/E/2/39.

Chapter 9 – Family Matters

1 CW's journal, 16 June 1836,
  ULDP, D/3196/E/2/39.
2 Dunraven 1865, 7n; CW's journal,
  16 June 1836, ULDP, D/3196/E/2/39.
3 The house was not completed until 1861.
4 CW's journal, 31 July 1841,
  ULDP, D/3196/E/2/43.
5 WHQ to CW, 6 November 1839,
  ULDP, D/3196/E/3/82.
6 Calculations by WHQ regarding
  William Monsell's income,
  ULDP, D/3196/E/10.

7 CW's journal, 28 June 1836,
  ULDP, D/3196/E/2/39.
8 AG to CW, 1 April 1833,
  ULDP, D/3196/E/7/15.
9 WHQ to Sir Matthew Barrington,
  14 July 1848, ULDP, D/3196/C/12.
10 CW to AMW, 16 July 1836,
  ULDP, D/3196/D/3/50.
11 Account book no. 4,
  ULDP, D/3196/J/3A/4; WHQ
  to EWQ, 10 February 1837, ULDP,
  uncatalogued item.

12 Thomas Phillips to WHQ, 30 January 1837, ULDP, D/3196/J/3B/4.

13 CW to AMW, 22 January 1837, ULDP, D/3196/D/3/59.

14 WHQ to EWQ, 10 February 1837, ULDP, uncatalogued item.

15 CW's journal, 1 September 1837, ULDP, D/3196/E/2/40.

16 CW's journal, 22 September 1837, ULDP, D/3196/E/2/40.

17 *The Era*, 26 May 1839.

18 *The Examiner*, 2 June 1839.

19 CW's reflections, January 1838, ULDP, D/3196/E/1/1.

20 CW's journal, 12 February 1837, ULDP, D/3196/E/2/40.

21 CW's reflections, January 1838, ULDP, D/3196/E/1/1.

22 CW's journal, 9 October 1837, ULDP, D/3196/E/2/40.

23 Bristol, England, select Church of England parish registers, CW's journal, 13 and 14 September 1822, ULDP, D/3196/E/2/23; Eliza Bolleau was married under the assumed name of Elizabeth Bell.

24 CW's journal, 31 May 1837, D/3196/E/2/40.

25 CW's journal, 24 June 1837, ULDP, D/3196/E/2/40.

26 *Morning Post*, 28 June 1837.

27 *The Globe*, 8 July 1837.

28 *Morning Chronicle*, 4 August 1837.

29 See, for example, *London Evening Standard*, 7 August 1837.

30 CW's journal, 3 August 1837, ULDP, D/3196/E/2/40.

31 See, for example, *The Standard*, 8 August 1837; *Morning Advertiser*, 10 August 1837; CW's journal, 4 August 1837, ULDP, D/3196/E/2/40.

32 Cornforth 1969, 1233.

33 Clarke 1998, 97.

34 Wedgwood 1985, 105. For a short but informative account of Willement's art see Wright 1964–5.

35 WHQ to CW, 9 May 1840, ULDP, D/3196/E/3/136.

36 WHQ to CW, 5 November 1839, ULDP, D/3196/E/3/81.

37 WHQ to CW, 13 November 1839, ULDP, D/3196/E/3/87.

38 WHQ to CW, 6 November 1839, ULDP, D/3196/E/3/82.

39 WHQ to CW, 16 November 1839, ULDP, D/3196/E/3/92.

40 Payne-Gallwey 1995, 90, n. 2.

41 *Adare Manor Ireland* (auction catalogue, 1982), II, 31.

42 WHQ to EWQ, 30 November 1837, ULDP, uncatalogued item.

43 WHQ to CW, 5 February 1840, ULDP, D/3196/E/3/107.

44 WHQ to CW, 5 February 1840, ULDP, D/3196/E/3/107.

45 Dunraven 1865, 17, 24; CW's journal, 25 September 1835, ULDP, D/3196/E/2/38.

46 *Freeman's Journal*, 25 November 1851.

47 WHQ to CW, 10 February 1840, ULDP, D/3196/E/3/109.

48 WHQ to CW, 22 October 1839, ULDP, D/3196/E/3/72.

Chapter 10 – A Dabbler in Architecture

1 CW to John Wick Bennett, 23 August 1838, ULDP, D/3196/D/3/78.

2 WHQ to EWQ, 22 February 1838, ULDP, uncatalogued item.

3 CW's journal, 15 February 1838, ULDP, D/3196/E/2/41.

4 CW to John Wick Bennett, 13 March 1838, ULDP, D/3196/ D/3/77.

5 WHQ to EWQ, 9 December 1833, ULDP, uncatalogued item.

6 WHQ to EWQ, 22 February 1838, ULDP, uncatalogued item.

7 Middleton 1985, 101–2.

8 CW's journal, 7 August 1839,

ULDP, D/3196/E/2/42.

9 *Report of the Oxford Society* (1841), 23.

10 Richardson 1837, 17.

11 Caroline first uses the new name in her reflections in January 1840 (ULDP, D/3196/E/1/1).

12 WHQ to CW, 23 March 1840, ULDP, D/3196/E/3/121.

13 WHQ to Sir Matthew Barrington, 14 July 1848, ULDP, D/3196/C/12.

14 WHQ to CW, 25 March 1840, ULDP, D/3196/E/3/122.

15 Windham is here referring to the so-called Second Barons' War of 1264–7, during which Simon de Montfort, sixth Earl of Leicester, led a group of barons into rebellion against Henry III and took Warwick Castle in a surprise attack.

16 Stephens 1969.

17 WHQ to CW, 25 March 1840, ULDP, D/3196/E/3/122. Some punctuation added by the author for clarity.

18 Hill 2007, 187.

19 WHQ to CW, 28 [?] March 1840, ULDP, D/3196/E/3/123.

20 WHQ to CW, 28 [?] March 1840, ULDP, D/3196/E/3/123.

21 Sigourney 1842, 160.

22 WHQ to CW, 29 March 1840, ULDP, D/3196/E/3/124.

23 Ibid.

24 Ibid.

25 WHQ to EWQ, 7 December 1833, ULDP, uncatalogued item.

26 WHQ to EWQ, 9 April 1835, ULDP, uncatalogued item.

27 EWQ to CW, 30 July 1835, ULDP, D/3196/E/7/17.

28 WHQ to EWQ, 1 July 1835, ULDP, uncatalogued item.

29 James Pain to WHQ, 19 February 1842, ULDP, D/3196/J/3/8.

30 WHQ to James Pain, 21 February 1842, ULDP, D/3196/J/3/8.

31 Myles 1996, 54.

32 Ibid., 38.

33 Quoted in Myles 1996, 46.

34 Myles 2001, 265–70.

35 Britton 1840, 36.

36 Myles 1996, 45.

37 Ibid., 51.

38 WHQ to EWQ, 1 July 1835, ULDP, uncatalogued item.

39 EWQ to CW, 30 July 1835, ULDP, D/3196/E/7/17.

40 Ferrey 1861, 86–7.

41 WHQ to CW, 25 March 1840, ULDP, D/3196/E/3/122.

42 WHQ to CW, 31 March 1840, ULDP, D/3196/E/3/125.

43 WHQ to CW, 4 April 1840, ULDP, D/3196/E/3/126.

44 Ibid.

45 WHQ to CW, 7 April 1840, ULDP, D/3196/E/3/128.

46 WHQ to CW, 4 Apr. 1840, ULDP, D/3196/E/3/126.

47 Ibid.

48 CW's journal, 18 July 1823, ULDP, D/3196/E/2/25.

49 CW's journal, 10 March 1835, ULDP, D/3196/E/2/37.

50 CW's journal, 14 October 1835, ULDP, D/3196/E/2/38.

51 Dunraven 1865, 160.

52 WHQ to CW, 9 May 1840, ULDP, D/3196/E/3/136.

53 WHQ to CW, c. May 1840, ULDP, D/3196/E/3/139.

54 WHQ to CW, 5 November 1839, ULDP, D/3196/E/3/81.

55 Dunraven 1865, 147.

56 WHQ to CW, 10 February 1840, ULDP, D/3196/E/3/112.

57 Dunraven 1865, 15.

58 Second Report of the Royal Commissioners on Technical Instruction (London, 1884), IV, 28.

59 Dunraven 1865, 15.

60 WHQ to CW, 22 February 1840, ULDP, D/3196/E/3/113.

61 WHQ to CW, c. May 1840, ULDP, D/3196/E/3/140.

62 WHQ to CW, after 7 April 1840, ULDP, D/3196/E/3/129.

Chapter 11 – Progress Through Adversity

1 CW's journal, 15 and 16 January 1844, ULDP, D/3196/E/2/47.

2 CW's journal, 19 October 1841, ULDP, D/3196/E/2/43.

3 EWQ to CW, 8 September 1846, ULDP, D/3196/E/8/7.

4 CW's journal, 2 November 1841, ULDP, D/3196/E/2/43.

5 Dunraven 1865, 2.

6 CW's journal, 26 and 27 January 1842, ULDP, D/3196/E/2/44.

7 CW's journal, 25 May 1839, ULDP, D/3196/E/2/41.

8 CW's journal, 21 February 1843, ULDP, D/3196/E/2/45.

9 CW's journal, 6 April 1843, ULDP, D/3196/E/2/46.

10 Now Dún Laoghaire.

11 CW's journal, 24 May 1843,
ULDP, D/3196/E/2/46.

12 CW's journal, 7 July 1843,
ULDP, D/3196/E/2/46.

13 CW's journal, 4 and 5 September 1843,
ULDP, D/3196/E/2/46.

14 CW's reflections, January 1846,
ULDP, D/3196/E/1/1.

15 CW's journal, 18 Apr. 1844,
ULDP, D/3196/E/2/47.

16 Browne 1846, 115–16; *Freeman's Journal*,
22 April 1844.

17 WHQ to EWQ, 26 April 1844,
ULDP, uncatalogued item.

18 CW's journal, 9 August 1845,
ULDP, D/3196/E/2/48.

19 CW's journal, 7 November 1845,
ULDP, D/3196/E/2/48.

20 CW's reflections, January 1847,
ULDP, D/3196/E/1/1.

21 *Morning Chronicle*, 24 April 1846.

22 CW's journal, 30 April 1846,
ULDP, D/3196/E/2/49.

23 See, for example, *Daily News*, 8 May 1847;
Preston Guardian, 22 May 1847;
The Standard, 25 May 1847 and
22 July 1848; and *Limerick Examiner*, 25
September 1847; CW's journal, 9 May
and 22 June 1847, ULDP, D/3196/E/2/50;
CW's reflections, January 1848, ULDP,
D/3196/E/1/1.

24 CW's journal, 20 December 1847,
ULDP, D/3196/E/2/50.

25 CW's journal, 31 October 1849,
ULDP, D/3196/E/2/52; *Freeman's Journal*,
5 November 1849.

26 CW's journal, 15 October 1849,
ULDP, D/3196/E/2/52.

27 CW to John Randall, November 1849,
ULDP, D/3196/M/8.

28 CW's reflections, January 1817,
ULDP, D/3196/E/1/1.

29 Dunraven 1865, 27.

30 EWQ to CW, 16 October 1843,
ULDP, D/3196/E/8/2.

31 CW's journal, 11 September 1844,
ULDP, D/3196/E/2/47.

32 CW's journal, 5 January 1847,
ULDP, D/3196/E/2/50.

33 CW's journal, 29 and 31 March 1848,
ULDP, D/3196/E/2/51.

34 CW's journal, 2 November 1848,
ULDP, D/3196/E/2/51.

35 CW's journal, 27 September 1849,
ULDP, D/3196/E/2/52.

36 CW's journal, 19 July 1849,
ULDP, D/3196/E/2/52.

37 CW's journal, 13 May 1849,
ULDP, D/3196/E/2/52.

38 CW's journal, 23 March 1846,
ULDP, D/3196/E/2/49.

39 Pugin 1841, 1.

40 Hill 2007, 144.

41 EWQ to CW, 17 October 1847,
ULDP, D/3196/E/8/8.

42 CW's journal, 19 May 1849,
ULDP, D/3196/E/2/52; CW's reflections,
January 1850, ULDP, D/3196/E/1/1.

43 Purcell 1900, I, 66. Phillips took the
additional surname of de Lisle in 1862.

44 Ambrose Phillipps to EWQ, 8 May 1845,
ULDP, uncatalogued item.

45 *Ibid.*

46 Hill 2007, 335–46.

47 EWQ to CW, 2 August 1845,
ULDP, D/3196/E/8/5.

48 EWQ to CW, 20 November 1845,
ULDP, D/3196/E/8/6.

49 Ferrey 1861, 136.

50 EWQ to CW, 23 April 1846,
ULDP, D/3196/E/8/6.

51 CW's journal, 28–30 April 1846,
ULDP, D/3196/E/2/49.

52 Pugin to WHQ, 18 May 1846,
ULDP, D/3196/J/5/2.

53 EWQ to CW, 25 June 1846,
ULDP, D/3196/E/8/6.

54 EWQ to CW, 15 August 1846,
ULDP, D/3196/E/8/7.

55 EWQ to CW, 14 January 1848,
ULDP, D/3196/E/8/8.

56 Pugin to WHQ, 23 January 1847,
ULDP, D/3196/J/5/8.

57 Pugin to WHQ, 18 May 1846,
ULDP, D/3196/J/5/2.

58 Pugin to WHQ, 4 August 1846,
ULDP, D/3196/J/5/3; also see 23 January
1847, ULDP, D/3196/J/5/8.

59 Pugin to WHQ, 15 September 1846,
ULDP, D/3196/J/5/5.

60 Pugin to WHQ, 4 August 1846,
ULDP, D/3196/J/5/3.

61 CW's journal, 20 May 1848,
ULDP, D/3196/E/2/52; Augustus Pugin
to Anne Pugin, *c.* 18 May 1848, in Belcher
2001–15, III, 688.

62 EWQ to CW, 13 September 1846,
ULDP, D/3196/E/8/7.

63 EWQ to CW, undated but *c.* December
1833, ULDP, D/3196/E/7/16.

64 WHQ to EWQ, 7 December 1833,
ULDP, uncatalogued item.

65 EWQ to CW, 29 October 1845,
ULDP, D/3196/E/8/6.

66 EWQ to CW, 14 December 1848,
ULDP, D/3196/E/8/10.

67 CW's journal, 12 February 1849,
ULDP, D/3196/E/2/51.

68 See PCH to EWQ, 24 January 1851,
ULDP, D/3196/J/6/5.

69 EWQ to CW, 22 June 1852,
ULDP, D/3196/E/8/14.

70 Telford and Telford to Captain
Curlay, 27 October 1901,
ULDP, D/3196/J/21/3; Dunraven
1865, 15.

71 EWQ to CW, 28 April 1852,
ULDP, D/3196/E/8/14.

72 EWQ to CW, 22 June 1852,
ULDP, D/3196/E/8/14.

73 EWQ to CW, 2 September 1855,
ULDP, D/3196/E/8/16.

74 EWQ to CW, 8 November 1849,
ULDP, D/3196/E/8/11.

Chapter 12 – Deaths and Duties

1 EWQ to WHQ, undated but *c.* May 1850,
ULDP, D/3916/E/7/17.

2 WHQ to EWQ, 30 May 1850,
ULDP, uncatalogued item.

3 WHQ to EWQ, July [1850],
ULDP, uncatalogued item.

4 CW's reflections, January 1851,
ULDP, D/3196/E/1/1.

5 WHQ to CW, 5 August 1850,
ULDP, D/3196/E/3/153.

6 CW's reflections, January 1851,
ULDP, D/3196/E/1/1.

7 *Limerick Reporter*, 13 August 1850;
Freeman's Journal, 13 August 1850.

8 CW's reflections, January 1851,
ULDP, D/3196/E/1/1.

9 *Freeman's Journal*, 8 August 1850.

10 Will of Windham Henry, second Earl of
Dunraven, Public Record Office, London,
PBOB 11: will registers, 1850–1852, piece
2125: vol. 1, quire nos 1–50 (1851).

11 See, for example, WHQ to John Randall, 7
November 1849, ULDP, D/3196/M/8.

12 WHQ to Sir Matthew Barrington, 14 July
1848, ULDP, D/3196/C/12.

13 Dunraven 1922, II, 2.

14 EWQ to CW, 17 December 1843,
ULDP, D/3196/E/8/2.

15 EWQ to CW, 2 February [1844?],
ULDP, D/3196/E/8/2.

16 EWQ to CW, 23 January 1868,
ULDP, D/3196/E/9/4.

17 Lenox-Conyngham 1998, 191; White 1980, 5.

18 James 1945, 210.

19 Potter 2009, 2–3, 43; CW's reflections,
January 1851, ULDP, D/3106/E/1/1.

20 *The Standard*, 23 December 1850.

21 CW's reflections, January 1851,
ULDP, D/3106/E/1/1.

22 Dunraven 1922, I, 4, 7–9.

23 AG to CW, 18 August [1856],
ULDP, D/3196/E/8/17.

24 EWQ to CW, 17 December 1856,
ULDP, D/3196/E/8/17.

25 EWQ to CW, 11 December 1856,
ULDP, D/3196/E/8/17.

26 EWQ to CW, 22 June 1852,
ULDP, D/3196/E/8/14.

27 *Cork Examiner*, 1 May 1854.

28 Quoted in Trappes-Lomax 1932, 306.

29 PCH to EWQ, 24 October 1850,
ULDP, D/3196/J/6/1.

30 EWQ to CW, 27 December [1851?],
ULDP, D/3196/E/8/18.

31 EWQ to CW, 20 July [1852],
ULDP, D/3196/E/8/14.

32 PCH to EWQ, 7 November 1856,
ULDP, D/3196/J/6/58.

33 PCH to EWQ, 12 April [1852],
ULDP, D/3196/J/6/29.

34 EWQ to CW, 2 October 1852,
ULDP, D/3196/E/8/14.

35 *Freeman's Journal*, 6 December
1854.

36 EWQ to CW, 22 June [1852],
ULDP, D/3196/E/8/18.

37 CW's reflections, January 1851,
ULDP, D/3196/E/1/1.

38 EWQ to CW, 18 June 1853,
ULDP, D/3196/E/8/15.

39 EWQ to CW, 15 July 1853,
ULDP, D/3196/E/8/15.

40 EWQ to CW, 1 November [1855?],
   ULDP, D/3196/E/8/18.
41 For Middleton's collaboration with
   Caroline see Torode 2008, 81–6.
42 CW's journal, 29 June 1863,
   ULDP, D/3196/E/2/65.
43 CW's journal, 25 May 1869,

ULDP, D/3196/E/2/68.
44 Swete, n.d. [1870], 162.
45 CW's journal, 1 November 1869,
   ULDP, D/3196/E/2/68.
46 CW's journal, 5 July 1856,
   ULDP, uncatalogued item.

Chapter 13 – Clerks of Works

1 CW's reflections, January 1851,
   ULDP, D/3196/E/1/1.
2 CW's journal, 7 August 1850,
   ULDP, uncatalogued item.
3 CW's journal, 13–16 September 1850,
   ULDP, uncatalogued item.
4 PCH to EWQ, 23 November 1850,
   ULDP, D/3196/J/6/2.
5 PCH to EWQ, 15 January 1851,
   ULDP, D/3196/J/6/3.
6 PCH to EWQ, 23 November 1850,
   ULDP, D/3196/J/6/2.
7 EWQ to CW, 11 May 1849,
   ULDP, D/3196/E/8/11.
8 Some ten years later, the small library
   between the dining room and drawing room
   was converted into a billiard room and the
   drawing room into a library.
9 PCH to EWQ, 23 November 1850,
   ULDP, D/3196/J/6/2.
10 PCH to EWQ, 24 October 1850,
   ULDP, D/3196/J/6/1.
11 PCH to EWQ, 24 January 1851,
   ULDP, D/3196/J/6/5.
12 PCH to EWQ, 19 February 1851,
   ULDP, D/3196/J/6/6.
13 *Ibid*.
14 PCH to EWQ, 15 January 1851,
   ULDP, D/3196/J/6/3.
15 PCH to James Connolly, 6 March 1851,
   ULDP, D/3196/J/6/7.
16 EWQ to CW, 24 March 1851,
   ULDP, D/3196/E/8/13.
17 EWQ to CW, 26 March [1851],
   ULDP, D/3196/E/8/13.
18 AG to CW, 8 [May 1853],
   ULDP, D/3196/E/8/14.
19 List of labourers employed at Adare Manor,
   August 1851, ULDP, D/3196/J/15/1.
20 EWQ to CW, 17 May 1852,
   ULDP, D/3196/E/8/14.
21 EWQ to CW, 24 March 1851,
   ULDP, D/3196/E/8/13.

22 EWQ to CW, 27 August 1851,
   ULDP, D/3196/E/8/13.
23 EWQ to CW, 24 and 26 March [1851],
   ULDP, D/3196/E/8/13.
24 PCH to EWQ, 24 October 1850,
   ULDP, D/3196/J/6/1.
25 PCH to EWQ, 2 January [1855?],
   ULDP, D/3196/J/6/48.
26 WHQ to Sir Matthew Barrington,
   14 July 1848, ULDP, D/3196/C/12.
27 EWQ to CW, 24 March, 4 and 5 April
   1851, ULDP, D/3196/E/8/13.
28 EWQ to CW, 5, 10 and 17 April 1851,
   ULDP, D/3196/E/8/13.
29 EWQ to WHQ, undated but *c*. June
   1850, ULDP, D/3916/E/7/17.
30 EWQ to CW, 10 June 1851,
   ULDP, D/3196/E/8/13.
31 PCH to EWQ, 21 June 1851,
   ULDP, D/3196/J/6/17.
32 EWQ to CW, 23 August 1851,
   ULDP, D/3196/E/8/13.
33 EWQ to CW, 7 July [1851?],
   ULDP, D/3196/E/8/13.
34 EWQ to CW, 18 June [1851?],
   ULDP, D/3196/E/8/18.
35 EWQ to CW, 7 June 1851,
   ULDP, D/3196/E/8/13.
36 EWQ to CW, 23 and 27 August 1851,
   ULDP, D/3196/E/8/13.
37 EWQ to CW, 24 March and 5 April 1851,
   ULDP, D/3196/E/8/13.
38 EWQ to CW, 6 July 1851,
   ULDP, D/3196/E/8/13.
39 EWQ to CW, 24 March 1851,
   ULDP, D/3196/E/8/13.
40 See, for example, *Dublin Evening
   Packet and Correspondent*, 9 October
   1851.
41 EWQ to CW, 29 January 1852,
   ULDP, D/3196/E/8/14.
42 EWQ to CW, 2 February 1852,
   ULDP, D/3196/E/8/14.

43 EWQ to CW, 12 February 1852, ULDP, D/3196/E/8/14.
44 EWQ to CW, 22 June 1852, ULDP, D/3196/E/8/14.
45 EWQ to CW, 2 July 1852, ULDP, D/3196/E/8/14.
46 EWQ to CW, 13 October 1852, ULDP, D/3196/E/8/14.
47 EWQ to CW, 22–25 September 1852, ULDP, D/3196/E/8/14.
48 EWQ to CW, 2 October 1852, ULDP, D/3196/E/8/14.
49 EWQ to CW, 31 October 1852, ULDP, D/3196/E/8/14.
50 EWQ to CW, 11 December 1852, ULDP, D/3196/E/8/14.
51 AG to CW, December 1852, ULDP, D/3196/E/8/14.
52 EWQ to CW, 16 December 1852, ULDP, D/3196/E/8/14.
53 AG to CW, December 1852, ULDP, D/3196/E/8/14.
54 PCH to EWQ, 16 March 1854, ULDP, D/3196/J/6/43.
55 Estimate dated 30 September 1852, ULDP, D/3196/J/8/32.
56 PCH to EWQ, 12 June [1851?], ULDP, D/3196/J/6/15.
57 EWQ to CW, 12 July 1856, ULDP, D/3196/E/8/17.

Chapter 14 – Finishing Touches

1 AG to CW, 12 and 13 September 1851, ULDP, D/3196/E/8/13. The glazing was subsequently removed by later generations.
2 PCH to EWQ, 15 December [1851?], ULDP, D/3196/J/6/25.
3 Bill from John Crace to Pugin, 2 April 1851, ULDP, D/3196/J/9/14.
4 Bill for wall hangings from John Crace, 27 December 1859, ULDP, D/3196/J/10/15; estimate for oak bookcases and doors by John Crace, June 1863, ULDP, D/3196/J/20/4.
5 PCH to EWQ, 11 June [1851?], ULDP, D/3196/J/6/14.
6 *Ibid.*
7 EWQ to CW, 17 November 1854, ULDP, D/3196/E/8/16.
8 EWQ to CW, 15 June [1854?], ULDP, D/3196/E/8/18.
9 PCH to EWQ, 20 February 1854, ULDP, D/3196/J/6/40.
10 For a bill and estimate for chimney-pieces in the dining and billiard rooms see ULDP, D/3196/J/9/2 and 76.
11 AG to CWQ, 21 March [1854], ULDP, D/3196/E/8/16.
12 EWQ to CW, 16 March 1853, ULDP, D/3196/E/8/15; E.W. Pugin to EWQ, 15 September 1853, ULDP, D/3196/J/5/11.
13 EWQ to CW, 14 January 1856, ULDP, D/3196/E/8/17.
14 For related lists and bills see ULDP, D/3196/J/13/2–3 and an unnumbered item between 17 and 18.
15 EWQ to CW, 5 November 1856, ULDP, D/3196/E/8/17.
16 EWQ to CW, 19 August 1857, ULDP, D/3196/E/8/17.
17 PCH to EWQ, 10 September 1857, ULDP, D/3196/J/6/60.
18 Bill from John Hardman, December 1860, ULDP, D/3196/J/9/33.
19 CW's journal, 27 February 1846, ULDP, D/3196/E/2/49.
20 Quoted in B. Roberts and P. Yunnie, The story of Rosser & Russell [n.d.] (http://www.hevac-heritage.org/electronic_books/rosser_&_russell-2/1-RR.pdf, accessed 10 October 2022), p. 6.
21 EWQ to CW, 8 June 1847, ULDP, D/3196/E/8/8.
22 EWQ to CW, 3 December 1847, ULDP, D/3196/E/8/8.
23 EWQ to WHQ, undated but *c.* June 1850, ULDP, D/3916/E/7/17.
24 WHQ to EWQ, 30 May 1850, DEC.
25 EWQ to CW, 14 January 1856, ULDP, D/3196/E/8/17.
26 EWQ to CW, 20 December [1864?], ULDP, D/3196/E/9/7.
27 For correspondence and estimates see ULDP, D/3196/J/19/1–21.
28 EWQ to CW, 19 November 1869, ULDP, D/3196/E/9/6.
29 EWQ to CW, 13 December [1854–5?], ULDP, D/3196/E/8/18.
30 EWQ to CW, 1 May 1852, ULDP, D/3196/E/8/14.

31 EWQ to CW, 8 May 1852,
ULDP, D/3196/E/8/14.

32 EWQ to CW, 16 January 1865,
ULDP, D/3196/E/9/2.

33 EWQ to CW, 19 November 1868,
ULDP, D/3196/E/9/4.

34 EWQ to CW, 29 January 1868,
ULDP, D/3196/E/9/4.

35 EWQ to CW, 21 December 1868,
ULDP, D/3196/E/9/4.

36 *Nottinghamshire Guardian*, 28
February 1868.

37 PCH to EWQ, 20 February 1854,
ULDP, D/3196/J/6/39.

38 EWQ to CW, 25 February 1854,
ULDP, D/3196/E/8/16.

39 EWQ to CW, 15 April 1851,
ULDP, D/3196/E/8/13.

40 EWQ to CW, 26 March 1855,
ULDP, D/3196/E/8/16.

41 EWQ to CW, 27 December [1856],
ULDP, D/3196/E/8/13.

42 EWQ to CW, 5 May 1855,
ULDP, D/3196/E/8/16.

43 EWQ to CW, 2 July 1853,
ULDP, D/3196/E/8/15.

44 *Morning Post*, 9 January 1855;
Dublin Evening Post, 13 January 1855.

45 AG to CW, 1 February 1855,
ULDP, D/3196/E/8/16.

46 EWQ to CW, 9 April 1855,
ULDP, D/3196/E/8/16.

47 Loudon 1840, 49.

48 EWQ to CW, 3 January 1857,
ULDP, D/3196/E/8/17.

49 PCH to EWQ, 1 November 1858,
ULDP, D/3196/J/6/64.

50 EWQ to CW, 3 January 1857,
ULDP, D/3196/E/8/17.

51 PCH to EWQ, 1 November 1858,
ULDP, D/3196/J/6/64.

52 EWQ to CW, 19 April 1857,
ULDP, D/3196/E/8/17.

53 PCH to EWQ, 21 February 1858,
ULDP, D/3196/J/6/62.

54 PCH to EWQ, 21 February 1858,
ULDP, D/3196/J/6/62.

55 PCH to M. Duggan, 9 February 1859,
ULDP, D/3196/J/6/70.

56 John Duggan to EWQ, 15 February 1859,
ULDP, D/3196/J/6/72.

57 William Spaight to PCH, 26 November
1858, ULDP, D/3196/J/6/69.

58 EWQ to CW, 4 January 1864,
ULDP, D/3196/E/9/1.

59 EWQ to CW, 6 March 1864,
ULDP, D/3196/E/9/1.

60 EWQ to CW, 20 December [1864?],
ULDP, D/3196/E/9/7; and 16 January 1866,
ULDP, D/3196/E/9/4.

Chapter 15 – *Quae Sursum Volo Videre*

1 EWQ to CW, 24 December 1863,
ULDP, D/3196/E/9/1.

2 PCH to EWQ, 29 March 1851,
ULDP, D/3196/J/6/8.

3 EWQ to CW, 13 May 1852,
ULDP, D/3196/E/8/14.

4 Dunraven 1865, 147–8.

5 Anon. 1872, 82.

6 Dunraven 1875–7, I, xiv.

7 EWQ to CW, 31 July 1851,
ULDP, D/3196/E/8/13.

8 *London Daily News*, 4 September 1851.

9 EWQ to CW, 23 July 1851, ULDP,
D/3196/E/8/13; Dunraven 1865, 156–7.

10 For related estimates and correspondence,
see ULDP, D/3196/J/16–17.

11 CW's journal, 6 August 1863,
ULDP, D/3196/E/2/65.

12 CW's journal, 21 August 1863,
ULDP, D/3196/E/2/65.

13 CW's journal, 5 and 23 December
1865, ULDP, uncatalogued item.

14 CW's journal, 31 October 1865,
ULDP, uncatalogued item.

15 CW's journal, 26 October 1866,
ULDP, D/3196/E/2/67.

16 CW's journal, 22 November 1866,
ULDP, D/3196/E/2/67.

17 *Freeman's Journal*, 13 March 1857;
London Daily News, 16 January 1858.

18 EWQ to CW, 20 March 1867,
ULDP, D/3196/E/9/4.

19 EWQ to CW, 16 February 1869,
ULDP, D/3196/E/9/6.

20 EWQ to CW, 20 May 1869,
ULDP, D/3196/E/9/6.

21 EWQ to CW, 8 December 1868,
ULDP, D/3196/E/9/4.

22 EWQ to CW, 28 December 1868,
ULDP, D/3196/E/9/4.

23 CW's journal, 10 January 1870, ULDP, D/3196/E/2/68.

24 CW's journal, 8 and 16 February 1870, ULDP, D/3196/E/2/68.

25 CW's journal, 26 and 27 September 1867, ULDP, D/3196/E/2/67.

26 Anon. 1872, 81; *Western Mail*, 28 May 1870.

27 *Western Mail*, 28 May 1870.

28 *Western Mail*, 3 June 1870.

29 *Tipperary Vindicator*, 3 June 1870.

30 *Western Mail*, 3 June 1870.

31 *Morning Post*, 27 Aug. 1870.

32 John Doherty to EWQ, 9 September 1870, ULDP, D/3196/J/3/29.

33 *Freeman's Journal*, 9 October 1871.

34 Woodberry 1894, 303–4.

Bibliography

Manuscripts

Dunraven Papers (D/3196), Special Collections and Archives Department, Glucksman Library, University of Limerick.
Dunraven Papers, in possession of the Dunraven family.
Dunraven Estate Records, National Library of Wales.
Public Record Office, London: will of Windham Henry, second Earl of Dunraven, PBOB 11: will registers, 1850–1852, piece 2125: vol. 1, quire nos 1–50 (1851).

Online Sources

Baggs, A.P. and Jurica, A.R.J. 1996 'Newland'. In C.R.J. Currie and N.M. Herbert (eds), *A History of the County of Gloucester, volume 5: Bledisloe Hundred, St Briavels Hundred, the Forest of Dean*, 195–231. London, British History Online, http://www.british-history.ac.uk/vch/glos/vol5/pp195-231 (accessed 10 October 2022.)
Brooke, J., 'Edwin (formerly Wyndham), Charles (d. 1801), of Llanmihangel Plas and Dunraven Castle, Glam.', http://www.historyofparliamentonline.org/volume/1754-1790/member/edwin-%28formerly-wyndham%29-charles-1801 (accessed 10 October 2022).
Bristol, England, select Church of England Parish Registers, 1720–1933, www.ancestry.co.uk (accessed 10 October 2022).
The correspondence of William Henry Fox Talbot, http://foxtalbot.dmu.ac.uk/letters/letters.html (accessed 10 October 2022).
Hagley Hall, 'The Long Gallery', http://www.hagleyhall.com/the-hall/the-state-rooms/the-long-gallery (accessed 10 October 2022).
'Hannan, Nicholas', *Dictionary of Irish Architects, 1720–1940*, http://www.dia.ie/architects/view/2371/HANNAN-NICHOLAS%2A (accessed 10 October 2022).
Herbert, N.M. 1981 'Cranham'. In N.M. Herbert (ed.), *A History of the County of Gloucester: volume 7*, 199–210. Oxford. (British History Online, http://www.british-history.ac.uk/vch/glos/vol7/pp199-210, accessed 10 October 2022.)
Jupp, P.J., 'Quin (afterwards Wyndham Quin), Windham Henry (1782–1850), of Adare, co. Limerick', http://www.historyofparliamentonline.org/volume/1790-1820/member/quin-%28afterwards-wyndham-quin-%29-windham-henry-%29-1782-1850 (accessed 10 October 2022).

Nicholas, C.H., 'Dunraven Park', *Cadw Parks and Gardens Register* (2006), PDF file, https://coflein.gov.uk/media/17/588/cpg249.pdf (accessed 10 October 2022).

Roberts, B. and Yunnie, P., *The Story of Rosser & Russell* [n.d.], PDF file, http://www.hevac-heritage.org/electronic_books/rosser_&_russell-2/1-RR.pdf (accessed 10 October 2022).

Robinson, D., 'Margam Park and Castle: A Landscape and Buildings with an Incredible Tale Spanning Millenia', https://www.countrylife.co.uk/architecture/margam-park-and-castle-a-landscape-and-buildings-with-an-incredible-tale-spanning-millennia-225344 (accessed 10 October 2022).

Sanders, L.C., 'Goold, Thomas (1766–1846)', *Oxford Dictionary of National Biography*, http://www.oxforddnb.com (accessed 10 October 2022).

Stephens, W.B. 1969 'The Borough of Warwick: The Castle and Castle Estate in Warwick'. In W.B. Stephens (ed.), *A History of the County of Warwick, volume 8: The City of Coventry and Borough of Warwick*, 452–75. London, British History Online, http://www.british-history.ac.uk/vch/warks/vol8/pp452-475 (accessed 10 October 2022.)

Thorne, R.G., 'Wyndham, Thomas (?1763–1814), of Dunraven Castle, Glam.', https://www.historyofparliamentonline.org/volume/1790-1820/member/wyndham-thomas-1763-1814 (accessed 10 October 2022).

Will of John Wyndham of Clearwell, 10 December 1724, the National Archives UK, *Prerogative Court of Canterbury and Related Probate Jurisdictions: Will Registers*; class: *PROB 11*; piece: *606,* https://ancestry.co.uk (accessed 10 October 2022).

Published Sources

Adare Manor Ireland. Christie, Manson & Woods auction catalogue (2 vols) (London, 1982).

Ainsworth, W.H. 1843 *Windsor Castle: An Historical Romance.* London.

Anon. 1823a 'Accounts Relating to Diocesan and Parish Schools in Ireland', House of Commons 1823 (229), vol. 16, 241–318.

Anon. 1823b 'Society for the Relief of the Peasantry of Ireland'. *The Inquirer* **2**, 156–60. London.

Anon. 1872 'The Late Earl of Dunraven'. *Archaeological Journal* **29**, 78–82.

Anon. 1911 'Some Forgotten Books and a Family of Architects'. *The Builder* (23 June 1911), 769–73.

Anon. 1942 'Editorial: Art Treasures Lost and Found'. *The Burlington Magazine for Connoisseurs* **80** (469), 80–2.

Arnold, D. 1998 *The Georgian Country House: Architecture, Landscape and Society.* Stroud.

Aspinall, A. (ed.) 1947 *The Diary of Henry Hobhouse.* London.

Beard, G. 2015 *Decorative Plasterwork in Great Britain.* Abingdon.

Belcham, E.F. (n.d. [1992]) *About Aberpergwm: The House of the Williams Family in the Vale of Neath, Glamorgan.* Glynneath.

Belcher, M. (ed.) 2001–15 *The Collected Letters of A.W.N. Pugin* (5 vols). Oxford.

Bence-Jones, M. 1987 *Twilight of the Ascendancy.* London.

Bence-Jones, M. 1988 *A Guide to Irish Country Houses* (revised edn). London.

Bence-Jones, M. 1996 *Life in an Irish Country House.* London.

Berry, S. 2012 'The Georgian Provincial Builder-Architect and Architect Amon and Amon Henry Wilds of Lewes and Brighton, *c.* 1790–1850'. *Sussex Archaeological Collections* **150**, 163–83.

Blackwood, W. 1828 'Notes of a Journey in the Kingdom of Kerry'. *Blackwood's Edinburgh Magazine* **23** (134), 48–54.

Bourne, J.M. 1986 *Patronage and Society in Nineteenth Century England.* Baltimore.

Britton, J. 1840 *Graphic Illustrations, with Historical and Descriptive Accounts, of Toddington, Gloucestershire, the Seat of Lord Sudeley.* London.

Browne, R.D. 1846 *Debate on the First Reading of the Protection of Life (Ireland) Bill.* London.

Bunbury, T. (n.d. [2019]) *Adare Manor: The Renaissance of an Irish Country House.* Adare.

Burney, M.C. 1825 *General Index to Journals of the House of Commons, vol. 54 (1801) to vol. 75 (1820).* London.

Clarke, S. 1998 'Abbeys Real and Imagined: Northanger, Fonthill, and Aspects of the Gothic Revival'. *Persuasions* **20**, 92–105.

Climenson, E.J. (ed.) 1899 *Passages from the Diaries of Mrs Philip Lybbe Powys of Hardwick House, Oxon., AD 1756 to 1808.* London.

Coghlan, A. 1836 'A Brief Description of the Gardens of Adare, the Residence of the Earl of Dunraven, in the County of Limerick'. *The Gardener's Magazine* (new ser.) **2**, 450–2.

Colvin, H. 2008 *A Biographical Dictionary of British Architects, 1600–1840* (4th edn). New Haven.

Cooke, I.K.S. 1992 'Whiteknights and the Marquis of Blandford'. *Garden History* **20** (1), 28–44.

Cornforth, J. 1969 'Adare Manor, Co. Limerick—The Seat of the Earls of Dunraven'. *Country Life* **165**, 1230–4, 1302–6, 1366–9.

Cotman, J.S. 1838 *Specimens of Architectural Remains in Various Counties in England but Principally in Norfolk* (2 vols). London.

Crisp, F.A. 1902 *Fragmenta Genealogica*, vol. 8. [N.p.]

Curl, J. 1990 *Victorian Architecture.* Newton Abbot.

Davis, Revd D. 1793 'Poetical Description of Tintern Abbey'. In C. Heath (ed.), *Historical and Descriptive Accounts of the Ancient and Present State of Tintern Abbey.* Monmouth.

De Vere, A. 1897 *Recollections of Aubrey de Vere* (2nd edn). New York.

Derrick, S. 1767 *Letters Written from Leverpoole, Chester, Corke, the Lake of Killarney, Dublin, Tunbridge-Wells, and Bath* (2 vols). Dublin.

Dooley, T., O'Riordan, M. and Ridgway, C. (eds) 2018 *Women and the Country House in Ireland and Britain.* Dublin.

Dunraven, Caroline, Countess of 1865 *Memorials of Adare Manor: With Historical Notices of Adare, by Her Son, the Earl of Dunraven.* Oxford.

Dunraven, Edwin Richard Windham Wyndham Quin, Earl of 1875–7 *Notes on Irish Architecture* (ed. M. Stokes) (2 vols). London.

Dunraven, Windham Henry Wyndham Quin, Earl of 1926 *Dunraven Castle, Glamorgan: Some Notes on Its History and Associations.* London.

Dunraven, Windham Thomas Wyndham Quin, Earl of 1922 *Past Times and Pastimes* (2 vols). London.

Evans, C.J.O. 1938 *Glamorgan: Its History and Topography.* Cardiff.

Faught, C.B. 2003 *The Oxford Movement: A Thematic History of the Tractarians and Their Times.* Pennsylvania.

Fenning, H. 2003 'The Cholera Epidemic in Ireland, 1832–3: Priests, Ministers, Doctors'. *Archivium Hibernicum* **57**, 77–125.

Ferrey, B. 1861 *Recollections of A.N. Welby Pugin, and His Father, Augustus Pugin; With Notices of Their Works.* London.

Franklin, J. 1981 *The Gentleman's Country House and Its Plan, 1835–1914.* London.

Gilpin, W. 1782 *Observations on the River Wye, and Several Parts of South Wales, &c. Relative Chiefly to Picturesque Beauty: Made in the Summer of the Year 1770.* London.

Girouard, M. 1978 *Life in the English Country House: A Social and Architectural History.* New Haven.

Graves, R.P. 1882 *Life of Sir William Rowan Hamilton* (3 vols). Dublin.

Grosart, Revd A.B. (ed.) 1876 *The Prose Works of William Wordsworth* (3 vols). London.

Grose, F. 1775 *The Antiquarian Repertory*, vol. 1. London.

Grose, F. 1786 *The Antiquities of England and Wales*, vol. 7 (new edn). London.

Guernsey, E. 1857 *Homeopathic Domestic Practice* (2nd edn). New York.

Hall, F.G. 1949 *The Bank of Ireland, 1783–1946.* Dublin.

Harris, J. and Banham, J. 1984 *William Morris and the Middle Ages: A Collection of Essays, Together with a Catalogue of Works Exhibited at the Whitworth Art Gallery, 28 September–8 December 1984.* Manchester.

Hick, V. 1989 'The Palatine Settlement in Ireland: The Early Years'. *Eighteenth-Century Ireland* **4**, 113–31.

Hill, J. 2011 'Gothic in Post-Union Ireland'. In T. Dooley and C. Ridgeway (eds), *The Irish Country House: Past, Present and Future*, 58–89. Dublin.

Hill, R. 2007 *God's Architect: Pugin and the Building of Romantic Britain.* London.

Hobhouse, H. 1977 'Philip and Philip Charles Hardwick: An Architectural Dynasty'. In J. Fawcett (ed.), *Seven Victorian Architects*, 32–49. Pennsylvania.

Hofland, B. 1819 *A Descriptive Account of the Mansion and Gardens of White-Knights: A Seat of His Grace the Duke of Marlborough.* London.

Holmes, G. 1801 *Sketches of Some of the Southern Counties of Ireland Collected During a Tour in the Autumn of 1797 in a Series of Letters.* London.

Hopkins, T.J. 1963 'Francis Grose's Tour in Glamorgan, 1775'. In S. Williams (ed.), *Glamorgan Historian*, vol. 1, 158–70. Cowbridge.

Ilchester, Countess of and Stavordale, Lord (eds) 1902 *The Life and Letters of Lady Sarah Lennox, 1745–1826* (2 vols). London.

Ingamells, J. 1997 *A Dictionary of British and Irish Travellers in Italy, 1701–1800.* New Haven.

James, L. 1945 *A Forgotten Genius: Sewell, of St Columba's and Radley.* London.

Jenkins, E. 1963 'Artists in the Vale of Neath'. In S. Williams (ed.), *Glamorgan Historian*, vol. 1, 44–53. Cowbridge.

Jenkins, E. 1978 'Rheola'. *Transactions of the Neath Antiquarian Society* (1978), 61–8.

Jenkins, P. 1983 *The Making of a Ruling Class: The Glamorgan Gentry, 1640–1790.* Cambridge.

Kelly, J. and Dymoke 2004 'Documents: Review of the House of Commons, 1774'. *Eighteenth-Century Ireland* **19**, 163–210.

Kingsley, N. 1992 *The Country Houses of Gloucestershire, volume 2: 1660–1830.* Chichester.

Knight, C. 1851 *Knight's Excursion Companion: Excursions from London.* London.

Laffan, W. (ed.) 2006 *Painting Ireland: Topographical Views from Glin Castle.* Tralee.

Large, D. 1958 'The Irish House of Commons in 1769'. *Irish Historical Studies* **11** (41), 18–45.

Lee, D. 2005 *James Pain, Architect* (ed. D. Jacobs). Limerick.

Lenox-Conyngham, M. 1998 'Rev. William Sewell 1804–1874'. In M. Lenox-Conyngham (ed.), *Diaries of Ireland: An Anthology, 1590–1987*, 191–8. Dublin.

Lewis, S. 1837 *A Topographical Dictionary of Ireland* (2 vols). London.

Loudon, J.C. 1840 'Fortis Green, Muswell Hill, the Villa of W.A. Nesfield, Esq.' *The Gardener's Magazine* (February 1840), 49–58.

Luddy, M. 1995 *Women and Philanthropy in Nineteenth-Century Ireland.* Cambridge.

Malcomson, A.P.W. 2006 *The Pursuit of the Heiress: Aristocratic Marriage in Ireland, 1740–1840.* Belfast.

Martin, J. (ed.) 1998 *A Governess in the Age of Jane Austen: The Journals and Letters of Agnes Porter.* London.

Martin, J. 2004 *Wives and Daughters: Women and Children in a Georgian Country House.* London.

Melville, L. 1910 *The Life and Letters of William Beckford of Fonthill.* London.

Middleton, C.R. 1985 'Irish Representative Peerage Elections and the Conservative Party, 1832–1841'. *Proceedings of the American Philosophical Society* **129** (1), 90–111.

Morgan, E.A. 1954 'The Wesleys and Fonmon Castle, Glamorgan'. *Bathafarn: The Journal of the Historical Society of the Methodist Church in Wales* **9**, 38–41.

Morrison, J. 1844 'Life of the late William Vitruvius Morrison, of Dublin, Architect'. In J. Weale (ed.), *Quarterly Papers on Architecture*, vol. 1, 1–8. London.

Mullen, R. and Munson, J. 2010 *The Smell of the Continent: The British Discover Europe.* London.

Myles, J. 1996 *L.N. Cottingham, 1787–1847: Architect of the Gothic Revival.* London.

Myles, J. 2001 L.N. 'Cottingham's Museum of Mediaeval Art: Herald of the Gothic Revival'. *Visual Resources* **17** (3), 253–87.

Nash, J. 1839–49 *Mansions of England in the Olden Time* (4 vols). London.

NicGhabhann, N. 2015 *Medieval Ecclesiastical Buildings in Ireland, 1789–1915: Building on the Past.* Dublin.

Nicholas, T. 1874 *The History and Antiquities of Glamorganshire and Its Families.* London.

O'Brien, G.R. 1991 *These My Friends and Forebears: The O'Briens of Dromoland.* Whitegate.

O'Brien, J. and Guinness, D. 1992 *Great Irish Houses and Castles.* London.

Ollerenshaw, P. 1987 *Banking in Nineteenth-Century Ireland: The Belfast Banks, 1825–1914.* Manchester.

Pakenham, V. 2000 *The Big House in Ireland.* London.

Parliamentary Debates from the Year 1803 to the Present Time, vol. 39 (London, 1819).

Parliamentary Gazetteer of Ireland, 1844–1845, vol. 1 (Dublin, 1846).

Payne-Gallwey, R. 1995 *The Book of the Crossbow.* New York.

Potter, M. 2009 *William Monsell of Tervoe 1812–1894: Catholic Unionist, Anglo-Irishman.* Dublin.

Prichard, T.J.Ll. 1824 *The New Aberystwyth Guide.* Aberystwyth.

Provost, Ven. Sir G. (ed.) 1891 *The Autobiography of Isaac Williams.* London.

Pugin, A.C. 1821–3 *Specimens of Gothic Architecture* (2 vols). London.

Pugin, A.W. 1836 *Contrasts: Or, a Parallel between the Noble Edifices of the Fourteenth and Fifteenth Centuries, and Similar Buildings of the Present Day; Shewing the Present Decay of Taste.* London.

Pugin, A.W. 1841 *The True Principles of Pointed Christian Architecture.* London.

Purcell, E.S. 1900 *Life and Letters of Ambrose Phillipps de Lisle* (ed. Edwin de Lisle) (2 vols). London.

Randall, H.J. 1961 *The Vale of Glamorgan: Studies in Landscape and History.* Newport.

Rees, R.D. 1964–5 'Electioneering Ideals Current in South Wales, 1790–1832'. *Welsh History Review* **2** (3), 233–50.

Report of the Oxford Society for Promoting the Study of Gothic Architecture for Hilary, Easter, and Trinity Terms (1841).

Reports from Committees of the House of Commons, vol. 5 (1819).

Repton, H. 1803 *Observations on the Theory and Practice of Landscape Gardening Including Some Remarks on Grecian and Gothic Architecture.* London.

Richardson, C.J. 1837 *Observations on the Architecture of England During the Reigns of Queen Elizabeth and King James I.* London.

Robertson, N. 1960 *Crowned Harp: Memories of the Last Years of the Crown.* Dublin.

Rolt, L.T.C. 1958 *Thomas Telford.* London.

Roscoe, T. 1844 *Wanderings and Excursions in South Wales: With the Scenery of the River Wye.* London.

Rowan, A. 1970 'Clearwell Castle'. In H.M. Colvin and J. Harris (eds), *The Country Seat: Studies in the History of the British Country House; Presented to Sir John Summerson on His Sixty-Fifth Birthday Together with a Select Bibliography of His Published Writings*, 145–9. London.

Rudder, S. 1779 *A New History of Gloucestershire.* Cirencester.

Rutter, J. 1823 *Delineations of Fonthill and Its Abbey.* London.

Second Report of the Royal Commissioners on Technical Instruction, vol. 4 (London, 1884).

Shaw, H. 1839 *Details of Elizabethan Architecture.* London.

Sigourney, L.H. 1842 *Pleasant Memories of Pleasant Lands.* Boston.

Somerville-Large, P. 1995 *The Irish Country House: A Social History.* London.

Suggett, R. 1995 *John Nash: Architect in Wales.* Aberystwyth.

Summerson, J. 1980 *The Life and Work of John Nash, Architect.* London.

Swete, H. (n.d. [1870]) *Handy Book of Cottage Hospitals.* London.

Swift, J. 1705 *A Tale of a Tub: Written for the Universal Improvement of Mankind* (4th corrected edn). London.

Temple, N. 1979 *John Nash and the Village Picturesque.* Gloucester.

Temple, N. 1996 'The Rustic Residence of William Todd'. *Garden History* **24** (1), 137–43.

Thomas, H.J. 1999 'The Manor and Castle of Fonmon, near Barry'. *Morgannwg: Transactions of the Glamorgan Local History Society* **43**, 63–82.

Thomas, H.M. (ed.) 1987 *The Diaries of John Bird of Cardiff, Clerk to the First Marquess of Bute, 1790–1803.* Cardiff.

Thomas, H.M. 1997 'Llanmihangel, near Cowbridge: A Tale of Family Fortunes and Misfortunes. *Morgannwg: Transactions of the Glamorgan Local History Society* **41**, 8–37.

Thorne, R.G. 1986 *The House of Commons, 1790–1820*, vol. 4. London.

Torode, B.E. 2008 *John Middleton: Victorian, Provincial Architect.* Zagreb.

Trappes-Lomax, M. 1932 *Pugin: A Medieval Victorian.* London.

Wallace, A.R. 1905 *My Life: A Record of Events and Opinions* (2 vols). London.

Walters, C. (ed.) 1897 *Bygone Somerset.* London.

Watkins, C. and Cowell, B. 2006 *Letters of Uvedale Price.* Cambridge, MA.

Watkins, C. and Cowell, B. 2012 *Uvedale Price (1747–1829): Decoding the Picturesque.* Woodbridge.

Wedgwood, A. 1985 *A.W.N. Pugin and the Pugin Family: Catalogue of Drawings in the Victoria and Albert Museum.* London.

Westgarth, M. 2009 *A Biographical Dictionary of Nineteenth Century Antique and Curiosity Dealers.* [Glasgow.]

White, G.K. 1980 *A History of St Columba's College, 1843–1974*. Dublin.

Williams, S. (ed.) 1963 *Glamorgan Historian*, vol. 1. Cowbridge.

Wilson, R. and Mackley, A. 2000 *Creating Paradise: The Building of the English Country House, 1660–1880*. London.

Woodberry, G.E. (ed.) 1894 *Selections from the Poems of Aubrey de Vere*. New York.

Wright, C.E. 1964–5 'The Work of Thomas Willement, Stained-Glass Artist, 1812–1865'. *British Museum Quarterly* **29** (1–2), 1–5.

Young, A. 1780 *A Tour in Ireland*. Dublin.

Index

Illustrations marked in **bold**

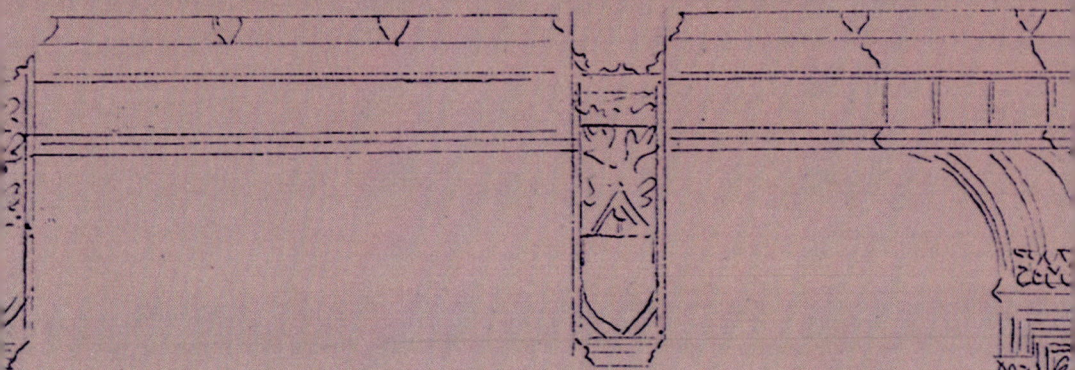